Working In Britain

203

Time Off

299

About Britain

313

Appendices

365

Preface

People have been heading to Britain for centuries. Way back in 55BC the Romans were among the earliest to recognise the potential of this small but productive island on the northern edge of Europe, but since then there has been wave after wave of immigrants coming to Britain's shores for various reasons. Fortunately in recent times they've had less of an urge to conquer the islands and take them for their own. In fact, people are attracted to Great Britain for a variety of far more peaceful reasons – to work, to be educated, to escape from persecution in less liberal and tolerant countries, to buy a holiday home or to make a permanent home in Britain.

The number of people moving to Britain is increasing, in line with a worldwide growth in international migration. In the last fifty years there has been a doubling in the percentage of current UK residents who were born overseas, and it now stands at more than 8%.

The growth of the European Union and the ease with which EU nationals can move freely to Britain has been an important boost to inward migration – among foreign-born residents, Europe is the most common area of birth with the Republic of Ireland being the largest single country of birth. However, Britain has attracted significant numbers of people from the other continents, despite the greater difficulties nationals from other countries face in respect of British immigration legislation.

A significant number of immigrants do not come for very long – around a third of foreign-born migrants stay for less than four years. The majority of these come either to work in Britain on short-term contracts, or to study in the universities.

For those who wish to study or gain work experience in Britain, the opportunities are greater now than they have been in the past. Foreign students are encouraged to come to Britain, and many are able to stay on after they have completed their courses while they look for work which will keep them in the country, using their new-found skills and qualifications. They are especially attracted to the burgeoning new industries, such as IT, electronics and life sciences, which have attracted many international companies to Britain.

The country's official title is the exhausting 'United Kingdom of Great Britain and Northern Ireland', often abbreviated to UK or GB, or given the generic name Britain. Although the UK is in many respects a single entity, its four nations – England, Scotland, Wales and Northern Ireland – are distinct, each having their own indigenous cultures, national characters and way of life. There are also differences between various aspects of the legal, political and education systems in each country. Land and property ownership and purchase, for example, are governed by different rules in different regions. These differences are explained clearly in this book and advice is given as to the best way to proceed with your move. Whether you wish to move temporarily or permanently to Britain, this book will help you achieve your aim.

Whatever your reason for moving to Britain, it has a great deal to offer – a liberal, tolerant, largely unrestrictive lifestyle; thriving modern cities; beautiful countryside; good educational and employment opportunities; and history and heritage by the bucketload. It is a unique country, and its people as diverse as its landscape.

Nicola Taylor, January 2008

Contents

Acknowledgements

The author would like to thank all those people who provided advice and encouragement during the writing of this book. In particular, Amy Burns; Roberth Lindholm; Joe Rawal; Susan Griffith; John Livesey; Dionne Rennie; Sue Hardie; Matthew Taylor and Anna Gorse who kindly served as case studies. Also those others, too numerous to list, who have supplied information or whose experiences feature elsewhere in the book. Finally, as always – thank you Charlie.

◣ TELEPHONE NUMBERS

International Telephone Codes. Throughout this book, UK telephone codes have been used. For those calling UK numbers from abroad, the international code is +44 (or 00 44) and the initial 0 is dropped. So 0131 222 5555 is + 44 131-222 5555 when calling from outside the UK.

While every effort has been made to ensure that the information contained in this book is as up-to-date as possible, some details are bound to change within the lifetime of this edition, and readers are strongly advised to check facts and credentials themselves. Readers are invited to write to the author c/o Crimson Publishing, Westminster House, Kew Road, Richmond, Surrey TW9 2ND with any comments, corrections and first-hand experiences. Those whose contributions are used will be sent a free copy of the next edition.

◣ PHOTOGRAPHS

With thanks to Beth Law, Lianne Slavin, Patricia Law, Jo Jacomb, Nicole Jackson and Virginia Palé-Parsons for their photographic contributions. Thanks also to iStock for the images used throughout the book.

Why Live & Work in Britain?

ABOUT BRITAIN

Although Britain is small it is an extremely diverse country. Within a comparatively compact space – the entire area is less than 100,000 sq. miles – there is an astonishing variety of landscape. From the welcoming white cliffs of Dover and rolling green expanses of the Downs in the south of England, to the rugged and wild northern coast of Scotland, to the amazing Giant's Causeway in Northern Ireland, its 40,000 basalt columns earning it the title of 'Eighth Wonder of the World' when it first became a tourist attraction in the 1700s.

Between these boundaries, the inland areas are equally diverse. If you were to drive the length and breadth of Britain you would find that, within the space of a few hours, you had passed through areas patchworked with fertile farmland and others of bleakly beautiful moor, seen impressive mountains dominating the changing skies, skirted serene inland lakes, driven beside clear sparkling rivers and spotted white surf crashing on golden beaches.

And that's just the rural landscape – the urban areas of Britain are equally varied, from the vast lively metropolitan area of London (one of the most densely populated cities in Europe, through sleepy English villages, bustling market towns, busy and sophisticated modern cities and smaller), ancient boroughs steeped in history, tiny Welsh hamlets, to scattered crofting townships in the Scottish Highlands where the population density is among the lowest in the world.

Britain's people are as diverse as the terrain. The natives of the UK (the English, Welsh, Scottish and Northern Irish) each have their own distinct characters and cultures and are fiercely proud of their home nations, often preferring to describe themselves in those terms, rather than as Typically British a Welshman or a Scotsman is more likely to display the Welsh Dragon or the Scottish Saltire than the Union Flag on national occasions. National pride has shown a resurgence over recent decades, as evidenced by the growth in the numbers of people learning the ancient Celtic languages of Gaelic (Scottish and Irish) and Welsh which had all but died out by the mid-20th century. Although English is the undisputed first language of Britain,

> I just love the way every area of Britain has its own special 'feel'. It's small enough, too, that it is possible to explore every region on short trips from my home in London.
> Jo Penfold, Australia

> When our two boys started school in a tiny primary school at the ages of six and four I was surprised they were taught some Gaelic as a matter of course. But now I've decided to learn too and am taking evening classes.
> Ally Wright, Scottish Highlands

many people are determined to preserve these older languages and the cultural heritage which goes with them.

The establishment of devolved regional governments for Wales, Scotland and Northern Ireland in 1999 is another sign of the nations of Britain asserting their differences far more than in the past, refusing to be submerged by what was perceived as the Anglo-centric desires of a centralised London government.

Aside from these original nationalities of Britain, the UK is home to many other races who have been attracted to its shores over centuries from around the world. A large percentage of these families are now several generations old, and therefore British themselves.

Top 20 nationalities of people living in the UK, 2005[*]
1. UK 55,589,150
2. Irish Republic 367,600
3. India 209,100
4. Poland 124,800
5. USA 118,600
6. South Africa 100,000
7. France 96,150
8. Pakistan 95,800
9. Italy 92,700
10. Germany 85,500
11. Former USSR etc 83,500
12. Portugal 78,800
13. Australia 78,300

14.	China 66,500
15.	Bangladesh 66,000
16.	Nigeria 62,900
17.	Phillippines 62,400
18.	Zimbabwe 58,400
19.	Somalia 58,200
20.	Spain 53,000

Annual Population Survey, Office for National Statistics.

REASONS TO LIVE IN BRITAIN

- **A green and pleasant land** With a variety of National Parks and areas of outstanding natural beauty, Britain is blessed with an extraordinarily varied and picturesque landscape. There are plenty of opportunities to enjoy the 'great outdoors' throughout the country, especially in the less populous areas of Wales, the Scottish Highlands, the North York Moors and the Peak and Lake Districts in England.

- **Lively, generally safe, cities** The capital cities of Britain's four member countries are thriving, diverse places. London is a hub for international business, but it's also at the heart of many other industries like film and fashion. Edinburgh is renowned as the host of an international theatre festival each August, while Cardiff and Belfast have enjoyed significant redevelopment and investment since devolution. Many other cities of the UK offer unique benefits – from Manchester's dynamic creative industries to Bristol's place as the home of many leading financial services firms.

- **Diversity: a multi-cultural, multi-ethnic society** Britain may be the land of picnics on the lawn and cricket in the park, but it's also home to a rich network of cultures. The Hindu and Muslim communities in cities such as Leicester, Bradford and Birmingham have forged new, richer identities for their adopted homes. One of the highlights of London's social calendar is the Notting Hill Carnival, once a byword for racial tension, but now a celebration of all that is diverse and inclusive in Britain today.

- **A prosperous nation** The UK is one of Europe's leading business and financial centres. Within the EU, the UK has the least restricted business environment, the least regulated marketplace and workforce, the largest international transport system, the best communications, the most widely spoken language, the lowest top rate of personal taxation, one of the lowest rates of corporation tax and the most cosmopolitan and culturally-diverse capital.

- **Good job prospects** Throughout the country, but especially in London, there are many opportunities for well-trained professionals to succeed. As the city through which most of the world chooses to trade, London is a particularly good base for anyone aiming to get on in finance or in the legal profession.

- **High wages** With good jobs come good rewards, and salaries are generally high in Britain. The average annual salary across the country is approximately £25,000 per year.

- **Good standard of living** The cost of living in the UK is relatively low, which means that life is generally good. There is an increasingly effective transport infrastructure as the train network gradually renews itself after many years of chronic under-investment–services

FACT

With good jobs come good rewards, and salaries are generally high in Britain. The average annual salary across the country is approximately £25,000 per year.

are now prompt, clean and reliable, albeit somewhat costly. Food is inexpensive and British supermarkets offer a dizzying range of products and services. Many are open 24 hours a day during weekdays.

National Health Service Since 1948, the National Health Service (NHS) has been at the heart of Britain's welfare state. Formed with the aim of providing all citizens with free access to medical, dental and optical care, the service has lost some of its egalitarian ethos over the years, but still boasts free medical and hospital treatment for all.

Welfare state In a broader sense, Britain's welfare state has also grown up from the post-Second World War era to become a safety net protecting and providing for the least well-off members of British society.

Excellent education system Britain is one of the best places in the world to study, with an education system which is among the best in the world. The high quality academic research coming out of Britain's universities means there is a thriving partnership between academia and business across the UK. Primary and secondary education in Britain is generally of a high standard, with a great deal of investment in schools and classroom technology over recent years.

- **Diverse business opportunities** The UK is renowned for its expertise in developing and nurturing new industries with many busi-nesses carrying out research and development in telecommunication, e-business, software and semiconductor development, biotechnology, industrial design, life and physical sciences.
- **The British Broadcasting Corporation (BBC)** The BBC remains a beacon of public service broadcasting that attracts the admiration of the world's broadcast media. The corporation's output is partly funded by a licence fee, payable by anyone who uses a TV or equipment that is capable of receiving a television signal. The BBC has a network of regional TV and radio stations based in cities and large towns around the country and a comprehensive website at www.bbc.co.uk.
- **One of the world's great centres of music** As a nation, Britain has an extraordinarily wide-ranging musical heritage. From the high culture of the Royal Opera House and Sadler's Wells in London to the popular music history of Liverpool and Manchester (via some surprise musical hotspots like the rock-influenced northern English cities of Sheffield and Leeds), Britain's musical story is rich and complex.

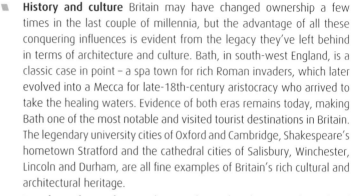

- **History and culture** Britain may have changed ownership a few times in the last couple of millennia, but the advantage of all these conquering influences is evident from the legacy they've left behind in terms of architecture and culture. Bath, in south-west England, is a classic case in point – a spa town for rich Roman invaders, which later evolved into a Mecca for late-18th-century aristocracy who arrived to take the healing waters. Evidence of both eras remains today, making Bath one of the most notable and visited tourist destinations in Britain. The legendary university cities of Oxford and Cambridge, Shakespeare's hometown Stratford and the cathedral cities of Salisbury, Winchester, Lincoln and Durham, are all fine examples of Britain's rich cultural and architectural heritage.

- **Freedom of speech** From the soap-box political orators of Speakers' Corner in London's Hyde Park to a largely independent press and the preponderance of alternative, single-issue political parties that spring at up every general election, Britain has a solid reputation for freedom of speech and thought. Recent anti-terrorist legislation has curbed the boundaries of acceptable free speech to eliminate the freedom to incite religious hatred, but, in essence, the average Briton has a high level of civil liberty.

- **Politeness** British politeness is another legendary (though over-estimated) virtue. Gone are the days of carefully-wrought phrases such as 'would you mind awfully passing me the sugar if it's no trouble?' but the British still strive to wrap formal social conversation in a comfort blanket of could/would/may and, of course, please and thank you. In contrast, informal language among friends is stripped down and often quite blunt. Politeness also manifests itself in queuing for buses, cinemas and at the bar of a pub.

- **British sense of humour** The British are renowned for their sharp, dry wit and humour is usually self-deprecating and sarcastic. There is a long tradition of physical comedy stretching back to medieval court jesters all the way to Mr Bean and situational comedy is a vital ingredient of British cultural life. For a crash course in the evolution of the British sense of humour over the last 40 years watch an episode of each of the following comedy shows:–*Dad's Army Fawlty Towers, Blackadder, The Fast Show*.

- **Wide range of leisure activities** As a great sporting nation, Britain has good facilities for football (soccer), rugby, cricket and tennis. Most large towns and cities have a range of private and council-owned well-equipped leisure centres and swimming pools. In spite of increased demand for housing land, parks and heaths are still prevalent and the island has the most incredible natural leisure resource in its many miles of beaches.

FACT

The opening of the new St Pancras International Train Terminal, London, in 2007 marked a new era for continental travel from Britain. The terminal and its accompanying high speed rail link, makes it possible to reach Paris, France in just over two hours.

◼ COMMON MYTHS ABOUT BRITAIN

- **Poor climate** The first thing many people think of in connection with Britain is the weather. It always rains, allegedly, and the sun rarely shines. Neither of these are actually true. You will find higher-than-average rainfall in the mountainous areas, but the south and east of England have a fairly dry climate, with water shortages sometimes being a problem in summer months. The south of England enjoys a respectable amount of sunshine during the year, and even the far north regularly sees settled summer weather where the sun shines every day. It has to be said that you may encounter rain every day for weeks in the winter – but this is unusual and the general pattern is for a good mixture of all types of weather throughout the year.

- **Densely populated** England is by far the most densely populated part of Britain, while Wales, Scotland and Northern Ireland are largely rural, with comparatively few areas of high population, which are concentrated in a few cities and large towns. The downside of this is that in these parts of Britain there is comparatively little in the way of industry, with implications for the quantity and type of employment available. With much land usage being classified as non-urban, there is a preponderance of small companies or 'one-man' businesses.

- **Traffic congestion** For the biggest choice and variety of jobs, immigrants–as well as domestic job-hunters–tend to head for London and the south east. This has caused the region to become increasingly densely populated, causing some problems, the most obvious and frustrating of which is traffic congestion. This produces its own problems, such as air pollution.

- **Pollution** It is notable that as one travels north towards Scotland and west into Wales the air becomes clearer. In the remotest areas, where even street lights are few and far between, light pollution is rare, so better views of the stars can be seen than elsewhere in Britain. When conditions are right, the Northern Lights (*aurora borealis*) can be seen in the more northerly parts of Scotland.

- **Property is expensive** While property prices are often prohibitively high in areas like London, the south-eastern counties such as Kent, Hampshire, Sussex and Surrey and the northern county of Cheshire, elsewhere in Britain, prices are reasonable, and public transport links are sufficiently good to allow an easy commute to work in any of the more expensive areas.

- **High taxes** Income tax in Britain has not been high since the upper level tax rate was reduced at the beginning of the 1980s. Over that period the base rate of income tax has declined and additional local taxation (council tax) has been altered to better reflect income and circumstance. Generally, the quality of public services represents reasonable value for the cost of taxation.

- **Racism** Racist violence in Britain isn't a thing of the past, but its focus has shifted from white youths attacking black youths to a much more complex reflection of a multicultural society. Gang violence among the young in cities like London and Manchester is a social issue, but it is much less racially-motivated than ever before. Overall, the positives of British multiculturalism far outweigh the negatives. Football crowds are an interesting barometer of the nation's mood, and thankfully racism has been all but eliminated at most clubs.

- **An island nation, so travelling abroad is not easy** The opening of the new St Pancras International Train Terminal in London marked a new era for continental travel from Britain. The terminal and its accompanying high-speed rail link, makes it possible to reach Paris, France in just over two hours. Britain's airports are also among the busiest in the world and cheap flights to European destinations are readily available. Ferries are fast and frequent to France, Belgium and Ireland.

Roberth Lindholm

Roberth, aged 36, came from Stockholm, Sweden in November 2006 to take up a six-month contract at an International Bank in Glasgow.

Why did you decide to come and work in Britain?

I was offered a contract that sounded interesting. And I grabbed the chance to get some experience from working abroad.

How did you find your job?

I was contacted by a contract broker that has been calling me on and off for a few years.

How would you describe your current job?

I'm a computer consultant at an International Bank, working as a product specialist on a few of the Middleware products used at the bank.

Describe the application and interview procedure you went through.

I received a call from the contract broker about an available contract here in the UK and they wondered if I was interested. I got a few days to think about it and then decided to take the step and try it out. I then had a short interview with people at the bank via telephone and they decided I suited their needs and would like me to join their team.

How long is your contract for? If it was extended would you be happy to stay longer?

The contract is for six months with an option to prolong it. If I was asked to stay longer I would have to think it over. But as it is now I like it here in Glasgow and wouldn't mind another six months or more.

Were there any difficulties with the immigration process or was it all plain sailing?

The move was not too difficult. As an EU citizen all you need to do is just pack your bags and move. The real hurdle was to get a bank account here in the UK. I needed both a personal one and a business account for the company I started to handle everything here in the UK.

Were there any difficulties with the moving process?

As stated above, banking is a real hassle. Just to open an account requires papers that are hard to come by when you recently moved into a home in the UK. As an example, they ask for a utility bill or similar as proof of address. Firstly, there is a delay before you get your first utility bills. And as I was renting a 'serviced apartment' at the beginning I didn't get any of that at all as everything was included in the rent. So after a month I moved to a long-term rental apartment.

How did you find somewhere to stay?

I got help from the Consult Service people at the Contract Broker firm to find links on the internet where I could locate somewhere to stay. Also I did some research on the internet. But it's hard when you're not at the location.

What are the advantages/disadvantages of short-term and long-term rental?

The disadvantage of short term is the lack of a 'stationary' address but that was about it. And in the long term it's a bit expensive. The advantage of the short term is that it's all handled for you. No need to worry about the TV licence, council tax and such.

The disadvantage of a long-term rental is that I need to handle all such things on my own – figure out how to get registered for council tax, electricity, TV licence and so on. The advantage is to get a permanent address and the possibility to leave stuff at the apartment even when I'm not there so I don't have to carry everything around everywhere. As I'm travelling a bit around Europe it's a big plus to be able to just have carry-on baggage. Also to sort the banking issues a permanent address is more or less required.

Would you consider buying a property if you have the chance to stay here longer?

I would probably continue to rent. But it all comes down to how long the period is. At present a permanent move might not be planned, but one never knows. And if I considered staying here for a longer period it might be a solution. But that's something that has to be decided when and if it happens.

Any comments on conditions of work and employment in your job?

The work is fine and I don't really have any problems with that.

What is your tax situation in your job – will you pay tax in the UK or in Sweden?

As I'm here for six months I'll be paying taxes here in the UK as that's the easiest way to handle things. This is an effect of the tax treaty between the UK and Sweden.

How long did it take you to acclimatise to both the way of life and the climate?

The way of life isn't really any different here, although it took a little while to understand the Scottish accent. It took around two weeks to be able to clearly understand what people said, even if there still are a few people that I have trouble understanding. The climate isn't too bad. It's a bit warmer than in Sweden generally during winter. But as I spend a lot of time in Malmo (a town to the very south) which is located at almost the same latitude it's no big difference. And I don't mind missing out on the -20C at my home town in Sweden during winter.

Did you find it easy to make friends?

That is of course a bit tricky when you move anywhere. It might be even more difficult when you move from one country to another. But I have good contact with a few of the other contractors at work and try to socialise as much as possible at work to get to know people.

Have you come across any 'anti-European' feeling from people?

No, haven't had any such experiences.

Have you suffered any 'culture shock'?

Not that I have noticed. The only thing would be the large amount of ready made convenience foods available at the grocery stores. Apart from that nothing is too different.

Have you any advice for others thinking of moving to Britain?

Yes. Look into the banking problem as soon as possible as I have found out is a constant battle against the banks due to the anti money-laundering regulations. There is a possibility to open an account in the UK with HSBC from your home country as they have something called

HSBC Passport. I would advise anyone moving here from abroad to look into that if needed as it really would make things a bit easier.

Also I would advise starting off with a short-term rental before starting to look at anything more permanent as it's much easier to do such things when you're actually here. It is really difficult trying to figure out which parts of a town are good or not, or even where it's located, when you aren't here.

What are your feelings about living in Britain?

I like it here. It's a bit different but not too much and everything is more or less as in Sweden.

How do you find the standard and cost of living in Britain?

There isn't a big difference compared to Sweden. Sure it's .a bit cheaper to eat out and go for a beer, but that's mainly due to taxes in Sweden being a bit high on such things. Food is more or less the same here, maybe a bit cheaper. Compared to Stockholm the rents are reasonable here, at least if you compare location and price.

I had a picture of UK living standards but was surprised. The living standard was much higher than I expected and have encountered further south. But then I've mainly stayed in cheap hotels before so that might explain it.

How do you find the social/community side of life in Britain?

I find it interesting and there is a lot to do around here in Glasgow if you have got the time for it. I haven't had too much time to explore everything but hope to get the time and see more of Britain.

Are you glad you came here?

Yes. It's been developing and interesting and I will have benefit from the experience in my line of work, wherever I work after the period here.

Amy Burns

Amy, aged 36, was born and brought up in Alabama. She had never been outside the USA before she came to Britain in 2006.

Why did you decide to move to Britain?

Interestingly enough, this question gave me reason to pause before answering. Fact is, my decision to move here wasn't based on a singular motivation, unless you will allow me to say that, in the grand scheme of things – there were several major aspects of my life that would benefit by making the move, both professionally and personally. I made a decision to quit a long-term, managerial position with a major American corporation in a heavily industrial field and return to a more creative career as a writer, editor, publisher... the list kept growing. My decision to change jobs was a success and put me in touch with several new business associates in the Britain and it was through my new contacts that I began learning more about the culture. I made my first business trip and as a consequence, I fell in love with the place. On that first trip, I also began investigating another long-hidden desire, to return to university to pursue a postgraduate degree. Needless to say, I was thrilled when asked to participate in the University of Glasgow's Creative Writing Program. So, before moving to Britain I knew I would be able to finally fulfil a lifelong dream of pursuing a postgraduate degree; I would be able to work with greater ease on writing/publishing projects with new business associates; and I would be able to continue down the much happier path I forged for myself when I walked away from the gruelling '14-hour-day' mentality in corporate America.

Did you look at other options besides coming as a student? Were any of them feasible?

When I realized that moving to Britain was indeed an attractive idea and seemed to fit into my 'life plan' for several reasons, I did investigate many options for acquiring a visa. Although attending university was my first choice, I had to consider the possibility (as badly as I hate to admit it) that the programme to which I was applying is highly competitive and there was a chance that I wouldn't be accepted. I needed to know what other options were available. Let me just say, I was lucky to be accepted at university, because otherwise... there were no options available. I did investigate the Highly Skilled Migrant Program and although I have no doubt that I would have qualified, it was not my intention to come to Britain in search of a typical job in the business world and when I began to understand all the requirements expected of a person setting up their own business, I realized that was far too complicated for what I had in mind.

How easy is it to move here as a US citizen?

Plainly and simply, it is not easy to move here as a US citizen. I spent hours reading websites and going back and forth from page to page trying to make sense of it all. The language seemed intentionally vague and in places downright contradictory. I spent a great deal of time speaking to, supposedly, knowledgeable people who were there to assist me... when in actuality what I found was that I was getting a different story from each and every person I spoke with, and each one of those stories differed slightly from what I could make out from the websites. I'd also spent a lot of money, as well, mainly because no matter what 'free' number they gave me it always directed me back to a number which required a credit card and billed a high per-minute fee for advice. Once I was clear on my options, it became even clearer that there was actually very little there for me to understand. As a US citizen, my options for entering Britain and staying for more six months as a visitor were practically none!

Why did you decide to do your Masters in Britain rather than the US?

There were practical issues at hand. The University of Glasgow offered a Masters in half the time at half the expense of most universities offering an equivalent degree in the US.
How did you find information about courses? Were there any difficulties with the immigration process or was it all plain sailing?
My basic source of information was email/internet. But even though the wonderful World Wide Web is indeed wonderful, I found that, on several occasions, it simply wasn't a suitable substitute for actual face-to-face interaction with the people I needed to communicate with so urgently. And on that count, I was lucky in the sense that I could rely on a little help from my friends already living in Britain. Quite often, they actually paid a visit to various offices, asked a few simple questions, and within minutes understood clearly and had answers to questions I'd been struggling with for days.

What made you decide on Glasgow University?

Needless to say the reputation of the University of Glasgow speaks for itself; however, I was particularly interested in the calibre of the Creative Writing program. And, aside from the fact that I was obviously attracted to the city and the university itself, there were several practical issues to consider in regard to time and financial matters. The University of Glasgow offered an absolutely brilliant opportunity to study with an amazing staff, while allowing me to attain a Masters degree in a year for less than half the cost of an equivalent degree in the US.

Were there any difficulties with the moving process?

The only major difficulty I can think of was actually getting my things from the US to Britain. Early on in the process, I ran into a virtual showstopper when I found out what was involved in bringing along my eight month old English Springer Spaniel, Chloe. The quarantine period, the long list of requirements, the expense involved in inserting a micro-chip, getting special shots, flying certain airlines, flying certain routes, buying Chloe a special ticket... I was amazed at the cost involved. However, the thing that I couldn't bear the idea of was the six month quarantine period. I know they have relaxed the rules to some extent and allow for some of the period to begin in the US now, but my schedule didn't have six months to spare. I decided not to move... that is, until I found a family with a huge farm and two little boys and a golf-cart which, from what I understand, Chloe loves to ride around in all day. So, although I miss my dog terribly, my story with her ended happily knowing that she has a good home. The regulations, however, are something to be considered carefully and EARLY if you are planning on bringing your pet!

Apart from that, shipping costs are outrageously expensive and for this very reason, I came to Britain basically empty-handed. I certainly wasn't able to bring across large items of furniture or anything of that nature. Luckily for me, I was able to pack my luggage creatively, pay a little extra at the airline for excess baggage and bring along a few of my most beloved books and things that would give me a good start in making my new flat in Britain feel like home.

How did you find accommodation?

I can't say that I braved meeting with estate agents or pounded the pavements to check out flats to rent. I was lucky again, in the fact that friends already living in Britain were able to lend great assistance on this count. I will say, though, that on my journeys through the city of Glasgow, I see no shortage of flats to let on both short-and long-term agreements, as well as signs indicating properties for sale. Just one look around and you'll see what a thriving, growing city it is. So I can't imagine finding accommodation would be a problem and from the adverts I have seen, the pricing is reasonable.

Will you be working while you are a student?

Yes, I am allowed to work for up to 20 hours per week as an overseas student. Since my hours are flexible, I have the ideal situation to accommodate both my work and my studies.

What are your feelings about living in Britain?

I'm very happy here. I felt an immediate affinity with the place when I arrived and although I haven't lost my sense of amazement with being in a new place, always awed by the architecture and beauty surrounding me, I have never once felt as if I was isolated in a foreign country.

Would you recommend it to other Americans?

Certainly! I've mentioned that I needed a change in my life: well, it wasn't only for professional reasons. I think I was suffering from a general social malaise affecting the US that I simply don't feel here for many reasons. Couple that with the extraordinary beauty found in Britain, both natural and man-made, and it is certainly enough to lift anyone's spirits and give them a reason to feel inspired and creative. Not to mention, there is great attention paid to the arts here, one is never at a loss for something wonderful to do whether it be a jazz show on Tuesday night, a quick stop by the Gallery of Modern Art or a show at the Royal Concert Hall.

How do you find the British – do they seem different from the Americans?

I find, for the most part, that the British seem a bit more reserved than Americans and less 'in your face'. I don't mean that they aren't friendly, my experiences here thus far have all been positive, however, in the US I very often couldn't escape the feeling that everywhere I went I was being accosted to some degree by this exaggerated sense of happy-happy, joy-joy... especially in the service industry – restaurants and shopping malls. I haven't found that here and it hasn't affected the efficiency of the service, rather it has added to the pleasure of an evening out.

Have you come across any anti-American feeling from people?

Regarding strong anti-American feelings in Britain ... yes, I have. I regularly pass protestors in the city centre who have set up peaceful demonstrations expressing their views on American politics and US involvement in the war in Iraq. I have had conversations with people here in which they have conveyed frustrations and sentiments that could definitely be considered anti-American. Most interesting, perhaps, is the idea that some of these sentiments seem to be directed at a phantom, a myth, an image of what the US is and isn't – an entity loping along at breakneck speed wrecking havoc throughout the world with a nation of people in tow that seem to know just as little about defining their own country as the rest of the world. I should mention that I've also come across plenty of anti-American feelings in the US, by the way.

How does life compare with life in the USA?

To me life here in Britain is much 'easier' on the senses and by that I mean... in the US it seems as though everything is geared toward a constant sell: from the time you walk out of your home in the morning until you go to sleep at night, you are subjected to a constant barrage of advertisements and hard sells and insinuations and people telling you what you need to buy to survive and to live the good life and to protect your family in case of a catastrophic event. Flashing neon signs, rolling marquees, huge roadside advertising billboards, pamphlets left on your car windshield, junk mail stuffed in your mail box and email, radio, television, door to door, you name it... almost everything has an angle to sell you some type of service. In Britain, it isn't like that. It certainly isn't that all those services aren't available – but it does seem as though the focus of life hasn't been completely consumed by this market driven obsession with the in-your-face hard sell.

Also, life in Britain is different in that I don't have access to my own car. In the US most people would think all life would come to a screeching halt if they had to give up their cars, however, the public transportation is so wonderful here that I've found no need to purchase a car. I have immediate access to trains, the subway, buses and taxis. Not to mention, I walk! It would have been unheard of to get out and walk to the bank or the post office from where I previously lived, it would have been dangerous – for many reasons. Here, it is just a way of life.

On balance, are you glad you made the move?

I couldn't be more pleased with my move to Britain. I enjoy the pleasures of living in a thriving city with beautiful architecture both historical and contemporary, while at the same time I live only a short drive away from some of the most strikingly beautiful, remote scenery in the world. The people I have met are a pleasure to know and I am looking forward to completing my Masters degree.

Susan Griffith

Susan came to Oxford in September 1976 as a graduate student. She had spent a summer at an international summer school a few years before and instantly loved the UK and Oxford in particular.

What other countries have you lived and worked in?

Canada till the age of 22; have spent two three-month periods living in Australia (Canberra in 1988, Sydney in 1999/2000). Have travelled extensively worldwide (e.g. several months in the Indian subcontinent on several occasions).

Which places have you lived in since being in Britain?

Oxford and Cambridge.

What jobs have you done since being here?

Graduate student (M.Phil. Eng lit), employee of Vacation-Work 1978-1990; freelance writer/editor since then.

How would you describe your current work?

Freelance writer/editor.

Now that you have been here for some time, what are your feelings about living in Britain?

I have been here so long that I hardly think of myself as a foreigner any more; in fact I feel much more foreign when I visit Canada. Despite retaining my Canadian accent almost totally, I am very seldom treated like a tourist in the UK, so am always surprised when (for example) someone working in a pub asks me how long I am visiting. For many years, I had a pronounced preference for life and culture in Britain, and was guilty of being dismissive of my country of birth. Have mellowed somewhat towards Canada, and am sorry to see a gradual 'Americanisation' of Britain.

Would you recommend it to other Canadians?

Yes, though many Canadians have a somewhat romantic view of 'the olde country' (a term they would never use) and would find living and job-hunting in London more stressful than they had anticipated.

How do you find the British?

Have always felt at home with the British sense of humour (= irony) and miss it when I have been back in Canada or travelling abroad for extended periods.

At least in Cambridge, Brits are always ready to celebrate an occasion (an important birthday, seasonal events) with great gusto.

When I first arrived, I did find the British bizarrely private, e.g. they seldom struck up conversations on trains, but now I have converted to thinking that that is preferable. Am now so used to the restrained service that you tend to get in shops and pubs that I feel slightly disapproving of the over-the-top (and often false) friendliness of shop and restaurant staff in North America.

Have you any advice for others thinking of moving to Britain?

Be sure to take advantage of Britain's easy access to the rest of Europe especially on no-frills airlines but also trains and ferries.

Try not to complain too loudly about the relatively high cost of living – it may be much more expensive to eat out here than where you came from, but everybody is in the same boat and if paying that spoils your pleasure, stay at home. There are other things that are MUCH cheaper than they would be from Toronto (like flying to Rome).

How do you find the standard and cost of living in Britain?

I have long since stopped comparing prices with equivalents in my homeland, though friends and family in Canada remind me of how much more expensive the UK is, especially property, petrol and eating out. By the same token, since I have been here, British salaries have risen and in many cases are proportionate to the high cost of living (e.g. minimum wage in UK now £5.35 but only C$7-$8 in Canada = £3-£3.50).

Did you have set ideas on what you intended to do when you moved to Britain?

When I came as a student, my plans were open-ended, and when my course finished, I automatically registered with the university employment service (which is how I got my job in publishing) partly because I was in a long-term relationship in England but also because the prospect of job-hunting in Canada was not in any way attractive to me. I have never once considered moving back (though I tried it in the winter of 1983 for relationship reasons and was very homesick for Oxford).

Has it turned out as you visualised or are you doing different things than you intended?

Since I had no plans when I arrived at a young age, I can't say things have panned out as expected or not. The folks back home have found it harder to fathom the decision to stay in Britain than I have.

How do you find the social/community side of life in Britain?

Splendid. It is very difficult to generalise but the neighbourhood spirit I have encountered has been wonderful with annual street parties, neighbourhood book groups, fund-raising ceilidhs, etc. Neighbours and local people met through the PTA (primary and secondary school) have become close friends over the years, which is just as well since if you work freelance, you can't depend on finding your friends among your colleagues.

What are the best things about living here?

I love the variety of topography, culture, accent, history, architecture, etc. between places that are relatively close together, e.g. Norfolk to the Fens, Birmingham to the Black Country. I never tire of exploring the nooks and crannies, comparing the churches and pubs, etc.

People walk and cycle far more than North America (though the car is in the ascendancy here). Ancient rights of way mean that people walk in the countryside – this doesn't exist in Canada.

The worst?

As recently reported in the UNICEF report, the innocence of childhood seems to pass too quickly in Britain. An obsession with drinking in youth culture is much worse than in Canada, which my teenage sons have noticed. The rules (e.g. of pubs and off-licences serving under-aged drinkers) are enforced less rigorously in the UK than in Canada. But this tendency to bend the rules is in other contexts an attractive aspect of Britain, i.e. it means it is completely different from (say) Germany, which is so bureaucratic and enslaved to following rules (e.g. ordinary citizens will reprimand you if you jay-walk).

Joe Rawal

Joe moved to Britain in October 2002 when he was 32, from Eritrea, East Africa.

Which countries had you lived and/or worked in before you came to Britain?

India, Egypt, Yemen, Cambodia.

Why did you decide to come and work in Britain?

This was purely by chance, I was offered a position with my employer which I gladly accepted.

How did you find a job in Britain?

The position in UK was connected to my previous job which was with the same organisation I worked for in East Africa. I work with a charity specialising in the removal of the debris of war. The application process took place in Eritrea where I first came across my current employer. I had a panel interview with the Director, programme manager and senior desk officer.

Were there any difficulties with the immigration process or was it all plain sailing?

It was pretty much straightforward since I had letters of support from my employer and the British embassy in Eritrea.

How did you find somewhere to stay?

Accommodation was provided by my employer when I first arrived. I then went about and purchased a flat in the neighbouring area after having spent a couple of years in the country and deciding to stay longer.

You have bought property in Britain. Can you give your feelings on the pros and cons of renting as opposed to buying?

I suppose the biggest advantage of renting is that you can pick up your bags and leave without much hassle and at very short notice. This is ideal for a short tenancy. The disadvantage of long-term renting is that it is not only expensive, but at the end of it all, you still do not own the property despite all the money spent on renting it. Additionally, one can never really settle in a rented property.

Any comments on employment in Britain?

I feel that, despite what people say, there is plenty of opportunity for someone to find work, if they have the will and are prepared to go out and search for it.

Now that you have been here for some time, what are your feelings about living in Britain?

Britain is a great place to live and work in. There are limitations and some of them are the weather, high cost of living, limited transport services, access to medical services and high taxes. But I would still recommend living and working here.

How long did it take you to acclimatise to both the way of life and the climate?

I had lived overseas in a few countries prior to coming to Britain, which was helpful to get used to a new way of life, but nothing had prepared me for the climate!

How do you find the British compared with other nationalities you have lived and worked with?

It depends, it can be difficult to get to know people and make friends as they tend to be quite reserved. The pace of life is fast, for some reason people do not really have the time and the social structure can get rigid.

Did you find it easy to make friends?

Yes and no. Besides friends at work, many of my close friends are people I met and know from outside the UK. It was through them that I met others. There is also a difference if you live in the city or a village. It is not as easy to make friends or to know people as it would be in Africa or Asia.

Did you suffer any 'culture shock' after you arrived?

Not really. My experiences gained by living and working abroad with people from different nationalities helped me a lot. But still, it took getting used to, especially living in a small village in the countryside where people are not used to having foreigners around and they tend to keep their distance.

Have you any advice for others thinking of moving to Britain?

Be prepared for long periods of very dull weather, especially if you come from very sunny climates! Be prepared for a hard and hectic lifestyle with little time for friends or family – it can get lonely. Unless you live in a big city with local amenities or a small shop nearby, be prepared to drive even for the newspaper! So make sure you can drive even before you enter Britain. Be prepared to save very little money – see most of it going into taxes!

What are your feelings about living in Britain?

I have lived here for five years now, but I'm still not sure if I would like to settle down here. In general, the standard of living is good as long as you can afford it.

How do you find the social/community side of life in Britain?

From my experiences so far, there is little community life in Britain. Some of the reasons for this can be listed as the unpredictable bad weather, hectic lifestyles and technology that mostly tend to keep people indoors.

What are the best things about living here?

For its size Britain is very multicultural and has plenty of opportunities to offer. I have had a good life, but mainly because I have had a good job to support my lifestyle. There are no restrictions and you are free to do most things as long as you are law abiding. There is plenty of choice for good quality education, careers and business opportunities. With its location, Britain also has very good access to most countries in Europe and the rest of the world.

Matthew Taylor & Anna Gorse

Matthew and Anna both work in Liverpool and have rented a flat there for a couple of years. They decided to buy their first house in 2007 when they realised a mortgage would not cost them much more than what they had been spending on rental.

Our first step when deciding to buy a house was to check the internet for how much we might be able to borrow. Anna and I went straight to our own banks' websites and used their mortgage calculator to get a ballpark figure for how much we might be able to borrow. These figures, as they turned out, were pretty much identical. Having started looking at a few decidedly dodgy properties in our chosen area in that price range we were then 'encouraged' by the estate agent to visit their own mortgage advisor. Despite our huge scepticism that he would try and push certain products at us he was actually a great help in explaining the 'extras' involved in a mortgage – valuation fees, early repayment, leaving fees, etc. He recommended two different mortgages which would actually lend us far more than we had expected.

We returned to the internet to read further and work out if the quotes were as they appeared. One invaluable website that we would recommend is www.moneysavingexpert.com – loads of advice for the complete novice or seasoned pro, helpful basic guides and extensive forums. As with anything, all advice should be checked and double checked but it helped us to understand the financial side of things a bit better. It advised using a fee-free, independent, whole-of-market mortgage broker to get an impartial view of what was right for us – we've used London and Country who have been nothing short of fantastic thus far. So, we actually found the financial side of things relatively straightforward. My biggest piece of advice would be to double and triple check everything you hear from anyone, be very wary of being pushed to pay for services or products you don't need.

Our real fun and games started when we found a property. We had a bid accepted for a house that needed a bit of work and were waiting to go to survey when I received a phone call from the estate agents. Apparently the vendor had fallen into arrears on his mortgage for the past six months and his lender was going to repossess the property. We were given the option of paying the shortfall (about £4,000 by the time our sale would have been completed) and re-negotiating the sale price based on that but, having failed to find that much money down the back of the sofa, we quickly did a runner.

Property number two was a smaller house that needed not a thing doing to it. After a short bidding process with another interested party we had a bid accepted at the asking price. Two days later we received a phone call from the estate agents informing us that the vendor had been contacted directly by the other party who, in floods of tears, had begged her to accept their offer at the asking price. Which she did. Despite our protestations that 'our bid was accepted first', the agents said it was not possible for them to get the vendor to drop the offer and the first survey to be completed would get the house. Not wanting to be hurried in such a massive purchase we again backed out. We also believed that the agents themselves had made the error, hence their unwillingness to get the vendor to reject the second offer, so told them we would not be dealing with them any further. Second piece of advice, estate agents are professional liars. Their role is to represent the seller and they will, we've found, tell you anything to push through a sale.

House number three we saw within 12 hours of it going on the market and put an offer in at the asking price straight after viewing. We were told by the agents that the vendors had more viewings that weekend and would get back to us on Monday. Monday came and we were told that there were six bids in total at the asking price and they were taking 'best and final offers' for 12 noon the following day. Having upped our offer to our maximum we were beaten by just one bid so lost that one as well.

We spoke to the same estate agents today and they are valuing another house in similar condition on the same road tomorrow and will let us know as soon as it comes on the market. Apparently we're in pole position, but then they would say that, wouldn't they? Our final piece of advice is to talk to the estate agents and get them to tell you when houses become available. By the time a house goes up in the window or on the website, it's often too late.

Dionne Rennie

Dionne started a small business in 2007 after she had some success selling her own jewellery designs. She is based in Scotland, but as she works from home and markets her wares through her website she could run it from anywhere with no difficulty.

My business is called Dionne Designs – I specialise in photography and jewellery making. You can find out more information about me at www.dionnedesigns.co.uk. I get a lot of business through friends, family and work colleagues. I provide a variety of photography services – weddings, portraiture, landscape prints and commercial work. I also sell ready-made jewellery as well as providing a very competitive commissioning service.

Starting your own business in Scotland doesn't have to be a giant pain in the neck. It's more like a dull ache. But with help it will go swimmingly. It took me a few years to finally decide to go ahead and start my business, which I think is for the best – you need to think things through and decide if it's really what you want. Once you do decide (hopefully it will take you less than the several years it took me!) go along and chat with a business advisor at Business Gateway (part of Scottish Enterprise).

The first thing you need to do is write a business plan. In the plan you'll give details about yourself, your skills, what kind of business you plan to run, who your customers will be, who your competitors are and give financial projections. This does sound rather daunting, but you will be given a template and the advisor will help you in collecting all the information you need. It has to be said that it can be a dull process, especially trying to work out the intricacies of 12-month financial projections, but this document is vital in getting funding and opening a business bank account. Once that's completed you'll feel very relieved and probably a bit excited, which is good because then it's time to look at money! Banks are usually keen to get your custom, so keep your eyes open for fee-free banking offers. The only difference to opening a personal bank account is that usually the bank wants to read your business plan and ask you some questions.

When you have your bank account up and running, your advisor will be able to help you with funding applications. Most of these require your bank account to be up and running, so that's why it's worthwhile to get that out of the way once your business plan is finished.

Don't forget to register with the Department of Revenue and Customs as self employed. All you need to do is call 0845 915 4515 and have your business plan and NI number to hand. They will take all the details and send you out a letter confirming your status with your all important individual reference number. Don't lose this letter whatever you do! This number is the holy grail of all your business information when it comes to applying for funding.

There's quite a lot of funding available and your advisor will be able to point you in the right direction. If you're under 30 then the world's your oyster as there are quite a few grants just an application form away. The most important thing to remember about these forms is to check and double check you've filled them in correctly – you don't want your money disappearing into someone else's bank account! It can take a while to get your funding, so be patient but don't be afraid to call for regular updates.

The next thing you want to look at is publicity and marketing. During your meetings with your advisor, this is something you will have discussed in some detail, thankfully! There are a lot of networking groups in Britain – a simple web search will show you what's available in your area. It's a great way to meet like minded people and hand out some information about your burgeoning business. Also a visit to the Scottish Enterprise website is a must, you'll find all sorts of useful advice and contacts on there to help you. Remember the value of friends and family in helping you to promote your business, they can help with vital word of mouth publicity.

All in all the process of setting up my business really wasn't as difficult as I anticipated. My advisor really helped get me thinking along the right lines, pulling together the right information and most importantly, filling out the forms correctly! The financial projections were possibly the most difficult part because you're dealing in uncertainties, but in the end I understood how things should work and I got excited about the future. Anything is possible if you try!

Before You Go

RESIDENCE AND ENTRY REGULATIONS FOR EU NATIONALS

UK Immigration Rules

> There were no restrictions on my entry to the UK. I was able to continue my work as a freelance IT consultant, keeping in contact online with my clients across the world.
> Frederik Ramm, from Germany

The rules and regulations relating to immigration apply equally across the UK. There are no border controls between England, Scotland, Wales and Northern Ireland, and once you have been granted admittance to the UK, residence in its different countries is unrestricted.

The European Economic Area (EEA) comprises the following EU countries: Austria, Belgium, Bulgaria, Cyprus, the Czech Republic, Denmark, Estonia, Finland, France, Germany, Greece, Hungary, Ireland, Italy, Latvia, Lithuania, Luxembourg, Malta, the Netherlands, Poland, Portugal, Romania, Slovakia, Slovenia, Spain, Sweden and the United Kingdom. In addition it includes Iceland, Liechtenstein and Norway, which are not members of the European Union. Although Switzerland is not in the EEA, Swiss nationals have similar rights to residence in the UK as EEA nationals.

Although other EU countries put some bureaucratic obstacles in the way of European immigrants, Britain puts few restrictions on EEA nationals wishing to relocate either temporarily or permanently. Nationals of most of the above countries have a right of residence (i.e. a right to live and work) in the UK if they are working in the UK or if they are not economically active in the UK but do have sufficient funds to support themselves during their stay without needing financial assistance from UK public funds.. This right was, until recently, unrestricted, but with the expansion of the EU in the past few years, there has been a far greater influx of people from the new member states than anticipated, and some restrictions have been put in place in certain circumstances.

Of the ten new states which joined the EU in 2004, nationals of the Czech Republic, Poland, Lithuania, Estonia, Latvia, Slovenia, Slovakia and Hungary must register with the Home Office and obtain a worker's registration certificate, but nationals from Malta and Cyprus have full free movement rights in line with other EEA nationals.

> The move was not too difficult. As an EU citizen all you need to do is just pack your bags and move.
> Roberth Lindholm, from Sweden

Bulgaria and Romania joined the EU in January 2007, and there have been some additional restrictions placed on nationals of those countries who wish to work in the UK. These effectively prevent low-skilled workers from taking up forms of employment other than that which is within existing quota schemes in the agricultural and food processing sectors. In these cases they must obtain an Accession Worker Card.

Individuals must register under the scheme as soon as they start work in the UK. They must complete an application form and send it together with a copy of a letter from their employer (confirming their employment); two photographs; a valid passport/ID card; and payment of £70. This should be addresed to Work Permits (UK) WRS, PO Box 492, Durham, DH99 1WU.

> *Diplomatic status had its advantages, of course, and I'm not sure how easy it would have been without it in those days. All this business about equal rights for EEC nationals was just starting then, but today there should be no difficulties whatever in that respect for nationals of EU member states, though it's more difficult for non-EU Europeans and for Americans.*
> *Rainer Thonnes, diplomat's son from Germany*

The application form is available on the internet at www.workingintheuk. gov.uk

Bulgarian and Romanian Nationals

Highly-skilled nationals of Bulgaria and Romania may work in the UK as long as they qualify under the Highly Skilled Migrants Programme, the Science and Engineering Graduate's Scheme, or the Fresh Talent: Working in Scotland Scheme. For more detailed information regarding the requirements for Bulgarian or Romanian Nationals see *Highly Skilled Migrants,* below. For further guidance on these schemes, see www.workingintheuk.gov.uk.

Family Members

Members of your family (including your spouse, dependent children or grandchildren, parents or grandparents) who are also EEA nationals, have the same rights as you to live and work in the UK. Family members who are not EEA nationals need to obtain a visa or an EEA family permit before entering the UK.

Members of your family who are non-EEA nationals may join you as long as they are granted an EEA family permit or suitable visa, which they must get before they travel to the UK if they are visa nationals (see the next chapter for more about visa nationals) and are coming to live with you permanently or on a long-term basis. If they try to enter the UK for this purpose without an EEA family permit, entry may be refused.

For these purposes your family includes:

- Your husband, wife or civil partner.
- Your husband's, wife's or civil partner's children or grandchildren (if they are under 21 years of age or if they are over 21 and are dependent on you).
- Dependent relatives, for example your husband's, wife's or civil partner's parents or grandparents.

If you are a student, only your husband, wife or civil partner and your dependent children can join you.

> *As I come from an EU country I did not need a student visa and paid the same tuition fees as a home student. It was useful being able to work to supplement my living costs, as I was not eligible for a UK student loan.*
> *Jeanne Dubois, from France*

An unmarried partner can apply for an EEA family permit, but not as a family member. They need to meet the relevant requirements of the Immigration Rules for Unmarried Partners. They do not have a right to join the EEA national in the UK like a family member, but their application can be considered.

Other relatives, such as brothers, sisters, cousins and so on, do not have an automatic right to live in the UK with you. However, applications for your other relatives to join you if you are working or coming to work in the UK will be considered if:

- They are dependent on you, and you live together in an EEA member state.
- They satisfy the Immigration Rules for other dependant family members.
- They are suffering from serious illness and require your care.

EEA family permits are free of charge. Non-EEA family members may visit you for up to six months without a family permit, as long as they are not visa nationals.

Your non-EEA family members can, if they want to, apply to the Immigration and Nationality Directorate for a residence card once they are in the UK. This is optional, and simply confirms that they have a right to live with you in the UK because you have a right of residence. Non-EEA family members who have a valid residence card do not need to get an EEA family permit each time they enter the UK after travelling abroad.

Family members of an EEA national living and working in Britain can work also, without the need for a work permit. Applications for a family permit may be refused if the authorities suspect the marriage is a marriage of convenience – i.e. only contracted in order to obtain the right to work in the UK for either party.

Your family could lose their right of residence in the UK if:

- You no longer have the right of residence in the UK.
- You leave the UK permanently.
- You are not working in the UK and you cannot live in the UK without getting help from public funds.

Your husband, wife or civil partner may also lose the right to stay in the UK if you are divorced/dissolve your civil partnership.

Application forms for family permits can be obtained from British Missions or downloaded from www.ukvisas.gov.uk. Online applications may be made at www.visa4uk.fco.gov.uk.

Documents needed:

- A recent passport-sized colour photograph.
- Supporting documents relevant to their application.

Acceptable supporting documents include:

- Proof of their relationship to you (e.g. birth certificate or marriage certificate)
- Evidence that you are in the UK, or intend to travel to, the UK.
- A certified copy of your EEA passport.
- Evidence of your employment in the UK or evidence that you can support them for the whole period of their stay in the UK.

 For more advice and information about visas contact:
UK Visas, London, SW1A 2AH | general enquiries: 0845 010 5555 | application forms: 020 7008 8308 | www.ukvisas.gov.uk/enquiries

Students

You may enter the UK for study or training as long as you can support and accommodate yourself and pay for your studies without recourse to public funds. Students will be given leave to enter and remain in the UK for the full length of their studies, unless there is a specific reason why they should not stay so long.

Students whose studies in the UK are longer than six months can work up to 20 hours per week during term time and full time in vacations. The income from part time work provided and guaranteed by a publicly-funded institution of further or higher education in the UK at which you are studying may be taken into account when assessing your financial means.

Any course of study followed should occupy at least 15 hours per week of organised daytime study and the student must intend to leave the UK on completion of their studies. When applying for entry clearance a letter from the educational establishment confirming acceptance on the course of study must be provided.

Further information can be found on the website of *The Council for International Education at:* www.ukcosa.org.uk.

Settling in the UK

There is no requirement to apply for settlement if you are a national of another member state of the EEA.

Those who may apply for settlement from other countries are certain non-EEA family members of a person who is already settled in the UK. These include their husband, wife or unmarried partner (including same sex partner); fiancée; children; parents, grandparents or other relatives dependent on them. There are different rules for these different family members. For instance, a husband, wife or civil partner will be allowed to stay in the UK and work for one year initially, at the end of which time they may apply to stay in the UK permanently, whereas a fiancée will only be allowed initially to stay for six months without working and may only apply to stay for a longer period once he/she is married. Children will not normally be allowed to settle in the UK while one parent lives abroad.

Arrival in Britain

Even if you have all the necessary visas and entry clearances for you and your family before arrival in Britain, you will still have to satisfy an Immigration Officer that you are entitled to enter Britain under whichever category of the rules you applied to enter. You must present your passport together with whichever of the following are applicable:

- A work permit.
- A letter from a bona fide educational establishment confirming you have been accepted on a course of study.
- A letter stating you have been offered work as an au pair, trainee or voluntary worker.
- Evidence that your qualifications are adequate for such a job or course of study.
- Evidence that you will be able to support yourself and your dependants during your stay without recourse to public funds.

Acceptable evidence of your financial status includes such things as:

- Bank statements.
- A letter from a bank.
- Travellers cheques.
- Credit cards.

If your stay is for a limited period you may have to confirm that you will leave at the end of that period.

If you leave Britain during your period of stay, you will be required to produce the same documents once again before you are readmitted to the country. EU nationals are given a form on arrival in Britain which they must produce if they stay for longer than six months.

If you are refused entry into Britain, you can appeal to an independent adjudicator and will be allowed to remain in Britain until the appeal has been heard. Appeals can take several months to be heard, so if you entered Britain for work or study it may be sensible to continue with your plans, although any long-term commitments, especially those involving substantial financial outlay or the signing of a binding contract – say, a long term lease on a property – would be unwise in case you lose your appeal.

If you arrive in Britain without entry clearance you will either be sent home immediately or will be given temporary admission of between

24 hours and a week or more while a final decision is made. This period allows you to gather any evidence you need to support your application to stay. If you are refused temporary admission you will be kept in an immigration detention centre or may be allowed to stay in private accommodation, until you can be deported.

If you are granted temporary admission you must surrender your passport and, provide the immigration officer with an address of where you will be staying. You will be told to report back to immigration at a certain date and time.

Immigration Advice

If you have any difficulties with the immigration process there are various bodies supplying help and advice. The first port of call should generally be the Immigration and Nationality Directorate. However, if you are unsure about your position, or feel your case has not been treated sympathetically, try speaking to a specialist immigration advisor. Ensure that any advisor you choose is regulated by the Office of the Immigration Services Commission (OISC), an independent public body responsible for ensuring that all immigration advisors follow good practice. Their website contains a database of approved immigration advisers.

If you are refused entry to Britain, contact the Immigration Advisory Service (IAS). Students may also contact UKCOSA, The Council for International Education.

You can appeal the decision on your case to the Immigration Appellate Authority. If you do transgress the immigration rules, it is viewed as a serious offence, and you could be deported back to your home country, so it is essential that you get advice if you are at all unsure about your eligibility.

Useful Addresses and Websites

Immigration and Nationality Directorate: 0870 606 7766 (Mon-Fri 9am-4.30pm); www.ind.homeoffice.gov.uk
UK Visas: www.ukvisas.gov.uk
Working in the UK: www.workingintheuk.gov.uk
Immigration Advisory Service (IAS): 020 7967 1200; www.iasuk.org
Immigration Appellate Authority (IAA): 0845 6000 877; www.iaa.gov.uk
British Consultates/British Missions: there are too many British Consulates and British Missions around the globe to list here. The Foreign and Commonwealth Office can give details and they have a full list on their website. 020 7008 1500; www.fco.gov.uk
Office of the Immigration Services Commission (OISC): 0845 000 0046; www.oisc.org.uk

UKCOSA, The Council for International Education: 020 7288 4330;
www.ukcosa.org.uk
Citizens Advice Bureau (CAB): Advice on immigration problems.
www.adviceguide.org.uk/index/your_rights/immigration
Northern Ireland Council for Ethnic Minorities: www.nicem.org.uk
www.scotlandistheplace.com
www.workingintheuk.com

■ RESIDENCE AND ENTRY REGULATIONS FOR NON-EU NATIONALS

The rules and regulations relating to immigration apply equally across the UK. There are no border controls between England, Scotland, Wales and Northern Ireland, and once you have been granted admittance to the UK, residence in its different countries is unrestricted. You may enter the UK through any of its constituent countries.

All overseas nationals who wish to enter the UK must satisfy the Immigration Officer at the point of arrival that they meet the requirements of the UK Immigration Rules. These rules allow or deny entry under a number of different categories and for varying lengths of stay. There are additions and amendments made to them on a regular basis, so you should always check the up-to-date position through the relevant websites.

The UK Immigration Rules are fairly complex, as there are many different categories of entry and rules regarding how long different people can stay in the country. However, the ease with which you can relocate to the UK depends ultimately on the country you come from.

Visitors from other countries must generally obtain entry clearance in the form of a visa, a work permit or an entry certificate if they wish to settle, work or set up a business in the UK. Those with a criminal record or who are subject to a deportation order may be refused entry, and people may also be refused entry on medical grounds. Visitors to the UK are not entitled to free medical treatment and should make sure they have adequate medical insurance to cover their stay. It can take up to two to three months for a visa or work permit to be approved, so allow adequate time for your application.

There are regulations regarding the maximum length of stay granted under different categories. Each application is taken on its own merits, but, if you are coming here to work, for example, you may initially be granted a one-year permission to stay, which you would then apply to renew before the end of that year.

There have been many waves of immigration to Britain from different countries. The country was shaped historically by settlers coming from elsewhere – the Romans invaded in 55AD, and were followed in succeeding centuries by settlers from Germany, Scandinavia and France. In the modern era, immigrants have arrived en masse from Ireland, Jamaica, Poland, Russia, the West Indies, the Indian Sub-continent and Asia at different times and for different reasons. As a result, the population of Britain has a diverse mix of nationalities, with the highest proportion of these in the larger cities. London alone has 270 nationalities living there, with over 250 languages spoken.

UK Immigration Rules

Those with the right of abode are completely free from UK immigration control and do not need to have their passports stamped by an immigration officer on entry to the UK. They may also live and work there without restriction.

All British citizens have the right of abode and can apply for a British Passport, possession of which will be sufficient proof of their right of abode.

Commonwealth citizens with a parent or grandparent who was born in the UK, and those whose partners have the right of abode, may also have the right of abode. Depending on their particular circumstances, they may be restricted to a maximum stay of four years, but they have the right to apply for an extension to their stay. This application must be made before the initial agreed period of stay has ended.

The following countries are members of the British Commonwealth:

Antigua and Barbuda, Australia, Bahamas, Bangladesh, Barbados, Belize, Botswana, Brunei, Cameroon, Canada, Cyprus, Dominica, Gambia, Ghana, Grenada, India, Jamaica, Kenya, Kiribati, Lesotho, Malawi, Malaysia, Maldives, Malta, Mauritius, Mozambique, Namibia, Nauru, New Zealand, Nigeria, Pakistan, Papua New Guinea, Saint Kitts and Nevis, Saint Lucia, Saint Vincent and the Grenadines, Samoa, Seychelles, Sierra Leone, Solomon Islands, South Africa, Sri Lanka, Swaziland, Tanzania, Tonga, Trinidad and Tobago, Tuvalu, Uganda, Vanuatu, Zambia.

In order to prove you have the right of abode, you may apply for a Certificate of Entitlement. This may be applied for by Commonwealth citizens who satisfy the above conditions, and by those British Citizens who are travelling on a foreign or Commonwealth passport. Application forms are available from any British mission (Embassy or Consulate) offering a visa service. There is a non-refundable fee payable.

ENTRY FOR US CITIZENS AND NON-EEA NATIONALS

The general position under the Immigration Rules is that overseas nationals (other than EEA nationals) coming to work in Britain must have work permits before setting out. The employer (not the employee) has to apply to Work Permits (UK), which administers the scheme. Permits are issued only for specific jobs requiring a high level of skill and experience for which residents of the country or EEA labour is not available. In other words, a UK employer will not receive a work permit for a non-EEA citizen unless it is a job for which there is no EEA National available.

The last 50 years have seen a major increase in economic migration to the UK. The country's immigration policy has evolved organically over this period and has been struggling to cope, both with the numbers of migrants and with the many and varied entry routes, there are more than 80 possible ways into the country to study, work or train). As a result of this complexity, Britain is now in the process of introducing a simplified points-based immigration policy, based on a model pioneered by Australia.

This new policy consists of a five-tier framework, through which all applications by non-EEA residents wishing to work, study or train in the UK will be judged. Tier one (dealing with highly trained professionals) and tier two (which focuses on skilled workers with a job offer in the UK), are being implemented in 2008, while tiers three to five, which deal with low skilled workers, students and temporary workers respectively, will be introduced over the course of 2008 and 2009. The system is expected to be fully operational by summer 2009 and until than, there will be a number of schemes running concurrently. In essence, the new scheme is intended to speed up and simplify the immigration process, but it will clearly take some time to be fully functional. In the meantime, entry regulations for certain professionals and for students may be subject to change. Consult the UK's Border and Immigration Agency website (details below) for the latest information. The information provided in this book is current as of March 2008.

The rules and regulations relating to immigration apply equally across the UK. There are no border controls between England, Scotland, Wales and Northern Ireland, and once you have been granted admittance to the UK, residence in its different countries is unrestricted. You may enter the UK through any of its constituent countries.

 http://www.bia.homeoffice.gov.uk/managingborders/managingmigration/apointsbasedsystem/howitworks

Entry Clearance

An entry clearance is a visa or an entry certificate issued to a passenger prior to travel to the UK. A person who has an entry clearance will not be refused admission as long as there has not been a material change of circumstances since the entry clearance was obtained.

Holders of entry clearances may be refused entry if they have a criminal record or if they are subject to a deportation order. They may also be refused entry on medical grounds. With few exceptions, visitors to the UK are not entitled to free medical treatment and a charge will be made for any treatment received. Visitors should make sure they have adequate medical insurance to cover their stay.

Application for entry clearance should be made through the British Mission in the country in which the applicant is living, or through the Immigration & Nationality Directorate website www.ind.homeoffice.gov.uk. Downloadable leaflets and application forms on all aspects of visa information are also available.

It should be noted that in all cases, long or short-term visitors to the UK must be able to support and accommodate themselves in the UK without recourse to public funds.

It is advisable to allow two to three months for a visa or work permit to be approved.

British Visas

Nationals of the following countries or territories must have a visa to enter the UK:

Afghanistan, Albania, Algeria, Angola, Armenia, Azerbaijan, Bahrain, Bangladesh, Belarus, Benin, Bhutan, Bosnia-Herzegovina, Burkina Faso, Burma, Burundi, Cambodia, Cameroon, Cape Verde, Central African Republic, Chad, China, Colombia, Comoros, Congo, Cuba, Djibouti, Dominican Republic, Ecuador, Egypt, Equatorial Guinea, Eritrea, Ethiopia, Fiji, Gabon, Gambia, Georgia, Ghana, Guinea, Guinea Bissau, Guyana, Haiti, India, Indonesia, Iran, Iraq, Ivory Coast, Jamaica, Jordan, Kazakhstan, Kenya, North Korea, Kuwait, Kyrgyzstan, Laos, Lebanon, Liberia, Libya, Macedonia, Madagascar, Malawi, Mali, Mauritania, Moldova, Mongolia, Montenegro, Morocco, Mozambique, Nepal, Niger, Nigeria, Oman, Pakistan, Peru, Palestinian Authority, Philippines, Qatar, Russia, Rwanda, Sao Tome & Principe, Saudi Arabia, Senegal, Serbia, Sierra Leone, Somalia, Sri Lanka, Sudan, Surinam, Syria, Taiwan, Tajikistan, Tanzania, Thailand, Togo, Tunisia, Turkey, Turkmenistan, Uganda, Ukraine, United Arab Emirates, Uzbekistan, Vietnam, Yemen, Yugoslavia, Zambia, Zimbabwe.

> Plainly and simply, it is not easy to move here as a US citizen.
> I spent hours reading websites and going back and forth from
> page to page trying to make sense of it all. The language seemed
> intentionally vague and in places downright contradictory. I spent
> a great deal of time speaking to, supposedly, knowledgeable people
> who were there to assist me... when in actuality what I found was
> that I was getting a different story from each and every person
> I spoke with, and each one of those stories differed slightly from
> what I could make out from the websites. I also spent a lot of money,
> mainly because no matter what 'free' telephone number they gave
> me it always directed me back to a number which required a credit
> card and billed a high per-minute fee for advice. Once I was clear
> on my options, it became even clearer that there was actually
> very little there for me to understand. As a US citizen, my
> options for entering Britain and staying for more than
> six months as a visitor allows were practically none!
> Amy Burns, from USA

People from these countries are known as visa nationals.
In addition, the following also need visas:

- persons who hold passports or travel documents issued by the former Soviet Union or the former Socialist Federal Republic of Yugoslavia; stateless persons; persons who hold non-national documents.

If entering as a visitor, you must show that you are able to support and accommodate yourself without working in the UK. This support and accommodation may be provided by family and friends in the UK but not from public funds. A visitor is not allowed to work in the UK, but may conduct business, and must intend to leave the UK after a maximum stay of six months.

Nationals of any other country do not need a UK visa for a visit or to study for up to six months but must obtain a visa or entry clearance if they wish to settle, work, set up a business or study for longer than six months. There are fees payable for visas and entry certificates.

Commonwealth Citizens

Commonwealth citizens with a grandparent born in the UK, Channel Islands or the Isle of Man qualify for UK ancestry. If they can show they are able to work and intend to seek work in the UK they will be granted entry for a period of four years and will not need a work permit.

Students

Currently, you may enter the UK for study or training as long as you can support and accommodate yourself and pay for your studies without recourse to public funds. Students will be given leave to enter and remain in the UK for the full length of their studies, unless there is a specific reason why they should not stay so long. They should apply for a student visa once they have been accepted on an eligible course of study in the UK. For details see www.ukvisas.gov.uk.

Students whose studies in the UK are longer than six months can work up to 20 hours per week during term time and full-time in vacations. Students whose studies involve a period of work placement, as with some vocational, engineering and scientific courses, do not need to obtain a work permit. The income from part-time work provided and guaranteed by a publicly-funded institution of further or higher education in the UK at which you are studying may be taken into account when assessing your financial means.

Any course of study followed should occupy at least fifteen hours per week of organised daytime study and the student must intend to leave the UK on completion of their studies. When applying for entry clearance a letter from the educational establishment confirming acceptance on the course of study must be provided.

Highly Skilled Migrants

The Highly Skilled Migrant Programme (HSMP) was established to encourage entry to the UK for successful people with sought-after skills who are seeking to work, invest or set up businesses. Highly Skilled Migrants currently working in the UK are the first category of foreign workers to be assessed under the UK's new points-based system for economic migrants, and applicants from India need to use the new system to apply from

April 2008. Later in the year, highly-skilled workers across the rest of the world will need to meet the pre-conditions of tier one of the points-based scheme, but until this scheme has rolled out fully, they can still apply under the terms of the HSMP.

Although the entry requirements for both the points-based system and the HSMP don't specify particular in-demand professions, both schemes favour young, highly-skilled individuals with a good level of qualification that is recognised by the British academic system. Initial applications to the HSMP involve a two-stage process. The first stage of the application is to pass the points-based and English-language assessments–called the HSMP application. You should apply using application form HSMP1. The second stage is to apply for permission to enter or permission to stay in the UK as a highly-skilled migrant. You will need to pay a fee when you make your application. This fee will not be refunded if your application is unsuccessful.

If you are granted entry clearance or leave to remain as a highly-skilled migrant you will be able to live and work in the United Kingdom for a maximum period of 24 months. When the end of this period approaches you will need to apply to extend your stay as a highly-skilled migrant.

If your first stage HSMP application is successful you will receive a HSMP approval letter and you can move onto the second stage of the process. If you are living overseas when you do this, you will need to make an application for entry clearance before you can travel to the United Kingdom. You must make this application within six months of receiving your HSMP approval letter. Entry clearance applications are processed by UK visas. You will need to make your application at the nearest British diplomatic post. The diplomatic post where you make your application will be able to provide you with full details on how to apply for entry clearance, the cost, and what supporting documents you need to provide.

If you are currently living in the United Kingdom under the HSMP, you should apply to change your status to tier one of the points-based system. Visit http://www.bia.homeoffice.gov.uk for the latest information from the Border and Immigration Agency on the scheme.

The basic requirement for entry under this scheme is a total score of 95 points made up of scores in a variety of areas:

■ Two essential prerequisites:
  – The English Language requirement: To show that you meet the required level of proficiency in English, you must either have passed an IELTS (International English Language Testing System) exam with a score of six or more within the last two years (visit www.ielts.org for details of tests, which can be taken at centres worldwide); completed a degree that was taught in English, or be a resident of a country in which English is the mother tongue (eg. Caribbean countries and the US). This category is worth 10 points.

- Sufficient demonstrable funds to maintain your life in the UK without recourse to state assistance (worth 10 points).

■ You must also have a combination of the following additional factors (adding up to a score of at least 75 points):
- The MBA (Masters in Business Administration) provision: To qualify for this provision, the applicant must have completed an MBA in a recognised, eligible institution. This provision is worth 75 points.
- Qualifications: You can earn up to 50 points in this section, with a PhD scoring the maximum points. Your qualification has to reach the standard set by the National Academic Recognition Information Centre (NARIC – www.naric.org.uk). Vocational qualifications that are demonstrably equivalent to UK alternatives may also be accepted.
- Previous earnings: You can earn up to 45 points in this category. Points may be awarded for your earnings before tax over a period of up to 12 consecutive months in the last 15 months. The number of points you are awarded will depend on your earnings and the country in which you were living and working.
- UK experience: You can earn up to five points under this category if you have had the relevant level of work or study experience in the UK over the last five years.
- Age: This category is worth up to 20 points if you are aged 27 or under with lower bands of points as age increases. Applicants aged over 32 score no points in this category.

The outgoing HSMP scheme consists of broadly the same points-based assessment procedure. For full details of the HSMP scheme and information on how to submit a first-stage application visit www.bia.homeoffice. gov.uk.

The Fresh Talent: Working in Scotland Scheme

This scheme was launched on 22 June 2005 and applies to overseas students who have been awarded a Higher National Diploma (HND), undergraduate degree, Master's degree or PhD from a Scottish university. They must also have lived in Scotland whilst studying.

Participants are granted up to two years leave after being awarded their qualification. During this time they can undertake any type of employment (paid or unpaid, self-employed or business) in the UK, without the need for a work permit or other permission from the Home Office.

Entry as an Employee

There are various categories of people entering the UK as an employee who do not need a work permit. These are Commonwealth citizens with a grandparent born in the UK and Islands (see above) and those whose employment falls into one of the following categories:

- A working holidaymaker or au pair.
- A minister of religion, a missionary or a member of a religious order.
- The representative of a firm with no representative in the UK.
- A representative of an overseas newspaper, news agency or broadcasting organisation on long-term assignment to the UK.
- A domestic worker or a member of staff on a diplomatic or consular mission.
- A domestic worker in a private household.
- A teacher or language assistant coming to a UK school under an exchange scheme.
- A member of the operational ground staff of an overseas airline.
- A postgraduate doctor or dentist coming for training.
- A seasonal worker at an agricultural camp.

US students seeking temporary work in the UK can benefit from the 'Work in Britain Program'. This allows full-time college students and recent graduates over the age of 18 to look for work in Britain; finding jobs through BUNAC listings or through personal contacts. Jobs may be pre-arranged, though most participants wait until arrival in Britain to job hunt. US students on study abroad programmes through an American University overseas are also eligible for the programme.

To qualify for the scheme, students must first obtain a BUNAC 'Blue Card' recognised by the British Home Office as a valid substitute for a work permit. The Blue Card must be presented to immigration on arrival in the UK. It is valid for six months and cannot be extended, although it is possible to obtain a second Blue Card in another calendar year if they again fulfill the eligibility requirements. The Blue Card costs $290 from BUNAC Connecticut. See www.bunac.org for more details.

All other intending employees will need a work permit, which must be applied for on their behalf by their intended employer in the UK. Your work permit must be obtained before travel to the UK or you will be refused entry. Visa nationals need a visa in addition to a work permit, and the visa cannot be issued until they have a work permit to show to the visa officer.

"Immigration was pretty much straightforward since I had letters of support from my employer and the British embassy in Eritrea."
Joe Rawal, from Africa

Entry as Self-Employed

Visitors to the UK are free to transact business during their stay. You may come to the UK permanently to set yourself up in business or self-employment, or to join as a partner or take over an existing business, pending you satisfy the following requirements. You must bring at least £200,000 of your own money to invest in the business and your investment must create new, paid, full-time employment for at least two people who are already settled in the UK. In addition you must show that there is a genuine need for the services you will be offering.

Writers, artists and composers who intend to support themselves by self-employment in their field may be admitted to the UK as long as they can satisfy the immigration authorities that they are bona fide and have a proven track record in their field in the country in which they have been living.

The Innovator Scheme is aimed at those who have a new business idea that will bring considerable economic benefits to the UK, particularly in the areas of information technology and telecommunications. To apply under the scheme you must have a business idea that is new and innovative; you must bring exceptional economic benefit to the UK; you must have sufficient funding in place or agreed in principle to establish the business; you must create employment for at least two people; you must have significant business experience; you must maintain at least a 5% shareholding of the equity capital in the business.

Investors

If you intend to come to the UK as an investor, you must have documentary evidence to show that you have capital of at least £1m and that you intend to invest not less than £750,000 in approved UK government bonds or companies. The UK must become your main home.

Retired Persons

Retired persons of at least 60 years of age must be able to show that they have an annual income of at least £25,000 which must be disposable in the UK. You must be able to support and accommodate yourself and any dependants indefinitely without working, without assistance from anyone else and without recourse to public funds.

In addition to the financial requirements you will also need to show that you have a close connection with the UK.

Working Holidaymakers

The working holidaymaker scheme allows young Commonwealth citizens the opportunity to come to the UK for an extended holiday which they may help fund by working in the UK for up to a maximum of two years. To qualify you must be a Commonwealth citizen, be aged 17 to 30 inclusive and either be unmarried, or married to a working holidaymaker who is taking the holiday with you.

During the period of stay, you may take employment incidental to a holiday but not set yourself up in or run a business. You can choose when to work and when to take your holiday breaks, but you are not allowed to work for more than a total of 12 months out of the 24. You must also be able to prove you have enough money for your accommodation and living expenses for the first two months after you arrive, or for at least one month if you can show that you have arranged a job in advance.

Council Exchanges and BUNAC run schemes which allow US and other citizens to work in Britain for limited periods. See the *Entry As An Employee section for further details.*

Au Pairs

The au pair scheme allows single people to learn English by living with an English-speaking family. In return for working in the home the au pair must be given a reasonable allowance and two days off each week.

To qualify as an au pair you must be aged between 17 and 27, be unmarried and have no dependants, be taking up a pre-arranged placement and be a national of one of the following countries: Andorra, Bosnia-Herzegovina, Croatia, The Faroes, Greenland, Macedonia, Monaco, San Marino, or Turkey.

The maximum time you may stay as an au pair is two years.

British Citizenship

Anyone who does not automatically qualify for British citizenship may apply, if over the age of 18, to become a British citizen. This process is also called naturalisation. To qualify the applicant must have lived legally in Britain for at least five years without being absent for more than 450 days and with less than 90 days absence in the year preceding the application. In addition the applicant must intend to continue living in Britain, have a good knowledge of English, Welsh or Gaelic and have no criminal record.

Anyone over 18 and married to a British citizen may apply for naturalisation if they have lived in Britain legally for at least three years without being absent for more than 270 days.

It is not necessary to give up your original nationality as you may have dual nationality under British law.

Entry Clearance Fees

Fees vary depending on the length of your proposed stay and the category under which you enter the UK. At the time of writing they vary between £22 and £260, and are subject to periodical review and amendment. For a full list and latest fee schedule see www.skillclear.co.uk. Entry fees are payable in the local currency of the country in which you are currently residing, so contact your nearest British mission, embassy or consulate for the fee that is currently being charged. These are listed on the Foreign & Commonwealth Office website at www.fco.gov.uk.

■ ARRIVAL IN BRITAIN

Even if you have all the necessary visas and entry clearances for you and your family before arrival in Britain, you will still have to satisfy an

Immigration Officer that you are entitled to enter Britain under whichever category of the rules you applied to enter. You must present your passport together with whichever of the following are applicable:

- Your visa or entry clearance.
- A work permit.
- A letter from a bona fide educational establishment confirming you have been accepted on a course of study.
- A letter stating that you have been offered work as an au pair, trainee or voluntary worker.
- Evidence that your qualifications are adequate for such a job or course of study.
- Evidence that you will be able to support yourself and your dependants during your stay without recourse to public funds.

Acceptable evidence of your financial status includes such things as:

- Bank statements.
- A letter from a bank.
- Travellers cheques.
- Credit cards.

If you leave Britain during your period of stay, you will be required to produce the same documents once again before you are readmitted to the country. If entering from certains countries you may also need to have immunisation certificates.

The Immigration Officer can send new arrivals for a routine heath check before allowing them to have their passport stamped and permitting them entry to Britain.

If you are refused entry into Britain, as long as you have entry clearance such as a visa, entry certificate, letter of consent or work permit, you cannot be sent immediately back to your home country. You can appeal to an independent adjudicator and will be allowed to remain in Britain until the appeal has been heard. Appeals can take several months to be heard, so if you entered Britain for work or study it may be sensible to continue with your plans, although any long-term commitments, especially those involving substantial financial outlay or the signing of a binding contract – say, a long-term lease on a property – would be unwise in case you lose your appeal.

If you arrive in Britain without entry clearance you will either be sent home immediately or will be given temporary admission of between 24 hours and a week or more while a final decision is made. This period allows you to gather any evidence you need to support your application to stay. If you are refused temporary admission you will be kept in an immigration detention centre or may be allowed to stay in private accommodation, until you can be deported.

If you are granted temporary admission you must surrender your passport, provide the immigration officer with an address of where you will be staying. You will be told to report back to immigration at a certain date and time.

THE LANGUAGES

The main language spoken in Britain is English. As you travel around Britain, you will find there is a big variation in the way English is spoken in different places. England, Scotland, Wales, and Northern Ireland all have distinctive accents which affect the way the same words are pronounced in the different regions, and there are also distinctive accents in the different areas of each country speak differently. Add to this the existence of regional dialect words and grammatical usages, and this can lead to difficulties with understanding what is being said – it can even be a problem for Britons themselves, let alone for foreigners.

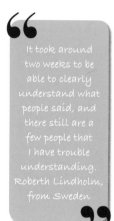

It took around two weeks to be able to clearly understand what people said, and there still are a few people that I have trouble understanding. Roberth Lindholm, from Sweden

Welsh

Welsh is a Celtic language which has experienced a major revival in recent years, notably since the Welsh Language Act of 1993. It now has equal status with English in the public sector in Wales, and all council documents are produced in English and Welsh, while road signs and signs on and in public buildings are bilingual. There are around 611,000 Welsh-speakers in Wales, plus another 133,000 in England, mainly along the Welsh border. The language is taught in all Welsh schools and schools in the western counties of Wales may indeed teach all classes and subjects in the medium of Welsh.

Gaelic

Gaelic, a Celtic language, is spoken in both Scotland and Ireland. The Gaelic language was originally introduced to Scotland from Ireland around the fifth century. Over the centuries, the language has mutated in both countries so that now there are distinct differences between Scottish and Irish Gaelic. These differences are mainly in the area of vocabulary and pronunciation – the latter clearly seen in the fact that in Scotland the word Gaelic is pronounced 'gallic' and in Ireland 'gaylic'.

Today, Scottish Gaelic is spoken by around 59,000 people, mainly in the Highlands and Islands. There has for some years been a movement to revive Gaelic, and children in Scotland have the option of taking their education in Gaelic. It is estimated there are about 168,000 Gaelic-speakers in Northern Ireland and many more in the Republic. It is an official language of the EU.

Scottish Dialects

The various forms of 'Scots' include Lowland Scots, Lallans and Doric, which is a group of dialects with a strong Scandinavian influence, spoken in Aberdeen and the north-east. Although they are, strictly speaking, dialects rather than full-fledged languages, the European Charter for Minority and Regional Languages recognises Scots as a minority language.

Other Languages

Because of the large number of races and nationalities living in Britain, there are many other languages spoken. Although there is no official source giving a detailed breakdown of how many people in the UK have English as a second language, more than 300 languages are spoken by schoolchildren in London.

Top 10 Languages Spoken by Children in London	
Language	**Speakers**
English	608,500
Bengali and Sylheti	40,400
Punjabi	29,800
Gujarati	28,600
Hindi/Urdu	26,000
Turkish	15,600
Arabic	11,000
English-based Creoles	10,700
Yoruba (Nigeria)	10,400
Somali	8,300

◣ BANKS AND FINANCE

There is a great deal of competition between the retail banks, and they offer a wide range of services to both personal and business customers. Accounts offered vary from bank to bank, but there are basically two kinds; current accounts and savings, or deposit–accounts. For personal customers, there are usually no charges made on either current or deposit accounts as long as you keep your account in credit. Bank opening hours vary from place to place, with some city centre banks staying open in the evening and on Saturdays. Core opening hours are Monday to Friday 9am–5pm.

Addresses and phone numbers of local bank and building society branches can be found in local phone books business pages or through the banks websites:

FACT

◣ Bank opening hours vary from place to place, with some city centre banks staying open in the evening and on Saturdays. Core opening hours are Monday to Friday 9am to 5pm.

Abbey: 0870 607 6000; www.abbey.com

Alliance & Leicester: www.alliance-leicester.co.uk

Barclays: 0845 677 0002; www.barclays.co.uk

HSBC: 0800 032 4738; www.hsbc.co.uk

Lloyds TSB: 0845 300 0000; www.lloydstsb.com

Natwest: 0800 015 4212; www.natwest.com

Bank of Scotland: www.bankofscotland.co.uk

The Royal Bank of Scotland: www.rbs.co.uk

First Trust Bank: 028 9032 5599; www.firsttrust.bank.co.uk

Northern Bank: 028 9024 5277; www.northernbank.co.uk

Egg: www.egg.com

Smile: www.smile.co.uk

Banking: an overview

Current accounts generally pay a low rate of interest on credit balances, which varies depending on the type of account. Cheque books are available free. Cheque guarantee cards will, as their name suggests, guarantee funds to cover the value of the cheque, usually £50 or £100 for a normal account. If your bank deems your account to be healthy enough to deserve a gold card, this guarantees to a maximum of £250. In 99% of cases, a cheque will not be accepted unless it is supported by a guarantee card.

The card will also usually allow you to withdraw cash, request a balance or statement or access other services from 'cashpoints' (ATMs). These are usually situated outside banks or in other outlets such as supermarkets or garages. Most of the main banks belong to the Link system which means you can use your card in a cash machine provided by another bank. There will be a daily limit on the amount of cash you can withdraw, which will vary depending on the type of account you have and the funds you normally have available. However, cash can only be withdrawn if there are funds in your account to cover the amount.

Overdraft facilities are available on current accounts, at a variable interest rate set by the bank on the basis of current Bank of England rates. Overdrafts must first be agreed with the bank, although some accounts have a basic agreed overdraft limit of around £100, in case of accidentally or temporarily going into the 'red'. Unauthorised overdrafts will be charged for, with service charges on transactions plus a high rate of interest, often equivalent to over 30% per annum.

Standing orders and direct debits can be arranged on current accounts for the automatic transfer of regular amounts of money for the payment of monthly bills and so forth. To compare the best current account deals available, visit a price comparison website such as www. moneysupermarket.com.

Deposit accounts are savings accounts which pay a higher rate of interest, often on a sliding scale so that the larger your credit balance, the higher the rate of interest payable. A basic deposit account will allow withdrawals or money transfers on demand, and may offer a cheque book and cash card facility.

Other savings accounts require 30 or 90 days notice for withdrawal of funds without loss of interest. These pay a correspondingly higher rate of interest. Some accounts offer other facilities and may charge a maintenance fee. Individual banks will provide details of their range of accounts on request, or they are available in most cases online.

Business accounts for small to medium-size enterprises are similar in type and operation to personal accounts–with the difference being that fees are charged on each withdrawal or deposit, whether made by cheque or electronically. These charges vary from bank to bank so it is best to shop around to find the best deal, although some banks will waive all charges for the first year of operation on the account in order to attract your business. If you run a one-man or woman business – such as running a holiday cottage, or working as a freelance writer – it is best, therefore, just to have a personal current and/or deposit account and avoid bank charges, which can be punitive.

Banks issue quarterly or monthly bank statements which are posted to your address and itemise all transactions on the account in the period. You may also request a statement at other times.

Tax is generally payable on interest earned on savings. There are, however, special savings accounts, called ISAs (Individual Savings Accounts) which allow you to save a specified maximum amount tax-free. ISAs currently allow a maximum of £7,000 per year to be saved, over a period of ten years.

Opening an Account

It is very hard to exist in Britain without a bank account, but organising an account from overseas is incredibly difficult. There are three main options. Firstly, you can arrange for an account to be set up before you arrive. Some banks offer a premium service to overseas customers which is most effective if you bank with a large international bank (such as HSBC) that has branches in your home country. HSBC, for example, can arrange all the practical elements of your UK bank account prior to arrival in UK, only requiring an identity check when you arrive in the country to activate the facility. The downside of this service is that it comes at a fairly high cost and can sometimes require a significant deposit prior to arrival.

> Opening a bank account is a pain if you move here from abroad. The anti money-laundering regulations require you to have certain proofs of address which you do not have when you have recently moved. There is a possibility to open an account in UK with HSBC from your home country as they have something called HSBC Passport. I would advise anyone moving here from abroad to look into that if needed as it really would make things a bit easier.
> Roberth Lindholm, from Sweden

The terms, fees and requirements vary from country to country and from bank to bank.

A second option is to go through a banking package company, such as 1stContact or Visa First, which aims 3 to make the process of applying for a bank account easier for migrants who can provide evidence of a fixed address in their home country, but not necessarily in the UK. This service is only offered to people coming from Australia, New Zealand, Canada, South Africa, the US and the EU, but it may provide a possible short cut for anyone from those countries-wanting to get set up quickly. Beware, however, that the costs of this type of 'quick-fix' matching service may again be high.

The third option is to wait until you arrive. This presents something of a catch-22, as you will need proof of address (such as a utility bill), as well as proof of identity (like a driver's licence or passport), but it can be hard to find accommodation if you don't already have a bank account. Application forms for the various different accounts are available from branches or, increasingly, online. You will need to supply personal details of name, address, date of birth, occupation and so forth.

If you are planning to work in Britain, you are most likely to be paid monthly and the money will be paid directly into your bank account with a payslip posted or handed to you separately by your employer. Some people are still paid weekly, and may be paid in cash, but this number is dwindling.

Plastic Money

Debit Cards

This allows money to be taken electronically from your card at poin of sale as long as there are funds to cover it currently in the account. There is no cost for the service and no interest payable. Debit cards have almost eliminated the need for paper cheques (which are now not accepted in most major supermarkets and at petrol stations) due to their ease of use.

Mail-order companies, traditional and online, will take debit card payments. Many shops now allow customers to obtain an advance of up to £50 in cash from their account, known as 'cash-back' when paying with a debit card.

Credit Cards

Credit cards are issued by most financial institutions including all banks and building societies and a range of other organisations such as car manufacturers, chain stores and charities. The most widely accepted credit cards in Britain are Visa and Mastercard (Eurocard).

Store-branded credit cards, such as those issued by retail giant Marks & Spencer, are mainly intended for use against purchases in that store, and offer incentives such as discounts on purchases in order to encourage shoppers to use them.

Credit cards allow you to spread repayments over a period, with interest payable on the balance owing, unless you pay off all outstanding balances at the end of each month, in which case no interest is charged. There may be an annual fee charged in addition to the interest; while those cards with no annual fee may charge a higher rate of interest, so it is advisable to read the small print of any cards you are considering. Store cards tend to carry a higher than average rate of interest.

Most credit cards are issued as ordinary, gold or platinum cards with different credit levels. The gold and platinum cards may also have extra benefits included in the package.

Chip and Pin

When using your credit card or debit card in a shop or to pay for services face to face, you enter your personal four digit security code (PIN number) into the electronic card reader. This replaces the requirement for a signature, and is regarded as a more secure system.

Charge Cards

The main difference between credit cards and charge cards is that with a charge card you must pay the total outstanding balance when it is due, otherwise you will incur penalty fee. Charge cards include American Express and Diners Club. They are far less popular in Britain, and to counteract this American Express introduced a UK credit card in 1995.

International charge cards, if lost or stolen, can usually be replaced at short notice, which may not be possible with a credit card. Gold and platinum cards may allow instant access to large amounts of cash or an unsecured overdraft facility at an advantageous interest rate.

Credit Card Websites
Mastercard: www.mastercard.com/uk
Visa: www.visaeurope.com
American Express: www.americanexpress.com/uk

> Setting up bank accounts and credit cards was particularly frustrating. I needed to supply letters from bank managers in Ireland and the US who would never have laid eyes on me. For a while, having no UK credit history was a real pain, but it gradually built up, more through having my name on the electoral roll, I guess. Funnily enough, while the bank was reticent in minding my money, the taxman had no such compunctions – gladly setting my tax codes with the minimum of fuss.
> Bob Grayson, from USA

Account options

Building Societies

In 1987, the regulations regarding financial institutions were changed, and now building societies offer much the same range of services as banks (and vice versa) and some of the bigger building societies have converted into banks.

Many building societies now offer current accounts with a cheque book, cheque guarantee card and all the other 'add-ons' offered by the banks. Rather than issuing statements, building societies usually issue you with a 'pass book' in which all transactions on your accounts are recorded. You need to take or send the book to the building society for it to be updated.

Post Office

The post office has its own bank, called the Giro Bank, which offers a range of different accounts. Cash can be withdrawn through the post office or can be obtained from cash machines (ATMs).

The post office also operates the National Savings Bank which has two main savings accounts; the ordinary account and the deposit account. These don't allow the use of cheques or cards, so are better for longer-term savings. The deposit account pays a higher rate of interest, on a sliding scale depending on the balance, because it requires 90 days notice for withdrawals.

Telephone and Online Banking

Banks now have telephone and online banking facilities. Both of these allow you, either through your telephone or your computer, to check recent transactions, make transfers of money between accounts and pay bills.

There are also some online banks which do not have physical branches. Applications for and administering of accounts is all done online, although you do need to mail them certain documents confirming your identity before they will open an account for you.

Loans

Personal and business loans are available through a variety of financial institutions, such as banks, building societies and credit card companies. In addition, other institutions such as mail-order catalogue companies and retailers such as Marks & Spencer and Tesco offer their own financial services, including loans. Interest rates can vary greatly, so you should always shop around carefully to find the best deal for your own circumstances.

Currency

The unit of currency is the pound (£) of 100 pence (100p). Coins are in denominations of 1p, 2p, 5p, 10p, 20p, 50p, £1, £2. Notes are in denominations of £5, £10, £20 and £50.

All these are acceptable in England, Scotland, Wales and Northern Ireland. All coins are issued by the Royal Mint and banknotes by the Bank of England, the main bank of issue. In addition, certain banks in Scotland and Northern Ireland issue their own banknotes. By a strange anomaly these banknotes are not technically classed as legal tender, but they are an authorised currency and have a status comparable to that of Bank of England notes.

It is best to avoid taking Scottish or Northern Irish notes abroad, because you may receive a lower exchange rate than for Bank of England notes.

The Euro

Britain has not yet joined the Euro, the Single European Currency. Before the decision is made whether to join or not, the UK Government has said they will see how the Euro performs. Once certain 'economic tests' have been met (determined by the Treasury) a referendum will be held for the UK people to decide whether to join the Euro zone or not. If there was a 'yes' vote it would take several years after that before the Euro was in use in Britain.

However, some businesses which trade within the Euro zone find it convenient to carry out their business using the Euro, and some large retailers will accept Euros for purchases. You would be given any change in pounds.

The EU's official multi-lingual website contains information about the Euro. http://europa.eu.int.

Foreign Currency

Britain has no currency restrictions, which means you may take out or bring in as much money as you wish in most currencies. The major banks will change most foreign bank notes, but will not exchange foreign coins. You will probably get a better rate of exchange for travellers' cheques than for bank notes.

When buying or selling currency, shop around for the best deal. Exchange rates are posted by banks and bureaux de change, and may vary from place to place. In addition, there is sometimes a commission charged on top of that, typically of around 1%–2% with a minimum charge of £2.50. Building societies and larger post offices also buy and sell foreign currency. You may need to order currency or travellers' cheques two or three days in advance. Take your passport if buying or selling foreign currency.

Transferring Funds

Money can be transferred to Britain by a banker's draft or a letter of credit. It may take up to two weeks to be cleared. Money can also be sent via a post office, by international money order, a cashier's cheque or by way of a telegraphic transfer such as Western Union. You will need your passport to collect money transferred from abroad or to cash a banker's draft or other credit note.

You can send money direct from your bank to another via an interbank transfer. Unless both banks are in the UK, both the sending and receiving bank will charge a service charge or a percentage of the amount transferred, so it may be expensive for small sums. An alternative option is to use an internet money transfer service, such as www.tranzfers.com or www.onlinefx.co.uk. These are fast and efficient and the fees are normally much more competitive than the traditional methods of transfer.

■ GETTING THERE

However you choose to travel to the UK, whether by plane, ferry, road or rail, you will almost certainly be able to book your tickets online. If you prefer not to use the internet, travel agents in your home country should be able to arrange your itinerary and tickets.

Flights within the UK and to selected international destinations, mainly within Europe, are becoming far cheaper than they have been in the past, especially since the arrival of low-cost 'no-frills' airlines including Ryanair and Easyjet. In March 2007 the skies between the UK and USA were opened to greater competition, having previously been restricted to very few airlines, so falling transatlantic prices may be seen in the future.

Coach travel is also becoming cheaper, with at least one company taking a leaf out of the book of the low-cost airlines and offering very cheap inter-city travel within the UK. By and large, train fares are not following suit, as this is still an expensive way to travel. It is estimated that on some long-distance routes within Britain rail travel is up to three times more expensive than in other European countries. However, you can take advantage of reduced fares if you are able to book in advance, either through an online service like www.thetrainline.com or in person at a train station. There are also family, senior citizen and young persons' railcards available for purchase which give a discount each time you buy train tickets.

UK Public Transport Information

There are a number of websites which have links to public transport providers throughout Britain, and these are a good place to start when planning your journey. Here are some of the best:

Seaview: Comprehensive details of ferry routes throughout Europe, with online booking service. www.seaview.co.uk

The Trainline: Details of train services, routes and timetables throughout the UK. Train tickets for all UK services can be bought online.
www.thetrainline.com

Translink: Bus and rail services within Northern Ireland.
www.translink.co.uk

Traveline: Impartial information on planning your journey, by bus, coach or train... or any combination of the three. www.traveline.org.uk/index.htm

UK Superweb Online: Site has details of and links to airports, airlines, and public transport throughout the UK. http://www.uksuperweb.co.uk/index.html.

By Air

If you are flying to Britain, you will most likely be flying into one of the main London airports – Heathrow or Gatwick – with connecting flights to regional airports if necessary. However, there are increasing numbers of

> *Always plenty of public transport choices. Obviously it would be preferable if trains etc. ran as reliably as on the continent. I love the easy access to Europe by air, and London is a hub of long haul airline routes.*
> Sue Hardie

> *Transport played a major role in our choice of location. Edinburgh was out because house prices were too expensive. Cornwall was out because the travel connections to London were not good enough. North east England was too rural and did not fulfil the kids' requirements. We were left with Stirling northwards, and in fact Inverness had the best travel connections with the south east, having the sleeper and planes.*
> Caroline Deacon

international flights available from regional airports, so you may choose to fly directly into Scotland, Wales or Northern Ireland if that is your ultimate destination. The main Scottish airports are at Glasgow, Edinburgh and Aberdeen, while Inverness airport has flights to many of the Scottish Islands. Cardiff airport in Wales, and Belfast airport in Northern Ireland both have international as well as domestic flights.

Major Airlines Operating in Britain

British Airways: 0870 850 9850; www.ba.com.
bmi: 0870 6070555; www.flybmi.com.
Easyjet: 0871 7500 100; www.easyjet.com.
flybe: 0871 700 0535; www.flybe.com.
Ryanair: 0818 303030; www.ryanair.com.
Virgin Atlantic: 0870 380 2007; www.virgin-atlantic.com.

Traditionally, domestic flights throughout the UK have been expensive. In recent years however, low-cost, no-frills economy flights have forced the larger airlines to compete, so prices have fallen across the board. Generally, the longer in advance tickets are booked, the cheaper the price.

British Airways fly to the greatest number of destinations, but you will pay higher prices for their services. However, on the plus side, you will get free meals and drinks on board. The no-frills airlines charge extra for drinks and snacks. Remember that the basic cost of the flight does not always include airport taxes, so the final price will be higher.

> The airport connections work fine. Flights to and from Sweden are a bit thin, but there are enough to get back and forth if needed. So far all the trains I have tried have been on time and easy to locate so it's good.
> Roberth Lindholm

By Rail

You can enter the UK by train. Eurostar runs passenger train services linking England and Europe via the Channel Tunnel. They run from London St Pancras and Ebbsfleet, Kent (and sometimes Ashford in Kent) to Paris, Brussels and Lille. There are connecting services running between London and Edinburgh.

Trains between London and Scotland run from either Kings Cross or Euston, while trains for south Wales run from London Paddington. The journey to Cardiff takes just over two hours. For a more relaxed rail journey to Scotland, Scotrail runs the Caledonian overnight sleeper service from London Euston to Glasgow, Edinburgh, Fort William, Aberdeen and Inverness.

An alternative to taking a short-haul flight from London to Belfast is to get a combined train and ferry ticket which can take you to Belfast or indeed most places in Northern Ireland. There are train+ferry tickets available from any UK railway station to Belfast, Londonderry, or any Northern Irish railway station via any of the main ferry routes. This will take you through the UK countryside by train and across the Irish Sea by ship. Fares start at £32.30 each way.

Ferry Routes Between Britain and Europe	
Country	**Routes Available**
Belgium	Hull-Zeebrugge
	Rosyth-Zeebrugge
Channel Islands	Poole-Guernsey-Jersey
	Weymouth-Guernsey-Jersey
	Portsmouth-Guernsey-Jersey
	Penzance-St Mary's
Denmark	Harwich-Esbjerg
France	Dover-Calais
	Newhaven-Dieppe
	Portsmouth-Caen/St
	Malo/Le Havre/Cherbourg
	Poole-Cherbourg/St Malo
	Plymouth-Roscoff
Germany	Harwich-Cuxhaven
Holland	Harwich-Hook of Holland
	Hull-Rotterdam
	Newcastle-Amsterdam
Irish Republic	Fishguard-Rosslare
	Pembroke-Rosslare
	Holyhead-Dublin/Dun Laoghaire
	Liverpool-Dublin
	Swansea-Cork
N. Ireland	Stranraer-Belfast
	Cairnryan-Larne
	Liverpool-Belfast
	Stranraer-Belfast
	Troon-Belfast/Larne
Norway	Newcastle-Bergen/Stavanger
	Lerwick-Bergen
	Aberdeen-Bergen
Spain	Plymouth-Santander
	Portsmouth-Bilbao
Sweden	Newcastle-Kristiansand-Gothenberg

Eurostar: 08705 186186; www.eurostar.com. Eurostar tickets can also be purchased online through www.raileurope.co.uk.
Caledonian Sleeper: 08457 550033; www.firstgroup.com/scotrail. Through-tickets between Scotland and France on Eurostar and the Caledonian Sleeper service are available.
National Rail Enquiries: 08457 484950 or buy online at www.thetrainline.com.
Northern Ireland Train + Ferry Enquiries: 0870 5455 455; www.seat61.com/NorthernIreland.htm.

For further details of train operators and services within Britain, see *Daily Life.*

By Sea

There are a number of passenger ferry operators sailing to Great Britain from continental Europe and Ireland, including Brittany Ferries, DFDS Seaways, Fjord Line, Hoverspeed, P&O Ferries, Sea France and Stena Line.

Comprehensive details of routes and operators, plus links to ferry operators' websites are on www.seaview.co.uk.

By Road

Coach

Eurolines in conjunction with National Express run frequent services by coach between Europe and the UK. Depending on your route, your coach will cross the English Channel either by ferry or through the Channel Tunnel on a train. If necessary, you will transfer from your coach to a train for the 31-mile (50.5km) trip through the tunnel.

Car

You can travel to the UK in your car via the Channel Tunnel (your car will travel on board a special train) or by ferry. There is a good network of long-distance roads (known as motorways) throughout England. Although in theory these are fast roads, congestion is becoming a big problem in and around the cities, especially in the south east, and you may encounter delays due to roadworks or simply because of the sheer volume of traffic. In the less populated areas of Scotland, Wales and Northern Ireland there are few motorways. However, away from the cities, traffic volume is far lower and you should experience far less congestion than in much of England.

 For details of coach semices operating in the UK.contact National Express. 08705 808080; www.nationalexpress.com. For further details regarding local and national services, see also *Daily Life.*

PLANNING AN INTERNATIONAL MOVE

There are a number of professional bodies which removal companies may belong to. When choosing one to do your move it is wise to ensure that they are members of one of these as you should then be covered by insurance and guarantees of safe delivery.

International Federation of Furniture Removers: 0032 2426 5160 (Belgium); www.fidi.com

Overseas Moving Network International: 01737 222022; www. omnimoving.com

British Association of Removers: 01923 699480; www.bar.co.uk

International Removals

It should take only a few days to have your belongings shipped from continental Europe, around four weeks from the east coast of the US, six weeks from the west coast. From Far Eastern countries it should take around six weeks and eight weeks or so from Australasia.

Make sure that you are adequately insured to the replacement cost in the UK of lost or damaged items. Your removal company will send you the UK Customs Form 3 for completion. A separate C3 must be completed for each shipment – for example if you are sending some by air and some by sea.

There are many companies which offer international removal services – to compare some of the leading firms around visit www.intlmovers.com

Storage Depots

If you are moving into rented accommodation temporarily you may need to arrange to have your belongings put into storage. If so, you must ensure your goods are properly insured. Storage is charged at a monthly rate depending on the size of the consignment. If you need to access any items during the storage period you will have to pay a fee to have the container opened, so it is as well to be sure you only put items you will not need for some time into storage. There are storage depots in most cities.

The only major difficulty with the 'moving process' was actually getting my 'things' across from the US. Shipping costs are outrageously expensive and for this very reason, I came to Britain basically empty-handed. I certainly wasn't able to bring across large items of furniture or anything of that nature. Luckily for me, I was able to pack my luggage creatively, pay a little extra at the airline for excess baggage and bring along a few of my most beloved books and things that would give me a good start in making my new flat in Britain feel like home.
Amy Burns

The largest UK firm of removers is Allied Pickfords. They also do international removals and have storage depots throughout the UK.

Removal Companies

Pickfords Ltd: www.pickfords.co.uk. Includes a branch locator listing over 100 branches throughout the UK, with their phone numbers.

British Association of Removers: 01928 699480; www.bar.co.uk. The website includes a searchable database of BAR members, national and international.

Customs Regulations

Used household goods and personal effects are allowed into the UK free of duty and value added tax (VAT), provided that they have been in your possession and used abroad at least six months prior to your arrival and that you have lived outside of the EU for at least 12 months. All items less than six months old are subject to duty and VAT. Keep with you any receipts/invoices for new and dutiable items as they may be required by Customs and Excise.

Customs clearance for goods from Europe are usually made without delay, but International Customs clearance can take up to two weeks. If your belongings are sent unaccompanied, the receiving freight or removal company will send you a customs form for completion when your goods arrive in Britain.

Importing your Car

You may bring your motor vehicle free of duty and tax provided you have used it in your home country for at least six months, you keep it for personal use and you do not sell or hire it out in the UK within 12 months.

Your removal company will supply you with a C104A customs form to complete. This should be supported by copies of your passport, utility bills to prove you have resided previously in another country, your car insurance policy and a purchase invoice.

If the motor vehicle is under six months old you will have to pay the full rate of duty and VAT, approximately 29% of the car's value.

Upon clearance and payment of any duties, you will be given a clearance form and registration instruction. These should be taken, together with proof of car insurance, to the nearest Department of Transport Vehicle Registration Office to get the vehicle licensed. A road tax disc will be issued and car registration plates can then be collected.

Even if your car is less than six months old, it may be cheaper to import it and pay duty rather than buy a car in the UK. Motor vehicles are expensive compared with most other countries, although UK prices have come down in recent years, largely as a result of the increasing numbers of UK residents buying vehicles in Europe, often via internet marketing sites. Even with the cost of import duties and tax you can save thousands of pounds compared with buying the same make and model of car from a UK outlet.

Useful Address

HM Revenue and Customs: 0845 010 9000; http://customs.hmrc.gov.uk. Offers advice on importing personal effects and goods into the UK.

Importing Pets

If you wish to bring family pets with you to Britain, there are stringent regulations involved, with hefty fines, or even the possibility of the animal being destroyed if you do not comply with all the requirements. You need to start the process of preparing to bring your pet with you many months in advance, or you may find that it cannot travel at the same time as you do.

The Government department responsible for all aspects of importing animals into the UK is the Department for Environment, Food & Rural Affairs (DEFRA).

The Pet Travel Scheme (PETS) allows dogs, cats and ferrets from specified countries, into the UK without the need to go into quarantine as long as they have undergone certain procedures to ensure the health.

The whole process of health checks and documentation can take up to six months and can cost around £200–£300. Once a pet is issued with a passport, its owner needs to ensure it is kept up to date by taking the animal to the vet for boosters by stated dates. If these procedures are followed, there are no requirements for further blood tests or a six month wait to take your pet in or out of the country, so it is important to keep these dates in your diary.

PETS Routes

Even if your pet has a pet passport, there are still restrictions on the route you use to bring it into the UK. You can only use specific approved routes and transport companies, which are frequently amended. For the current list see www.defra.gov.uk.

> Early on in the process, I ran into a virtual showstopper when I found out what was involved in bringing along my eight month old English Springer Spaniel, Chloe. The quarantine period, the long list of requirements, the expense involved in inserting a microchip, getting special shots, flying certain airlines, flying certain routes, buying Chloe a special ticket... I was amazed at the cost involved. However the thing that decided it was the six month period required to complete PETS or quarantine. My schedule didn't have six months to spare and I almost decided not to move... and then I found a family with a huge farm and two little boys and a golf-cart, which from what I understand, Chloe loves to ride around in all day. So, although I miss my dog terribly, my story with her ended happily knowing that she has a good home. The regulations, however, are something to be considered carefully and EARLY if you are planning on bringing your puppy!
>
> Amy Burns

Quarantine

Animals which are not from the qualifying countries or are not otherwise eligible for entry under PETS must be detained in quarantine for six months. The animal's owner should choose where this will be from a list of authorised premises available from DEFRA. The cost of keeping a pet in quarantine is £900–£1,500 for cats; £1,500-£2,000 for dogs.

You or the quarantine premises should complete Form ID1 'Application for a licence to import a dog or cat for detention in quarantine'. This form may be downloaded from the Defra website; See *Defra*: 0870 241 1710; www.defra.gov.uk.

Dangerous Dogs

In Great Britain, some breeds of dogs are prohibited and it is illegal to bring them into the country. Pit bull terriers, Japanese tosas, dogo Argentinos and fila Brazilieros brought into the country may be seized and destroyed.

Setting Up Home

■ HOW DO THE BRITISH LIVE?

FACT

■ There has been a significant change in the balance between owner-occupied and rented accommodation in Britain. In 2003-04, 70% of dwellings (18 million) were owner-occupied, which was an increase of 45% since 1981. Currently, in the rental sector 21% of homes are social housing with the rest being in the private sector.

In Britain, over three-quarters of people live in houses rather than apartments (usually called 'flats' in the UK). In larger cities there is a higher proportion of flat or apartment dwellers, either living in purpose-built apartment buildings, or conversions of older properties. In Scotland the picture is slightly different, with the balance being far more even between house and flat dwelling. Historically, a high proportion of Scotland's city-dwellers lived in 'tenements' (apartment blocks) and this is a pattern which continues today. In recent years, however, there has been a great drive to redevelop with attempt to made to Britain's decaying inner-cities, encourage people to live there. As a result high numbers of new apartments are being built throughout Britain, so it seems inevitable that the proportion of flat dwellers will rise in years to come.

Generally flats will have one, two or three bedrooms, with a living room and dining area, a kitchen and a bathroom or shower room. Often, especially in newer properties, the living, dining and kitchen areas will be open plan.

Studio apartments have a single main room, which contains the sleeping area, sometimes with a bed which folds away into the wall. The bath or shower room is often off the main room.

Housing options

There has been an increasing trend in recent years for residents of either houses or flats to be owner-occupiers, due both to easier access to home loans and the increasing numbers of council tenants buying their properties. Rentable properties, furnished or unfurnished, are available in both the public and the private sectors. Traditionally, local councils provided the only public sector housing (often known as 'social housing'), but in recent years these have been augmented in many areas by housing association properties, provided via a mixture of public and private funding.

Since the UK government introduced legislation in 1979 giving council tenants the right to buy their council house at less than the market value, over 40% of council stock has been sold and there is now a shortage of council housing in many areas. Some councils have now banned tenants from buying their homes, in order to safeguard their dwindling stock of social housing.

Households by Type of Dwelling, 2001–2002					
Region	Detached	Semi-detached	Terraced	Purpose built flat	Converted flat
UK	21%	31%	28%	16%	4%
England	21%	32%	28%	14%	4%
Wales	29%	30%	32%	7%	2%
Scotland	15%	21%	21%	39%	2%
N. Ireland	36%	24%	32%	6%	2%

People on a budget, such as students, may live in a rented 'bedsit' (short for bed-sitting room) bedsits a single room with a shared bathroom and kitchen. In some cases the room has a small kitchen area. Bedsit are normally in converted houses and are legally classed as 'houses in multiple occupation' (see below).

Houses in Britain are either detached, semi-detached (two connected houses sharing a party wall) or terraced (streets of houses joined together in long rows).

There has been a significant change in the balance between owner-occupied and rented accommodation in Britain. In 2003-04, 70% of dwellings were owner-occupied, which was an increase of 45% since 1981. Currently, in the rental sector, 21% of homes are social housing with the rest being in the private sector.

◼ RESIDENTIAL AREAS OF LONDON

London is a huge, diverse, and somewhat daunting place. Within its 33 boroughs, living standards can vary enormously – from the tree-lined avenues of Kensington to the multicultural, up-and-coming areas of Brixton and Hackney. Londoners will rarely refer to the borough they live in; more often referring to an area, which gives a much better indication of the type of place they live. Monthly rental costs can also vary hugely within a borough – even within a few hundred metres – and most estate agents will work by traditional neighbourhoods of London (Clapham and Battersea, for example, instead of Lambeth and Wandsworth).

Each area of London has a distinct personality, and many have a community 'feel ' that some are surprised to find in the capital of England. There are

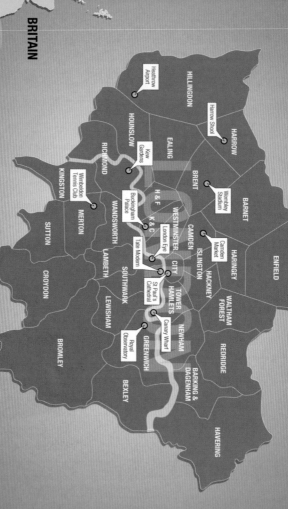

BRITAIN

LONDON

Heathrow Airport

HILLINGDON

Harrow School

HARROW

HOUNSLOW

EALING

BRENT

BARNET

Wembley Stadium

ENFIELD

Kew Gardens

RICHMOND

H & F

WESTMINSTER

CAMDEN

HARINGEY

Camden Market

Wimbledon Tennis Club

KINGSTON

Buckingham Palace

K & C

London Eye

ISLINGTON

HACKNEY

WALTHAM FOREST

MERTON

WANDSWORTH

Tate Modern

CITY

St Paul's Cathedral

TOWER HAMLETS

NEWHAM

REDBRIDGE

SUTTON

LAMBETH

SOUTHWARK

Canary Wharf

BARKING & DAGENHAM

CROYDON

LEWISHAM

Royal Observatory

GREENWICH

BEXLEY

HAVERING

BROMLEY

> ## Price factor
>
> The prices given in the following section are rental costs per month. You will notice these are comparatively higher than the rest of Britain, and so the 'price factor' indicated refers to London only. Rental prices you can expect to pay bear a close relationship to house prices in each area.

some areas more suitable for young families, with good schools and parks, while others tand to attract young professionals who demand great bars, shopping, and a metropolitan way of life.

England's capital can be divided up into 'inner' and 'outer' London. While in inner London the capital is on your doorstep, the suburbs of outer London are becoming increasingly popular. With a comprehensive public transport system in place (although admitiedly sometimes struggles to cope with the mass of people it carries!), commuters are discovering pleasant and good-value areas outside of the inner boroughs.

Inner London

Camden

Lively, young and cosmopolitan, this area is popular and trendy. Camden Town is famous for its extensive and eclectic weekend street markets which attract London residents and tourists alike. The locks on the river are a cool hang-out for music-lovers, with some excellent bohemian-style pubs and lively bars. In the same borough is Hampstead, one of the few areas in London that has succeeded in retaining its village identity, full of delightful and very large period houses. As a result, it is packed with celebrities and the seriously rich. Hampstead Heath, London's largest area of parkland, is well-used by locals for dog-walking, jogging and picnics, with ponds you can swim in! A touch more central, Bloomsbury and Regent's Park are also attractive, wealthy areas, and wonderful views can be had from Primrose Hill. More affordable homes are to be found in West Hampstead and Kentish Town. £850–£900 won't get you much more than a small one-bedroom flat in Hampstead, compared with £750 in Kentish Town for a similar property. A four-bedroom detached house in Hampstead is £19,600.

> One-bed Flat: £345 – £17,200
> Three-bed House: £920 – £34,400

City of London

'The City' or 'Square Mile' as it is sometimes known, is the heart of the capital's business centre and one of the biggest financial centres in the world. Amongst the office blocks, its main tourist landmark is St Paul's Cathedral. In the last decade there has been a growth in the residential market here; around the Barbican, concrete buildings initially built as social housing now hide luxury apartments. The area is still however, predominantly business-based however and it is not a major residential area. The Smithfield area is the hippest in the City, with excellent restaurants and pubs, and a young population. Despite renovation initiatives, the resident population of The City is still less than 10,000. It becomes somewhat deserted at weekends, as without the custom of city workers, many shops close. A studio apartment in the Barbican can be found for £1,000 a month, while a stylish two-bedroom penthouse with roof garden and stunning views in Clerkenwell is a touch under £6,000.

> One-bed Fat: £1,550– £7,125
> Three-bed House: £1,720 – £7,580

Greenwich

Stretching along the south side of the river, Greenwich is a World Heritage Site, with attractions including the Royal Observatory, the Millennium

Dome and beautiful Greenwich Royal Park within its borders. It is easy to see why this area is popular with both tourists and residents. With its good rail and underground links providing its easy access to the City. New developments on the river provide contemporary alternatives to the Georgian, Victorian and 1930s houses situated elsewhere in the borough. Further to the east is the 'new town' of Thamesmead with new homes, a school and retail park. Rents here are lower than in the older parts and good for those on tight budgets. A three-bed room apartment within the Royal Park is £5,400, compared with a two-bedroom house in Thamesmead at £750.

One-bed Flat: £675 – £1,850
Three-bed House: £1,075 – £5,460

Hackney

Hackney has had a bad press for decades. With high unemployment and crime rates, no tube line, and not many green spaces, it is cited as one of the worst places to live in London. However, some southern areas in the borough–notably Hoxton and Shoreditch–have developed and become more desirable. In the 1990s, derelict warehouses and factories that were redeveloped into loft apartments became popular with artists, and it is now a centre for arts, music and fashion. Stoke Newington has become a trendy and somewhat expensive village area, which attracts families looking for the borough's best schools. The forthcoming Olympics and an expected extension of the Underground both promise the area a brighter future. A one-bedroom conversion in a Victorian mansion in Clapton Park is just £640. In contrast, a penthouse in Hoxton, in a converted chocolate factory, is £3,000.

One-bed Flat: £585 – £2,365
Three-bed House: £920 – £2,795

Hammersmith and Fulham

Fulham is especially popular with young professionals and families, due to its good restaurants, fashionable shops, and pubs. Just down the road from Kensington and Chelsea, it is far more affordable than the more upmarket areas to the east, yet still offers a trendy lifestyle sought by many. Hammersmith also provides employment opportunities in a number of large companies including Disney, Coca-Cola and AOL.

Most of the housing in the borough is Victorian; from large substantial houses to smaller terraces and flat conversions. Hammersmith and Fulham have great transport links into the centre, both tube and bus routes, though traffic is often heavy and does sometimes affect the roads. A furnished one-bedroom flaton Fulham Palace Road would cost around £800, while a six bedroom semi-detached house in Hammersmith would be in the region of £5,200.

> One-bed Flat: £480 – £1,900
> Three-bed Flat: £1380 – £3,400

Islington

One of the trendiest of boroughs, this is particularly popular with young professionals. The popular Upper Street is packed with cool bars and restaurants and is perfect for those seeking an urban edge to their area. Warehouses converted into loft apartments suit those looking for a modern style, but there are also plenty of more traditional houses and flats. Canonbury and Clerkenwell are the most upmarket areas, while Holloway and Tufnell Park offer good value for money. A recently refurbished studio apartment in a Georgian terrace in Islington is £800 while a quaint early-Victorian two-bed room cottage £1,880.

> One-bed Flat: £430 – £3,850
> Three-bed House: £1,500 – £10,750

Kensington and Chelsea

If you can afford to live in this area, do. There is a great quality of life here, with 23 parks as well as a wealth of museums and galleries, top-class restaurants and excellent boutique shops. This is, of course, reflected in accommodation prices; it is the most expensive area of London, attracting wealthy business people, foreign dignitaries and celebrities alike. It is easy to find original town houses here, unlike other central areas where most have been converted in to flats, so it is appealing to wealthy families. There are also a number of very expensive private schools is the area which can cater for their children.

The hustle and bustle of London is found here, as cultural landmarks attract hoards of tourists. There are cheaper areas, such as Earls Court and North Kensington, which can be more affordable. Small studio flats in Chelsea start at £1,000 while in Earls Court one would be £650. A large family home in Chelsea could be as much as £30,000.

One-bed Flat: £495 – £17,200
Three-bed House: £1,230 – £21,500

Lambeth

Home of the London Eye, this borough has improved tremendously in recent years. After street riots in the 1980s, Brixton was seen as a no-go area, and this affected nearby Clapham and Streatham. Today, Clapham, with the extensive Common at its heart, is popular with young professionals and has expensive shops and restaurants with a lively nightlife. Multicultural Brixton is increasing in popularity with both shoppers and the informed young professional, and, while Streatham has for a long time been viewed as 'rough', it is on the up. Transport links towards Waterloo Station are excellent, and the substantial Victorian terraces and conversions provide good living spaces. A spacious studio apartment in Clapham can be found for £760. £1,000 will get a split-level two-bedroom conversion with private garden in Streatham.

One-bed Flat: £775 – £6,450
Three-bed House: £1,465 – £5,800

Lewisham

The most desirable and expensive part of Lewisham is Blackheath Village, which has a traditional village green – 'the heath' – at its centre. There are loads of trendy bars and restaurants here making it popular with wealthy young professionals. Although much of the rest of the borough has been neglected for decades, since the Docklands Light Railway was extended here, transport into the City is far quicker and easier, making it an affordable option for commuters. A one-bedroom flat conversion with original Victorian features can be found for £725. In Blackheath, £4,000 will get you an elegant four-bedroom apartment on the edge of the heath.

One-bed Flat: £600 – £1,300
Three-bed House: £900 – £1,700

Southwark

This area has seen much regeneration in recent years and is now home to some very desirable areas to live in. Near the river, derelict warehouses which once blighted the area have been reborn as trendy loft apartments while the acclaimed Borough Market attracts wealthy foodies to sample its diverse fresh produce. An old power station, now the Tate Modern, and the replica of Shakespeare's Globe theatre, make this a culturally rich destination. To the south of the borough, Dulwich has good schools and is seen as a safe environment, attracting families (especially in the sought-after area of Dulwich village), while Camberwell and Peckham provide cheaper alternatives. A Georgian three-bedroom house packed with original features here could be yours for £2,900. A one-bedroom conversion in Peckham is £750.

One-bed Flat: £750 – £2,860
Three-bed House: £1,175 – £3,330

Tower Hamlets

Found to the east of the City, this is a borough of extremes. Redevelopment of the docklands to the west of the borough has pumped money into the area and brought swanky new housing, offices and shops, but plenty of below-standard flats remain. One of London's oldest landmarks, Tower Bridge, is now dwarfed by its newest, the Canary Wharf complex on the Isle of Dogs, which has the three tallest buildings in the UK. High-powered financial services, law, media and technology firms are based here. The area has one of the highest average incomes in the UK, while there are also pockets of extreme poverty and high unemployment. Ahead of the 2012 Olympics, the worst areas are being improved. A small, basic studio flat in Bethnal Green costs £500. A luxury three-bedroom Docklands flat can be as much as £10,750.

One-bed Flat: £600 – £4,295
Three-bed House: £1,290 – £12,040

Wandsworth

This borough has seen an influx of residents priced out of neighbouring Clapham and Fulham, and has now become a desirable area for young professionals. Fringing Clapham Common, and with its own Wandsworth

Common, the area has green spaces and leafy streets of solid Victorian houses, many of which have been converted into flats. 'Between the commons' is a desirable place to live, and is an affordable alternative to its neighbouring boroughs. Putney is famous for rowing on the Thames and Battersea chic riverside are sought after development. There are still, however, areas of neglect. A Thames-side one-bedroom flat can be had from around £1,500, while a four-bedroom house in Putney is good value at £2,500.

> One-bed Flat: £820 – £17,200
> Three-bed House: £1,475 – £12,880

City of Westminster

The heart of tourist London, famous landmarks are found round each corner – from the Houses of Parliament and Buckingham Palace to China Town and Soho. The West End is famous for shopping on Oxford Street, as well as for the 40 theatres around Shaftesbury Avenue which make up 'Theatreland'. Residents are steps away from central London's nightlife and numerous art galleries, and can live amidst the buzz of activity. There are several university campuses here, and swarms of students needing plenty of bedsits and flatshares. The cheapest areas are Paddington and Kilburn in the north, while Belgravia, Westminster and Pimlico are the most expensive. Being so central means rents are high: a two-bedroom apartment overlooking Hyde Park will set you back £2,000 and a four-bedroom terraced house in Fitzrovia is £8,800. There are some very wealthy people living here who pay as much as £24,000 for a large property in the right area.

> One-bed Flat: £470 – £17,200
> Three-bed House: £920 – £32,250

Outer London

Barking and Dagenham

The average house price here is the lowest of all 33 London boroughs, with good reason. High crime rates and low-quality housing have made this an area to avoid if possible. Things are improving, however, with a major regeneration programme shortly to start, but it is not due to be completed until 2025. Rents here are cheap London prices as go. You could find a one-bedroom flat for £600 or a three-bedroom house for £1,000.

> One-bed Flat: £490 – £3,225
> Three-bed House: £750 – £1,250

Barnet

With good, but very busy, transport links and close to green spaces this is a solidly middle-class borough, and attracts celebrities such as pop stars and footballers to its wealthier areas, Totteridge and Hampstead Garden Suburb. This area is also home to three of the UK's top independent schools. It has a large Jewish community in Golders Green, which has many Jewish shops and synagogues. Brent Cross shopping centre offers an all-encompassing shopping experience, but also makes this area traffic-heavy. One-bedroom flats in Edgware start at £650, while a six-bedroom house in Hampstead Garden Suburb with views over a golf course is £5,200.

One-bed Flat: £580 – £1,290
Three-bed House: £990 – £2,170

Bexley

Situated on the eastern outskirts of London, south of the river, this is a popular commuter area. The underground does not reach this far, but there are train and bus services into central London. Quaint Victorian cottages are found around Old Bexley, which has a village feel, while much of the rest of the borough is more modern. The area has been expanding since the 1930s to cater for the seemingly unstoppable growth of London, and continues to close, with numerous new housing developments being built on the marshland at Thamesmead. Two-bedroom apartments start at about £750 and you should expect to pay £1,200 upwards for a substantial three-bedroom house.

One-bed Flat: £650 – £750
Three-bed House: £950 – £1,350

Brent

An extremely multicultural borough, around half the residents in this area are from ethnic minorities. These include sizeable Asian, Afro-Caribbean and Jewish communities. The largest commercial and retail area of Brent is Wembley (famous for its football stadium) which was rebuilt in 2007. The west side of the borough is more affluent than the east, which has some deprived areas, but with people always looking for more affordable areas of London, these, too are on the up. A large number of studio apartments are available from around £700 in Neasden and Cricklewood. For a decent-sized one-bedroom flat, expect to pay £850 upwards.

One-bed Flat: £750 – £950
Three-bed House: £1,100 – £6,235

Bromley

Geographically the largest London borough, the majority of it is green belt land, so development is restricted under planning laws. Consequently much of this area has a rural feels, though Bromley town has a large shopping centre and is well-served by transport links. Its wide range of property types and local facilities mean it is popular with families, commuters and older couples. Modern one-bedroom flats in Bromley start at around £650, while a modern three-bedroom detached house in a quiet part of the town is £1,000. At the upper end, a detached house in Farnborough Park is £4,000.

One-bed Flat: £635 – £2,795
Three-bed House: £900 – £1,800

Croydon

The southernmost London borough, Croydon also has the largest population. Being on a major rail artery, it is popular with commuters and there is also a tram service. These transport links have attracted large businesses and office complexes to the area. Croydon town is also the largest retail centre in the south-east, after central London. This diverse borough offers everything from million-pound houses in exclusive settlements, more modest family homes on leafy streets, and flats of all shapes and sizes. Croydon is not, however, the hippest place to live and those seeking style and fashionable areas tend to steer clear. A one-bedroom modern apartment in Croydon can be had for £600, a three bedroom terrace for £1,000.

One-bed Flat: £500 – £850
Three-bed House: £850 – £4,515

Ealing

Another diverse borough, Ealing is popular with young professional and office workers due to its good transport links and several tube stations. Solid converted Victorian properties and plenty of green space also make this area good or families. This is a diverse area, with a large Asian population in Southall, which also has some great ethnic shops. This borough, does however also have many deprived areas and a lot of traffic around. A modern one-bedroom flat on Ealing Broadway is £815, while a three or four bedroom house is around £2,000.

1-bed Flat: £495 – £1,050
3-bed House: £1,100 – £16,000

Enfield

This borough has a mixture of semi-rural areas in the west, where it borders Hertfordshire, and some run-down council estates to the east. Hadley Wood is smart, and one of the most expensive areas of the UK, with several Tottenham and Arsenal footballers (other celebrities as well as number of) in residence. Enfield town is cheaper, yet still has a rural feel. The cheapest areas are Edmondton and Ponders End, where disused industrial sites blight the banks of the River Lea. These are earmarked for redevelopment. A one-bedroom flat in Enfield can be found for £625, while a five-bedroom family home set in a lovely garden comes is at approximately £3,500.

One-bed Flat: £470 – £850
Three-bed House: £750 – £4,730

Haringey

Areas in this borough once again vary greatly, so you will want to pick carefully. While there are a few very desirable and trendy areas with a village feel, such as Highgate, Crouch End and Muswell Hill, these leafy suburbs contrast strongly with deprived areas such as Tottenham, where rates of unemployment and crime are high. Although popular, transport links to the centre are surprisingly poor in hungry. An unfurnished studio apartment in the heart of Highgate Village can be found for £760, while a one-bedroom flat in Tottenham is offered at £607.

One-bed Flat: £590 – £1,505
Three-bed House: £1,610 – £4,730

Harrow

This borough is best known for its public school, situated in Harrow-on-the-Hill, which attracts wealthy families to its solid Victorian and Edwardian houses.

Apart from Stanmore and Pinner Hill, where some of the grandest houses are to be found, the rest of the borough has more modest properties, and is popular with commuters and families seeking green spaces and good schools – other independent schools here are ranked among the top in the country. This area is also becoming increasingly multi-cultural, adding a new flavour. One-bedroom flats in Harrow start at around £750 while a newly-built three-bedroom semi-detached house is £1,375.

One-bed Flat: £625 – £850
Three-bed House: £900 – £1,850

Havering

To the east of London, this suburban area includes the towns of Romford, Upminster and Hornchurch. This is an area with a good quality of life. Set amid open fields and marshland, there is plenty of space here, with a low population density for London. Much of the borough is protected from development to preserve these green spaces. Other plus points are the lowest unemployment rate in Greater London and one of the lowest crime rates. One-bedroom apartments start at about £650. Expect to pay £1,000 upwards for a substantial three bedroom house.

One-bed Flat: £650 – £750
Three-bed House: £775 – £1,350

Hillingdon

Hillingdon is the westernmost borough. Much of it lies in the green belt and it is also the most thinly populated. On the downside, Heathrow Airport is here, so there is aircraft noise and pollution to contend with in addition to the weight of road traffic heading to and from Europe's busiest airport. Due to their proximity to the airport, Hillingdon and Hayes are fairly industrial towns, while Uxbridge is the main retail centre. The more attractive areas are to the north of the borough, at Northwood and Ruislip. A one-bedroom flat in Hillingdon is £725, and a three bedroom semi-detached house at Ickenham can be found for £1,050.

One-bed Flat: £625 – £950
Three-bed House: £825 – £5,375

Hounslow

This is a large and diverse borough, ranging from the village-like and desirable areas of Chiswick, Isleworth and Osterly Park, to Hounslow itself, Hanworth and Feltham, which are unexciting and further out and so consequently cheaper. Brentford is going up in the world as the riverside warehouses are being converted into smart flats. Heathrow Airport is just down the road and a huge employer, but bear in mind the borough is under its flight path. A one-bedroom flat in Chiswick's most desirable area is £1,000, whereas you could get one in Hounslow for £600.

> One-bed Flat: £550 – £1,000
> Three-bed House: £900 – £5,590

Kingston upon Thames

At the south-western tip of Greater London, this borough is good for commuters. Trains into London are frequent and nowhere is longer than a 30-minute journey into town. The Thames runs through Kingston town, where lively restaurants and bars can be found along the riverfront. Surbiton has some original art deco architecture, and a number of large modern housing estates, but residents must head to Kingston for a night out. A four-bedroom house in Surbiton can be found for £3,000, while a modern two-bedroom flat close to Kingston town centre is £1,350.

> One-bed Flat: £775 – £1,650
> Three-bed House: £900 – £2,900

Merton

This borough has a distinct split personality. There is Wimbledon Village and Common in the north, providing luxurious housing and good restaurants for middle-class professionals, with the world-famous tennis tournament close at hand, but the rest of the borough is unexciting suburbia, whose main advantage is its reasonable transport links into London. A four-bedroom apartment with period details and parking in Wimbledon is £4,300, while a two-bedroom house in Mitcham is £1,200.

> One-bed Flat: £820 – £3,180
> Three-bed House: £1,000 – £6,500

Newham

Situated five miles east of the City, Newham is the most ethnically diverse district in England and Wales though unfortunately it is also one of the most deprived areas of London. The area is being regenerated with new homes, schools, offices and shops planned and transport links are good, with the Docklands Light Railway, London City

Airport and a new Channel Tunnel link all in the area. You could find a one-bedroom flat for £600, or a three-bedroom terraced house for £1,050.

One-bed Flat: £430 – £860
Three-bed House: £900 – £1,250

Redbridge

Located on the fringe of Epping Forest, there are plenty of green spaces here. The borough is home to a wide cultural mix, with large Asian and Jewish communities. It is one of the wealthiest areas of east London, attracting well-paid residents with its good schools and transport links. Gants Hill and Hainault have more affordable housing than the wealthier towns of Redbridge and Woodford. With a high level of owner occupancy, rents are less easy to find here. Location affects price greatly – a two-bedroom apartment in Redbridge could cost between £750 and £3,600 depending on its position.

One-bed Flat: £700 – £3,010
Three-bed House: £860 – £1,590

Richmond upon Thames

The only borough to straddle the Thames, Richmond has 21 miles of river frontage, lined with expensive properties. It also has over 100 parks and green spaces, including the extensive Richmond Park, and in all has five times more open space than any other London borough. Hampton Court Palace and Kew Gardens are popular tourist attractions, and Twickenham, the home of English rugby, is a draw for sporting types. Richmond Green is delightful, surrounded by historic buildings. A one-bedroom flat in Twickenham is around £780, while a three-bedroom penthouse with river frontage in St Margaret's is £6,500.

One-bed Flat: £775 – £3,225
Three-bed House: £1,000 - £5,000

Sutton

A solidly middle-class area with plenty of green space, Sutton attracts commuters and families mainly due to the high standard of schools in the area. Carshalton and Carshalton Beeches are the wealthiest, and nicest, areas, usually attracting City business types. A two-bedroom bungalow in Carshalton Beeches can be found for £1,100, and a one-bedroom flat in Sutton for £650.

One-bed Flat: £600 –£925
Three-bed House: £950 – £5,160

Waltham Forest

One of the more deprived areas, Waltham Forest has a high proportion of immigrants and social housing.It should, however, receive a boost from the 2012 Olympics as the London Velopark is being constructed here. As its name suggests, there are plenty of green spaces, and it is close to the countryside surrounding London. A modern one-bedroom flat in Chingford is around £750, and a three-bedroom terraced house in Leyton £1,150.

One-bed Flat: £550 – £3,120
Three-bed House: £710 – £4,840

Young Families

Popular top-end areas	
Blackheath	Highgate, Crouch End and Muswell Hill
Chiswick	Kensington and Chelsea
Dulwich	Putney
Fulham	Richmond, Kew
Greenwich	Wimbledon
Hampstead	

Popular mid-priced areas	
Bromley	Pinner and Stanmore
Ealing	Redbridge
Enfield	Sutton
Kingston	Thamesmead

Young Professionals

Popular top-end areas	
Borough	Islington
Clapham Common	Kentish Town
Earls Court and North Kensington	Shoreditch
Fulham	South Wimbledon
Highgate, Crouch End and Muswell Hill	West Hampstead
Hoxton and Shoreditch	

Popular mid-priced areas	
Battersea	Peckham
Bethnal Green	Ruislip
Bromley	Stoke Newington
Ealing	Streatham and Brixton
Holloway and Tufnell Park	Wembley and Neasden
Lewisham	

Students

Popular areas	
Bethnal Green	Hounslow, Hanworth and Feltham
Brixton	Neasden and Cricklewood
Camden	Paddington and Kilburn
Clapton Park	Stoke Newington
Edgware	Smithfield

◣ OTHER UK CITIES

Although much of the focus of the UK jobs market is on London, many of the country's other cities can stake a reasonable claim as thriving financial and business centres in their own right. They all have distinct identities and characteristics and the following is a brief guide to some of the more sizeable and popular destinations outside of London.

Birmingham

Britain's second largest city, with a population in the region of 1,000 000, is a model of successful regeneration. Typified by the iconic shopping precinct known as 'The Bullring', which has blossomed from a concrete monstrosity into a stylish chrome-clad modernist icon, Birmingham is a fine example of money well spent.

The city is located in the West Midlands region of England, and is blessed with excellent transport links, as it is the point where two of the main arterial motorways of the UK – the M5 and M6 – intersect. There is a booming international airport, good rail links to all parts of the UK and good access to areas of natural beauty, including the Cotswolds to the south, Stratford-Upon Avon to the East and the Welsh borderlands to the West. Birmingham also sits astride an impressive network of canals - a link to its history as a centre of trade in many industries, including textiles. Now the

canals are used mainly for pleasure sailing and as a popular destination for walkers.

Birmingham's main shopping area, centred around New Street, is filled with major retail stores. The city's cultural life is partly defined by its multicultural community, with curry a particular local speciality. Many fine curry restaurants are to be found in the so-called 'Balti Triangle', an area of the city dominated by Asian migrants, some of whom are now second-or third-generation UK residents. The nightlife in Birmingham is also lively and varied.

Culturally, Birmingham sets a standard that few cities outside of London can match. With a selection of widely-reputed theatres, including the renowned Hippodrome and stunning Symphony Hall, Birmingham's artistic credentials are hard to beat. Birmingham's Museum and Art Gallery is also huge and extremely well stocked.

It's hard to define Birmingham's dominant industry– as a scaled-down version of the capital it also apes London's business diversity. The city has two universities; the long-established University of Birmingham and the more recently formed University of the West Midlands.

Like all large cities, Birmingham has its good and bad residential areas, from relatively affluent areas such as Bournville, Moseley and Edgbaston or, further afield, Sutton Coldfield, to more deprived areas such as Handsworth.

In terms of everyday entertainment, Birmingham has its fair share of retail and leisure parks, situated around the edges of the rather domineering motorway network. It is a big football city with a handful of leading teams, including Aston Villa, Birmingham City and West Bromwich Albion.

Birmingham is affectionately known as 'Brum' and its residents as 'Brummies'. The distinctive regional accent is often derided by other Brits and can be hard to follow at first, but as a rule, Birmingham's residents have a reputation for generosity of spirit, openness and friendliness.

Manchester

Manchester is situated in the north west of England, close to the port city of Liverpool, with a population just short of half a million. It is the ninth biggest city in the UK, but it ranks much higher in terms of its significance as a centre of business and culture.

The first thing most visitors to Manchester think of is football. The brand of Manchester United is a truly global phenomenon and is undoubtedly the city's greatest export since the city was first established during the industrial revolution in the 1800s. Manchester has much more to offer as a home. It is a proud city, and the local residents, dubbed 'Mancunians', are fiercely competitive, especially when sparring with their neighbours in Liverpool. However, the city also has a very strong creative streak and a great tolerance of difference and alternative culture.

Beyond football, Manchester's most iconic feature is the huge Beetham Tower, a mixed-use high-rise building that is part hotel, part office space and entirely representative of the city's desire to stand out from the crowd.

As might be expected the creative industries stand out in Manchester; Public Relations, Marketing and Advertising agencies abound and the city centre offers an extremely vibrant and dynamic environment.

Culturally, the city is blessed with a fine orchestra-in-residence, the world-renowned Halle Orchestra. There are excellent theatres in the form of The Royal Exchange and The Library, and the nightclub culture, defined through the 1980s and 1990s by the iconic Hacienda club, is still going strong. Manchester is a big music city and was the birthplace of many fine rock groups, including The Stone Roses, The Happy Mondays and Oasis.

Manchester is also well known for its lively gay scene. The so-called Gay Village is a network of excellent clubs, bars and restaurants in the city centre which are 19 popular with the gay community but welcoming and inclusive to all. The bars and clubs around Canal Street in Manchester are particularly good.

The cultural identity of Manchester is also shaped by its migrant population, with a large Chinese quarter and a significant Jewish community.

Shopping in Manchester is on a grand scale and there is the giant Trafford Centre near by. This is one of the largest shopping complexes in Europe, featuring almost every leading brand retailer.

Getting to Manchester is easy. Road and rail links are excellent, and the orbital M60 motorway makes travel around the city relatively painless. Manchester airport is also one of the UK's busiest airports outside of London.

As with Birmingham, Manchester has its trouble spots, with the Moss Side area of the city in particular suffering from the worst excesses of gun crime and urban deprivation. Other areas which may be better avoided include Cheetham Hill, Levenshulme and Eccles. These are balanced out by attractive residential areas such as Didsbury, Prestwich and Worsley.

FACT

■ Culturally, the city is blessed with a fine orchestra-in-residence, the world-renowned Halle Orchestra. There are excellent theatres in the form of The Royal Exchange and The Library, and the nightclub culture, defined through the 1980s and 1990s by the iconic Hacienda club, is still going strong.

Leeds

The city of Leeds is Britain's fastest-growing metropolis. With a population just short of half a million it is comparable in size with Manchester, but is expanding at a far greater rate. This is due in no small part to Leeds' reputation as a hub for the financial sector, particularly in the area of personal finance.

Leeds dues, however, also cultural significance and is home to the West Yorkshire Playhouse theatre have a Opera North, the Northern Ballet Theatre, and a wide range of museums and galleries which celebrate the city's rich architectural heritage.

Like Birmingham, Leeds has been undergoing a fair degree of redevelopment over recent years. In Leeds' case the transformation is still incomplete, but with more shopping facilities and cultural centres planned, it seems that Leeds is destined to rival Birmingham as a financial powerhouse. And while Manchester has its Beetham Tower, Leeds has Lumiere, a 171m skyscraper, due for completion in 2010.

Leeds is close to Manchester and another major northern city, Sheffield; a geographical situation that is being exploited by the business communities of these cities to their mutual advantage. With closer co-operation and a more commercial focus, this triumvirate of cities is set to dominate the creative and financial industries in the UK over the coming decades.

Leeds has a large student population and an accompanying nightlife, with arguably the best clubs in the north of England. Rather like Birmingham, Leeds has a large Asian migrant population and this is reflected in an excellent selection of restaurants offering food from around the world.

The city is well situated for travel around the region, being connected with London via the M1 motorway and with Manchester via the M62. It is also a good base from which to explore the national parks of the Peak District to the south, the North York Moors to the north east and the Lake District to the north west.

As a thriving city, there's also no shortage of accommodation for the new arrival. While Leeds is generally a quieter city than either Birmingham or Manchester, certain areas have higher crime rates, including Chapel Allerton, Beeston, Harehills and Gipton. Temple Newsam and Killingbeck are more attractive areas, although it might be better to travel further afield to some of the outlying suburbs and villages if you're looking for a quieter and more picturesque area to live.

Bristol

With a population similar in size to Leeds and Manchester, Bristol is situated in the south west of England, close to the historic city of Bath. Bristol has a strong maritime history and the harbourside is now one of the city's main cultural attractions. Well connected to London and Wales by the M4 motorway, Bristol also has good rail links to the north. Like Leeds, Bristol has profited from a boom in the financial services industry and is home to many major companies. Culturally, the city is well served by the Old Vic Theatre and by a variety of cinemas, arts centres and galleries.

Liverpool

Renowned as the home of The Beatles and Liverpool Football Club, the port city on the north-west coast of England has a population in excess of 400,000 and is also a major centre of commerce and finance. Unsurprisingly, given its seafaring connections, Liverpool is a major centre for the insurance industry, though while many of the companies may have grown up insuring against losses at sea, they are now firmly rooted on dry land. The city's Albert Dock area, once a hive of manual activity, is now a smart retail and business complex. Liverpool was awarded the European City of Culture title for 2008, and the city is home to a Philharmonic Orchestra with a good reputation and, of course, to a rich musical heritage. Road and rail links are good and the city is also well connected to Ireland by means of ferry travel.

Newcastle

Another urban regeneration success story, Newcastle is a very distinctive city located in the north east of England, with a population in excess of a quarter of a million. The residents of Newcastle are colloquially known as 'Geordies', with a distinctive regional accent that is among the strongest in the country. Newcastle is an extremely welcoming city, popular with students, and blessed with an excellent night life. Thanks to regeneration capital, Newcastle's quayside is now an area of business and cultural importance, with some architectural gems, including the Tyne bridge and Sir Norman Foster's Sage music centre, situated in the neighbouring city of Gateshead– an important partner in Newcastle's new-found economic prosperity.

Southampton

On the south coast of England, Southampton is a port city with a significant past in international trade. A former hub of the boat-building industry, Southampton has been forced to adapt to survive after much of the historic city was destroyed in the Second World War. Now Southampton is more of a cultural capital for the region rather than an industrial centre, with nearby Portsmouth taking on the bulk of the international sea trade. Southampton still has a massive dockside area, but much of this has been turned over to retail use in recent years. Service industries such as insurance and retail are strong in the area, and the city is linked to London via the M3 motorway. The city also has a large Polish community.

Glasgow

The UK's second city ad the largest city by far in Scotland with a population well in excess of two million, Glasgow is a tough trading city which has had its fair share of social problems in the past, but which has now entered a new age of prosperity and cultural standing. Glasgow is home to many of Scotland's major companies and is a major centre of business and finance. One the UK's fastest growing economies, it is also a rapidly expanding location, with more new jobs created here than anywhere outside of London. The main growth areas are financial services, the creative industries and sciences, although the city still maintains its strong links with heavy industries, especially shipbuilding. Culturally, the city may not have the glamour of Edinburgh, but it has many fine arts venues and a vibrant nightlife, as well as two extraordinarily passionate football teams in Rangers and Celtic!

Edinburgh

Scotland's capital city is dwarfed by Glasgow in terms of population, but it more than holds its own as a centre of commerce and culture. The city is divided into the New and Old Town, though in reality both date back to the 18th century. The city's architecture is stunning and its outlook is cosmopolitan. This is typified by the festival, held every August, which welcomes the international theatrical ad artistic community. Edinburgh is bit more cut off from the rest of the UK than Glasgow in terms of transport links, and this comparative isolation makes the city feel more exclusive. The nightlife and culture are excellent. Edinburgh is also the home of the Scottish parliament.

■ RENTING

It is a far less complicated process to rent a property than to buy one so it should not take more than two to four weeks to arrange. The part of the process that is likely to take the longest is finding a suitable property. The rental market in Britain is comparatively small – less than 10% of private homes are available for the purpose. There is a shortage of properties to rent in many areas, particularly those with three or more bedrooms.

FACT

■ There is a shortage of properties to rent in many areas, particularly those with three or more bedrooms. One bedroom flats or one-room studios are easier to come by, especially in cities

One bedroom flats or one-room studios are easier to come by, especially in cities.

Bedsits or flatshares are generally easiest to find in student areas that are, close to universities and colleges. They are either privately owned or provided by the educational establishment. Universities normally have an accommodation office which keeps lists of properties available for students to rent.

The vast majority of properties to rent are furnished. The reason for this is historical: until the law was changed in 1989, landlords had greater legal protection if their properties were let furnished. Although this is no longer the case, in many areas, unfurnished properties are still hard to come by.

Furnished accommodation is more expensive, and if you have your own furniture already, this may need to go into storage, which is an additional cost. The problem you may find with furnished property is that, unless you are looking at the luxury end of the market, the furnishings may not be of a very high standard. Generally, unfurnished properties do include carpets, curtains and kitchen appliances such as cooker and fridge.

How to Find A Rental Property

In order to find which properties are to let, you should contact all the estate agents and letting agents in the area you are interested in, in addition to looking in the local papers where you may find privately advertised properties. 'Free-ads' papers, where private sellers and lessors can advertise items and property free of charge carry details of rental properties as well as building sites and houses for sale. Taking a walk around your preferred area is a good way to check out properties with 'to let' signs outside. The internet is a growing resource for the property hunter, especially in the lettings market, which can move much quicker than residential sales. Most estate agents have separate lettings departments with comprehensive online listings. See below for information on how to find properties for sale.

Rental costs will vary considerably depending on the size and age of a property, its condition and most importantly, its location. In city areas, rents tend to be high. In rural areas they will be far lower, but the saving on rent may be offset by other costs, such as higher fuel costs and higher prices in local shops. As a rule of thumb, the more remote a property is, the lower the rent will be.

If you need to fix up accommodation from abroad, the internet is the obvious place to look, but it is very difficult to assess the standard of the accommodation or the local area. If you can get the help of somebody in Britain – either a friend or a relocation agency – you can avoid making a mistake. Alternatively, if you can wait until you arrive, given the relatively quick set-up period for rental accommodation it might be advisable to take on a short-term let of a holiday home, serviced apartment, or even

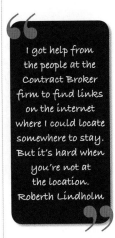

> I got help from the people at the Contract Broker firm to find links on the internet where I could locate somewhere to stay. But it's hard when you're not at the location.
> Roberth Lindholm

> I was lucky that friends already living in Britain were able to lend great assistance on this count. I will say, though, that on my journeys through the city I see no shortage of flats to let. So I can't imagine finding accommodation would be a problem and from the adverts I have seen, the pricing is reasonable.
> Amy Burns

a room in a bed and breakfast hotel while you are searching. Holiday accommodation, expensive and over-subscribed in peak season, is often available on low rents over a longer period out of season. A month in a rented holiday home could be long enough to give you the chance to set up fixed accommodation in your desired area.

Sources of Rental Properties

Loot: Free-ads publication/website for England. www.loot.com/property

Scot Ads: 08457 434343; Free-ads publication/website for Scotland. www.scot-ads.com

Letting Web: A very useful website which advertises properties to let via letting agents throughout Great Britain. www.lettingweb.com

Property News: Properties to rent throughout Northern Ireland. www.propertynews.com

Relocation Agencies: You can employ a relocation agency to find a suitable property for you, but it is wise to compare the costs of different agencies, as these can be quite high. The Association of Relocation Professionals can provide a full list of their members. 08700 737475; www.relocationagents.com

The Flatshare and Roommate Website: www.housepals.co.uk

Easy Roommate: www.easyroommate.com

Tenancy Agreements

In England and Wales there is no legal requirement to have a written tenancy agreement – a contract detailing the basic rules and regulations of the tenancy that should be signed by both the tenant and the landlord – though you may have an oral one. In Scotland, in most cases the agreement must be written; in Northern Ireland all tenancy agreements must be written. However, it is strongly advised that you do not take on the rental of any property unless you have a written agreement as if there are any problems later on it puts you in a stronger position if you wish to take your landlord to court.

A written tenancy agreement is a legal contract, so both parties who sign it agree to abide by the conditions contained within it and if they fail to do so the other party can take legal action. For this reason it is essential to read the tenancy agreement closely, and to obtain the advice of a solicitor if there is anything you are unsure or unhappy about.

The tenancy agreement will require the tenant to hand the property back to the landlord in the same condition it was in at the start of the tenancy. You should be given an inventory at the outset which outlines the state of the property and what items were provided. Before you sign the tenancy agreement you should walk around the property with the landlord and go through all the points in the inventory. This is an extremely important process as it gives you a strong legal position in the event of any disputes at a later stage. It also allows you to check, in the landlord's presence, for any potential trouble areas, such as leaking pipes or damp, which may affect or damage furniture.

Your landlord should also be able to provide you with written evidence that the appliances and services connected in the property, such as the gas boiler, any heating appliances and the mains electricity supply, have been checked to the standards required for rental property. Any plumbing or gas equipment repair should have been carried out by a tradesman registered by UK standards body CORGI, which gives you a degree of protection as a tenant. Similarly, all electrical maintenance must be performed by qualified and registered electricians. The central heating/hot water boiler in the property should be serviced annually.

Generally, both tenant and landlord are required to give a period of notice (usually a month) if they wish to terminate the agreement.

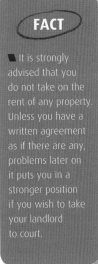

What a Tenancy Agreement Should Contain

◼ Your name, your landlord's name, the address of the property which is being let.

◼ Your landlord's contact details, including address and emergency contact phone number

◼ The date the tenancy began.

◼ Details of whether other people are allowed the use of the property, and if so, which rooms.

◼ The date the tenancy ends.

◼ The amount of rent payable, how often, when it should be paid, and how often and when it can be increased.

◼ What the rent includes, for example, council tax or fuel.

■ Whether your landlord will provide any services (e.g. laundry, maintenance or meals) and whether there are service charges for these.

■ The length of notice which you and your landlord need to give if the tenancy is to be ended.

■ Details of your landlord's obligations to repair the property.

You can contact the Office of Fair Trading if you think there are unfair terms in your tenancy agreement, such as:

■ Adding in charges for repairs which are the landlord's responsibility.

■ Charging you extra penalty costs for late payment of rent.

■ Unfair rent increase clauses.

Assured Shorthold Tenancies (AST)

These are tenancies of not less than six months, in England, Wales and Northern Ireland. In Scotland the equivalent agreement is know as a 'short assured tenancy'. After the initial fixed period (usually six months) the landlord has the right to regain possession on giving notice to the tenant, whether or not the tenant has observed the terms of the tenancy agreement.

During the initial agreed fixed term, both parties are contractually bound – the tenant(s) to pay rent for the full term, and the landlord to allow the tenant(s) exclusive possession. Once the fixed term has expired, unless a new fixed term is agreed, the tenancy automatically becomes a periodic tenancy. The tenancy then continues with the rent being paid at agreed periods – weekly or monthly, for example – until either party wishes to end the agreement and gives the appropriate notice. In this case, an agreed length of notice must be given – normally a month – after which time the tenant will leave.

If there is no written tenancy agreement, or if the tenancy agreement does not state that it is an assured tenancy (see below), it is treated in law as an assured shorthold tenancy.

Assured Tenancies

An assured tenancy gives greater rights to a tenant as it is for an indefinite period. As long as the landlord does not live on the premises and the tenant observes the terms of the tenancy agreement, the landlord cannot evict the tenant unless he obtains a court order on certain grounds specified in the Act. These include such things as unpaid rent, damage to the property, or otherwise breaking the contract with the landlord.

A court may serve you with written notice to leave if the landlord offers you a similar property, needs the property for himself or needs vacant possession in order to sell the property.

These sort of tenancies are most likely to be used by housing associations and other public sector landlords.

Houses in Multiple Occupation

Certain rental properties are classed as 'houses in multiple occupation' (HMOs). The landlords of these premises must be licensed in order to ensure that they are a 'fit and proper person' and that standards within the property are acceptable.

The following properties are classed as HMOs:

- An entire house or flat which is let to three or more tenants who form two or more households and who share a kitchen, bathroom or toilet.

- A house which has been converted entirely into bedsits and which is let to three or more tenants who form two or more households and who share kitchen, bathroom or toilet facilities.

- A converted house which contains one or more flats which are not wholly self contained (i.e. the flat does not contain within it a kitchen, bathroom and toilet) and which is occupied by three or more tenants who form two or more households.

- A building which is converted entirely into self-contained flats if the conversion did not meet the standards of the 1991 Building Regulations and more than one third of the flats are let on short-term tenancies.

- In addition, the property must be used as the tenants' only or main residence. In the case of students and migrant workers it will be treated as their only or main residence.

To find out whether a property is licensed, contact your local housing authority which holds a register available for public inspection. If you think that you are living in a property which should be licensed and is not you should notify your local housing authority. If your landlord proves to be unlicensed, you cannot withhold rent. However, in certain cases, you or the local housing authority may apply to a residential property tribunal to reclaim rent.

When sharing a property with other tenants normally all of the individuals sign a joint tenancy. If one or more tenants abscond, those remaining become liable for all the rent and expenses. It is therefore essential to be sure you can trust everybody you share a tenancy with.

Credit Checks and References

Before you are accepted as a tenant there may be various checks made to ensure you will not cause problems to the landlord. You may be asked for references from previous landlords as to your suitability as a tenant, to check whether you behaved well, did not cause damage, and paid your rent on time.

A letting agency will almost certainly carry out a credit check on you to ensure your creditworthiness.

In some cases, particularly with younger tenants, they may be asked to provide a guarantor. This is a person who will guarantee paying the rent to a landlord if the tenant, for any reason, does not pay the rent. A guarantor is legally responsible to for any rent payments outstanding and can be taken to court by a landlord in cases where a tenant has failed to meet any rent payment. A guarantor is most likely to be the parent or guardian of the tenant, but another responsible adult would generally be acceptable as long as they will agree to take the risk.

In the absence of a guarantor it might be possible to negotiate alternative guarantees about rent payments so long as you can provide references from employers and a credit reference check.

Rental Costs

Your tenancy agreement should detail how often and in what form the rent is to be paid. This is normally payable in advance for one or three months at a time. You may need to set up a UK bank account to make the payments. The agreement will state the length of time the tenant agrees to take the property, and rent is then payable for the whole of this period. The landlord should issue you with a receipt for all rent paid. This provides evidence if there is ever a dispute about payments. If the tenant leaves early, he or she will have to continue to pay the rent and outgoings for the property until a new tenant is found. The tenancy agreement may state a period after which your rent may be reviewed or increased.

As was mentioned earlier, there are legal protections against unexpected increases in rent. Within the period of a current contract, rent can only be increased with the agreement of both landlord and tenant. Where there is no contract or a contract has ended, rent can be increased by service of a valid notice of rent increase or by provision of a new contract.

In addition to the monthly rental, tenants are usually responsible for paying for other outgoings such as council tax and contents insurance, as well as for gas, electricity, water rates and telephone bills. The building's insurance will normally be paid by the owner.

Deposits

In addition to the rent, a tenant pays a deposit to the landlord or letting agent at the commencement of the tenancy. This is a sum of money, usually equivalent to about four or six weeks' rent, which should be kept in an interest-bearing account until the end of the tenancy when it will be used to pay for any rent arrears or any damage to the property during the tenancy. The balance, and interest, if any, is then returned to the tenant. The tenancy agreement should state these conditions, so before you sign it or hand over any money, do check it to see what your deposit will cover and how it will be returned as the return of all or part of deposits, let alone of interest due, has long been a cause of disputes between landlords and tenants.

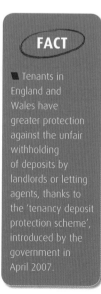

FACT

Tenants in England and Wales have greater protection against the unfair withholding of deposits by landlords or letting agents, thanks to the 'tenancy deposit protection scheme', introduced by the government in April 2007.

Tenants in England and Wales have greater protection against the unfair withholding of deposits by landlords or letting agents, thanks to the 'tenancy deposit protection scheme', introduced by the government in April 2007. This applies to assured shorthold tenancies only, although the legislation may be extended to cover the rest of the UK in future. There is further information on deposit protection below.

When you sign your tenancy agreement always check the details to see what your deposit will cover and how it will be returned. Ensure that you agree with the terms and conditions of the tenancy before you hand any money over.

Deductions can be made from a deposit when a tenant leaves a property for the following reasons:

- Rent arrears.
- Damage that is more than fair wear and tear.
- The property not being cleaned.
- Outstanding bills.
- Failure to return keys.
- Leaving before the end of a fixed term of a contract.
- Failing to give proper notice or agreeing surrender.

Tenancy Deposit Protection

All deposits taken for an assured shorthold tenancy are protected by a government-authorised scheme which allows tenants to get all or part of their deposit back when they are entitled to it and encourages tenants and landlords to make a clear agreement from the start on the condition of the property.

There are two types of tenancy deposit protection scheme available for landlords and letting agents. All schemes provide a free dispute resolution service.

Insurance-based Schemes
- The tenant pays the deposit to the landlord or letting agent.
- The landlord or letting agent retains the deposit and pays a premium to the insurer.

Custodial Schemes
- The tenant pays the deposit to the landlord or letting agent.
- The landlord or letting agent pays the deposit into the scheme.

In either case, within 14 days of receiving a deposit the landlord or letting agent must give the tenant the details about how their deposit is protected including:

- The contact details of the tenancy deposit scheme selected.
- The landlord or letting agent's contact details.
- How to apply for the release of the deposit.

- Information explaining the purpose of the deposit.
- What to do if there is a dispute about the deposit.

At the end of the tenancy there are minor differences on how to release the deposit, depending on which type of scheme is used. Under an insurance-based scheme:

- If an agreement is reached about how the deposit should be divided, the landlord or letting agent returns all or some of the deposit.
- If there is a dispute, the landlord must hand over the disputed amount to the scheme for safekeeping until the dispute is resolved.
- If the landlord fails to comply, the insurance arrangements will ensure the return of the deposit to the tenant if they are entitled to it.

Under a custodial scheme:

- If an agreement is reached about how the deposit should be divided, the scheme will return the deposit, divided in the way agreed by both parties.
- If there is a dispute, the scheme will hold the Deposit until the dispute Resolution Service or courts decide what is fair

The interest accrued by deposits in the scheme will be used to pay for the running of the scheme and any surplus will be used to offer interest to the tenant (or landlord if the tenant isn't entitled to it).

If your landlord isn't protecting your deposit you can apply to your local county court which can order the landlord or agent to either repay the deposit to you or protect it in a scheme. If your landlord or agent has not protected your deposit, they will be ordered to repay three times the amount of the deposit to you.

At the end of the tenancy, you should, of course, leave the property and its contents in the condition in which it was let to you, allowing for fair wear and tear. All rent and any other expenses should be paid up to date. Then agree with your landlord or agent how much of the deposit should be returned to you. You should receive the agreed amount of the deposit within ten days.

Scheme Providers

There are three government-authorised Tenancy Deposit Scheme providers.

Custodial Scheme

The Deposit Protection Service (DPS): 0870 707 1707; www.depositprotection.com

Insurance Backed Schemes

Tenancy Deposit Solutions Ltd (TDSL): 0871 703 0552; www.mydeposits.co.uk

Tenancy Deposit Scheme (TDS): 0845 226 7837; www.thedisputeservice.co.uk

Ending a Tenancy

When a landlord wishes to end a tenancy he must provide notice, giving legal reasons why he wants the tenant to leave. The notice must be in writing, dated, and must provide details of property, tenant, landlord, and the date by which the tenant is expected to leave. The minimum period of notice required must be observed – this may vary, depending on the reason why the landlord wishes you to leave.

If a tenancy has ended or a notice has been served and the tenant has not left, the tenant continues to remain liable to pay rent. A non-resident landlord is lawfully obliged to claim repossession at court.

Advice and assistance on these matters can be obtained from your local council's Housing Advice Service.

Letting Agents

Many rented properties are let through letting agencies, which act as an intermediary between the landlord and tenant. They collect rents from tenants and pass them onto the landlord. However, you should check any letting agent out carefully as they have an even poorer reputation than estate agents. Anybody can set up as a letting agent and there are numerous tales of unscrupulous letting agents collecting rents and deposits and keeping them in their own accounts rather than passing them on to the landlord. Amazingly, there is very little redress in law against such behaviour, and any legal action you do take is likely to be protracted and expensive, so the best way to protect yourself against this is to make enquiries about the agents first before entering into an agreement with them. Try to deal only with a member of the Association of Residential Letting Agents (ARLA), which insists that members have insurance cover to safeguard rental income and deposits. They have a website which includes a searchable database of letting agents by area.

Letting agents usually ask for a reservation fee, deductible from the deposit when you sign a rental agreement.

Agencies can charge for a number of services provided to tenants so it is important to establish what fees will be charged before using an agency. These fees may include:

- Drawing up a tenancy agreement.
- Carrying out credit reference checks and securing references
- Negotiating with the landlord on the tenant's behalf about the contract

Letting agencies may not charge for registering the names and housing requirements of prospective tenants or supplying the addresses and details of available accommodation. If you are charged for this service contact the local council's Housing Advice Service.

Useful Contacts

Association of Residential Letting Agents: 0845 345 5752; www.arla.co.uk

Advice Guide: The Citizens advice Bureau information about all aspects of renting property on their website, Advice Bureau. www.adviceguide.org.uk/

Directgov: Offers UK Government advice and information about buying and renting your home offers . www.direct.gov.uk is available on the general website

Housing Net: Website contains a searchable database of Housing Associations throughout the UK. Also has details of local authorities. www.housingnet.co.uk

■ BUYING A HOME

Procedures for buying a home vary from country to country, so below you'll find an introduction to buying a home in Britain; from finding a property and getting a mortgage to the hidden costs involved in purchasing your new home

Finance

In the UK, mortgages can be taken out through a number of different types of institutions. Traditionally, building societies were the sole source of mortgages, and were available only to those who saved regularly with them. Today, due to changes in the law relating to financial institutions, banks and insurance companies, others can supply mortgages, and building societies will lend to anyone who satisfies their criteria regarding security – you no longer have to be an established saver with any particular building society. This is in part due to the fact that in recent years the distinction between building societies and banks has become blurred, with each taking on functions of the other. Indeed, increasing numbers of building societies are now formally converting to banks.

A recent phenomenon, with the advent of telephone and online banking, has been the 'direct mortgage' company, which does not do business face to face with the customer. As they will arrange mortgages over the phone, through the post, and over the internet, their overheads are low compared with companies with expensive high street properties and staff to maintain, so they can offer mortgages at a competitive rate.

Because of these changes, financial services in the UK are generally becoming more and more competitive and the range of choice is becoming larger. It is important to be aware of all the different options available when borrowing money to buy a property or a building plot and to understand the advantages and disadvantages of each.

FACT

◼ Today, due to changes in the law relating to financial institutions, banks and insurance companies, others can supply mortgages, and building societies will lend to anyone who satisfies their criteria regarding security – you no longer have to be an established saver with any particular building society.

Mortgages

Although there are many different mortgages on the market, there are just two main types available; the repayment mortgage, where both the interest on the loan and the capital are repaid over a period of years, and the interest-only mortgage where only the interest on the loan is paid, and another payment is made into some sort of investment plan which is used to repay the capital amount at the end of the mortgage period.

In Britain, borrowers can usually borrow up to 90 or 95% of the value of a property. This percentage is usually termed the 'maximum loan to value' (LTV). It may be possible to get a 100% mortgage, particularly if you are a first-time buyer, but most lenders will want a deposit of at least 5% of the cost (i.e. they would allow you a 95% mortgage). A 100% mortgage is likely to attract high-interest rates. If you have other savings or security, you may take out a mortgage for a portion of the house value, so you may buy a house for £100,000 with a £70,000 mortgage. The remaining £30,000 will then be paid for from other sources.

The amount that any particular borrower will be allowed is calculated on the basis of their annual income. Lenders will usually offer around three

> *Our first step was to check the internet for how much we might be able to borrow. Anna and I went straight to our own banks' websites and used their mortgage calculator to get a ballpark figure for how much we might be able to borrow. These figures, as they turned out, were pretty much identical. Having looked at a few decidedly dodgy properties in that price range we were then 'encouraged' by the estate agent to visit their own mortgage advisor. Despite our scepticism that he would try and push certain products at us he was actually a great help in explaining the 'extras' involved in a mortgage – valuation fees, early repayment, leaving fees, etc. He then recommended two different mortgages which would actually lend us far more than we had expected.*
> *Matthew Taylor and Anna Gorse*

times your annual salary, or 2.5 times the joint income of a married couple. So, someone earning £34,000 per year could take out a mortgage of around £102,000. Another, earning £15,000, would be allowed up to £45,000.

Many people are denied mortgages because of bad credit ratings or uncertain income. Self-employed people in particular may have problems finding a mortgage. Many lenders will not lend to the self-employed. They will, at the very least, need to produce three years' accounts so a lender can determine the risk they may pose. These groups of people very often can only resort to lenders who charge relatively high interest rates and impose large penalties if borrowers fall into arrears. If you are in this position, it is worth trying to persuade mortgage lenders you are a good credit risk by using other means, for instance, by showing them evidence of paid bills and invoices, direct debit agreements which you have never defaulted on, and so forth.

For those who are self-employed or have variable incomes, it may be possible to obtain a 'self-certification mortgage', which enables you to set up a loan without the need for payslips, bank statements or accounting records. The interest will almost certainly be higher in this case.

Useful Contact

Any mortgage lender or broker should agree to follow the guidelines laid down in 'The Mortgage Code'. It is on the website of the Council of Mortgage Lenders: 020 7437 0075; www.cml.org.uk.

Repayment Mortgages

The loan is repaid gradually over the length of the mortgage, usually 25 years, although this could be longer or shorter, depending on circumstances. Monthly repayments comprise interest on the outstanding loan and repayment of part of the loan. The amount of interest paid fluctuates according to the periodic rise and fall in interest rates.

Interest-only Mortgages

The loan amount on interest only mortgages remains the same throughout the mortgage term, again usually 25 years. Interest is paid on the total amount of the loan for the whole of the mortgage period, the interest fluctuating with changes in interest rates. Alongside the mortgage, regular payments are made into an investment plan, and at the end of the mortgage period the capital is repaid in a lump sum from the money accrued in the investment plan.

There are three main types of interest-only mortgage, depending on the type of investment plan involved: ISA, Pension or Endowment Mortgages.

Endowment Mortgages

Alongside the interest payments to the lender, a life insurance endowment policy is taken out. Monthly premiums, less charges, are paid to an insurance company which invests them in shares, bonds and other assets. Premiums are set at a level which should ensure that the accumulated investment funds pay off the loan at the end of the mortgage period. There is no guarantee, however, that the final sum will pay off the mortgage in full – you may end up with a shortfall. It is also possible that you may end up with a surplus, which is payable as a lump sum at the end of the mortgage period.

It is strongly advised that you get good advice from a mortgage broker before deciding on an endowment mortgage. In recent years some endowment mortgages have not been performing well enough in the current low inflationary environment to pay off the full amount of the mortgage.

Part of the monthly premiums payable on an endowment mortgage, typically around 5%, goes to provide life insurance cover. In the event of the death of the mortgagee, the mortgage is paid off in full. Where there is more than one party to the mortgage, for instance, if a married couple take out a joint mortgage, the mortgage may be paid off in the event of the death of either party, so the surviving mortgagee owns the property outright even if the mortgage still has a period to run.

Pension Mortgages

Monthly interest is paid off on the loan but premiums are paid into a pension plan which pays off your mortgage on retirement and also pays you a pension. There are tax advantages with this type of mortgage, as payments into the pension plan qualify for tax relief. There are, however, disadvantages, including the fact that you may no longer be eligible to make contributions to the pension scheme if you should join a pension scheme at work or you become unemployed. In this case, another means of building up capital to pay off the mortgage would be required.

ISA Mortgages

With these, the loan is linked to an Individual Savings Account (ISA). An ISA can be used to invest in a wide range of investments including cash in the form of bank, building society and National Savings accounts; investment-type insurance plans and stocks and shares. The ISA is used to build up a capital lump sum which pays off the loan at the end of the term. These are more flexible than other endowment mortgages because profits can be taken from the ISA at any time, rather than having to wait for any surplus to be paid at the end of the mortgage period. The disadvantage is that the value of the ISA may be depressed as a result of low-share prices at the time repayment of the loan is due. There is no life insurance included in an ISA mortgage, so a policy must be taken out separately if life cover is required.

Flexible Mortgages

A comparative newcomer to the mortgage scene, a flexible mortgage allows the borrower to pay off varying amounts depending on current financial circumstances. By paying increased monthly payments for a period, you can later take a break in their monthly repayments, reduce them, or borrow back any money you have previously overpaid. By overpaying each month you can pay off your mortgage far more quickly and cheaply because less interest will be charged.

Self-Build Mortgages

One of the biggest problems faced by self-builders is managing cash flow during the course of the build. With a self-build mortgage, stage payments can be made in advance of each stage. The mortgage can be used for both traditional and timber-frame builds, as well as for renovation and conversion projects. Typical stage payments will include land, foundations, wall plate or erection of the timber frame, watertight/roof on, plastered, and completion.

Generally, you may borrow up to 95% of land purchase price; up to 95% of the building costs and up to 95% of the end value.

For more information on self-build properties, see the Self-Build section later in the chapter.

Building Societies and Banks

These are some of the largest lending institutions active in Britain, but there are many smaller ones. A full list is available from the Council of Mortgage Lenders. Telephone 020 7437 0075 or visit www.cml.org.uk.

Addresses and phone numbers of local bank and building society branches can be found in local phone books or business pages or on their websites.

Abbey: 0870 607 6000; www.abbey.com
Alliance & Leicester: www.alliance-leicester.co.uk
Barclays: 0845 677 0002; www.barclays.co.uk
Lloyds TSB: 0845 300 0000; www.lloydstsb.com

NatWest: 0800 015 4212; www.natwest.com
Bank of Scotland: www.bankofscotland.co.uk
The Royal Bank of Scotland: www.rbs.co.uk
First Trust Bank: 028 9032 5599; www.aibgroup.com
Northern Bank: 028 9024 5277; www.northernbank.co.uk
Internet banks include Egg: www.egg.com and Smile: www.smile.co.uk

Mortgage Rates

Every month, the Bank of England reviews its base interest rate, which applies to the whole of the UK. They may move it up or down, or leave it at its existing rate. Since 2000 the property market in Britain has been booming, at times threatening to 'overheat'. By adjustments to the base rate the Bank of England has attempted to walk the tricky path of not allowing prices to rise too high, thus encouraging inflation, while not depressing the market too much, in order to avoid encouraging stagnation. There have been fluctuations in the base rate as a result, with periods of an unchanging rate having been followed by a number of small rises in quick succession.

Banks and building societies set their own interest rates on the basis of the Bank of England. Their various mortgage products will offer differing rates depending on the particular conditions of the mortgage and the situation of the borrower.

Fixed or Variable Rate

With a fixed-rate mortgage, the interest rate is, as is suggested by the name, fixed for a number of years. The longer the fixed rate period, the lower the interest rate offered. The advantage is that you know exactly what

> Once we had a couple of mortgage quotes we returned to the internet to read further and work out if the quotes were as they appeared. One invaluable website that we would recommend is www.moneysavingexpert.com – loads of advice for the complete novice or seasoned pro, helpful basic guides and extensive forums. As with anything, all advice should be checked and double checked but it helped us to understand the financial side of things a bit better. It advised using a fee-free, independent, whole-of-market mortgage broker to get an impartial view of what was right for us – we've used London and Country who have been nothing short of fantastic thus far. So, we actually found the financial side of things relatively straightforward. My biggest piece of advice would be to double and triple check everything you hear from anyone, be very wary of being pushed to pay for services or products you don't need.
> Matthew Taylor and Anna Gorse

your repayments will be every month for that period. The disadvantage is that you need to gamble that interest rates do not fall significantly during that period, as this would mean you would end up paying over the odds. Of course, if interest rates rise appreciably in that period, you can save yourself a great deal of money. At the end of the fixed term, the normal variable rate is paid.

With a variable rate mortgage, as the name suggests, your interest payments will fluctuate as mortgage rates vary.

Discounted Rate

In this case a borrower pays a lower rate of interest in the earlier years, which can be useful for people such as first-time buyers where money may be tight for the early years of the loan. These deals should be approached with caution, however, as sometimes the discount is not genuine and the interest saved in the earlier years is just added to the outstanding loan.

Tracker Mortgages

With tracker mortgages, the interest rate 'tracks' the Bank of England base rate. There are three basic types of tracker mortgage: those which track the base rate for the whole life of the loan; those which run at an agreed differential to the base rate (either above or more rarely below it) for a set period before reverting to the standard variable rate; and finally those in which the lender promises that the margin between the base rate and the mortgage interest rate will not go beyond a set level.

Buying Land

If you satisfy requirements regarding income and so forth, there should be no difficulty getting a mortgage if you wish to buy a plot of land and build a house on it immediately. The amount of the mortgage would be based on the combined value of the land and the house you build, together with the cost of running services such as mains water and electricity to the site. However, if you wish just to buy a building site, with the intention of building on it at some later date, you would not be granted a mortgage on the land alone.

Advice and Information

There are a variety of mortgage products available for house buyers in Britain. It is obviously important that you find the one that is best for you in your individual circumstances, so it is strongly advised that you get the advice of an independent mortgage broker, who will be able to source the best mortgage for you. On the internet, Find Financial Directory has links to mortgage brokers; www.find.co.uk.

Always treat mortgage advice given by lenders with caution. They will be on commission for the numbers and types of mortgages they sell, so the temptation for them to 'miss-sell' mortgages – i.e. to sell you a mortgage which is not the best one for you in your circumstances – is often there. There is evidence that the miss-selling of mortgages is not an uncommon phenomenon, so you must do your homework carefully.

It is wise to ensure that anybody you borrow or take advice from is a member or associate member of the Council of Mortgage Lenders. Any complaints you have regarding the advice or service you are given can then be reported to them for investigation.

The Times and *Sunday Times,* plus most other weekend papers, publish lists of the best variable, fixed-rate and discount mortgages and the *Electronic Telegraph* publishes them at www.telegraph.co.uk. The website www.aboutmortgages.co.uk has tables of the best value mortgages currently available.

An excellent website giving information, advice and current facts and figures on all aspects of house buying, including current mortgage rates is www.houseweb.co.uk.

High street banks and building societies have free leaflets outlining the mortgages they have on offer. The same information is also explained on their websites.

As was mentioned previously, there are a number of building societies that operate without high Street branches, conducting their business instead through the post and the internet. Because of their lower overheads they have been able to offer competitive rates for savers and borrowers.

Internet banks have their own mortgage products available. The rates they offer are competitive with more traditional banks and building societies.

Buying a Home

The sections which follow explain the process of finding and buying a house in England, Wales and Northern Ireland. The law relating to house purchase is different in Scotland. Here, the legal procedure attached to the purchase or sale of houses is called conveyancing, a process which in Scotland can only be undertaken by a solicitor. In other parts of Britain, there are certain stages of the conveyancing process that a purchaser can undertake himself or can engage a licensed conveyancer to do on his behalf. In Scotland, however, the entire process must be carried out by a solicitor qualified to do so.

The other main difference between the house purchasing system north and south of the border, is that in Scotland conveyancing is carried out only after an offer has been accepted. Once an offer has been made and accepted, this forms a contract which is legally binding on both parties. If either side wishes to withdraw after this stage there can be substantial financial penalties and legal costs payable. For a full explanation of Scottish procedures plus specific information and advice about finding property for sale there this still happening?

> We found a house we loved and, after a short bidding process with another interested party, we had a bid accepted at the asking price. Two days later we received a phone call from the estate agents informing us that the vendor had been contacted directly by the other party who, in floods of tears, had begged her to accept their offer at the asking price. Which she did. Despite our protestations that 'our bid was accepted first', the agents said it was not possible for them to get the vendor to drop the offer and the first survey to be completed would get the house. Not wanting to be hurried in such a massive purchase we backed out. We also believed that the agents themselves had made the error, hence their unwillingness to get the vendor to reject the second offer, so told them we would not be dealing with them any further. In our opinion some estate agents are professional liars. Their role is to represent the seller and they will, we've found, tell you anything to push through a sale.
>
> Matthew Taylor and Anna Gorse

Estate Agents

Most property in Britain is sold through estate agents, who advertise and sell properties on commission for owners. Normally, their fees are a percentage of the amount they sell the house for, although some charge a flat fee. For those wishing to buy, they provide details of and arrange visits to properties, and will keep you updated with details of suitable properties if you inform them of your requirements. They nearly all advertise their properties online as well as in their offices.

As estate agents are not required to have any professional qualifications nor be a member of any professional body, it is essential that you are sure they are trustworthy before you do business with them.

For all below contacts, more description so it precedes contact details.

Useful websites

Your Move: www.your-move.co.uk. Company with branches throughout Great Britain.

Right Move: www.rightmove.co.uk. Displays properties for sale throughout the UK.

Countrywide: Has links to websites of agencies across Great Britain. See www.countrywideplc.co.uk/estate_agency/sales_list.asp

Property Sale Wales: www.propertysalewales.co.uk. Has links to estate agencies across Wales.

Scottish Property SSPC: www.sspc.co.uk. Website has links to branches throughout Scotland.

Northern Ireland Property: www.niproperty.net. Website has links to estate agencies throughout Northern Ireland.

Property Window: www.propertywindow.com

UK Homes For Sale: www.homes-uk.co.uk
Property Finder: www.propertyfinder.com
The House Hunter: www.thehousehunter.co.uk

 The National Association of Estate Agents requires its members to complete a minimum entry qualification and binds them by rules of conduct. It 01926 496800; www.naea.co.uk.

Types of housing

Listed Buildings

Any building which is considered of special architectural or historic interest is 'listed' by the Government. Buildings on the list are assigned a category, A, B or C, according to their relative importance. If you are looking for something out of the ordinary, such as a historic house, or even a church or a castle, there are a number of listed buildings for sale in the UK. If a building is listed, this should be made clear in the estate agents' detailed information on the property.

There are fairly stringent controls placed on the alterations which can be made to listed buildings and their immediate surroundings, so you must take these restrictions into account when considering buying one. The planning authorities must always be consulted before doing any work on a listed building – it is a criminal offence to undertake unauthorised works to demolish, significantly alter or extend a listed building. Grants towards the repair, maintenance or sympathetic improvement of listed buildings may be available through central or local government. Contact the local authority planning department for advice.

 Pavilions of Splendour Ltd: 020 8348 1234; www.heritage.co.uk. Estate agent specialising in the buying and selling of listed buildings.

> We spent some time looking at houses and putting in offers, but we kept getting outbid. It was awkward to keep flying up and looking at places, as my husband Mark and I had to do this separately, and then we would not get the place. Finally we found an estate about to be built, and we were able to secure a house not yet built for a £100 deposit, which would be ready around the time we wanted and would be within our budget. Then we had to sell our house which took longer than expected as the sale kept falling through. We still had not sold before I had to move up with the kids in order to allow them to start school, while Mark stayed down south to sell the house, which was pretty scary, but we did eventually sell it for the amount we needed that autumn.
> Caroline Deacon

New Property

There are certain advantages in buying a new house. They tend to be built to higher standards than older houses and come with thermal insulation, double glazing, modern central heating, and adequate ventilation, which may not always be the case with an older property. They are often sold complete with luxury fitted kitchens, bathrooms and bedrooms, together with the full range of kitchen appliances such as fridges, freezers, dishwashers and so forth. They tend to be built as small 'estates' or 'developments' of from around a dozen up to scores of similar houses. In rural areas, new developments are correspondingly smaller – maybe half a dozen or so houses – because of the smaller population.

New properties are generally sold directly by the builders, most of which are large concerns with developments in various parts of the country. You can contact them direct for details of properties currently available or under construction.

The process of buying a new house is exactly the same as buying any other property but it has the advantage that you will not find yourself caught in a chain of buyers – i.e. where the house you want to buy will not be available until its current occupants can take occupation of the house they are buying. If the owners of that house are negotiating on a house which is also still occupied you can find yourself in a chain of several different parties, who are all waiting on the party at the top of the chain reaching the stage of vacating their property. If any one of the 'links' in such a chain pulls out, this can result in all the other sales falling through.

Useful Websites

New Homes UK: (Great Britain) www.new-homes.co.uk
Daft: (N. Ireland) www.daft.ie
Barratt Construction: www.barratthomes.co.uk
Bett Homes: www.betthomes.co.uk
Redrow Homes: www.redrow.co.uk
Persimmon Homes: www.persimmonhomes.com

Self-Build

The term 'self-build' does not mean that you have to physically design and construct the house yourself – although those who have the skills may do all or part of the building or fitting-out work themselves. You may hire a building contractor to undertake all the work, or you may wish to employ a number of different tradesmen and craftsmen to do various parts of the project. But it means that you have overall control of the build from start to finish and you can work with an architect or builder to produce a building to suit your individual requirements.

One thing which might make building a new house preferable to the alternative of renovating and enlarging an older house is that value added tax (VAT) is charged on changes to an existing house. If you build from new, you can claim back all the VAT paid on materials as a single sum on completion of the project and without having to register as a VAT trader.

Despite this, self-build is not necessarily a cheaper option. In addition to the cost of the building there are the costs of buying the land and of installing services such as electricity, water and sewerage on site to take into consideration.

On the other hand, as the re-sale value of your self-built house can be at least 25% greater than the cost of the project including the purchase price of the plot, it is an option worth considering. Providing you occupy the house for at least a year before selling on, it will be classed as your principle residence and any profits made on the sale will therefore be tax-free.

Useful Publications and Websites

Homebuilding & Renovating Magazine and sister publication *Plotfinder* are both available in newsagents or by subscription from Ascent Publishing Ltd. Subscribe by telephoning 01527 834406 or visit the website at www.homebuilding.co.uk. The website includes a self-build directory which lists products, suppliers and services. It also has a database of plots for sale throughout the country.

Build It: 020 7770 8300; fax 020 7772 8584; www.self-build.co.uk. Available through newsagents or by subscription; this 12 issues around £40.

Building Plot: www.building-plot.org.uk. Prices of plots vary widely, as with every other aspect of property-buying, depending on location.

House Prices

It is a feature of the UK housing market that there is a cyclical trend, with periods of rising prices followed by stagnation or even falling prices. There are also large variations in house prices between different areas of the UK, so it is difficult to give a true picture using average figures. However, currently the general overall trend is upwards, after a slump in the early 1990s. By 1996 house prices had started to move again in the south east of England, followed by other areas of England, Wales, Scotland, and Northern Ireland. In the ten years since then there has been a massive rise of 187% in average house prices across the UK. London and Northern Ireland showed the greatest increase during the period, with rises of 240% and 231% respectively.

December 2006 saw the average UK house price break the £200,000 barrier for the first time, having risen 9.9% during the month. However, this includes a wide range of prices in different regions with about half of them still at below the £200,000 mark. Scotland is the cheapest country of the UK to buy in – but again, you would pay much more in Edinburgh, for example, than you would for an equivalent property in the Highlands. In 1996 Northern Ireland was the cheapest country to buy in, but due to its exceptionally strong growth during the decade, it has overtaken Scotland.

Average House Prices by Region	
Region	**Price**
England	
South East	£322,104
South West	£248,003
East Anglia	£216,999
Greater London	£210,116
East Midlands	£193,400
West Midlands	£163,225
Yorks & Humber	£154,917
North West	£153,112
North	£143,388
Wales	£172,152
Scotland	£142,355
Northern Ireland	£162,821
United Kingdom	£201,090

England and Wales: figures for the period October to December 2006.
Scotland and Northern Ireland: figures for the period July to September 2006.
United Kingdom: as at December 2006.

Purchasing Process

In England and Wales, most properties are offered for sale at a set price. This does not mean that you have to offer that price – you may offer the sellers a lower price, or if you are desperate to buy the house and other potential buyers are interested, you may choose to go over the asking price. If your first offer is not accepted, you can make a higher offer – and can make as many offers as you wish until the sellers accept or you decide they are asking more than you wish to pay. Oral offers are not legally binding – and a written offer made once your price has been accepted is always made 'subject to contract' so you can back out before contracts are signed if you change your mind.

Sometimes sellers ask for 'offers in the region of £X' and again you can offer above or below that amount. In Scotland and Northern Ireland, many houses are advertised for sale at a price 'offers over £X'. This is to encourage higher bids. However, if you can't afford £X, this does not mean that you are precluded from making another, lower offer. Offer only the amount you think that a property is worth. Many properties are sold at less than the 'offers over' price, and the longer the property has been on the market, the cheaper you are likely to get it. Take the 'offers over' point only as the point at which bargaining starts.

When you are making your offers they should always be made through the Estate Agent. In England and Wales, nothing is legally binding on either party until contracts have been signed, and this may be as long as seven weeks after your offer is made. If another person offers a higher bid during this period, the seller could choose to accept that instead of yours. This process is known as 'gazumping', and is frowned upon, but does happen.

Decide if you wish to have the property surveyed – in most cases this is advisable. If the survey comes back with information about defects in the house you were not aware of, you may decide to make a lower offer to cover the amount you would need to pay to rectify those faults Alternatively, you may decide to back out of the deal altogether and look for another property. See the section below entitled 'Surveys' for more information.

If you need to arrange a mortgage to buy the property you should do this now. It normally takes about three weeks from making a mortgage application to receiving a formal offer from the lender.

Freehold or Leasehold?

When buying a property in England or Wales you should check whether it is freehold or leasehold. Most houses are freehold, which means you fully own the property and all repairs and maintenance are your responsibility.

Most flats are leasehold, which means you own the property for as long as specified in the lease. After this period, ownership reverts to the freeholder. Many leases are originally granted for up to 999 years, but when you buy it the existing lease is likely to be shorter. You should not buy, and a mortgage is unlikely to be granted on, anything with a lease of less than 60 years. The lease will stipulate who is responsible for repairs and maintenance of various parts of the property and may impose other conditions on residents. You will also have to pay ground rent each year to the owner.

Surveys

It is advisable to obtain a survey on any property you contemplate buying, as there is, at the time of writing, no requirement for the seller

> We had a bid accepted for a house that needed a bit of work and were waiting to go to survey when I received a phone call from the estate agents. Apparently the vendor had fallen into arrears on his mortgage for the past six months and his lender was going to repossess the property. We were given the option of paying the shortfall (about £4,000 by the time our sale would have been completed) and re-negotiating the sale price based on that but, having failed to find that much money down the back of the sofa, we quickly did a runner.
> Matthew Taylor and Anna Gorse

to tell you about any defects in the building. There are three main types of survey available, which vary in how detailed an inspection of the property is made.

- **Valuation Survey.** If you are applying for a mortgage, your lender will carry out an independent valuation on the property to ensure that it provides sufficient security for the loan. This is paid for by the mortgage applicant, whether the purchase eventually goes through or not.

  A valuation must be carried out by a qualified surveyor, but it is simply an assessment of the value of the property, not a structural survey. You can go ahead with the purchase on the basis of just the valuation report, but it gives no guarantee that the property is structurally sound.

- **Homebuyer Report.** This is a more in-depth survey on the condition of a property, together with a valuation. Any major defect in the property will be listed, including such items as whether the property displays evidence of dampness, rot or woodworm. Recommendations for remedial work and any further investigations may be made.

- **Building Survey.** Previously termed a full structural survey, this is advisable for older properties and those which are particularly large or unique. The surveyor will inspect everything that is accessible. It may involve negotiations with the vendor to allow the surveyor access to the roof space, to pull up carpets to examine floorboards and so forth.

  If the surveyor's report shows that a property is in poor condition or has structural faults you may be able to negotiate a reduction in the price to cover the cost of remedial work. If a property is particularly poor, the lender may refuse to provide a mortgage on it.

  More detailed specialist surveys may be carried out if it is an especially old or unique building, or if there is particular cause for concern in a specific area.

 Property surveys must be undertaken by a qualified surveyor who is a member of the Royal Institution of Chartered Surveyors: 0870 333 1600; www.rics.org.

Choosing a Conveyancer

Once an offer has been made and accepted, the process of conveyancing begins. This refers to all the legal and administrative processes involved in transferring the ownership of land or property from seller to buyer. In England and Wales conveyancing may be done by:

- A solicitor.
- A licensed conveyancer.
- Yourself.

In Northern Ireland you may not use a licensed conveyancer; in Scotland all conveyancing work must be done by a solicitor. Any solicitor should be a member of the relevant law society. Details of members are available from the below websites:

The Law Society of England and Wales: 0870 606 6575; www.lawsociety.org.uk

The Law Society of Scotland: 0131 226 7411; www.lawscot.org.uk.

The Law Society of Northern Ireland: 028 9023 1614; www.lawsoc-ni.org

A licensed conveyancer must be licensed by **The Council of Licensed Conveyancers:** 01245 349599; www.theclc.gov.uk

There is no set scale of fees for conveyancing so always compare costs. Check that the fee quoted includes stamp duty, search fees and land registration fees as well as the conveyancer's fee.

Home Information Packs

From December 2007, all house sellers in England and Wales must legally supply to potential buyers a Home Information Pack (also know as a 'Home Sellers' Pack'). This contains a number of documents – *required* documents, which are mandatory, and *authorised* documents which may be included at the seller's discretion.

The required documents are:

- An index (i.e. a list of the contents of the Pack)
- A sale statement (summarising terms of sale)
- Evidence of title

Standard searches (i.e. local authority enquiries and a drainage and water search)

- An Energy Performance Certificate
- Where appropriate, commonhold information
- Where appropriate, leasehold information (including a copy of the lease, information on service charges and insurance)
- Where appropriate, a New Homes Warranty
- Where appropriate, a report on a home that is not physically complete

The **authorised** documents include:

- A Home Condition Report
- Guarantees and warranties
- Other searches

The Home Condition Report is an objective report on the condition of a home written in plain English and in a standard format. It covers the general condition of the property taking account of its age, how energy efficient the home is and any defects or other matters requiring attention. For further information see the government website: www.homeinformationpacks. gov.uk.

Scotland

The Scottish Executive will also be introducing a mandatory information pack for property sales north of the border, but the details will vary slightly from the England and Wales version and will be known as the Single Survey Scheme or Purchasers' Information Pack (PIP). At the time of writing the date of introduction has not been announced, although some voluntary pilot schemes have been carried out in various parts of Scotland.

Northern Ireland

There are no plans as yet to introduce a similar scheme in Northern Ireland.

The Conveyancing Process

A draft contract will be prepared by the seller's solicitor containing details of the seller and the buyer, the price offered and any deposits payable, and information from the title deeds. This is sent to your conveyancer.

The title deeds of a property name its owner, describe its exact extent and include any conditions relating to the property, such as any restrictions on business use, or a requirement to contribute to the maintenance of common ground with a neighbour.

Your conveyancer will examine the title deeds to ascertain that:

- The seller is actually the owner of the property and that there are no restrictions on his or her right to sell.
- The property and the land upon which it stands as described in the deeds are precisely what you think you are buying.
- Any conditions in the title are acceptable to you. If there are deemed to be unnecessary or unfair restrictions, it may be that steps can be taken to amend or remove those conditions.

Your conveyancer will carry out a local authority search, designed to discover if there are any planning proposals which may affect the value or desirability of your new property in the future, such as:

- New roads.
- Changes to road layout.
- Building developments in the vicinity.
- Alterations to land use or public rights of way.
- Changing the status of the land – e.g. putting your home into a conservation area or National Park.

Both parties agree a completion date on which the balance of the money is paid, you get the keys and the seller must vacate the property. The completion date is usually set for two to four weeks after exchange of contracts.

All these things are negotiated between the buyer's and seller's solicitors/conveyancers and may take some time to finalise. The whole process will take eight to 12 weeks, depending on the complexity of the details. It is hoped that Home Information Packs, which were introduced in June 2007, will speed up the process.

Exchange of Contracts

Once you are satisfied with the results of all enquiries made, a formal mortgage offer has been made (if required) and the completion date agreed, a final contract is drawn up. Each party signs a copy, and the contracts are exchanged. The sale is now legally binding and if you drop out after this stage you will lose your deposit.

Completion

After the bargain is concluded, all outstanding matters are settled and entry is gained to your new house, your conveyancer forwards the title deeds for registration in the Land Registry. On their return, he forwards them to you or your lender. If you have bought the property outright, the deeds remain in your possession. If you have taken a loan or a mortgage to buy the property, the deeds are lodged with the lender until such time as you have paid off the loan.

Buying a Flat

The foregoing sections apply in most respects to buying a flat. There may be additional conditions in the deeds in respect of obligations regarding the cost of repair and maintenance of the building. For instance, in a building which contains several flats or apartments, there may be a requirement for tenants to share the costs of repairs to the roof or to communal car parking areas.

Scotland

As mentioned above, the law relating to house purchase in Scotland varies in certain respects, although the systems are broadly similar. In addition, much of the Highlands and Islands are made up of traditional townships which are subject to crofting law. If you buy a house or a building plot on croft land the Crofters Commission need to be satisfied that you are a suitable person to live and work a croft.

Further Information

Citizens Advice Bureau: www.adviceguide.org.uk
Home Buyer Guide: www.home.co.uk/guides/buying

The Costs of Buying Property

The cost of buying property involves the paying of separate fees to most of the parties involved. Often the amount payable bears little relationship to the amount of work involved, as the fees are generally a percentage of the selling price of the property, so the larger the house, the higher the total fees payable. This is a rough breakdown of the level of fees for various elements of the transaction.

Solicitors and Conveyancers

Their fees cover the preparation of legal documentation, negotiation of contract with the seller's solicitor, plus the administration involved in such things as arranging for stamp duty to be paid, setting up a mortgage and passing monies to the mortgage lender. The level charged is normally up to 1% of the purchase price, plus value added tax (VAT), currently at 17.5%.

Estate Agents

The buyer of a house should not have to pay anything to the estate agent or solicitor who is selling it. They charge fees only to the vendor.

Deposits

On acceptance of your offer, a 'holding deposit' may be payable to the estate agent, usually a maximum of £500, to show you are serious about proceeding with the purchase. It is repayable if the sale should not go ahead.

On exchange of contracts, a deposit is payable, normally between five and 10% of the house price. Both these deposits are advance payments on the price agreed for the property, so are not extra costs.

Stamp Duty Land Tax

This is a government tax levied on the buyers of all property valued at over £125,000.

Tax rate	Cost of property
0%	£0-£125,000
1%	£125,001-£250,000
3%	£250,001-£500,000
4%	Over £500,000

Land Registry Fees

Once a property has changed hands, the details of the new owner are recorded in the Land Registry. There is a sliding scale of charges for this depending on the price paid for the property.

Fee	Cost of property
£40	up to £50,000
£60	£50,001-£80,000
£100	£80,001-£100,000
£150	£100,001-£200,000
£220	£200,001-£500,000
£420	£500,001-£1,000,000
£700	over £1,000,000

Valuation Fee

You must pay for a lender to value a property before they offer you a loan. Fees vary depending on the lender and the value of the property. Typically you will pay around £200–£250 for a house valued at up to £100,000 and £300–£350 for one valued at £200,000.

Survey Fee

The cost of a Homebuyer Report varies depending on type and value of the property. As a guide, a survey of a house valued at £100,000 will cost around £400–£450. One at £200,000 will cost around £500–£550+ vat.

A full Building Survey may cost you as much as £1,000 depending on its complexity.

Arrangement Fee

Variously called an arrangement, application or acceptance fee, this may be charged by a lender for arranging a mortgage and is typically around £300 to £350.

Lender's Legal Fees

Any legal fees charged by your lender's solicitor are payable by the borrower. If the same solicitor acts for both lender and borrower the fees may be lower.

Buildings Insurance

A condition of any mortgage is that the property is fully insured against structural and other damage for the full term of the loan. Premiums payable vary depending on individual circumstances, the area in which you live, the size and type of the property and the insurance company.

Life Insurance

You may be required to take out a life insurance policy to pay off your mortgage in full in the event of your death. The lender may arrange life insurance, but the borrower is entitled to arrange the necessary cover elsewhere, and this may work out cheaper.

■ COUNCIL TAX

All residents of England, Scotland and Wales must pay council tax, which is levied by local councils to pay for services such as education, road maintenance, police, refuse collection, and so forth. Each council fixes its own tax rate based on the number of residents and the income needed to supply those services. The amount payable is based on the value of your home as rated by your council.

Council tax has never been introduced in Northern Ireland, where householders pay rates based on the rental value of their homes. This system, which has been in place since the 1970s, is about to change. From April 2007 a 'house price tax' is being introduced, where householders pay a percentage of the value of their home each year. The level which has been set is 0.633%.

Council tax rates are set every year – and generally go up each year, although since 2007, some councils have frozen their rates. They vary considerably between different council areas. They also vary by country – in 2007 the average Band D rate in England was £1267.03; in Wales it was £962.05; and in Scotland it was £1,128.68.

When a property changes hands, the new occupant takes over payment of the council tax. It may be necessary to contact the local council to arrange this. In rented accommodation it is the tenant, not the landlord, who is liable for the council tax. It is not included in the rent.

Council tax is payable by weekly or monthly instalments or as a lump sum. It can be paid by standing order or direct debit through your bank account, by cheque or postal order or in person at council offices.

■ SERVICES AND UTILITIES

For many years utilities in Britain were nationalised (state-owned) industries. This first changed in 1986 when, over a period of years, they began become privatised. Since then a number of private companies supplying electricity, gas, water, and telephone supplies have emerged.

There have been large increases in fuel prices in recent years, and there is now big competition between companies to enlarge their market share. Even where the name of the company makes specific reference to gas or electric, just about all of them now supply and offer discounts for customers getting supplies of both from the one company. These are called 'dual fuel' accounts. Discounts are also available for having an online account where you do not get paper bills through the post.

The situation in Northern Ireland is less competitive, with the market dominated by a couple of big players, and dual fuel is not generally an option. As a result, gas in Northern Ireland is two thirds more expensive than in England.

Electricity, gas and telephone are generally billed quarterly, but payments may be made by monthly direct debit through a bank account. This allows for easier budgeting as regular equal payments are made throughout the year, levelling out the fluctuations of large fuel bills in the winter and smaller bills in the summer months. They all levy a standing charge for their services in addition to the payments for actual consumption. This is added to the quarterly bill.

When moving into a property, you will need to have the meters read and new accounts set up in order to ensure that you do not pay for electricity, gas or telephone calls used or made by the previous owner or tenant. You should give the company two weeks notice to arrange this. Where a property has been left empty for some time, services may have been disconnected. There may be a small reconnection charge

Electricity

The electricity supply is 240 volts AC, 50 hertz (cycles), single phase. Standard plugs have three flat pins and are generally fitted with three, five or 13 amp fuses depending on the wattage of the electrical equipment. Some equipment from Europe or the US may be usable with adapters, but generally it is advisable to buy new equipment in the UK. Light fittings use a wide variety of bulbs, some screw-in, some with push-in 'bayonet' fixings.

Gas

Mains natural gas is available in all cities and most urban areas, but some rural areas do not have piped gas. Some gas appliances are adapted for use with bottled propane or butane gas (usually Calor Gas) which is available from local suppliers who will deliver to your door. In areas on the mains, most central heating is gas-fired.

'Green' Energy

Some companies are offering accounts which use fuel from renewable energy sources. These are generally more expensive but worth investigating if you want to do your bit to prevent global warming.

Energy Supply Companies

Dual Fuel

British Gas: 0845 600 6113; www.house.co.uk
npower: 0800 316 2604; www.npower.com

Powergen: 0800 052 0346; www.powergen. co.uk
Scottish Power: 0800 027 5812; www.theenergypeople.com
Scottish and Southern Energy: 01738 456000; www.scottish-southern.co.uk

'Green' Suppliers

Ecotricity: 0800 0326 100; www.ecotricity. co.uk
Green Energy UK: 0845 456 9550; www. greenenergy.uk.com

Bottled Gas

Calor Gas: 0800 626626; www.calorgas. co.uk. This website has a searchable database of UK suppliers. They also offer an online gas cylinder ordering service.
Gleaner Oil and Gas: 01343 557400; www.gleaner.co.uk

Northern Ireland

Energia: 028 9068 5900; www.viridianenergia.co.uk
Northern Ireland Energy: 0457 643643; www.nie.co.uk
Phoenix Natural Gas: 08454 555555; www.phoenix-natural-gas.com

Oil

In areas off the mains, the majority of central heating systems are oil-fired. Local suppliers will deliver oil which must be stored in approved tanks outside the property.

Oil Supply Companies

BP Oil: 0845 607 6943; www.bp.com
Gleaner Oil and Gas: 01343-557400; www.gleaner.co.uk
Highland Fuels: 0800 224224; www.highlandfuels.co.uk

Solid Fuel

Coal, smokeless fuel, and logs for open fires, solid-fuel cooking and heating appliances are available from local suppliers. In the Highlands and Islands and in Northern Ireland some people still dig and burn peat from their traditional peat cuttings. This is now dying out, but some local firms will supply ready-bagged peat – worth trying at least once. The smell of peat-smoke is wonderful! Peat doesn't produce a great deal of heat on its own, so generally it is best augmented with coal. See your local *Yellow Pages* for local suppliers.

Water & Sewerage

England and Wales

Water and waste water services in England and Wales are provided by regional private companies. Most domestic customers pay their water and sewerage charges at a level based on the value of their property, and this is collected along with the council tax. However, increasing numbers of consumers are now on water meters and charged for their actual consumption. At the time of writing this applies to about 30% of consumers. Householders can choose whether they have a meter installed and begin to pay according to their consumption. Meters are installed free of charge, and householders have the right to revert to unmeasured charging within the first twelve months after installation.

Scotland

Water and sewerage services in Scotland are provided by the public water authority, Scottish Water. Most domestic water and sewerage charges are based on the council tax banding of the property.

There is a gradual move throughout Scotland to introduce water metering where actual consumption, plus a standing charge, will be paid for. This is in its early days, and currently householders have the choice whether to have a meter installed or to continue with the existing arrangements.

In all urban areas and many rural areas, mains sewerage is available. However, in remote areas domestic waste is discharged via a septic tank. In such cases, there is no sewerage charge on the water rates, but a charge is made on each occasion the septic tank requires emptying.

Northern Ireland

The Water Service is an executive agency within the Department for Regional Development. They provide water and sewerage services to domestic and commercial customers throughout Northern Ireland and have divisional offices in Belfast, Ballymena, Londonderry, and Craigavon.

The Water Service is funded by public funds and through direct charges to consumers, who pay for their usage over and above an annual domestic usage allowance of 200 cubic metres. Payments are made as a proportion of the rates paid on properties.

Water Supply Companies
Northern Ireland Water Service: 08457 440088; www.waterni.gov.uk
Scottish Water: 0845 601 8855; www.scottishwater.co.uk

Water UK: 0207 344 1844; www.water.org.uk. Represents water and waste water service suppliers across the UK and contains links to all regional water companies.

Refuse Collection

All residents have a regular refuse collection. This is a local authority service and is paid for through the council tax. This is free for domestic premises but there is a charge made for business collections. In most areas, wheeled refuse containers called 'wheelie bins' are supplied by the local authority. Depending on the authority, collections of landfill waste (non-recyclable refuse) may be made weekly or fortnightly. Local authorities may also have regular collection services for recyclable items such as cans, bottles, cardboard, newspapers and garden cuttings (grass, hedge trimmings etc.) Separate containers will be provided free of charge by the local authority to store all recyclable waste. If your local authority doesn't offer a roadside collection service for recyclable goods, you can dispose of these goods at public recycling areas.

Telephones

The telephone industry in Britain is dominated by British Telecom (BT), but since their monopoly was ended in the 1980s many more telephone companies have come into the market, introducing competition and thus driving down prices. Mobile phone usage has grown exponentially over the past five years and there is fierce competition between all the companies to secure their share of the market. Some are now offering discounts on calls, and in some cases free calls in off-peak periods, in order to attract

customers. All schools and libraries and the majority of businesses and private homes are now connected to the internet.

All telephones have Subscriber Trunk Dialling (STD) and International Direct Dialling (IDD). All areas now have high-speed internet available.

The technology involved with mobile phones is also advancing extremely quickly. The latest models include camera and video facilities, email and text messaging. There are 62.5 million mobile phones in use in Britain; more than one per person!

Generally, your phone bill will include an element of regular monthly charges, plus a cost per minute billing for all calls made. Cheaper calls are available in the evening and at weekends. Local, regional and international calls are charged at different rates and some providers offer free local calls at off-peak times.

Mobile phones are available either on a contract or pay-as-you-go basis. With a contract, the handset is usually free but the customer commits to keeping the phone for at least 12 months at a set fee per month. This fee will include a specified number of free phone calls and text messages, after which these are charged at a standard rate. With pay-as-you-go, the customer buys a handset, then buys electronic 'top-ups' which allow a certain value of calls and texts to be made from the phone. Top-ups are sold in units of £5, £10, £20 and £50.

Calls from landline phones to mobile phones are charged at a higher rate, and calls between mobiles on different networks are more expensive than those between phones on the same network. Some mobile phone providers offer free calls and texts to other phones on their network.

New technology is destined to change the way telephone calls are made and paid for in the not too distant future. With access to broadband in most homes, systems such as Skype and Freecall are now available which allow people to make local, national and international telephone calls across the internet: either free or at a fraction of the price charged by traditional companies.

Telephone Numbers

Landline telephone numbers are normally 11-digit numbers, composed of an area code followed by a local number. If phoning a number in the same local area, the area code does not need to be dialled.

Mobile phone numbers are also 11-digit numbers, always beginning with 07.

Public Telephones

With the growth of mobile phone usage, these are becoming less well used and BT are removing many of them. They can still be found in places such as airports, railway stations and hotel reception areas, and BT are obliged to keep at least one operating in most communities, where they will be found alongside residential streets, often close to a post office or other shop.

Emergency Services

The fire service, police, ambulance, coastguard, mountain rescue or cave rescue can be contacted on 999 or 112.

Installing a Telephone

Nearly all telephone lines throughout Britain are owned and maintained by British Telecom (BT). In some areas, telephone services can also be provided through cable TV networks. If you move into a house or apartment which has been previously occupied, there will probably be a phone line already installed. Re-connection is free. Where a new line has to be run into the property, a standard charge of £124.99 is made, payable in five quarterly payments if desired.

Since deregulation of the telephone industry, other companies have come into the market. They provide either 'direct access' or 'indirect access' telephone services. Direct access companies provide you with physical telephones lines which connect to the telephone network. Indirect access companies redirect your calls over their own network, but you will still have to pay line rental to your direct access company, such as BT.

There are numerous mobile phone companies operating in Britain. Mobile phone coverage has improved greatly in recent years but is still not complete. Inevitably, it is the remote areas which will be the last to get full coverage.

Internet

Connection to the Internet is available through any one of a large number of Internet Service Providers (ISPs). These fall broadly into two groups: 'free' services which charge no monthly subscription but apply telephone call charges for the time you are connected; and the others which charge a monthly subscription but have no call charges.

Dial-up internet connection over a standard telephone line is currently being replaced by broadband connections which enable connection to the Internet and email much faster than through dial-up. Broadband coverage in the UK is practically universal now, with more than 99.8% of the population able to access it. More than 40% of homes have a broadband connection.

Broadband is delivered to homes and businesses using various technologies, including high speed ADSL telephone lines via telephone exchanges, wireless connections using radio repeater stations, satellite and cable systems. Setting up broadband access to your home is easy – you simply choose your preferred supplier and apply direct. The process of connecting you to broadband facilities will normally take about two weeks. You will receive a broadband router and leads to connect your computer as well as all the relevant start-up discs. The set-up process is simple and intuitive.

Major Internet Service Providers	
BT Internet	www.bt.com
Orange	www.orange.co.uk
Tiscali	www.tiscali.co.uk
Virgin Media	www.virginmedia.com

Details of, and links to a wide range of UK ISPs, can be found at www.egrindstone.co.uk/technoISP.asp.

Useful Addresses

British Telecom (BT): For residential enquiries) 0800 800150; www.bt.com

British Telecom (BT): For business enquiries) 0800 800156; www.bt.com

O2 Mobile Phone Service: 0870 567 8678; www.o2.co.uk

Orange Mobile Phone Service: 0800 079 2000; www.orange.co.uk

Vodafone Mobile Phone Service: 0808 040 8408; www.vodafone.co.uk

Onetel: 0845 818 8000; www.onetel.co.uk

Favourite UK Telephone Companies: www.ourfavouritecompanies.com

Regulatory Bodies

If you have complaints about services or charges with regard to any of you utilities, you should contact the regulatory body for that industry. They exist to promote competition and protect customers' interests in relation to prices, security of supply and quality of services.

Office of Communications (Ofcom): Telephone regulation authority. 020 7981 3000; www.ofcom.org.uk

Office of Gas and Electricity Markets Scotland (Ofgem): 0141 331 2678; www.ofgem.gov.uk

Ofreg: Gas and electricity regulator, Northern Ireland; 028 9031 1575; http://ofreg.nics.gov.uk

Water Industry Commissioner for Scotland: 01786 430200; www.watercommissioner.co.uk

Water Services Regulation Authority (Ofwat): Regulator for England and Wales. 0121 625 1300; www.ofwat.gov.uk

Useful Books and Websites

Websites

Conveyancing Solicitors and Licensed Conveyancers throughout the UK are listed on www.conveyancing-cms.co.uk.

Up My Street is a guide to various facts and figures regarding different areas of the UK, including property prices, top schools, crime figures, and council performance. See www.upmystreet.co.uk.

Houseweb is a comprehensive site including wide-ranging advice, guides and services relating to all aspects of house buying and selling. See www.houseweb.co.uk.

UK-Mortgages This websites provides advice about mortgages, free quotations and offen a directory of the UK's most competitive mortgage companies and brokers has. See www.uk-mortgages.uk.com.

Letting Web Internet letting portal. See www.lettingweb.com

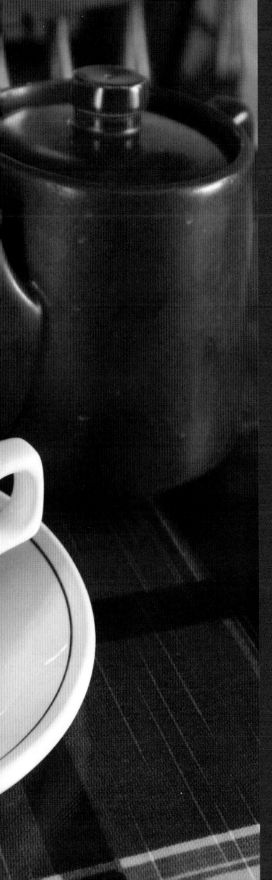

Daily Life

◼ CULTURE SHOCK

I t is hardly surprising that, having moved from a familiar culture to one where the environment and behaviour are different, some people find themselves feeling disoriented. The first few months in a new country can be an emotional time as you adjust to so many new experiences all at once.

It can affect your health, causing stress reactions such as headaches, stomach aches, sleeplessness, irritability or tearfulness.

How to Overcome Culture Shock

There are various things you can do to lessen the effects of culture shock:

- ◼ Make friends with someone in a similar situation, and/or find somebody to talk to about it, who will listen sympathetically.

- ◼ Keep in touch with home by email, letter or phone, but don't go home too often, as this may make it even harder to settle into your new life.

- ◼ Don't shut yourself away and become isolated – make an effort to socialise and make new friends.

- ◼ If you find self-help methods aren't working, contact a doctor or professional counsellor. Most of all, accept that these are normal feelings, and do your best to embrace the differences, explore your new country and grow to enjoy it.

> " I'm very happy living in Britain. I felt an immediate affinity with the place when I arrived and although I haven't lost my sense of amazement with being in a new place, always awed by the architecture and beauty surrounding me, I have never once felt as if I was isolated in a foreign country.
> Amy Burns, USA "

> " My experiences gained by living and working abroad with people from different nationalities helped me a lot. But still, it took getting used to, especially living in a small village in the countryside where people are not used to having foreigners around and they tend to keep their distance.
> Joe Rawal, Africa "

■ SOCIALISING

If you are prepared to put yourself out to make the first move, it is not difficult to make friends. There are many ways to meet and mix with others, whether you are in a city or in a small rural community.

Going out with work colleagues for lunch, or for a drink after work, can often ignite close friendships. If you are a parent, your children can be an excellent way of meeting new people. The parents of your children's friends may become your friends.

If you prefer more organised ways of getting to know people, there's a wide range of clubs and other activities you can get involved in. Depending on the area in which you live, you may find and decide to join a sports club or leisure centre, the Women's Institute (a community-based organisation that meets monthly for talks and presentations), a drama group, church group or any number of other organisations for enthusiasts of specialist activities and pastimes. Joining the Parent-Teacher Association (PTA) of your local school is a good way of getting to know people while performing a useful function.

Relationships

If you want to get to know someone for a more serious relationship, dating is a fairly relaxed business. Gone are the days of repressed Englishmen and no sex before marriage. Going on a date doesn't necessarily imply any commitment – indeed it's a good way of seeing what's out there.

Many people meet their partners at work, but starting a relationship with a work colleague can be fraught with problems. Some bosses dislike workplace romances, fearing they may lead to favouritism, disruption and charges of sexual harassment. Some firms have made employees sign 'love contracts' that oblige them to report relationships with other members of staff, while others try to ban office romances altogether. The majority take a more relaxed view, but it is sensible to be discreet about your relationship keep it in your own time, outside work hours.

> The neighbourhood spirit I have encountered has been wonderful with annual street parties, book groups, fund-raising ceilidhs, etc. Neighbours and local people met through the PTA (primary and secondary school) have become close friends over the years.
> Susan Griffith

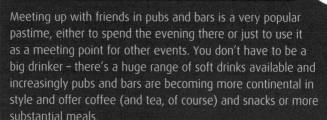

Establishing a social life

Meeting up with friends in pubs and bars is a very popular pastime, either to spend the evening there or just to use it as a meeting point for other events. You don't have to be a big drinker – there's a huge range of soft drinks available and increasingly pubs and bars are becoming more continental in style and offer coffee (and tea, of course) and snacks or more substantial meals.

Other places to socialise are restaurants, cinemas, theatres, or concerts. If you like to dance, most towns and cities have nightclubs that cater for a range of tastes and age ranges. If you would like to learn traditional, Latin or ballroom dancing, there are classes and ceilidhs (a Celtic traditional dance event) or barn dances to be found throughout Britain.

Entertaining people at home in the evening, whether for a dinner party or for drinks and light snacks, is another common way of relaxing.

> It can be difficult to get to know people and make friends as they tend to be quite reserved. The pace of life is fast, people do not really have the time and the social structure can get rigid.
> Joe Rawal

With people often working long hours, many find it hard to meet somebody special outside of the work environment. But there are plenty of organised ways to meet people:

- There are many singles clubs, both straight and gay, where you can meet to eat, drink or dance.
- 'Speed dating' is an organised 'interview', where you spend an evening in a bar or club, and have three-minute 'dates' with 15-20 other singles.
- You could sign up to a dating agency who will match you with potential partners and fix up dates with them.
- You can put a 'personal ad' in local newspapers or on dating websites, with brief details about yourself, inviting others to contact you for a date.

Gender Issues

British women have equal status with men in all areas of life and have more independence and responsibility than in some other cultures. It is acceptable for them to enter public places unaccompanied or with their female (and/or male) friends. It is perfectly acceptable for women to eat alone in a restaurant, or to drink beer.

There are few taboos concerning social circles and men and women mix freely, both socially and at work.

■ FOOD AND DRINK

In the towns and cities of Britain, there are numeroces restaurants serving a wide variety of foods. Indian, Chinese and Italian restaurants do particular, abound, as well as the ubiquitous burger chains. However, you can also choose to eat in Japanese Sushi bars, and panish tapas bars as well as in Mexican, Thai, Indonesian and French restaurants.

The increased quality of restaurant food hasn't been reflected in a dramatic increase in price – if anything, greater choice has brought good news for the consumer. Many restaurants offer set-price meaus on weekdays and pubs often reduce prices for diners eating before 7pm.

Lunch bookings are generally taken between noon and 3pm and dinner bookings between 7pm and 9pm in most restaurants. Pubs and cafes usually serve food all day.

A service charge is often included in hotel and restaurant bills – it should say so on the menu or the bill. If the credit card slip is left open for you to include a gratuity it is best to ignore this – tips taken in this way often do not reach the staff, so it is far better to give a cash tip of 10-15% to the waiting staff direct.

The relatively low cost of eating out hasn't impacted too much on the takeaway food market, which is still strong. Takeaway meals of all kinds are popular; from fish and chips to Chinese and Indian pizzas, kebabs, and burgers. Prices for a take-away meal usually range from £8-£20, and a takeaway is still a regular feature of the British Friday night.

At home, the British have taken to the new trend for gastronomy and now cook a range of culturally-diverse dishes. It is still traditional to round off the week with a roast dinner at Sunday lunchtime, and this is often a common excuse for a family gathering. Thanks to an increasingly canny

farming community, markets around the country are now supplied with a huge range of high-quality fresh produce and this is also reflected on the nation's dining table.

The British often go to pubs and bars to drink and socialise, without necessarily eating and this is one reason why drunkenness is sometimes a problem. The traditional dark ale known as bitter, served at room temperature, can be an acquired taste for the novice, but cold lagers and Guinness are also served in all pubs and bars. Younger drinkers often prefer spirits and mixed drinks. The traditional English-style pub (public house), with oak-beams and horse brasses is still a common sight, particularly in rural areas, but in town and city centres, most pubs have a cleaner, more modern image.

In the UK, all premises selling and/or serving alcohol must have a licence to do so. In 2005 the previous regime of restricted opening hours was replaced with the potential for premises to remain open for 24 hours a day, seven days a week. However, every pub, bar, club or other place serving alcohol has to apply for a licence and the opening hours allowed at each premises is decided on the basis of impact on local residents, businesses and other considerations. In practice, very few business have been granted 24-hour licenses, and most continue to close at the previously set time of 11pm on weekdays, with an hour or two extension on Friday and Saturday nights.

You must be 18 or over to buy and consume alcohol on licensed premises. Children aged 14 or over are allowed on licensed premises if they do not consume alcohol. If the establishment has a children's certificate, under 14s are allowed into specified parts of the establishment to eat, as long as they are accompanied by an adult.

A total ban on smoking in enclosed public spaces, including pubs and clubs, was introduced in Scotland in 2006, followed by England, Wales and Northern Ireland in 2007. Most pubs and bars provide covered and heated smoking areas outside for their smoking patrons.

■ SHOPS AND SHOPPING

Out of town shopping centres have changed the face of British shopping in recent years. Now most towns and all cities offer a variety of leading-brand shops in accessible retail parks. While these sites present a fairly

Farmers' markets

i

There has in recent years been a great growth in Farmers' Markets where local food producers sell their wares direct to the public, cutting out the middle man and benefiting both seller and buyer in the process. These are the places to find superb quality meat, vegetables, dairy products, and preserves, often organic, and always lovingly produced. However, if your main requirement of food is that it is cheap, you need to stick with the supermarkets, as their huge size allows them to negotiate rock-bottom prices with their suppliers, sometimes at not much above the cost of production, and pass these on to their customers. It is this process which has forced many a food producer to stop supplying the giants and head for the Farmer's Market.

homogenous experience for the shopper, they are, at least, convenient is that they offer a wide range of shops under one roof. The downside of the growth in retail parks is the gradual decline of the traditional high street – a town's main shopping street and traditional home of independent retailers such as butchers, bakers, and gasters. These shops still exist in quieter towns around the country and in certain 'artisan' quarters of the cities. Many traditional shops have had to adapt their location to survive and some can be found working together from farm shops or rural outlets and sometimes from attractive converted industrial units that have been turned into small arcades of specialist shops. From a former needle makers' workshop in Lewes in the south of England to a converted general hospital in Shrewsbury in the north west, examples of this kind of urban regeneration are changing the retail landscape once again.

Open-air and undercover markets are a feature of many towns, and some of them have held regular weekly markets for centuries. At these markets you can find versions of most of the things you would visit the large chain stores for, but generally at a cheaper price – although, be warned, the quality can be variable.

In rural areas, many small communities have just one general store, and others have none at all, as they struggle to compete with the shops in neighbouring towns, which are easily accessible now access to transport that everybody has transport.

In these areas, there are still, however, some alternatives to travelling to the 'big city' for anything more than basic supplies. Certain services are

brought to your door in areas such as the Highlands and Islands, with butchers, fishmongers, banks, and libraries travelling to remote communities on a set day and time each week.

Mail order and internet shopping have grown tremendously in recent years. Just about everything you could think of can be bought over the phone or online, and delivered within a day or so. The latest growth area is online supermarket shopping. Tesco, Asda and Sainsburys are the biggest of these. There are, however, still some rural areas where the supermarkets will not deliver.

Shopping on a Budget

If you have a limited budget, the most economical place to do your shopping is likely to be at one of the large supermarket chains. Their size allows them to sell food and other items very cheaply indeed. The biggest chains have their own-brand budget ranges of food and household goods: Tesco call theirs the 'Value' range; Sainsburys have a 'Basics' range; Somerfield's equivalent is 'Simply Value' and so on.

In recent years there has also been an influx of ultra-cheap 'warehouse-style' supermarkets from Europe where prices are very low. These include Lidl and Aldi (from Germany), and Netto (from Denmark).

> In the US it seems as though everything is geared toward a constant sell, from the time you walk out of your home in the morning until you go to sleep at night, you are subjected to a constant barrage of advertisements and hard sells and insinuations and people telling you what you need to buy to survive and to live the good life and to protect your family in case of a catastrophic event. Flashing neon signs, rolling marquees, huge roadside advertising billboards, pamphlets left on your car windshield, junk mail stuffed in your mail box and email, radio, television, door to door, you name it... almost everything has an angle to sell you some type of service. In Britain, it isn't like that. It certainly isn't that all those services aren't available – but it does seem as though the focus of life hasn't been completely consumed by this market-driven obsession with the in-your-face hard sell.
> Amy Burns

Inexpensive clothes can be found at stores such as Primark and H&M as well as some of the supermarkets – Tesco and Asda in particular are good for reasonable-quality clothes at unbeatable prices.

Matalan and TK Maxx both have good value clothes and household goods and can be found like the other stores, in most town and city centres or in retail parks on the edge of town. Check the branch locators on their websites for details.

For furniture and many other items for the home, Ikea is another store which offers very good value. They have massive warehouse-style shops in towns and cities across the UK.

If you're looking for bargain-priced good quality clothes, there are a range of retail parks known as 'Designer Outlet Villages' which are in fact shopping malls specialising in designer label 'seconds'.These are items which don't quite reach the standard required by the label but which may fall short only because of a little bit of uneven stitching which you wouldn't notice. You can save up to 50% on the full price of these clothes. For information about bargains available in a whole range of shops, register with Simple Saver (see details below).

Finally, if you are happy to buy second-hand goods, search out the car boot sales which take place across the country, usually at weekends. You can find all sorts of bargains there – but make sure you get there early as the best buys get snapped up quickly.

Useful Websites

Aldi: www.aldi-stores.co.uk – low budget supermarket selling a wide range of foods and consumer goods

Asda: www.asda.co.uk – part of the US giant Wal-Mart, Asda is primarily a food shop, but also sells a wide variety of goods, from clothes to electrical items and toys.

Car Boot Junction: www.carbootjunction.com – an advice and information site for car boot sale enthusiasts

H&M:www.hm.com – low priced clothing for all the family

Ikea: www.ikea.co.uk – cheap, stylish flat-packed furniture and a wide range of accessories for the home.

Lidl: www.lidl.co.uk – low budget supermarket selling a wide range of foods and consumer goods

Matalan: www.matalan.co.uk – low priced clothes and house wares

Morrisons: www.morrisons.co.uk – medium sized supermarket chain, principally a food retailer

Netto: www.netto.co.uk - low budget supermarket selling a wide range of foods and consumer goods
Primark: www.primark.co.uk – low priced clothing for all the family
Sainsburys: www.sainsburys.co.uk – one of the UK's big three supermarkets, selling clothes, food and electrical goods.
Simple Saver: www.simplesaver.co.uk – a portal for shoppers intent on making savings
Somerfield: www.somerfield.com – medium sized supermarket chain, principally a food retailer
Tesco: www.tesco.com - one of the UK's big three supermarkets, selling clothes, food and electrical goods.
TK Maxx: www.tkmaxx.com – low priced clothes and house wares

Opening Hours

The larger supermarkets have recognised that many people prefer to shop after they return from work, so they stay open late into the evening. Some large branches of stores such as Tesco and Asda are open 24 hours a day from Monday morning until Saturday evening (or, in Scotland, 7 days a week).

Traditionally, smaller shops open from around 9am to 5.30pm, Monday to Saturday, ensuring they stay open while the shoppers are around. Sunday opening, which was resisted for years by the retail trade, is now commonplace, but outside Scotland shops of any size are still restricted to opening for only six hours on a Sunday. On Sundays supermarkets generally choose to open from 10am to 4pm, while shops in town centres prefer to open from 11am to 5pm.

◤ POST

Over recent years post offices have begun to offer an increased range of services. As well as the traditional facilities available through the Post Office, including the collection of pensions and social security benefits; payment of bills such as gas, electricity, telephone; paying for motor vehicle licences; applying for passports and buying foreign currency, they are now offering many more services. You can withdraw cash from your bank, buy travel and house insurance or take out a loan, to name a few of the services on offer.

But the main business of the post office remains postal deliveries, and these are normally made to households and business premises once a day, Monday to Saturday. Mail is posted in post boxes which are found outside post offices, by the side of roads and in some large shops or shopping centres throughout the country. Collections are made several times a day from large town centre post-boxes, while in rural communities one collection every day except Sunday is the norm.

Letters can be sent either first class or second class, which vary in their cost and speed of delivery. First class mail, costing 34p for a standard letter, is usually delivered the next working day, while second class mail, at 24p, is usually delivered within three working days. Although these delivery times are what the Royal Mail aims at, and in most cases achieves, they are not guaranteed. In remote areas delivery times may be slower. Larger and heavier items may be charged more postage – check at the post office counter if you are unsure of the correct size and weight requirements.

Recorded or Special Delivery are useful if you are posting important documents, valuable items or documents which must be delivered quickly. Both require a receipt from the post office on posting and a signature of the receiver on delivery, while Special Delivery guarantees delivery the next working day. Compensation is paid for non-delivery of items based on their value.

> *Life in Britain is different in that I don't have access to my own car. In the US most people would think all life would come to a screeching halt if they had to give up their cars, however, the public transportation is so wonderful here that I've found no need to purchase a car. I have immediate access to trains, the subway, buses and taxis. Not to mention, I walk! In the US, it would have been unheard of to get out and walk to the bank or the post office from where I previously lived, it would have been dangerous – for many reasons. Here, it is just a way of life.*
> *Amy Burns*

The Royal Mail aim to deliver airmail letters within three working days inside Western Europe, four days to eastern Europe and five working days to destinations outside Europe. Small packets and printed papers may be sent by surface mail, and should be delivered within two weeks in Western Europe, four weeks to eastern Europe and up to eight weeks outside Europe.

Postage stamps can be purchased from post offices and in a wide range of shops. Stamps can also be bought in bulk through the Royal Mail website. Parcel Post rates vary on a sliding scale based on the weight and destination of the parcel.

Contact Details
Royal Mail: 08457 740740; www.royalmail.com
Post Office: Telephone numbers of local branches are in the phone book; www.postoffice.co.uk

■ HEALTH

World Health Organisation figures put the United Kingdom 14th in the world for Disability-Adjusted Life Years (DALE). This system calculates the number of years that a person can be expected to live in full health. The figures for the UK are 71.7 years overall (69.7 for men, 73.7 for women). Top of the list is Japan, with 74.5 years, followed by Australia (73.2) and France (73.1). The USA comes 24th, with 70 years.

The biggest killers in the UK are coronary heart disease and strokes, followed by various cancers, especially lung, breast and prostate cancers. There are health education initiatives which are ongoing. This is part of an attempt to cut down on the levels of drinking and smoking within the population, and to improve the nation's diet. These initiatives led to a fall in mortality rates due to heart disease and strokes have and a reduction in cancer deaths, but there is still a long way to go.

Scotland imposed a total ban on smoking in enclosed public spaces in March 2006. Similar smoking bans were introduced in the rest of the UK in 2007. Although this ban is still relatively new, it is hoped that it will be a big step towards cutting levels of smoking generally among the population, as well as minimising the effects of passive smoking on those non-smokers who previously had to work in smoky surroundings. Smoking is an important risk factor in all three of the main killers – heart attacks, strokes and cancer – so cutting levels of smoking is sure to have a beneficial effect on the nation's health.

However, while these areas of health improve, obesity is increasing, and more people than ever are becoming ill and even dying of alcohol-related causes. Nearly 30% of adults in Britain exceed the recommended daily maximum of alcoholic drinks at least once a week, while 22% of men and 9% of women are defined as heavy drinkers. Excessive drinking occurs most frequently amongst the 16–24 age group. There is also a worrying increase in drinking among children from age 11 upwards. Recent changes to the licensing laws in Britain have allowed pubs and bars to stay open longer, with the intention of introducing a more continental, responsible approach to drinking. Although it is too early to assess its effect, first signs are that it is going to take more than relaxation of drinking hours to improve the nation's attitude to alcohol.

Although more people are aware of the need to eat fresh fruit and vegetables, changing long-ingrained habits is hard, and obesity in adults and children, together with associated illnesses, is on the rise. In the UK, about 66% of adults are overweight, and of these, 22% of men and 23%

> An obsession with drinking in youth culture is much worse than in Canada, which my teenage sons have noticed. The rules (e.g. of pubs and off-licences serving under-aged drinkers) are enforced less rigorously in the UK than in Canada.
> Susan Griffith, from Canada

of women are classified as obese. The incidence of adult obesity has tripled in the past 20 years, and is still rising. In children it has doubled in six year olds (to 8.5%) and trebled among 15 year olds (to 15%).

National Health Service

The major healthcare provider in Britain is the National Health Service (NHS), which allows residents of the UK, including immigrants, to access free healthcare services in local surgeries, hospitals and other clinics. There are also home visit services available for the young, the old, the chronically sick, and the disabled. The cost of running the NHS has risen inexorably over time, This is no small part due to the fact that so many more conditions can be treated now than in the past (some of them with the use of extremely expensive medicines); that people are living longer; and that they have come to demand better levels of medical care as the standard of living has risen generally, due to the UK becoming more prosperous. In order to help 'balance the books', there are now charges for some NHS services, such as prescriptions (though there are no prescription charges in Wales) and some dental and ophthalmic treatments. However, children, the elderly, pregnant and nursing women, people with certain chronic health problems and those on low incomes, are exempt from all or some of these charges.

The NHS has a workforce of around 1.3 million people, making it Europe's biggest organisation. Its budget – around 76 billion pounds in 2006 – is the largest item of central government expenditure after social security. Even so, every year the NHS overspends – in 2006 the deficit at the end of the financial year was around £750.

It is a national pastime to criticise the NHS, and it is inevitable that such a large organisation, offering such a range of care through so many institutions, will have certain failings. One of the biggest bugbears of the British public in relation to the NHS are the waiting lists for consultations and operations. The government is forever introducing targets for all sorts of aspects of the service, but it is the waiting list targets which always hit the headlines. They have pledged that by the end of 2008 patients will have to wait no longer than 18 weeks for an operation, and in many cases will be treated far sooner. In the past it was not uncommon for patients to wait two years for some non-urgent operations.

How to Find a Doctor

All areas of Britain are well-served by family doctors (known as General Practitioners or GPs) working from local practices running regular surgeries – typically Monday to Friday, sometimes with special surgeries for urgent cases. GP practices deliver services to patients who live within a recognised practice boundary – in other words the practice(s) you can register with are limited by where you live, as they only serve a specific geographical area. They all have a practice leaflet providing information about the services and clinics available at the practice. They should also have details of the names of the doctors in the practice. This information may help you decide where to register. In rural areas, however, you will usually find that there is only one practice for the area.

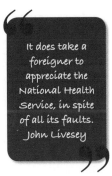

It does take a foreigner to appreciate the National Health Service, in spite of all its faults.
John Livesey

You need to register with a GP practice before using their services, although any GP will see non-registered patients in an emergency. Registering with a practice involves completing a form with your personal details. Take your NHS medical card, if you have one. If you do not have one, you will be issued with an NHS number when you register. This number will stay with you whenever you access NHS treatment or when you transfer to another GP. GPs are not obliged to accept everybody who wishes to register if they have a good reason for refusing you – for example, each practice has a maximum number of patients they can take, so if they are over-subscribed, they may refuse to accept you as a patient. Sometimes they may agree to take you as a temporary patient. In these cases, it's worth trying another practice nearby as they may have spare capacity.

If you need a medical consultation but have not yet registered with a doctor, some cities and towns have free access 'walk-in clinics' where medically-trained staff can provide advice and support for a wide range of concerns. Pharmacists in the UK are also highly skilled and can often prove to be a good source of advice for minor ailments.

All those who are classed as 'ordinarily resident' in the UK are entitled to free treatment on the NHS, by GPs or in hospitals. In practice, this means those who live for at least six months per year in the UK. There are no charges to anyone who has lived here permanently for more than a year, or for residents of the European Economic Area (EEA). NHS services can be accessed by other overseas visitors, but they will be charged for all services with the exception of accident and emergency treatment.

In order to visit your GP you will need to make an appointment. It may be several days before you can have an appointment, but if you have an urgent need to see a doctor, you should always be able to see one the same day, as long as you are prepared to sit and wait until there is a break in his/her scheduled workload.

For treatment and advice outside surgery hours your call to the surgery will be diverted to the local or regional out of hours service. They will take your details and arrange for a nurse to call you back and give you advice or arrange for a doctor to visit.

For more specialised treatment, GPs will refer patients to NHS hospitals as either out-patients (attending clinics) or in-patients (staying in the hospital while tests and treatments are carried out).

GP practices may offer other services, such as 'well woman' or 'well man' clinics where preventive health checks are made, and baby clinics which offer advice and support for mothers with new babies. They will usually have a practice nurse who may assist with routine matters such as changing dressings, taking blood, giving inoculations etc.

> ### *i* Medical Emergencies
> If you have a severe medical emergency you should phone the emergency services on 999 or 112.

Drugs and Medicines

If a GP decides you require drugs or medicines you will be given a prescription which you take to your local dispensing chemist (pharmacist). In rural practices where there is no local chemist, drugs and medicines may be dispensed from the surgery. Most drugs prescribed are available on the NHS, in which case you pay a set prescription charge per item prescribed, except in Wales. The Welsh Assembly, after reducing prescription charges year on year since 2004, abolished charges for all on 1st April 2007. Proposals are on the table to abolish all prescription charges in Scotland.

In England, Scotland and Northern Ireland prescription charges are set each year, usually on 1st April. From 1st April 2007 the charge was £6.85 per item. There are several groups of patients who are exempt from

NHS Direct

The NHS in England, Wales and Scotland have online services giving health advice and information. You can look up symptoms in their online encyclopaedia, or email health queries to an information team. There is also a telephone helpline you can ring, 24 hours a day. Arrangements will be made for a doctor to visit you in your home, or for you to go to hospital, if it is deemed necessary.

England: 01234 273473; www.nhsdirect.nhs.uk
Wales: 01234 273473; www.nhsdirect.wales.nhs.uk
Scotland:08454 242424; www.nhs24.com

prescription charges, including children below 16 and those between 16 and 18 who are in full time education; those above state retirement age; pregnant women and those who have had a baby in the past year; those in receipt of certain social security benefits; and patients suffering from certain specified medical conditions. Full details are given in booklet HC11, 'Help With Health Costs', available from doctors' surgeries.

Some drugs and medicines are not available on the NHS, in which case the doctor will give you a private prescription and the full cost of the drugs must be paid. Contraceptives are free for all patients, whether you are normally exempt from charges or not.

Prepayment certificates are available for those who need a number of medicines regularly and are not exempt from prescription charges, in which case they may represent substantial savings. If you think you will have to pay for more than five prescription items in four months or 14 items in 12 months, you may find it cheaper to buy a pre-payment certificate (PPC). In 2007 a 3-month PPC cost £26.85. You can apply for prepayment certificates via your doctor or health board or 0845-850 0030.

Hospitals

When referred to a hospital, the patient will be put onto a waiting list. Waiting lists have been coming down in recent years, and the government has charged the NHS with bringing the maximum length of wait for an operation to 18 weeks by the end of 2008.

Major hospitals with a range of departments providing diagnosis, treatment and care for in-patients, day patients and out-patients, are usually called General Hospitals. Typically they will have an accident and emergency (or casualty) department, maternity department, surgical, psychiatric, paediatric, and geriatric departments, and a range of outpatient clinics.

Accident and emergency departments operate on a first-come, first-served basis – although life-threatening emergencies will obviously jump the queue. This can mean that there are often long waits in these departments.

NHS Websites
England: www.nhs.uk
Scotland: www.show.scot.nhs.uk
Wales: www.wales.nhs.uk
Northern Ireland: www.healthandcareni.co.uk

Private Healthcare

Because of the prevalence of the NHS, there is a relatively small demand for private healthcare within Britain, with only 3.5% of total health spending being on private health insurance. It is more popular in England

Private medical care

The long working lists are one of the main reasons for patients choose private medicine over the NHS. In most cases the quality of medical treatment and care will be no better, although private patients benefit from nonessentials such as a private room with TV, telephone, en-suite bathroom, and room service.

than in Wales, Scotland and Northern Ireland, but it is on the increase generally. Lengthy waiting lists and the perceived poor state of some hospitals have led to many more affluent Britons taking out private health insurance.

Private health insurance may be part of an employer's package when you take a job, although this would generally only be for employees working at an executive level or above. Private insurance typically costs £50–£150 per month for an individual, with the elderly paying the higher rates. Most private health insurance schemes pay only for specialist and hospital treatment, and don't include routine visits to GPs and dentists. These you will have to pay for yourself if you do not wish to be treated under the NHS.

NHS GPs are not permitted to take private patients, but there are doctors in private practices who may be consulted for specialist matters. Private clinics offer a range of services including second opinions, health checks and screening. As they become more acceptably mainstream, there is also a growth in people paying for complementary and alternative health therapies.

Contact Details

Private Healthcare UK: www.privatehealth.co.uk. Lists private hospitals, nursing homes and the major private health insurance companies operating in the UK, with contact details and links to their websites.
AXA PPP Healthcare: 0870 608 0850; www.axappphealhcare.co.uk
British United Provident Association (BUPA): 0800 600 500; www.bupa.com
BMI Healthcare: 020 7009 4500; www.bmihealthcare.co.uk
Capio Healthcare UK: 01234 273473; www.capio.co.uk
HSA: 0800 197 6999; www.hsa.co.uk

Dentists

Every dentist is allowed to provide both NHS and private dental care, although some choose to provide exclusively one or the other. Those who do provide NHS services have a quota of NHS patients they can take, and if the dentist you choose has filled his quota he will not be able to treat you, unless he agrees to take you as a private patient. For NHS treatment you need to register using your medical card, as with a GP.

Dental treatment on the NHS is not free, but it is subsidised. There are a number of exemption categories, generally in line with the exemptions from prescription charges. Local dental practices can be found in the telephone directory or through your local Health Board. Contact them if you have difficulty finding a dentist who can treat you on the NHS.

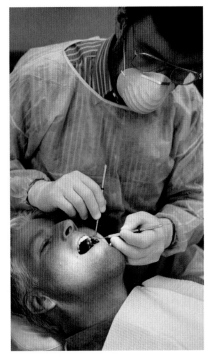

> Be prepared to wait for weeks, even months for a simple dentist appointment!
> Joe Rawal

Contact Details
British Dental Association: The UK dentists' governing body. www.bda.org
British Dental Health Foundation: Word of Mouth Helpline deals with enquiries from the public about their dental health or treatment; 0845 063 1188.

Opticians

You do not need to register with an optician. Their addresses can be found in the telephone directory. You must have your eyes tested by a qualified

NHS Dental Charges	
Examples of courses of treatment	**Total cost**
Examination, diagnosis, and preventive advice	£15.50
Examination, diagnosis, preventive advice and one or more fillings	£42.40
Examination, diagnosis, preventive advice, one or more fillings and one or more crowns	£189.00

practitioner who will give you your lens prescription. You can then either buy your spectacles or contact lenses from that practitioner, or you can take the prescription to have your glasses or lenses made up at another dispensing optician. The costs of frames and lenses vary widely, but generally you should expect to pay £75 upwards for a pair of spectacles and around £85 upwards for contact lenses.

Scotland has abolished charges for eye tests and they are free for everyone. In England, Wales and Northern Ireland they are free if: you are over 60, under 16, or under 19 and in full-time education; if you receive certain social security benefits or allowances; if you have diabetes or glaucoma; if you are aged 40 or over and have a close relative who has glaucoma; or if you are registered blind or partially sighted. If you are not entitled to free eye tests you will be seen as a private patient and the test will usually cost between £17 and £30.

Contact Details
General Optical Council: Regulator of the optical profession in the UK; 020 7580 3898; www.optical.org

Alternative Medicine

Alternative therapies and complementary medicines are booming in the UK. Many people swear by the results achieved by using such treatments as acupuncture, homeopathy or naturopathy. Although scorned by the medical profession for many years, recently there has been a noticeable increase in the number of doctors who have admitted albeit grudgingly, that there might be something in some of these therapies. In an increasing number of cases, GPs may suggest patients try certain alternative therapies alongside the traditional medical approach – hence the term 'complementary'.

It is rare to find any of these therapies available on the NHS, so you would have to pay as a private patient. As some courses of treatment can be extensive, it is often a rather an expensive option. Most alternative therapies in the UK have some form of governing body, so it is always wise to go to a practitioner who has been approved by their particular professional association.

Addresses of practitioners of various therapies can be found in the telephone directory or *Yellow Pages*.

i **Complementary Healthcare Information Service:** The UK's guide to alternative and complementary medicine, self development and natural health; www.chisuk.org.uk.

◼ EDUCATION

British education has a global reputation for its quality and the standard of qualifications received. Those qualifications are recognised worldwide, and as a result many international students are attracted to come to study in the United Kingdom. All schools and institutions of further and higher education are regularly inspected and monitored to ensure that standards are maintained and improved where necessary. Whichever government is in power at any time, the education system is always one of the major political focuses, with a constant claim that standards need to be improved. As a result there have been many changes in the system over the years. This desire for change – often just for the sake of it, it seems, although always it is stated to be in the interests of improving standards – has reached a positive frenzy in recent decades, with new curricula, examinations and performance monitoring systems being introduced every few years.

The Structure of the Education System

Responsibility for education is a devolved issue, so it lies variously with the Secretary of State for Education and Skills in England; the Minister for Education, Lifelong Learning and Skills in Wales; the Scottish Executive Education Department and the Northern Ireland Education Minister. Their departments formulate policies and aim to maintain consistency in educational standards throughout their respective countries. On a day-to-day basis, most school education is locally administered, so although regional governments are responsible for the broad allocation of resources, local authorities make many of their own expenditure decisions, taking into

accant other issues of financial concern is the area. Support for higher and further education and other specialised areas of education comes directly from the central government.

The education system is not uniform across the UK. England and Wales follow exactly the same system, while that in Northern Ireland is largely similar but has some significant differences. Scotland, however, has had a distinct education system for many centuries and there are substantial differences there compared with the rest of Britain. For a detailed discussion of the Scottish system.

In the UK, the academic year runs from early September to late July (mid-August to the end of June in Scotland). The year in which children start at school is determined by their age on 1st September in England and Wales; 1st March in Scotland; and 1st July in Northern Ireland. Children who are five after this date will start primary school at the start of the following academic year. Children move up to secondary school at the age of 11 (age 12 in Scotland) and pupils may leave once they are 16. Alternatively, or they can choose to undertake one or two further years of schooling, leaving at the age of 17 or 18.

At secondary level in England and Wales, children go on either to comprehensive schools, which take children of all levels of ability, or grammar schools, which have systems of selection to choose brighter children. Some areas chose to retain their grammar schools when the

School leaving age

Schooling across Britain is compulsory for all children between five and 16 years. After this age they have the option of staying on and pursuing further studies for one or two years. This allows then to gain either academic qualifications for entry to university, or vocational qualifications for specific careers. The current government has recently stated its intention to raise the leaving age to 18 by 2013, but the history of education shows that the successive raising of the leaving age to the current 16 has taken many more years to achieve than originally intended, for various political and practical reasons. Thus this that may be a target which proves difficult to hit.

comprehensive system was introduced in the 1970s, but most have only comprehensive schools.

Northern Ireland has retained its grammar school system, and once pupils finish primary school, they sit on 11-plus test to determine whether they go to a grammar school or a secondary school.

The decision was recently taken to introduce a form of comprehensive education in Northern Ireland, effective from 2008. Although many schools in the province are segregated along religious lines – Catholic and Protestant – there has been significant growth in the development and provision of integrated education throughout Northern Ireland, bringing together, in one school, pupils, teachers and governors from Catholic and Protestant traditions.

The Scottish secondary system has always been comprehensive in nature with no system of selection at the end of primary school – secondary schools, usually called either high schools or academies, take pupils of all levels of attainment.

Although generally children will attend a school in whose geographical catchment area they live, parents may express a preference for a particular school elsewhere by making a 'placing request'. This must be satisfied if the school is not already oversubscribed.

All schools are required to make specific information freely available, including things such as public examination results, truancy rates and the destinations of leavers.

Private and State Schools

The majority of schools are provided by the state and charge no fees to pupils, being financed by local government through a combination of central government grants and local taxation. Independent schools receive their funding from non-governmental sources, mainly through the fees charged to pupils. They are subject to government registration and HMI inspection. Most independent schools are known as 'private schools' but there are a few which, for historical reasons, are confusingly known as 'public schools'. These are the highest status schools, charging extremely high fees and attracting those children from the upper echelons of society. These include such famous schools as Eton, Rugby, Harrow, and Winchester.

There are a few grant-aided schools, mainly providing education for those with special educational needs, which receive grants direct from the relevant Education Department.

Pre-school and Nursery Education

Education before the age of five is not compulsory, but many parents choose to send their children to nurseries or pre-school play groups either part-time or full-time. Local authorities have a duty to ensure there is a free, part-time nursery place for all three and four-year old children whose parents want one. If you wish to send your child to pre-school before they are three years old, your local authority may be able to accommodate this, but you may be required to meet the costs. Over two thirds of children attend some form of pre-school education. Nursery schools and nursery classes in primary schools take children from two to five years old. These are run by trained teachers. Contact the relevant local authority for details of state-run nursery classes.

There are also numerous mother and toddler groups run on a voluntary basis in public and church halls throughout the country, where mothers can take their young children for a couple of hours a week, to chat and drink tea while their offspring play together.

Childcare for the remainder of the time and for younger children can work out expensive – it is estimated that the average cost of a full-time nursery place is £7,400 per year. Families do receive some help towards childcare costs either through the working tax credit for low income families, or through child care vouchers which are provided by employers in lieu of £50 per week in pay, which gives them a

discount of up to £800 per year in tax and National Insurance contributions.

Many parents make informal arrangements for the care of their children, by asking a relative or neighbour to look after them while they work. This is usually the cheapest, and sometimes the most convenient, option.

For those who do not have family living nearby or who cannot call on friends or neighbours, there are a variety of options. Workplace nurseries are provided by some large employers, often with rates varying depending on the individual's salary level. For school-age children, after-school clubs take care of children after school and in the holidays. Younger children, from birth to five years of age, may be sent to private nurseries either full or part time. These must be registered with the local authority. This can be an expensive option, but some offer lower rates for a second child or for lone parents. Some parents prefer to send their children to a childminder who looks after children in their own home. Childminders must register with their local authority, which will check that their home meets safety standards and has good facilities for the care of children.

Alternatively, parents choose to employ people to look after their children in their own home. Au pairs are young people from abroad who learn English while living in a family home and help with childcare and housework in exchange for their board and lodging. Another option is to employ a nanny who may live in the family home or not. The best nannies have childcare qualifications and are likely to be the most expensive option. The cost of a nanny can be lessened by sharing with another family.

Useful Contacts
National Day Nurseries Association (NDNA): 0870 774 4244; www.ndna.org.uk
The Pre-school Learning Alliance: 020 7833 0991; www.pre-school. org.uk

> I found there was a reasonable choice of pre-school options wherever I was, from child-minders and crèches while I was working, to mother and toddler groups to formal nursery education. This allowed me to choose whatever suited my life best at the time – as well as, more importantly, what suited each particular child best. Each one is different, and while my first child was very independent and ready for nursery education quite early, the youngest one was not happy leaving me until he was a year or two older, so the mother and toddler group in the local church hall was best for both of us. I was working from home at that time so it fitted in fine with my lifestyle.
>
> Sarah Bradshaw

Wales Pre-school Playgroups Association: 01686 624573;
www.walesppa.org
Scottish Pre-school Play Association: 0141 221 4148; www.sppa.org.uk
Northern Ireland Pre-school Playgroups Association: 028 9066 2825;
www.nippa.org
National Childminding Association (England and Wales): 0845 880
0044; www.ncma.org.uk
Scottish Childminding Association: 01786 449063;
www.childminding.org
Northern Ireland Childminding Association: 028 9181 1015;
www.nicma.org

Primary Education

Primary education begins at the age of five and is usually conducted in mixed classes of boys and girls. Generally, primary schools are divided into infants' classes, for the five to sevens, and primary classes for the seven to 11s (12s in Scotland). Many schools also provide nursery classes for children under five. The standard school hours are from approximately 9am to 3.15pm with some local variations designed to cut traffic congestion. Most primary schools have a basic uniform, which can be as simple as a common style of sweatshirt and the requirement to wear black or grey trousers or skirts.

National testing is carried out on core areas of the curriculum, to produce standardised results of achievement across the country's schools in various basic subject areas, such as English and mathematics.

In schools where there is a large population, there is normally one class for each age group and there are normally around 30 children per year group. In rural areas where the population, and therefore the school intake, is small, the distinction between age groups is less clear cut. There are many schools in the Highlands and Islands, for instance, which have

Rural schools

A consideration for families moving from urban to rural areas is how well their children will settle into a small school. There have long been debates on optimum class sizes, many driven by local authority needs to cut costs, but overall the high teacher to pupil ratio in small schools is seen – by parents at least – as a good thing. Specialist subjects such as art, music and physical education (PE) are provided by teachers who travel round all the schools in the region.

> When I started at Inverasdale Primary School, which had 23 pupils, after my school in England which had 300, there was initially a big culture shock, but I soon found it has massive advantages. In such a small school you mix with all the age groups and make lots of friends. It meant too that we all received far more individual attention from the teacher than I had been used to. The benefits continued when I moved to the brand new High School at Gairloch. There were plenty of resources to go round and class sizes were small. When I reached the sixth form, I was the only pupil taking the Certificate of Sixth Form Studies in English, so I had one-on-one teaching, and consequently achieved a good result.
> Matthew Taylor

primary schools of fewer than 50 pupils, some with only a dozen or so. In these cases they will have just one or two teachers teaching mixed age classes.

Secondary Education

Children move up to secondary school at 11 or 12 and stay until they are at least 16. Those who wish to can stay on for one or two further years, although the government has formally stated a desire to introduce compulsory education for all up the age of 18. Most British secondary schools are co-educational – i.e. they take both boys and girls – although there are some single sex schools. Most of these are in the independent sector. Comprehensive schools provide a full range of courses appropriate to all levels of ability from first to sixth year while Grammar Schools concentrate on the more academic subjects. There may be some restrictions on the courses that can be followed in smaller schools where the smaller number of teachers can produce timetabling difficulties when it comes to providing the widest range of options. Secondary schools are often called 'High Schools'. Secondary school hours are similar to primary school hours, with classes usually running between 9am and 3.30pm. Uniforms are also common for children up to the age of 16, with blazer-style jackets and ties for boys and formal dress codes for girls.

Despite the legislation allowing parents the right to choose the schools their children attend, you are limited to what is available in the local area. Certainly, in sparsely populated areas there is no choice in practice, unless you want to send your children away for their schooling.

National Curriculum

The National Curriculum is a required range of subjects studied by pupils in state schools in England and Wales, as follows:

Age 5–11:

- English
- Mathematics
- Science
- Information and Communication Technology (ICT)
- History
- Geography
- Art and Design
- Music
- Design Technology
- Physical Education
- Personal, Social and Health Education (PSHE)
- Welsh (Wales only)

Age 11–14:

- English
- Mathematics
- Science
- ICT
- Geography
- History
- Art and Design
- Design Technology
- Modern Foreign Language
- Music
- Physical Education
- Careers Education
- Welsh (Wales only)

Age 14–16:

- English
- Mathematics
- Science
- ICT
- Physical Education
- Citizenship
- Religious Education *
- Careers Education
- Welsh (Wales only)

* Parents can choose to withdraw their children from these lessons.
Schools may teach other subjects in addition to these subjects if they wish. All schools in Northern Ireland follow the Northern Ireland Curriculum which is based on the National Curriculum used in England and Wales.

School Curriculum in Scotland

Although there is no national curriculum as such in Scotland, with content and management of the curriculum being the responsibility of education authorities and individual head teachers, there are guidelines which give recommended hours of study for a selection of core subjects. There are separate guidelines regarding the curriculum from age 5–14 and 14–16.

In May 2005 a new Scottish Survey of Achievement was introduced which uses a representative sampling approach to assess the attainments of pupils aged 5–14 in the areas of English, Mathematics, Science, and social subjects. It is based on teachers' assessments of their pupils, and replaces the previous system of national testing which was unpopular with the majority of Scottish teachers and many parents.

 Schools Web Directory: Database of all UK school websites; www.schoolswebdirectory.co.uk

Special Education

Children with special educational needs, as a result of physical or mental disabilities, are assessed and a 'statement of special needs' produced. On the basis of this, parents, together with education authorities, decide where the child should be schooled and arrange for any special requirements to be satisfied. Wherever possible, children with special needs are integrated into mains streem schools and classes. In addition, there are special schools and special classes within mainstream schools thand classes for those children who require a different environment or specialised facilities.

Parents should contact the relevant local authority education department for further information on provision for special education.

Independent Schools

There are around 2,500 independent schools in Britain, attended by 625,000 children. They cater for all ages and include day and boarding schools. Although many are traditional in outlook and approach, there are some experimental schools which follow different models of education from the norm. Some independent schools are established and run by religious or ethnic minorities.

Most independent schools offer a similar range of courses to state schools and enter pupils for the same examinations, details of which are given overleaf. The majority are single–sex schools, although an increasing number have mixed sixth forms. Some parents prefer to move their children from a state school to a private school for their pre-university courses and examinations.

Independent schools receive no public funds. They charge fees to pupils and are managed under special trusts. Profits are used for the benefit of the school.

> We wanted to move before our eldest started secondary schooling; we wanted to find somewhere where the kids could have access to everything teenagers wanted, where they could go out and about under their own steam without having to be ferried everywhere by car, so it had to be in a town centre with facilities; and we wanted good state schools nearby. Finally we were able to buy a new house within our budget in the catchment area for schools we liked, and in reach of the town centre.
> Caroline Deacon

  Independent Schools Council: 020 7766 7070; www.isc.co.uk
Scottish Council of Independent Schools: 0131 220 2106; www.scis.org.uk

Examinations

At the age of 14, pupils select which subjects to continue to study for General Certificate of Secondary Education (GCSE) examinations. Currently it is compulsory to study English, Mathematics, Science, Religious Studies, and Physical Education, although a full GCSE course does not have to be studied for the latter two. In Northern Ireland it is also compulsory to study a modern foreign language (usually French, German or Spanish), a requirement which was scrapped in England and Wales in 2004. In addition, pupils usually elect to continue with other subjects and many study for eight or nine GCSEs, some as may as 10 or 11. They follow the GCSE course for two years, sitting the examinations when they are 16. It is not compulsory to take the examination, although the subjects must be studied. However, many schools insist all pupils take at least the English, Maths and Science examinations.

GCSEs are marked and graded from A* (A-star) through to G. Generally a grade of A*, A, B or C allows the student to continue to study the subject at A level. In addition to written and practical examinations there is a coursework component to many GCSE courses. GCSEs mark the end of compulsory education in England, Wales and Northern Ireland.

Post-16 Education

Pupils who continue their studies beyond the compulsory years have various options for this stage of their education: they may stay at school and attend the sixth form for one or two more years; go to sixth form colleges; or enrol at further education colleges. They can study courses leading to a variety of academic or vocational qualifications. The more academic students will generally study three or four subjects at AS and A2 levels. Eligibility for university entrance is based on the grades achieved in these courses. A levels are awarded pass grades of A to E, with a U (unclassified) grade meaning fail.

Post-16 Qualifications*

■ Entry Level

■ Basic Skills

■ Key Skills

■ AS Levels

■ A/A2 Levels

■ Advanced Extension Awards (AEAs)

■ General National Vocational Qualification (GNVQs)

■ Vocational A Levels (AVCEs)

■ National Vocational Qualifications (NVQs)

■ Foundation Modern Apprenticeships (FMAs)

■ Advanced Modern Apprenticeships (FMAs)

*England, Wales, Northern Ireland

Scottish Examinations

Scotland's system of public examinations is distinct from that of England, Wales and Northern Ireland's. The Standard Grade of the Scottish Certificate of Education is taken at the end of the fourth year at secondary school, about the age of 16 (this is roughly equivalent to the GCSE taken in England, Wales and Northern Ireland). Most pupils take seven or eight Standard Grade examinations (Standards), but they will take them at different levels depending on their abilities. Students who require more support with their learning can take Access courses.

Pupils aged 17 and over then take the next level of examinations. Higher Grade examinations (Highers) are taken at the end of the fifth year after one year of study. Pupils take up to five Highers in this year. Highers are awarded grades A–D and No award. D means the Higher has been failed, with the next level down, Intermediate 2, being awarded instead. 'No award' is an outright fail.

Scottish Vocational Qualifications (SVQs) aim to teach students practical skills in a particular occupational field. They are based on National Standards drawn up by people from industry, commerce and education and are designed to meet the needs of potential employers. There are SVQs for nearly all occupations in Scotland. They are available at five levels of difficulty to suit people who are just starting to study in that field as well as those who already have years of experience. They can be taken at schools or colleges, or they can be taken part time while in employment.

All these awards are administered and awarded by the Scottish Qualifications Authority (SQA): (0845 279 1000; www.sqa.org.uk).

International Schools

There are a number of international schools in Britain, open to both local and expatriate children. Most offer the International Baccalaureate while some allow students to study for British qualifications. Fees vary, but are generally over £20,000 per year for full boarding and less for weekly boarding or day attendance. For full details and links to individual schools see the websites below.

> *i* **ISBI Schools:** 01980 620575; www.isbi.com
> **London International Schools Association:** www.lisa.org.uk

School Transport

Free transport to and from school is provided for children who live beyond walking distance from their school. If a child lives more than three miles from the nearest school (two miles for the under eights), he or she is picked up and dropped off close to home. Free transport is also provided for those who, for medical reasons or because they are disabled, cannot walk to school.

School Meals

School meals at competitive prices are provided at lunchtimes within schools. To encourage healthy eating habits, schools are encouraged to provide a range of nutritious meals for students, ranging from traditional meat and vegetable meals to salads, pizzas and pasta. Sandwiches and snacks may also be available. Families with a low income may be eligible for free school meals. Alternatively, most schools allow children to take packed lunches from home which they can eat in the school dining room.

Further Education

The term 'further education' refers to all education provided for individuals over the age of 16, relating to those courses which lead to A levels, Highers, and their equivalent as well as the various work-based vocational qualifications available. Courses are taught mainly at the 465 colleges of further education throughout the UK. Of these, 102 are sixth form colleges. Courses are offered are both full time and part time courses. Applications for further education courses are generally made direct to the colleges concerned.

> **HERO:** This website has links to most further education colleges in the UK, plus information and advice about all aspects of further and higher education: www.hero.ac.uk

Higher Education

This term is used to describe education above A level, Higher and Advanced Higher grades and their equivalent. It is provided in universities and colleges of higher education of which there are over 100 in the UK. In 1992, the distinction between universities and certain other classes of higher education institution was removed, since which time all UK polytechnics have adopted the title of university and now award their own degrees. Despite this apparent equality between the institutions now, there is still a perception that the quality of education at the longer-established universities is better. Certainly, the entry requirements for the 'ex-polytechnics' tend to be lower, so they lead to attract less able students. It is open to debate whether this is because the education they provide is actually of a lower standard, or whether the public perception that this is the case means that there is less demand for places at these institutions. Employers are certainly more impressed by degrees from the older universities, so for the foreseeable future these are going to remain the elite of higher education establishments in Britain.

The UK government wants to encourage increased participation in higher education and has set a target that 50% of 18–30 year olds should be in higher education courses by 2010.

Useful Websites

UCAS: Brief details of all the universities, including student numbers, courses available, accommodation costs etc. Also has links to all UK university websites.

Active Map of UK Universities and Colleges: www.scit.wlv.ac.uk/ukinfo

Universities and Colleges in Northern Ireland: www.nidex.com/unis.htm

Open University

The Open University (OU) offers degrees by distance learning. It admitted its first students in 1971 and claims to be the UK's largest university with 200,000 students enrolled. This figure may be a little misleading because

> When I came as a postgraduate student to Oxford University, my plans were open-ended, and when my course finished, I automatically registered with the university employment service (which is how I got my job in publishing) partly because I was in a long-term relationship in England but also because the prospect of job-hunting in Canada was not in any way attractive to me. I have never once considered moving back (though I tried it in the winter of 1983 for relationship reasons and was very homesick for Oxford).
>
> Susan Griffith

nearly all the students are part-time as degrees can be taken over a period of many years. Unlike other universities, undergraduate level courses do not require any entry qualifications, so it does provide access to degree courses for those who might otherwise not have the opportunity.

Courses are conducted through correspondence, TV programmes and videos, summer schools at various universities throughout the UK, some face to face seminars and interactive online studying.

> ℹ **The Open University:** 0845 300 6090; www.open.ac.uk

Courses

The main higher education courses available are first degrees and postgraduate degrees. Most undergraduate courses lead to the title of Bachelor of Arts (BA) or Bachelor of Science (BSc), followed by graduate degrees of Master of Arts (MA) or Master of Science (MSc). Most undergraduate courses in England, Wales and Northern Ireland are three years in duration, while in Scotland students gain an ordinary degree after three years, but have to do an additional year to gain an honours degree. Professional courses in subjects such as medicine, dentistry and veterinary science take longer, sometimes up to seven years.

Postgraduate courses vary in length depending on whether they are taught or research degrees. A taught MA, for example, may take just one year, whereas research projects leading to a Doctorate (PhD) have been known to take up to ten.

Admissions

Applications for admission to courses of below postgraduate level at most universities and higher education courses are made through the *Universities and Colleges Admission Service* (UCAS). This is a central clearing house which allows potential students to apply to an unlimited number of institutions simultaneously. UCAS provides information, through its website and publications, about courses on offer at all participating institutions in the UK. It operates an online application system for potential students, and passes applications to the institutions concerned.

> "After I graduated I stayed on as a post-graduate student for a year, in the same university department, and was then offered a temporary post there. This was followed by another temporary extension, and so it went on until somewhere along the line I was made permanent.
> Rainer Thonnes, from Germany"

The individual institutions then indicate whether they wish to make the student an unconditional offer of a place on their chosen course; an offer conditional on them achieving certain minimum grades in their examinations; or to refuse them. They may call the potential student for interview before making an offer. On the basis of this information, the student then decides which course at which institution to take up.

The Open University and a few higher education colleges conduct their own admissions. Applications should be made direct to these bodies.

Most applications for admission as a postgraduate student are made to individual institutions, but there are central clearing houses for postgraduate courses in the fields of teacher training and social work.

Initial teacher training courses in Britain are taken either in colleges of education or universities. Details of courses on offer can be obtained from UCAS.

Entry Requirements

The formal entry requirements for most undergraduate degree courses are two or more A levels at grade E or above (or the equivalent), and to HND courses one A level (or equivalent). In practice, however, most courses will require higher requirements, and, of course, the more popular the course and the institution, the higher the grades asked for. UCAS converts all grades to a numerical equivalent, so that different qualifications can be compared.

Applicants without any, or enough, or the 'right kind' of, formal educational achievements may still apply if they have less quantifiable experience and skills. Mature students, for example, may be accepted on the basis of work and life experience together with work-based training courses and the like.

> *i* **UCAS:** 0870 112 2211; (Monday to Friday, 8:30am–16:00pm) or ac.UK
> **Graduate Teacher Training Registry (GTTR):** 0870 112 2205;
> www.gttr.ac.uk

Tuition Fees and Student Loans

Since the 1980s, a number of changes have been made to the arrangements regarding the payment of tuition fees and living expenses for students in higher education. Prior to this, UK students made no contribution towards the costs of their tuition, and means-tested local education authority grants were available to help with student living expenses. The system of non-repayable grants was first replaced by student loans, which were repayable by the student once he or she graduated and was earning above a certain level. In 1998, the UK Government announced that in future UK students would also pay an annual amount towards their course tuition.

The requirement for UK students to pay tuition fees was, and has continued to be, a huge political issue, with MPs from all parties divided on the issue. The general public too are divided on the matter – the main division being between those who are, or whose children are, university students, and those who are not!

The position regarding the level of fees payable, and who pays them, now varies depending on which part of the UK students live or study in.

Maximum Maintenance Loans 2007-2008		
	Per Year	**Final Year Students**
Living at home:	£3,495	£3,155
Living away from home outside London	£4,510	£4,175
Living away from home in London	£6,315	£5,750

England

In 2003, the UK Government introduced so-called 'top-up fees' in England and Wales, which allow universities to charge variable undergraduate tuition fees, a proportion of the whole cost. In 2007 the maximum which can be charged is £3,070. Details of fees for particular courses are available from the individual universities. These fees do not have to be paid upfront as there are fee loans available.

There are no regulations regarding the level of tuition fees for part-time students. These are set by individual institutions for each course. You may be eligible to receive a non-repayable fee grant and/or course grant. Eligibility for, and level of grant available, is based on household income and also takes into account factors such as whether you have dependent children, are married, in a civil partnership or live with a partner. In 2007-08 the maximum amount you could receive is £1,400. There are other forms of funding which may be available if you are on a low income, are disabled or have a learning difficulty. Grants and other funding must be re-applied for each year of the course.

Non-repayable maintenance grants are available for students from lower-income households. Student loans for maintenance (living costs) are also available. The amount you can borrow is assessed on the basis of yours, or your parents', household income and where you will be living when you undertake the course. Maintenance loans have to be re-applied for each year of the course. There may also be bursaries and scholarships available from your university or college.

Loans for fees and maintenance do not have to be repaid until the student has finished the course and is earning over £15,000 per year. Repayments are 9% of your earnings over £15,000. If your earnings drop back below £15,000 at any time, you stop repaying the loan. The interest rate is linked to inflation so you repay in real terms the same amount as you borrowed. Outstanding loans are written off once you reach 65, or after 25 years.

Wales

The situation in Wales is broadly similar to that in England, although different grants are available. Universities in Wales can, like English universities,

Student finance ℹ️

For further details about student finance, fact sheets and application forms, see www.directgov.gov.uk/studentfinance or contact the Local Education Authority in the area where you will be studying.

charge up to £3,070 per year in tuition fees. However, in 2007, Wales introduced a non-repayable tuition fee grant of up to £1,845 a year. The remainder of any fees due can then be covered by the student taking out a Student Loan for Fees, as in England.

An Assembly Learning Grant of up to £2,700 is available for eligible students from low-income households.

Student maintenance loans are available to help with living costs on the same basis as in England.

Scotland

The introduction of tuition fees was a major issue in Scotland during the Scottish Parliament elections in 1999, and a proposal to abolish them was one of the first matters considered by the new parliament. After a process of consultation and the production of the 'Cubie Report' by an independent committee set up to report on the matter, it was decided that tuition fees for full-time Scottish domiciled undergraduate students studying at Scottish institutions would be paid by the Student Awards Agency for Scotland (SAAS).

When 'top-up' fees were introduced in the rest of the UK in 2006, Scotland did not follow the same course. UK students from outside Scotland studying at Scottish institutions are liable to pay £1,700 in tuition fees, although loans and grants should be available as per the arrangements in their home country.

Students are liable to pay a Graduate Endowment at the end of their degree course in recognition of the higher education benefits they have received. The funds will go towards student support for future generations. The amount payable is set at the beginning of the course. For courses starting in 2006-2007 the Graduate Endowment payable after the end of each course was £2,289.

Means-tested student loans are available to help with living costs. There is an additional loan of £560 available to young students from low-income homes. There is also a range of bursaries available for eligible students.

Northern Ireland

As with Waks the situation in Northern Ireland is broadly similar to that
in England, although different grants are available. A non-repayable
maintenance grant of up to £3,265 is available for students from low-
income families. Universities and colleges charging the full £3,070 tuition
fees provide bursaries of at least £300, and an average of around £1,000,
to students eligible for the full maintenance grant.

There is also a non-repayable Special Support grant of up to £3,200 per
year available for students who are eligible for benefits such as Income
Support and Housing benefit while they are studying.

EU Students

EU students are charged the home student rate appropriate to the institution
and the country they are studying in. Scholarships to assist with fees may
be available; enquire to institutions direct or see their websites for details.
EU students are not eligible to apply for a student loan to assist with living
costs but they may apply for a tuition fee loan.

For further details, contact the relevant universities direct. Information for international students is contained on the university's website and in their prospectus. Some universities also have an international office specifically to assist overseas students. See www.ucas.co.uk for links to all university websites.

International Students

Non-EU students are required to pay full tuition fees. These vary depending on the course and the institution, but typically are between £8,500 and £12,500 per year. Scholarships to assist with fees may be available. Enquire to institutions direct or see their websites for details.

International students are not eligible to apply for a student loan to assist with living costs. For further details, contact relevant universities direct. Information for international students is contained on websites and in prospectuses, and some have an international office specifically to assist overseas students. See www.ucas.co.uk for links to all university websites.

Adult and Continuing Education

This covers a wide range of options including non-vocational general interest courses, vocational courses providing skills needed in industry and commerce and degree-level study at the Open University.

Most courses are part-time and are provided by a number of bodies including education authorities, further and higher education colleges, universities, residential colleges, and several voluntary bodies.

Local adult education evening classes, both vocational and non-vocational, are provided by local education authorities and take place in local centres including schools and community halls across Britain.

> The course [at St Andrews University, Scotland] cost about the same as studying at a state university out-of-state in the US. It is without doubt a far better bargain, as I get a masters degree after four years at a prestigious university while most Americans might study for five years to get a bachelors degree at a mediocre university. I really don't understand why more Americans don't take advantage of opportunities to study overseas, particularly at Scottish universities, which seem to welcome Americans more than the English. I found most of my information on Scottish universities over the internet – advisors and administrators at my high school were completely ignorant of overseas universities, and I was the only one of a graduating class of 640 to study abroad. I found the admissions process much easier and more objective than that of most American universities.
> Sam White

Useful Contacts

Workers Educational Association (WEA): The largest voluntary education body in the UK; 020 7426 3450; www.wea.org.uk

National Institute of Adult and Continuing Education (NIACE): Works in England and Wales to promote the study and general advancement of adult continuing education; 0116 204 4200; www.niace.org.uk

Lifelong Learning UK: Brings together organisations working throughout the UK; 0870 757 7890; www.lifelonglearninguk.org

Learn Direct: Offers courses including online courses, throughout the UK; 0800 101 901; www.learndirect.co.uk

Trans-national Education and Training Programmes

There are a number of schemes for those wishing to come to study in the UK. The European Union runs a wide range of programmes for education, training, youth, culture, and citizenship. For a full list of programmes available see the European Commission website: http://ec.europa.eu.

UK Socrates-Erasmus Council: 01227 762712; www.erasmus.ac.uk

Council On International Educational Exchange (CIEE): Creates and administers programmes that allow US high school and university students and educators to study and teach abroad. Toll-Free: 1 800 40 STUDY; www.ciee.org

British Universities North America Club (BUNAC): BUNAC runs a Work in Britain scheme. 020 7251 3472; www.bunac.org. BUNAC has various partner organisations running schemes for students to work in Britain. In Canada this is done through SWAP (Student Work Abroad Programme): 011 44 20 7251 3472 www.swap.ca. BUNAC's partner in Australia and New Zealand is International Exchange Programs (IEP). IEP (Australia): (03) 9329 3866; www.iep.co.au. IEP (NZ): (09) 366 6255; www.iep.co.nz. There are links to all relevant national websites from the main BUNAC website.

Another comprehensive source of information on studying in the UK is the British Council: 0161-957 7755; www.britishcouncil.org. The British Council has offices around the world, details of which can be found on their website.

US nationals should contact British Council United States: 0800-488 2235; www.britishcouncil.org/usa-education.

> " I began investigating a long-hidden desire, to return to university to pursue a postgraduate degree. The University of Glasgow offered a Masters in Creative Writing in half the time at half the expense of most universities offering an equivalent degree in the US.
> Amy Burns "

■ SOCIAL SERVICES

Social work services are administered by local authorities. They assess the needs of the population and provide, or commission others to provide, the care required.

Services for the elderly, the disabled, the mentally ill, and those with learning difficulties, are designed to enable them to remain living in their own homes or in the community wherever possible. Local authorities provide support in the home, short-term care, day centres and respite care in order to allow carers (usually close family), temporary breaks from their responsibilities.

Further information regarding social services in each area is supplied by the relevant local council.

Social Security Benefits

State benefits are paid to residents of the UK via the Department for Work and Pensions (DWP). There is a wide range of benefits to which recipients' entitlement is assessed depending on their situation, their income or the amount of National Insurance contributions they have made.

Income-related benefits take into account both income and savings and include Income Support, Family Credit, Housing Benefit, and Council Tax Benefit.

Situation-related benefits depend on such things as your health, or whether you are caring for a child or a chronically ill or disabled person. They include Child Benefit, Disability Living Allowance, Invalid Care Allowance, and Industrial Injury Compensation. Child benefit is paid weekly for each child in full time education, with a higher rate for the first child than for subsequent children.

National Insurance related benefits depend on the amount of National Insurance contributions made, and include Jobseeker's Allowance, Maternity Allowance, Statutory Sick Pay, Invalidity Allowance and the State Retirement Pension. Jobseeker's Allowance is in the form of a weekly cash payment for up to six months from the date you are unemployed, as long as you are actively looking for a job.

These benefits are governed by many rules and provisos, and are payable at different rates depending on personal circumstances, so it is not possible to give a definitive run-down here. Levels of benefit are set each year, usually in April, broadly in line with the retail Price Index.

◣ CARS AND MOTORING

Approximately 73% of households in Britain have one or more cars, but, in rural areas the figure may be as high as 80%.

 Full details of benefits available and current rates can be found on the DWP website: www.dwp.gov.uk

Roads

There are over 243,000 miles (391,000 km) of roads in Great Britain. Roads in Britain are classified using an alphabetical system. Motorways are high speed, multi-carriageway roads. They are indicated by M followed by a number: e.g. M1, M25. They are marked on road maps in blue and the road signs on motorways have a blue background with white markings. Major roads are 'A' roads: e.g. A6, A517. They are subdivided into 'Primary routes' which are marked in green on road maps and the road signs have green backgrounds with yellow markings. Other A roads are marked in red on maps and the road signs are generally white with black markings. Warning signs have a red border. Smaller roads are indicated by B followed by a number: e.g. B778. They are marked on maps in yellow. Other minor roads are not numbered.

There are generally no charges for travelling on the network of motorways and trunk roads in the UK, but there are some road bridges on which tolls are payable.

Britain is suffering the effects of high car ownership and the health risks of traffic congestion. Road transport is responsible for about 80% of all transport emissions, with CO_2 emissions rising fastest. With traffic predicted to rise by 38% over the next 20 years it is a problem that will become intolerable if measures are not taken to cut traffic levels in busy areas. With air pollution now a matter of international concern, the UK is committed to reducing CO_2 by 20% from their 1990 levels by 2010, and is currently negotiating a legally-binding target of reduction of six greenhouse gases, including CO_2.

Across the UK, councils in urban areas are examining schemes to discourage drivers from taking private cars into towns and cities. These include proposals such as 'road pricing' schemes, where drivers pay for the privilege of driving into towns; restricting access to certain vehicles on certain days of the week; and car-sharing schemes. Many towns and cities already have 'park and ride' schemes, where you park your car in a specific parking area outside the town, then continue your journey into the town centre on a free and frequent bus service.

> *It's a nightmare! So much traffic. The M25 motorway which rings London is notorious for traffic jams – not for nothing has it been called 'the world's biggest car park'!*
> *Jo Penfold*

A congestion charge was introduced in London in 2003. Motorists must pay £8 a day to drive into a designated area of the capital between 7am and 6pm, Monday to Friday. Other cities are sure to introduce similar charges in the coming years, despite the fact that such schemes are extremely unpopular with motorists. In February 2007, as a result of government proposals to install tracking devices in all road vehicles and charge for usage of the national road network by the mile, an online petition to oppose any such move attracted 1.8 million signatures.

Driving Regulations

UK vehicles are right-hand drive and motorists drive on the left. Overtaking is permissible only on the right. Speed limits are generally 70 miles per hour (mph) (112kph) on motorways and dual carriageways, 60mph (96kph) on unrestricted single carriageways and 30mph (48kph) or 20mph (32kph) in built-up and residential areas. Camper vans and caravans are restricted to a maximum of 50mph (80kph).

However, there is a national campaign to improve road safety in the UK and you will find that lower speed limits are indicated on certain stretches of roads. In recent years hundreds of speed cameras have been installed throughout the UK to catch speeding drivers, so it is essential to be vigilant while driving, as you can be fined heavily and get endorsements on your driving licence for exceeding the speed limit.

Seat belts must be worn by drivers and all passengers (front and rear seat) of cars and crash helmets by drivers and passengers of motorcycles.

It is illegal to drive on a public road without a current driving licence, vehicle excise duty, vehicle insurance cover and MoT certificate of roadworthiness. (See below for further details about these requirements.) The full rules of the road can be found in *The Highway Code* at a price of £1.49 from *The Stationery Office:* 0870 6065566; www.tso.co.uk.

FACT

Seat belts must be worn by drivers and all passengers (front and rear seat) of cars and crash helmets by drivers and passengers of motorcycles.

Driving Tests

Drivers of motorised vehicles must pass a driving test administered by the Driving Standards Agency (DSA). It is an executive agency of the Department of the Environment, Transport and the Regions and is responsible for approving driving instructors as well as carrying out driving tests.

The law states that you cannot learn to drive a car before you are 17, with the exception of disabled persons who are in receipt of mobility allowance, who can take their test at 16.

The car driving test consists of a theory test taken using a computer at a DSA Theory Test Centre, and an in-car practical test of around half an hour with an approved DSA driving examiner. There are certain standard manoeuvres and procedures you will be required to perform satisfactorily before you can pass the test.

Your eyesight will be tested – you must be able (if necessary, with spectacles or contact lenses) to read a car number plate at a distance of 20.5 metres. It is illegal to drive if your eyesight does not meet the minimum standard. If you suffer from certain medical conditions you may be required to also have a medical test.

Additional driving tests must be taken for those individuals wishing to drive large lorries or buses.

To drive a moped or motorcycle on a public road you must have completed and passed a Compulsory Basic Training (CBT) course provided by a DSA-approved training body.

There are fees payable for these various tests. They vary depending on the vehicle and when you take the test – there is a higher evening and Saturday rate. This ranged, in 2007, from £85.02 for cars to £107 for lorries and buses. The theory test costs £21.50. Tests for drivers of invalid carriages are free.

Driving Licences

Residents with a licence issued in the above countries must register their details with the Driver and Vehicle Licensing Agency (DVLA) but can continue to use their licences until the holder is aged 70 or for three years after becoming resident, whichever is the longer. Vocational licence holders can use them until they are aged 45, or for five years after becoming resident. If you are over 45 (but under 65) you can use your licence until you are aged 66, or for five years after becoming resident. If you are aged 65 or over, you can use your licence for 12 months after becoming resident. To continue driving after these periods, a British driving licence must be obtained.

A full Northern Ireland driving licence can be exchanged for a GB licence or can be used until it expires, at which time you may apply for a GB licence.

Licences issued in Australia, Barbados, the British Virgin Islands, Canada, Gibraltar, Hong Kong, Japan, Kenya, Malta, New Zealand, Cyprus, Singapore, South Africa, Switzerland and Zimbabwe are valid for 12 months from the time you become resident. After this time you must stop driving or exchange your licence for a British licence. You will need to fill out form D1 (available from www.dvla.gov.uk) and send it to DVLA along with a cheque for £45 and a passport-sized photo. This can be done up to five years after becoming resident. The rules for licences issued in Jersey, Guernsey or the Isle of Man are the same except that you can exchange them for a British licence up to ten years after becoming resident.

Licences from all other countries entitle you to drive for up to 12 months after becoming resident but you must obtain a provisional Britsh licence and pass the Britsh driving test before the 12-month period elapses.

Foreign driving licences

Visitors to Great Britain who hold a valid licence issued in the following countries can drive any vehicle indicated on the licence for as long as it is valid:
Austria, Belgium, Czech Republic, Denmark, Estonia, Finland, France, Germany, Greece, Hungary, Iceland, Ireland, Italy, Latvia, Liechtenstein, Lithuania, Luxembourg, Malta, Netherlands, Norway, Poland, Portugal, Republic of Cyprus, Slovakia, Slovenia, Spain, Sweden.

The DVLA is responsible for issuing driving licences.

Before beginning driving lessons on a public road, you must have a provisional licence. The relevant forms are available from post offices and, once completed, should be sent to the DVLA. Learner drivers must be supervised at all times by someone over 21 who has held a full licence for at least three years. A provisional licence currently costs £38.

After you have passed your driving test, your licence changes to a full licence. There is no additional fee payable. Your licence covers you for a wide range of vehicles including provisional motorcycle entitlement, upgraded to full entitlement if you pass your motorcycle test. Provisional motorcycle entitlement, where you do not hold a full car licence, lasts for two years and is then suspended for one year before you can apply for it again.

Driving licences stay valid for different periods for different categories of vehicle: for family cars and motorcycles, generally a driving licence stays valid until your 70th birthday, while for larger vehicles, it is valid until your 45th birthday. After this it is renewable every five years until you are 65, after which it is renewable annually.

If you need to apply for a licence renewal for reasons of age or for medical reasons, the replacement is free. Failure to inform the DVLA of any medical condition which may affect your fitness to drive, or of change in an existing condition, is a criminal offence with a fine of up to £1,000. There is a fee charged to replace a driving licence after disqualification or if it is lost or stolen.

Useful Addresses

The full rules of the road can be found in *The Highway Code,* which it can be purchased online at www.highwaycode.gov.uk.
Driving Standards Agency: 0115 901 2500; www.dsa.gov.uk
British School of Motoring; 0845 276276; www.bsm.co.uk
DVLA: 0870 240 0009; www.dvla.gov.uk

Endorsements and Disqualification

There are a whole range of traffic offences which may result in 'penalty points' being added to your driving licence. These may ultimately cost you the right to drive. The number of points added to your licence is decided by a court on conviction for a specific offence. These points remain on your licence for eleven years from the date of conviction for offences relating to driving while under the influence of drink or drugs, and four years from the date of the offence or of conviction in other cases. If a total of 12 points is built up within three years, the driver is automatically disqualified from driving for a minimum of six months, or one year if the driver was disqualified in the previous three years. In addition, every offence for which you can be given penalty points carries a discretionary disqualification, decided by the court at the time of conviction. This is usually between a week and a few months. Serious offences such as dangerous driving and drink driving carry a mandatory disqualification of 12 months or more and are likely to result in a prison sentence if injury or death was caused. If you drive while disqualified you can receive a prison sentence and your car may be confiscated.

i For a full list of offences incurring penalty points, plus the number imposed for each offence, see: www.dvla.gov.uk.

FACT

If a total of 12 points is built up within three years, the driver is automatically disqualified from driving for a minimum of six months, or one year if the driver was disqualified in the previous three years.

Motor Vehicle Licences

All motor vehicles are registered with the DVLA and a record is kept, doucmenting of changing ownership during the vehicle's lifespan. When you change your vehicle, its registration documents must be sent to the DVLA for the new car to be registered to you.

Vehicles must display a vehicle licence disc, valid for six months or twelve months at a time. This disc, often called a 'tax disc' is available from post offices on payment of vehicle excise duty (VED). In order to encourage the use of cars which cause less pollution, there is a lower charge for smaller vehicles. Vehicle excise duty increases most years, with the new rates announced in the UK Government's March Budget. In 2007 the annual rate for cars with an engine size of 1549cc or less was £110, while those above 1549cc paid the 'standard rate' of £175 per year. New cars registered after March 2001 attract discounts on their car tax levels depending on the levels of carbon dioxide emitted. The more environmentally friendly vehicles, including gas and electric-powered cars, have the biggest discounts, while diesel cars are the most expensive. For example, the VED on a low-emission alternative fuel car is currently just £30 for 12 months.

Motorcycles are charged VED on a sliding scale, depending on engine size. In 2007 this was £15 per year for those 150cc or lower, £31 for 151cc–400cc, £46 for 401cc–600cc and £62 for those exceeding 600cc.

Some vehicles are exempt from car tax. These include cars driven by disabled drivers, vehicles constructed before 1973, and agricultural machines.

Insurance

The law requires that vehicles using public and private roads in the UK must be covered by insurance. The minimum cover they must have is third party insurance, which includes cover for injury to other people. Some insurance companies may insist you take comprehensive insurance which covers all risks, such as fire and theft, or damage to your car. This insurance pays personal accident benefits and medical expenses where necessary.

The cost of car insurance varies greatly, because there are so many factors taken into account. These include the age and sex of the driver, the type of vehicle and its age and size of engine, in addition to the area in which you live. Insurance premiums are generally lower in rural areas because there is a lower rate of accidents and because car thefts are far less common than in urban areas.

Discounts are awarded on premiums payable if you have not previously claimed on your car insurance. This 'no claims bonus' is lost for succeeding years when you do make a claim. Drivers who have claimed more than once may have correspondingly heavier premiums to pay in future years.

A 'Green Card' providing western European cover for a maximum of three months a year is available at extra cost and it is not included in British motor insurance packages. The Green Card is, in effect, a certificate which gives proof that the driver has car insurance which complies with the minimum insurance requirements of the countries they drive through.

There is a lot of competition between insurance companies, so it is advisable to 'shop around' for the best quote. Motoring organisations such as the AA (Automobile Association) and the RAC (Royal Automobile Club) have their own insurance schemes, or you can get insurance from high street or internet insurance companies. If you don't want to do it yourself, insurance brokers will shop around to find a good deal for you. Ensure they are a member of the British Insurance Brokers' Association.

Useful Websites

Direct Line: One of the UK's leading car insurance providers; 0845 246 3761; www.directline.com

esure.com: Another of the UK's leading car insurance providers; 0845 603 7874; www.esure.com
Automobile Association: 0800 316 2456; www.theaa.com
UK Car Insurance Directory: Contains comparisons of, and links to, a wide range of insurance providers; www.ukcarinsurancedirectory.co.uk.
British Insurance Brokers Association: 0901 814 0015; www.biba.org.uk

MoT Tests

All cars, motorcycles, motor caravans and light goods and dual-purpose vehicles over three years old must have an annual test of roadworthiness. This is called an 'MoT test' because it was originally administered by the Ministry of Transport. Nowadays the MoT testing scheme is administered by the Vehicle Inspectorate.

MoT tests are carried out at official test centres. Most large garages and many small ones are approved as test centres, and there are also local authority test centres. Some will test your car while you wait, although you may need to book in advance. The test normally takes about 20 minutes and covers a specified list of checks which must be made of the condition and cleanliness of the car. Those indeed the state of the lights, brakes, suspension, tyres and wheels and seat belts. If any of the items tested are not up to standard, a test certificate will not be issued until the fault has been rectified. This will be done by the same garage, if you wish. If the test centre issues a 'warning' on any defect, you will only be allowed to drive the vehicle home, or to a garage for repair. It is an offence, otherwise, to drive a vehicle without a valid test certificate.

The police also have the power to carry out roadworthiness spot checks on vehicles, and if your vehicle is found to be not roadworthy, the possession of a valid test certificate is no defence. The cost of the MoT test in 2007 was £50.35 for cars and £27.15 for motorcycles.
Useful Address
Vehicle & Operator Services Agency: 0870 6060440; www.vosa.gov.uk
Car Owner's Guide to the MOT: www.motester.co.uk

Motoring Organisations

The two main motoring organisations in the UK are the Automobile Association (AA) and the Royal Automobile Club (RAC). There are smaller ones for specific groups of people, such as the Civil Service Motoring Association (CSMA). There are also organisations which provide breakdown services, wherever you may be in the country. Green Flag Motoring Assistance is one such.

These organisations offer all or some of the following services to members: vehicle insurance cover, breakdown services with recovery anywhere in the UK, free public transport or car hire, hotel charges, home start and legal advice and aid. These organisations charge from around £30 per year for the basic recovery service, up to around £150 for their full service which includes transport of the vehicle plus passengers to any destination in the UK if necessary.

Useful Websites

Automobile Association (AA): 0870 600 0371; www.theaa.com
Civil Service Motoring Association (CSMA): 0845 345 7444;
www.csma.uk.com
Green Flag Motoring Assistance: 0845 246 1557; www.greenflag.co.uk
Royal Automobile Club (RAC): 0800 731 7090; www.rac.co.uk

Breakdowns, Theft and Accidents

If you have an accident in which a person or a horse, cow, ass, mule, sheep, pig, dog or goat is injured, you must call the police. You must also contact the police if the road is blocked or if damage is caused to the property of a person who cannot be contacted. You should, if possible, move your vehicle off the road. On a motorway, you should, if possible, pull on to the 'hard shoulder' along the left-hand side of the road and stay with your vehicle. It is best to wait on the embankment beyond the hard shoulder, or on nearby land, rather than sitting in the car – a surprising number of accidents occur where other vehicles run into cars on the hard shoulder. If you have a mobile phone or can reach an emergency phone beside the road, call the police and/or the emergency services on 999, or contact a breakdown service if there is only vehicle failure or damage. If you cannot do this, wait until the police arrive, as they will do eventually. With most people now having a mobile phone, the police and emergency services are usually inundated with calls about every accident from passers-by, so you won't be ignored!

Note that it is against the law to use a hand-held mobile phone while driving. It is a punishable offence resulting in three penalty points on the driver's licence and a £60 fine. If you wish to use your phone while in the car, you must pull over and turn your engine off. Hands-free mobile phones are not subject to this law.

You should exchange your details and those of your insurance company with any other drivers or pedestrians involved; if not, you should inform the police within 24 hours. It is an offence punishable by a fine and penalty points on your licence to fail to stop after an accident, to fail to give your particulars or to report the accident to the police. You should inform your insurance company also of any accident, even if you don't intend to make a claim – this will allow you to make a claim later if you wish. Your own insurance company may handle a claim against another driver for you, or you may need to write to the other driver's insurers to make your claim.

> Cars are expensive to buy, and then there are the running costs – insurance, tax, fuel, maintenance and repairs, car parking costs – which easily come to a couple of thousand or more per year, depending on your vehicle and how far you drive.
> John Livesey

If you are a member of a motoring organisation, you will have a contact number to ring if you break down. They will arrange to send a repair person or recovery vehicle from the locality. If you do not belong to an organisation, other breakdown services are available. Motorway breakdown services are notoriously expensive, so if your vehicle is less than reliable membership of the AA or similar might be a good investment.

If your vehicle is stolen, you may (but are not obliged to) report it to the police. If you intend to claim for it on your insurance, however, your insurer will require you to report the theft to the police. Car theft is a huge problem in the UK which has the highest per capita rate in Europe.

Driving Under the Influence of Drink or Drugs

The police have the right to stop any vehicle whose driver they suspect of being under the influence of drink or drugs. A 'breathalyser' test may be given at the roadside to measure the amount of alcohol in the driver's system. The individual blows into a small machine which analyses the breath. If the reading is above the legal maximum level, it is followed by a blood or urine test at a police station. If a driver is involved in a road traffic accident, they may be breathalysed as a matter of course.

The legal limit for alcohol is 35 micrograms in 100 millilitres of breath, which is equivalent to 80mg in 100ml of blood or 107mg in 100ml of urine. This equates to around 2 pints of normal strength lager or beer. However, the alcohol level is dependent on matters such as body weight, so the only safe way is not to drink at all if you are planning to drive.

Drivers may also be prosecuted for driving under the influence of drugs. To test for the presence of drugs, a suspected driver is asked to do the following tasks:

- Counting out 30 seconds – drug users either under-read or over-read time
- Walk in a straight line nine paces forward and then back
- Raise a foot in the air – designed to test balance
- Touch their finger to their nose with their eyes closed – tests co-ordination

Penalties for driving under the influence of drink or drugs are harsh, and cover all the options – penalty points, fines and imprisonment. The penalty of was increases in severity depending on the quantity of drink or drugs the driver has ingested, whether an accident has occurred, and whether injury or death occurred as a result of the accident. Causing death by dangerous driving under the influence of drink or drugs carries a maximum penalty of 14 years' imprisonment, for example.

Servicing your Vehicle

Garages are generally open 9am–5.30pm, although in larger towns they may be open for longer hours and some attached to large supermarkets are open 24 hours a day. In rural areas many local garages have had to close down in recent years due to the uneconomic viability of such small businesses which require expensive machinery.

Costs of labour vary between main dealers in large towns and smaller garages which may be slightly cheaper, but they are generally expensive; between £25 and £45 an hour. At a small rural garage, you will often find you have to leave your vehicle in overnight, to allow for even everyday spare parts to be delivered from a large town. Consequently, you might find you have to pay more for parts in rural areas. Large garages in towns may be able to carry out the work while you wait.

Addresses of garages can be found in local phone books and in the *Yellow Pages.*

Car Rental

Car hire firms can be found in all big towns and cities. There are a number of international companies such as Avis, Budget, Europcar, and Hertz, as well as some large independents such as Kenning, Swan National and Arnold Clark.

All those companies can be found in the *Yellow Pages* under 'Car Hire-Self Drive' or on www.yell.co.uk. It is advisable to ring round for a selection of quotes, because prices can vary widely depending on the size and type of vehicle, the period you require it for, and so on. Hire charges are usually based on a daily or weekly rate. You will collect the car with a full tank of fuel and should fill it up before you return it.

There may be restrictions on the type of vehicle you can hire if you are below 21, and you may also be required to take out a higher level of insurance. If you have endorsements on your licence for careless driving, you may be refused car hire. It is also very difficult to hire a car if you are over the age of 70, as car hire companies may not cover you with their insurance. You may be able to arrange car hire cover through your own car insurers but this is likely to be expensive.

Some car insurance policies include free car hire for the period you are without your vehicle as a result of an accident.

Car Hire Websites
Europcar: 0845 758 5375; www.europcar.co.uk
Hertz Rent-A-Car: 08708 44 88 44; www.hertz.co.uk
National Car Rental: Website has links to many car hire companies; www.nationalcar-europe.com.

> " Living in the city I have no need for a car on a daily basis as I walk or use public transport.
> I often hire a car for a few days when I'm off to explore more of the country.
> Jo Penfold "

Fuel

Vehicle fuel is expensive throughout Britain, and in rural areas, especially in the far north, it is more expensive than in towns and cities. This is brought about by a combination of the high level of tax imposed by the government – over 76% of the pump price – with increased unit costs associated with low-volume sales in remote areas, and less competition from other suppliers.

Diesel used to be significantly cheaper than petrol which led many people in recent years to switch to diesel-engined vehicles to take advantage of the savings. However, once scientists produced evidence that diesel was less environmentally friendly than unleaded petrol, the government increased the tax on diesel too, and it is now the most expensive form of fuel.

The AA give the average daily price of fuel in Britain on their website (www.theaa.com). In a typical month a February 24th 2007, the average price of unleaded petrol was 87.1p per litre. Diesel was 91.1p per litre. For example.

Due to environmental concerns, leaded petrol was been banned in 1999. The UK has belatedly begun moves to adopt liquefied petrol gas (LPG) as an alternative vehicle fuel. It is, environmentally, far cleaner than the existing options and is also far cheaper. However, there are few cars in Britain capable of running on LPG Autogas, although many of the major car companies are introducing dual fuel models. It is possible to have other cars converted, though this costs around £1,600.

Useful Websites

Fuel Card Group: Discount cards for the main UK fuel companies; 0113 295 0420; www.fuelcard-group.com.

LPG Autogas: FAQs about LPG and details of over 1,200 LPG outlets throughout the UK; www.lpga.co.uk;

Buying a Car

Most local newspapers have a motoring section which runs at least once during the week. Here you will find both private sellers and car dealers

Buying fuel

Because of high overheads and low volume sales, many rural villages do not have a petrol station because it is not economically viable to run one. In some areas this can mean a round trip of twenty miles or more to fill up. If you run a business, even a very low-key bed and breakfast, you may be able to obtain a fuel 'agency card' which allows you to buy petrol and diesel at a discounted UK price.

advertising the vehicles they have for sale. There are also national magazines for car buyers and sellers, such as *Auto Trader*, available from newsagents and online at www.autotrader.co.uk.

Car dealers in large towns tend to cluster together, usually on the outskirts of town. Literally thousands of new and used vehicles are lined up on the forecourts of dozens of dealers. Some dealers specialise in specific makes, others will buy and sell anything.

Many car dealers now have their own websites, which can easily be found through the major internet search engines.

When you buy a new or used car you must ensure your insurance has been transferred to the new vehicle before you drive it away.

Selling a Car

If you have imported a car, you can not sell it within 12 months of arival without paying import duty and other taxes. If you wish to sell your car privately, you can advertise it in local newspapers, 'free-ads' papers or on local noticeboards. If it is an expensive or collectors' car, it might be worth advertising nationally in the motoring press. The internet is also a good place for advertising a car, whether via an appropriate website or on a motoring newsgroup.

Most car dealers will sell you a new or used car on a part-exchange basis, where they give you a discount depending on the value they put on the car you are wishing to trade. It is illegal to sell a car in an unroadworthy condition unless you are selling it as a 'non-runner' without an MoT test certificate. A potential buyer can only test drive your car if he or she is covered by your or his own insurance. When you have sold it your car, you must inform your insurance company and either cancel your insurance or transfer it to a new car. There is a portion of your vehicle registration papers which you must complete and send to the Driver and Vehicle Licensing Agency (DVLA). The new owner must also register his/her ownership with them.

◼ PUBLIC TRANSPORT

Bus and Coach

There is an extensive network of road passenger services in Britain. Local and regional bus services run several times a day – often several times an hour – in areas where there is a relatively high population. This falls to once a day or even less in the remotest rural areas. National coach services cover longer routes, generally travelling between large towns and cities, with stops along the way at smaller places. Bus and coach services throughout the UK are provided by the private sector, although local authorities subsidise 'socially necessary' routes which private companies could only otherwise run at a loss.

Information on local bus routes and timetables can be obtained from bus stations, local councils, tourist offices, and sometimes online.

Bus and Coach Companies
National Express Coach Services: 08705 808080; www.nationalexpress.com
Scottish Citylink Express Coach Services: 08705 505050; www.citylink.co.uk
Stagecoach: 0870 608 2608; www.stagecoachbus.com
Megabus.com: 0900 160 0900; www.megabus.com

Taxis

Taxis (or cabs) are easy to come by in large towns and cities. There will be a taxi stand at most railway stations and airports where you can hire a taxi to take you to your destination. Alternatively, local taxi firm numbers can be found in public telephones, or in your phone book, so you can ring to arrange for a taxi to collect you in advance.

Although taxis are a relatively expensive form of transport, they have the advantage over other public transport of delivering you right to your destination. Most are licensed by local authorities and will have a meter, so you can be sure that the fare you are charged is fair. If they do not have a meter, you should always agree a fare before you start the journey, to avoid being asked for an exorbitant amount when you arrive. Higher prices are charged after midnight.

Air

There are regional airports throughout the UK, all offering domestic flights.

The Ten Busiest Airports	
1.	London Heathrow
2.	London Gatwick
3.	Manchester
4.	London Stansted
5.	Birmingham
6.	Glasgow
7.	Edinburgh
8.	Luton
9.	Belfast International
10.	Bristol

Budget airlines offer cheap flights between certain UK airports, but by no means all. This means that you may find yourself paying a few pounds to fly, say, from Gatwick to Glasgow, but hundreds of pounds to fly from Inverness to Manchester. You may also find that you can save yourself a great deal of money on the same route simply by flying with a different airline. It is therefore essential to shop around and research comparative costs carefully.

 The following websites give you at-a-glance comparisons for the cost of flights from different airlines:
Travel Supermarket: www.travelsupermarket.com
Skyscanner: www.skyscanner.net

Be aware that flight prices may be shown without airport taxes (air passenger duty), which must be paid on all flights from and within Britain. On domestic flights this is £10 for Economy class flights and £20 on Business

or First Class flights. There are exemptions from this duty on certain 'lifeline' routes beginning and ending within the Scottish Highlands and Islands.

Airlines

British Airways: 0870 850 9850; www.ba.com

bmi: 0870 6070555; www.flybmi.com

easyJet: 0871 7500 100; www.easyjet.com

flybe: 0871 700 0535; www.flybe.com

Ryanair: 0818 303030; www.ryanair.com

For further details on international flights from and to the UK, see the section Getting There in Before You Go.

Rail

> Be sure to take advantage of Britain's easy access to the rest of Europe, especially on no-frills airlines but also on trains and ferries.
> Susan Griffith

The railway infrastructure in Britain is owned and managed by Network Rail, which is also responsible for devising and publishing a national timetable of services. Train services themselves, however, are operated by private sector train operators, of which there are 25 in total.

Despite the great national pastime of complaining about the railways, they are well used. In 2004-2005 there were 2.2 billion passenger journeys taken in Great Britain. As part of their strategy to cut down congestion and traffic emissions, there is a commitment by the UK government to improve services and to increase use of the railways for passengers and freight. To this end, a Strategic Rail Authority has been set up. There are Rail Users' Consultative Committees which monitor the policies and performances of train and station operators in their area. These have a legal right to make recommendations for changes.

Train tickets on all services can be bought online through The Trainline (wwwthetrainline.com). The website includes timetables, allowing you to find your preferred route and time.

Timetable, ticket and fare information are also available on the National Rail Enquiry 24 hour service; 0845 748 4950.

As well as online, ticket may be booked by telephone with rail companies, or bought in person from railway stations.

There are a number of railcards available which give discounts on rail travel throughout Britain. These include the Young Persons Railcard for people between 16 and 25 (or those 26 plus who are in full-time education); the Family Railcard for up to 4 adults and four children; the Senior Railcard for the over 60s; and the Disabled Persons Railcard (which gives discounted travel for the disabled person and one travelling companion). They currently

cost £20 each (£18 for the disabled persons card) and they give a one-third discount on rail travel for adults and 60% discount for children travelling on a family railcard. It is possible to save the cost of the card just on a single journey. For full details see www.railcard.co.uk.

London Underground

Colloquially known as 'The Tube', this is the oldest underground railway system in the world, with the first services, on the Metropolitan Line, running 10 January 1863. It currently has about 253 miles (408km) of track, only 45% of them underground, despite its name. It serves 275 stations on 12 interlinking lines and on 7 December carried a number of 4.17 million passengers on the one day. Fares are calculated on a geographical zoning basis, with Zone 1 in the centre, and Zone 6 the outermost. Fares are the highest in the world for comparable systems, but you can benefit from discount prices by buying one of the many travelcards available. The most popular payment system is the Oystercard. As oystercard is a available pre-paid smartcard that allows you to get cheaper travel on buses, trams, underground and standard rail networks within London. The advantage of an oystercard is that it makes fully-integrated public transport around London easier for the commuter. For more information on oystercards, visit the Transport for London website at www.tfl.gov.uk.

Tickets and travelcards are bought from Underground stations, either from ticket booths or machines. Travelcards can also be bought online at www.londontravelpass.com.

i **Transport for London:** 020 222 1234; www.tfl.gov.uk/tube.

Glasgow Subway

The only other underground railway system in the UK, the Glasgow subway was originally opened in 1897, though was reopened following modernisation in 1980. It has 15 stations, around 6.5 miles (10.4km) of track and carries over 13 million passengers a year. Due to the colour of the coaches and the circular track, it is sometimes known as the Clockwork Orange.

A single journey is always £1, a return £2, no matter where you're going. Off-peak Discovery tickets are available after 9.30am, allowing an unlimited day's travel for £1.90. There are also multi-journey tickets and season tickets at discounted rates. Tickets are bought at stations, from ticket booths or machines.

 The subway is operated by Strathclyde Passenger Transport: 0141 332 6811; www.spt.co.uk

Ferries

Ferry services run between the British mainland and its many offshore islands, including Northern Ireland. In Scotland there are also, in certain places, short hops across sea lochs on the mainland – for instance, from Gourock (Strathclyde) to Dunoon (Cowal). If you time your journey right, you can cut hours off the travelling time by taking advantage of these 'inland' crossings on the west coast.

For a very useful at-a-glance guide to domestic ferry routes and timings, see Sail and Drive, www.sailanddrive.com/routebritain.aspx.

 Ferry Crossings UK: Low-cost ferry crossings and has or online booking facility. 0871 222 8642 | www.ferrycrossings-uk.co.uk.

UK Public Transport Information

Traveline: Journey planners for bus, coach or train; 0870 608 2608; www.traveline.org.uk

National Express Coach Enquiry Service: 08705 808080; www.nationalexpress.com

National Rail Enquiry Service: For all rail in England, Scotland and Wales (except heritage railways); 0845 748 4950; www.nationalrail.co.uk

Scottish Citylink Coach Enquiry Service: 0870 505050; www.citylink.co.uk

Travel Supermarket: www.travelsupermarket.com

Translink: Bus and rail services in Northern Ireland; 028 9066 6630; www.translink.co.uk

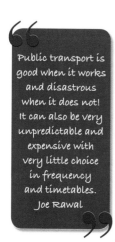

Public transport is good when it works and disastrous when it does not! It can also be very unpredictable and expensive with very little choice in frequency and timetables.

Joe Rawal

CRIME AND THE POLICE

Britain has the sixth highest level of crime in the world, at 85.5 crimes per thousand population per year, according to www.nationmaster.com. However, levels of crime vary widely from region to region, with the highest crime rates in cities, the lowest in rural, sparsely populated areas. The remotest areas – Shetland, the Western Isles and Orkney – report the lowest crimes rates of all.

In large areas of the Highlands and Islands there is almost no crime against property recorded, and as a result people feel safe leaving their houses and cars unlocked. This contrasts strongly with what is perceived to be the massively rising crime rates in the central belt of Scotland and south of the border. Some adults feel unsafe leaving home after dark and many do not like their children to go out alone, for fear of crime.

Even within the cities and towns, crime rates vary dramatically between one area and the next. Certain districts may be known as 'rough' and best avoided by those unfamiliar with the area. City centres, where a large number of pubs, clubs and bars are found, may also be best avoided at night, as they are often taken over by hordes of, generally young, people 'out on the town' and drinking heavily. This regularly leads to disorder and violence when the drinking venues close.

Throughout the UK, drug use is on the increase; the biggest problems are seen in the most deprived areas of cities.

The Police

There are over 50 police forces in the UK, responsible for all day to day policing matters in their area. In total, there are around 166,000 officers, although there are wide variations in the strength of individual police forces. The largest force is the Metropolitan Police Service in London, with over 30,000 officers, and the smallest the Dumfries and Galloway Constabulary in Scotland, with just 478.

Of the three main branches of the police force that most people will come across, the uniformed officers who investigate complaints of offences and misdemeanours are those from whom the famous 'bobbies on the beat term' was drawn. Today, their beats are far more likely to be patrolled in cars than on foot or bicycle, although many would like to see an on-foot patrol return. The Criminal Investigation Department (CID), usually plain clothes officers, will take over ongoing crime investigations, while the traffic police, who do wear uniform, deal with all traffic emergencies, accidents and breakdowns where injuries, traffic obstruction or other difficulties are caused. They can be seen patrolling the motorways and major roads of the country, often in highly-visible Land Rovers.

Most towns throughout Britain have their own police station, while cities tend to have several. In sparsely-populated rural areas, one police station, with just one or two officers, may cover a large area.

There are also three specialist police forces: the British Transport Police who deal with incidents on public transport vehicles or premises; the Ministry of Defence Police; and the Civil Nuclear Constabulary, who are responsible for protection of civil nuclear sites and nuclear materials.

 UK Police Service: This website has links to the websites of all UK police forces and related organizations, plus information about recruitment, appeals for information and a non-urgent crime reporting syste; www.police.uk

The UK Legal System

The legal system throughout the UK, makes a distinction between criminal law and civil law. However, in other respects, the legal system in Scotland differs significantly from the rest of the UK. The system in Northern Ireland is broadly similar to that in England and Wales.

Judicature of England, Wales and Northern Ireland

Civil cases in England, Wales and Northern Ireland are dealt with in county courts, heard by a judge or district judge. They deal with a wide range of cases and including landlord and tenant disputes, consumer disputes, personal injury claims, race, sex and disability discrimination cases and debt and employment problems.

Criminal cases are heard in magistrates' courts by justices of the peace (magistrates), who are unqualified and who are paid only expenses, or by district judges who receive payment. In Northern Ireland, cases are heard by paid magistrates only.

All criminal cases start in the magistrates' court. Some go on to the Crown Court for trial by jury, while others – known as summary offences – are dealt with only in the magistrates court. Some offences allow the defendant to elect whether their case is heard in the magistrates' court or in the Crown Court before a jury. The decision to prosecute in criminal cases is taken by the Crown Prosecution Service (CPS) in England and Wales, and by the Director of Public Prosecutions in Northern Ireland.

The Crown Court deals with more serious criminal offences, appeals from the magistrates court, and convictions in the magistrates court that are referred to the Crown Court for sentencing.

The High Court deals with civil cases and hears appeals in criminal cases. It also has the power to review the actions of individuals or organisations to make sure they have acted legally and justly.

The Court of Appeal deals with civil and criminal appeals from the High Court and the county court.

The House of Lords is the highest court of appeal and tends to deal mainly with appeals from the Court of Appeal, or direct from the High Court, where the case involves a point that is law of general public importance.

The Scottish Judicature

Scotland's legal system is separate from the English system, and it differs widely from it in many respects. The Lord Advocate is the head of the public prosecution system who are is independent of the police. The police have no say in the decision to prosecute.

Scotland is divided into six sheriffdoms which are themselves divided into sheriff court districts. Sheriff courts are the lowest criminal courts, in which legally-qualified sheriffs may either sit with a jury of 15 members to try more serious cases or, sitting alone, may try less serious cases under summary procedure. Minor summary offences are dealt with in district courts presided over by lay justices of the peace or, in Glasgow, by stipendiary magistrates.

More serious matters will be heard at the High Court of Justiciary, which is also where cases go for appeal. These cases are tried by a High Court judge sitting with a jury of 15, in Edinburgh or on circuit in other towns.

Prosecutions in the High Court are prepared by the Crown Office and conducted in court by a solicitor advocate. In the inferior courts the decision to prosecute is made by lawyers called procurators fiscal, subject to the directions of the Crown Office.

European Courts

In cases where legislation has not been implemented properly by a national government, where there is confusion over its interpretation, or if it has been ignored, a case may be referred to the European Court of Justice (ECJ), based in Luxembourg. The European Court of Human Rights, based in Strasbourg, deals with cases in which a person thinks their human rights have been contravened and for which there is no legal remedy within the national legal system.

Useful Contacts
Her Majesty's Courts Service: 020 7189 2000 or 0845 456 8770; www.hmcourts-service.gov.uk
Crown Prosecution Service: 020 7796 8000; www.cps.gov.uk
Scottish Court Service: 013 129 9200; www.scotcourts.gov.uk
Crown Office and Procurator Fiscal Service: 0131 226 2626; www.crownoffice.gov.uk
Northern Ireland Court Service: 028 9032 8594; www.courtsni.gov.uk
Public Prosecutions Service (N.I.): 028 9054 2444; www.cjsni.gov.uk

Working In Britain

■ THE EMPLOYMENT MARKET

Employment rates in Britain are currently very high, with around 75% of people of working age in employment. This equates to over 29 million, the highest level since comparable records began in 1971.

The unemployment rate was 5.5% at the end of 2006, which was up just slightly over the year, signs that there might just be the start of a downturn in the economy.

This 'headline' rate of British unemployment disguises differences between regions and between the sexes. There has been an ongoing increase in women's employment as more take on full-time and part-time jobs rather than, and a corresponding fall in male employment, especially among the over-50s. There are also wide differences between regions: in Spring 2005 the UK unemployment rate was 4.7%, with the highest rate in London (7.2%) and the lowest rate in the south west (3.4%). In Scotland, Northern Ireland and Wales the unemployment rates were 5.7%, 4.9% and 4.5% respectively.

Despite high employment rates, there are some sectors which often have difficulties filling job vacancies, for a variety of reasons. Employers

estimate that 17% of all vacancies are due to skill shortages in the labour market. Sectors with particular difficulties in recruiting include the construction and building engineering industries, environmental and land-based industries, hospitality and tourism services and social care employers. Construction and hospitality and tourism alone account for almost a fifth of skills-shortage vacancies.

The National Federation of Builders estimates that 430,000 additional construction workers will be required up to 2009. The National Health Service has been plagued for years by shortages of skilled staff. In addition to having difficulties satisfying requirements for doctors and nurses, there is also a need for occupational therapists, physiotherapists, dentists, and pharmacists. Veterinary surgeons too are in short supply, as are teachers.

■ SOURCES OF JOBS

Employment Service

The UK Employment Service runs Jobcentres which can be found in most towns in Britain. Here you will find advertisements for a wide range of job vacancies in that particular area. You can also register your details with the Jobcentre, who should then ensure that you are sent details of any relevant vacancies as they arise. Employers may advertise jobs for free in Jobcentres, so it is a good place to start job-hunting if you are already in the UK.

Useful Contacts
The address of your local Jobcentre is in the local phone book. Alternatively, contact.
Jobcentre Plus: 0845 6060 234; www.jobcentreplus.gov.uk
European Job Mobility Portal: Job huntes from the EU can visit http://europa.eu.int/eures

Newspapers

Job vacancies are advertised in local and national newspapers. They often have a specific jobs supplement once a week, in some cases related to specific professions. *The Times Educational Supplement* (TES), for example, lists teaching and academic vacancies. Online versions of newspapers also have job vacancies advertised – see the *Internet* below for details of some.

Professional and Trade Publications

There are over 4,000 UK trade, technical and professional publications, which are a good place to look for job vacancies in specific fields. Names and addresses of these publications can be found in *Willings Press Guide and Benn's Media Directory*, which are available in libraries. There are also many magazines on sale in newsagents, aimed at a more general readership, some of which include job advertisements. If your experience lies in the IT field, for example, take a look at the plethora of computer and internet publications. The main ones are listed in *The Writers' & Artists' Yearbook* and *The Writers Handbook*. These can be purchased online through Amazon (www.amazon.com, or www.amazon.co.uk).

UK professional and trade bodies (see details above) should also be able to point you in the direction of publications carrying job vacancies.

The Internet

A very effective way of finding UK vacancies from abroad is, of course, the internet. There is a large number of websites including job databases searchable by type of job and/or geographical area. Some of them also allow you to input your own details, so you can be emailed about suitable vacancies as they arise, and so that potential employers may even come direct to you.

Here is just a selection of such sites, but if you search for 'jobs uk', you should find many more.

- **All Jobs:** 0870 7460400; www.alljobsuk.com
- **Guardian Jobs:** http://jobs.guardian.co.uk
- **Jobs.ac.uk:** Jobs in research, science, academic, and related professions. www.jobs.ac.uk
- **Jobserve:** www.jobserve.com
- **Recruitment UK:** www.recruitmentuk.net
- **Telegraph.co.uk:** http://jobs.telegraph.co.uk/
- **Times Online:** http://jobs.timesonline.co.uk/Jobs

Employment Agencies

Private employment agencies take on the job of matching job vacancies to applicants. Some deal with general vacancies, some specialise in temporary workers to cover for holiday, sickness and maternity vacancies at short notice (generally known as temp agencies), and others deal with recruitment in specific areas, such as IT, or with professional and executive posts.

One of the biggest employment agencies in the UK is Manpower Employment *Services:* www.manpower.co.uk. Another nationwide employment agency is Reed: www.reed.co.uk.

There are many employment agencies which only advertise jobs in their local areas while others which specialise in specific types of job. Details of local and national agencies can be found on the directory and listings website www.yell.com.

Company Transfers

Although companies seldom recruit with the idea of international transfer in mind, it may be worth applying for a job in your home country which has branches or subsidiaries in Britain. If the idea of working in Britain is one you

> I would certainly recommend working in Britain to other Canadians, although I have to say many of them have a somewhat romantic view of 'the olde country' (a term they would never use) and would find living and job-hunting in London more stressful than they had anticipated.
>
> Susan Griffith

hope to pursue via the company it may be worth discussing at the initial interview. Then at least both sides know where they stand. Multinational companies with offices or subsidiaries in Britain can be found in directories of companies such as *Who Owns Whom*, available in libraries. Some are listed at the end of this chapter in the *Directory of Major Employers*.

Job Wanted

Another approach to try is to place advertisements in the British press or on the internet ideally in the area(s) in which you would prefer to live, detailing your qualifications and experience and the sort of job you are looking for. This gives employers the opportunity to approach you instead of vice versa.

The internet is becoming a highly effective means of letting employers that know you are in the job market. You can place your details on one of a number of databases, which can be searched by potential employers who are on the lookout for new talent.

■ TEMPORARY WORK

Tourism

Tourism is a sector providing many temporary jobs. Hotels, bars and restaurants need temporary workers during the summer season, particularly in tourist areas. Holiday camps, activity centres and theme parks are also fruitful areas for short-term work. Board and lodging may be included as an element of the wage. Outdoor activities, including hiking, skiing, nature study, and various sporting activities, fishing and golf in particular, are popular with tourists, and there are opportunities for temporary employment in all these fields.

Useful Contacts

Temporary jobs are advertised by a number of online recruitment agencies.

Jobsword: www.jobsword.co.uk/hospitality.html
Jobs1: www.jobs1.co.uk/directory/recruitment_leisure.html

Working as an Au Pair

There are numerous agencies arranging to put au pairs and nannies in touch with those who wish to employ them. They can be found very easily on the internet, by searching for 'au pairs'.

Useful Contacts

Au Pair World: +49 5603 917817; www.aupair-world.net

Almondbury Au Pair and Nanny Agency: 01803 380795; www.aupair-agency.com

Nannyjob: www.nannyjob.co.uk

Agriculture and Fishing

During the summer months, fruit and vegetable pickers are required on farms. Fish farms may take on extra workers at various times of year, particularly when the fish are being harvested.

Useful Contacts

Land-Force.Com: Land-based jobs online. 0870 770 1107; www.land-force.com

Total Jobs: www.totaljobs.com

Secretarial and Clerical

Temporary clerical and secretarial work can be found throughout the year. It generally requires you to be available at short notice, in order to cover for permanent employees on leave of various kinds. It is a good idea to register with private 'temping' or job agencies. Addresses can be found in the local phone book or at the Jobcentre. Good word-processing skills are much in demand for such jobs.

Useful Contacts

Agency Central: Database of recruitment agencies. www.agencycentral.co.uk

Tip Top Job: www.tiptopjob.com

Total Jobs: www.totaljobs.com/administrative

Teaching

Supply Teaching

Qualified teachers who do not wish to work full-time can sign on with their local authority as supply teachers to cover for absent staff. This may involve you in the odd few days here and there, or in full-time cover for a number of months while a permanent teacher is absent on long-term sickness or maternity leave. Supply teachers must be registered with the General Teaching Council for the relevant county.

Further information, resources and links can be found on the government website www.teachernet.gov.uk/supplyteachers

Teaching English

There are opportunities, for teaching England as a foreign language (TEFL) in the UK. There are companies running language summer schools, for example, for foreigners wishing to learn the language, for example. Your own standard of English would have to be high to be suitable for such posts so ideally English would be your mother tongue. You would, in most cases, also be expected to have completed a TEFL or equivalent training course – there are details of these on the websites listed below, as well as job vacancies.

Useful Contacts

British Council Teaching English: www.teachingenglish.org.uk
Saxoncourt Training and Recruitment: 020 7491 1911;
www.saxoncourt.com
TEFL.com: 0709 216 5424; www.tefl.com

Shop Work

Temporary shop work is often available in tourist areas during the summer months which are one of their busiest periods. In the towns, supermarkets and other high street stores see their peak sales during the run up to Christmas, and often take on temporary staff during this busy period.

Useful Contacts

Job Site: www.jobsite.co.uk/retail
Jobs in Retail: www.jobsinretail.co.uk
Retail Careers: www.retailcareers.co.uk

Factory Work

There may be seasonal demand for temporary labour in food processing factories. They tend to be busiest during the summer when freshly picked foods need to be canned or frozen quickly. Confectionery firms take on extra staff in the late summer, when they start increased production in the time for Christmas. Approach the personnel departments of factories to enquire about such opportunities.

Jim Finder: www.jimfinder.com
Total Jobs: www.totaljobs.com/manufacturing
Work Gateways: www.workgateways.com

Research

Research assistants in all disciplines are required from time to time at educational institutions, for those suitably qualified. Current requirements are advertised in the TES, local and national newspapers and can also be accessed direct from universities or via their websites.

Useful Contacts

Seltek, Clinical Research Jobs: 01784 473823;
www.clinicalresearchjobs.co.uk
Jobs in Research, Science and Academic Professions: 024 7657 2839;
www.jobs.ac.uk
Times Higher Education Supplement: 020 7782 3000;
www.thesjobs.co.uk/research_jobs.htm

Voluntary Work

While you are studying, looking for paid employment, or even while travelling around Britain, there are many opportunities for voluntary work with charities who are always looking for willing helpers. In some cases, you may be entitled to some pocket money or travelling expenses while working for a voluntary project.

The rules about foreigners taking voluntary work are the same as for paid work. People from the EEA can take voluntary work without any restrictions. If you have a student visa you can volunteer part-time, provided that you work less than 20 hours a week during term time, and no more than 40 hours a week in holidays.

If you are not a student but wish to do full-time voluntary work in the UK for up to one year, you can apply for a volunteer's visa. You can receive travel expenses, a small amount of pocket money, and possibly food and accommodation. You will need a letter from the charity that you will work for, and you will need to prove that you have enough money to live.

If you are already in the UK and are a non-visa national you can apply to extend your visa to work as a volunteer by completing the form FLR(O), which can be downloaded from the website of the Immigration and Nationality Directory: www.ind.homeoffice.gov.uk.

Most UK charities have their own websites where you will find volunteering opportunities advertised. Charity shops are common in towns across Britain and these are always looking for volunteers to help out – just call in and ask.

Useful Contacts
UK Charities Directory: www.charitychoice.co.uk
Direct Gov: www.direct.gov.uk Government website with advice and online search facility for volunteering opportunities.
Time Bank: 0845 456 1668; www.timebank.org.uk
Volunteering England: 0845 305 6979; www.volunteering.org.uk

■ PERMANENT WORK

Professional & Executive

There are a wide range of opportunities available for anyone with professional or vocational qualifications, such as lawyers, architects and engineers. As well as positions which arise within professional practices, large companies such as those in the oil industry, for instance, need professionals to work 'in house'. Local authorities also have their own departments dealing with legal matters, planning departments need qualified surveyors and architects, and so forth.

These jobs are advertised in a variety of places: professional associations have their own journals; local authorities advertise vacancies in the local

press and on their websites; there are agencies dealing specifically with executive recruitment; recruitment newspapers and websites also carry advertisements for such positions. Most high prestige and high salary jobs are advertised in the quality newspapers such as *The Times* and *The Telegraph*.

Professional qualifications are not always transferable across the border. Because of the different legal systems in different parts of the UK, lawyers have to retrain to work under the Scottish or Northern Ireland systems. Salaries for executive and professional posts tend to be lower in the UK than elsewhere in Europe and in the US. Posts in London are likely to attract higher remuneration than those in other regions – however, it also costs a lot more to live in London, so your disposable income may not be much different.

Civil Service

The Civil Service is one of the largest employers in the UK, employing around 542,000 people in over 60 departments and 100 executive agencies. Civil Servants work for the Crown and perform their functions through the elected Government of the day, while remaining politically impartial. All posts in the Civil Service carry nationality requirements. The three-quarters of posts classed as 'non-reserved' are open to Commonwealth and EEA nationals. 'Reserved' posts are only open for applications from UK nationals, a category which includes British citizens, some Irish and Indian citizens with dual nationality, and British Dependent Territories citizens acquiring their citizenship from connection with Gibraltar. The Diplomatic Service only takes entrants who are British citizens.

Graduates can enter the Civil Service through the 'Fast Stream Development Programme'; 01276 400333; www.faststream.gov.uk.

Entry as Junior Managers can also be made through Departmental Recruitment schemes. In addition there are short-term placements for graduates through sandwich course placements, vacation employment and vacation visits. For more on these, see *Temporary Work*. Non-graduates with suitable qualifications may apply to enter Departmental and Agency recruitment schemes. Vacancies are advertised on the Civil Service website, as well as in the press, relevant professional journals and Jobcentres. See www.careers.civil-service.gov.uk. Experienced professionals are also welcomed in Civil Service roles at various levels. Again, application would be made for specific advertised vacancies.

Most recruitment is carried out by individual departments and agencies. Advertisements for posts are placed in national newspapers as well as local and/or specialist press. University careers services and Jobcentres may also hold details of recruitment schemes. For government departments in specific geographical areas, see the local phone book.

Financial and Business Services

Insurance, banking and finance is the strongest sector in the British economy. London is one of the largest financial centres in the world,

and Edinburgh is also a big player in the field, being one of Europe's top cities for finance services. Many large finance companies have their head offices in these two cities and in others around Britain. There are also dozens of smaller investment trusts, insurance companies and others supplying business services based in cities around the UK.

There are high salaries on offer for good workers in the financial institutions, particularly among the city traders in London. In addition, record annual bonuses have recently been paid to high achievers in the financial services industry.

Useful Websites

Jobs Board: www.insurancejobsboard.com
The following sites have links to a wide number of specialist business and finance recruiters:
Jobs1: www.jobs1.co.uk
JobsWord: www.jobsword.co.uk
City Jobs: www.cityjobs.com. Allows you to add your CV so vacancies can be emailed to you.

Administrative

Those with good secretarial and clerical skills, and to a lesser extent those with administrative experience, should have no difficulty finding a job in Britain. The local authorities are among the biggest employers in the country and have a high demand for such skills.

Jobs can be found in the local and national press, in recruitment newspapers, in Jobcentres, on local authority websites, and the websites of other organisations. For instance the National Health Service has a need for administrators, and posts may be advertised on their websites. General recruitment websites also have sections listing administrative opportunities.

> I had only been to Edinburgh once before, on a school trip, but moving over for what was meant to be a six-month period did not hold any real worries or fears. I had just finished an 18-month stint in the eastern US, so being comparatively close to home, with the promise of frequent work trips back to Dublin, softened the pill. Now, several years after those six months elapsed, I'm still here – how did that happen?
>
> Bob Grayson

Medical

The 21st century is a good time to get into the National Health Service (NHS) in Britain. After years of under-funding leading to an inevitable decline in standards and conditions of work, with many health professionals leaving the NHS in favour of work with better pay and conditions, the Labour Government has addressed the issues and has put extra money into the health service. Consequently, there has been record growth of around 7% per year in the past five years, with a rise of £8 billion of funding in England alone during 2007-2008. Much of the extra money has been and will continue to be spent on increased numbers of doctors, nurses and other staff.

Vacancies within the NHS are generally advertised on an area by area basis, so the best way to find out about what is currently available is to contact the local health board or NHS Trust. Information about job vacancies in particular areas is be available from the websites of the regional primary care organisations and hospital trusts – you'll find links to all the regional sites via the main NHS website for each member country of the UK. Full details are below:

England: www.nhs.uk
Scotland: www.show.scot.nhs.uk
Wales: www.wales.nhs.uk
Northern Ireland: www.healthandcareni.co.uk

Useful Resources

The following medical publications are available by subscription. Their websites may also carry current job vacancies.

British Journal of General Practice: 0845 456 4041; www.rcgp.org.uk
British Medical Journal: 020 7383 6270; www.bmj.com
Nursing Times: 0870 830 4964; www.nursingtimes.net
The Practising Midwife: 01752 312140; www.roundash.com/practisingmidwife

> There are also jobs websites with specific healthcare listings, advertising job opportunities within the NHS and the private sector. One with a comprehensive selection regularly advertised is www.medic8.com/MedicalJobs.htm

Teaching

There are around 509,000 teachers employed in the public sector in the UK. Although the private education sector is comparatively small, there are also job opportunities there. In reality, one of the easiest ways for overseas teachers to get into the education system is through supply and part-time teaching, although permanent vacancies do exist, particularly in the areas of science and mathematics.

All teachers in publicly maintained schools (i.e. those run by local authorities) must be registered with the General Teaching Council (GTC) for England, Wales, Scotland or Northern Ireland as appropriate. Registration is a requirement for teaching in all local authority nursery, primary, secondary, and special schools in the UK. If you are registered to work as a teacher in Scotland or Northern Ireland you are not eligible to work in England and Wales (or vice versa) until you have been approved by and registered with the relevant GTC. Similarly, if you have worked in the independent sector in the UK, you must be registered with the relevant GTC before you can work in a state school. For full details of the process in each GTC (they vary slightly) see the websites (details below).

Only graduates are accepted as entrants to the teaching profession. They are eligible for registration as primary teachers if they have gained an ordinary or honours degree at any UK university plus a one-year full-time postgraduate course (or equivalent) at a teacher education institution, provided their training related to the primary curriculum (3-12 age range).

EU Nationals who are recognised as teachers in any European Member State are eligible for registration in Britain provided that the course of teacher education leading to such recognition was of not less than three years' duration. Such teachers may initially be registered conditional on completing an aptitude test or period of adaptation.

Teachers qualified outside the EU should have qualifications which would have entitled them to university entry in their own country. They should also have completed a period of higher education at a university or equivalent institution of at least three years' duration leading to an acceptable degree, as determined by the UK National Academic Recognition Centre (NARIC). To be eligible for teaching in the secondary sector, applicants must have studied at least one academic subject in considerable depth over a substantial period of time. Those whose first language is not English must satisfy the GTC as to their proficiency in English.

All teachers wishing to work full time in England and Wales must apply for Qualified Teacher Status (QTS). The same regulations do not apply in Scotland and Northern Ireland, although in practice, the GTC Scotland and NI pre-qualification requirements amount to the same thing. But in practice, if you are coming to England or Wales to teach permanently, you will need to obtain QTS within four years of arrival. You can gain QTS by enrolling on the employment-based OTT (Overseas Trained Teacher) programme of study which allows you to become qualified while you work. Visit the training ad development agency for schools website at www.tda.gov.uk for more information.

Useful Contacts

General Teaching Council for England: 0870 01 0308; www.gtce.org.uk
General Teaching Council for Northern Ireland: 028 9033 3390; www.gtcni.org.uk
General Teaching Council for Scotland: 0131 314 6000; www.gtcs.org.uk
General Teaching Council for Wales: 029 2055 0350; www.gtcw.org.uk

Teaching vacancies are advertised in the *Times Educational Supplement* (TES): 020 7782 3000; www.tes.co.uk. They are also advertised in local newspapers and can be obtained directly from local authority education departments. They may be accessible through local authority websites. For a full list of addresses, see General Introduction. For jobs in the private sector, contact the schools direct, or see TES. The recruitment website Jobsword lists teaching vacancies; www.jobsword.co.uk/teaching.html

Academia

Historically, academics in the UK have been generally lower paid than their counterparts in other European countries and, particularly, in the USA and Canada. However, a recently negotiated national pay rate has been introduced for staff in higher education, and now UK academic salaries compare well with most other relevant comparator countries (except perhaps the US), and there has been significant improvement in starting salaries for academic staff in recent years.

Academic posts are advertised in the Times Educational Supplement (TES), a weekly newspaper for the education profession and in national and local newspapers. They can also be obtained by applying directly to the institutions or through their websites. (See list of university addresses in *Daily Life*.)

Terms used for equivalent academic posts vary between countries, and also between the UK Universities and UK 'new' Universities (these were originally the polytechnics). Even more confusing, the oldest universities such as Oxford and Cambridge use their own arcane systems.

Computers and IT

There has been a massive expansion in the opportunities for employment within the computing and information technology sectors. With the rapid growth in company and domestic access to the internet since the late 1990s, there seems to be an insatiable demand for those with expertise in the area. Jobs are available for those with computer knowledge and qualifications

to work on the computer infrastructure within traditional companies; to work within hi-tech companies; to join website design companies; and to work in the computer hardware and software development, production and supply sectors. Of the dozens of internet access providers, and the many computer hardware and software producers and suppliers, the vast majority have telephone and online 'Help Centres' which need technically qualified operatives to assist with the constant queries from those less computer literate.

IT job vacancies can be found in all the usual sources of information. For obvious reasons, there are thousands of IT jobs advertised on the internet, in online recruitment agencies and newsletters as well on the websites of large companies who need in-house staff.

Because of the nature of computer and internet work, allowing remote working, there may be relatively more jobs outside the main centres of population than will be found in other industries. In rural areas, computers and the internet are becoming increasingly essential for domestic users and small businesses. These people have difficulty accessing expert assistance when their computer crashes, so those with such skills in rural areas are much in demand.

Useful Websites

Cerco IT Recruitment: 0500 828274; www.cercoitrecruitment.co.uk
Computing Careers: www.computingcareers.co.uk
Planet Recruit: www.planetrecruit.com/IT
Purely IT: www.purelyit.co.uk. Jobs vacancies plus the facility to upload your CV.

Police Service

Applicants to British police forces must be a British Citizen, a citizen of the EEA, or a Commonwealth citizen or foreign national with indefinite leave to remain in the UK. They must be not less than 18 and must have a good standard of physical fitness. There is now no minimum height requirement.

Although no formal qualifications are required, you must complete various written and other tests as well as one or more interviews, if you pass the test. New recruits are taken on as uniformed constables who serve a probationary period which includes training courses and basic duties.

Selection for promotion depends on ability and merit, and officers will not be considered for promotion until they have passed the appropriate qualifying examination which they may sit after completing their probationary period satisfactorily. Graduate entrants and serving officers who display high potential for high rank may be accepted on an accelerated promotion scheme (this goes under different names in different regions of the UK). Further details are available from the recruiting departments of the various forces.

Vacancies for police officers vary from force to force: at any one time some will have no vacancies while others may be having a recruitment drive. From time to time a force may run a Recruitment Fair in their area, with the aim of publicising the police as a career and attracting new entrants.

In England, Wales and Scotland, applications should be made to the Recruiting Department of a specific force. Check the vacancies and eligibility criteria for each force before applying as these may vary. In Northern Ireland recruitment is handled by an independent body, 'Consensia'.

For links to recruitment for all UK police forces, start at www.police.uk/recruitment.asp.

Oil and Gas Industry

The UK oil and gas industry is located mainly off the east coast of Scotland and England, but fields have also been developed in the Irish Sea, west of the Shetland Islands, and in the English Channel. About 18,000 people work offshore on a regular basis on fixed production platforms, mobile drilling rigs, or floating production storage and offloading units. The industry provides three quarters of the UK's primary energy and employs 380,000 people both offshore and onshore. Aberdeen in the north of Scotland has grown rich on the oil and gas fields in the North Sea and the bulk of jobs in the industry are based there. However, there is also a demand for workers in other areas of the country.

Useful Websites

The Grampian Oil and Gas Directory: www.oilandgas.co.uk. Online information about Scottish-based providers of products and services to the industry, and links to their websites.

Association of British Offshore Industries: 0171 928 9199; www.maritimeindustries.org/about/aboi.jsp

Oilcareers: Information about and vacancies in the industry. www.oilcareers.com

Tourism

Tourism is an important sector in the British economy, with the UK being ranked as the sixth major tourist destination in the world and attracting over 27 million tourists per year. It employs about 28 million people in various capacities. Many of these jobs are seasonal, but today tourism in the UK is pretty much year-round, so there are many opportunities for permanent jobs in the industry, and also for setting up small tourism businesses. The tourism industry is highly fragmented, with a large number of small businesses. It is estimated there are around 125,000 businesses in total, 80% of which have a turnover of less than £250,000 per annum. Around three million people are self-employed within the industry.

Businesses involved in the industry to a greater or lesser extent include:

- Hotels and other tourist accommodation.
- Restaurants, cafes, etc.
- Bars, public houses and night-clubs.
- Travel agencies and tour operators.
- Libraries, museums and other cultural activities.
- Sports and other recreation activities.

The various tourist boards employ a substantial number of staff, while hotels, bars and restaurants need staff year round. Efforts have been made over recent years to increase the length of the holiday season, and spring, autumn and winter breaks are now more popular than they were in the past. This means that visitor attractions and other services are busier for longer periods during the year, with implications for employment.

Tourist Boards

Enjoy England: 020 8846 9000; www.enjoyengland.com
Visit Wales: 08708 300306; www.visitwales.co.uk
Visit Scotland: 01463 716996; www.visitscotland.com
Northern Ireland Tourist Board: 028 9024 6609;
www.discovernorthernireland.com

Agriculture and Fishing

The agriculture sector in the UK is fairly small, and being highly mechanised, there is not a huge demand for agricultural workers on a permanent basis. The sector is also characterised by lack of job security, with the vast majority of jobs being short-term contracts.

Fish farming, particularly of salmon, provides many jobs in Scotland, but the industry is contracting from its peak, due to competition from elsewhere in Europe, Norway in particular. Fish farms do provide an important source of jobs in the Highlands and Islands, but they tend to employ local people, so there are not many openings for those who have just moved to the area.

Sea fishing is in decline throughout the country, with many life-long fishermen leaving the industry. Declining fish stocks, together with stringent European fish quotas designed to protect stocks of some species and allow others to recover to previous levels, have had a serious effect on the numbers employed.

Useful Contacts

Land-Force.Com: Land-based jobs online. 0870-770 1107;
www.land-force.com
Total Jobs: www.totaljobs.com/Jobseeking/AgricultureFishingForestry_f3.html

Construction

The construction industry in Britain provides employment to a large workforce of skilled and unskilled workers. Again, they suffer from lack of job security and wages are generally low. Most workers are on short-term contracts, liable to be laid off by their employer at the end of a project, to be re-hired when a new construction project comes along. However, there is a skills shortage within the construction industry, so skilled tradespeople stand a good chance of getting jobs with building firms. There is a constant demand for housing throughout Britain, so there are always new housing projects on the go in all areas. Run-down city centre areas are being transformed with prestigious new developments of residential, office, retail, and leisure premises so the demand for construction workers will remain high for some years to come, especially as London builds for the 2012 Olympics.

Recent efforts to repopulate rural areas, made possible by new technology which allows more people to work in remote areas and transact business across the internet, have brought about a growth in new housing. Councils are also putting money into renovating semi-derelict traditional houses in rural communities and providing affordable housing to help to address the housing shortage for lower income families in such areas. Architects, planners, builders, and other tradespeople all benefit from the increased workload.

Useful Contacts

Careers in Construction: www.careersinconstruction.com
Construction Industry Jobs Board: 01323 872810;
www.constructor.co.uk
Constructions Skills: 01582 727462; www.bconstructive.co.uk
Contract Journal: 020 8652 4805; www.contractjournal.com

Environment

With hundreds of thousands of hectares of Britain protected under various environmental designations, the environment sector is a large provider of employment. There are 4,900 organisations in the environmental conservation sector, employing over 56,000 people. The vast majority of these jobs are in the public sector, and there is also a significant number in the voluntary sector, accounting together for four out of five jobs in the industry. Many are temporary jobs, for people working on short-term projects. For further details on these opportunities, see *Temporary Work*.

Useful Contacts

Lantra: The Sector Skills council for the environmental and land-based sector; 024 7669 6996; www.lantra.co.uk

Scottish Natural Heritage: 01463 725000; www.snh.org.uk

Media and Creative Arts

The massive expansion in the entertainment and leisure industry over recent years means there are plenty of opportunities for employment with the media and arts in the UK. There are many new digital TV and radio channels all needing programming to fill them and people to work on those programmes. The explosion in the number of websites on the world wide web has brought about a huge demand for journalists, writers and designers for them. The digital arts too are becoming bigger and more sophisticated – in particular, computer game design and production, an industry which needs, in addition to IT people, composers and writers to provide the stories and music.

In the more traditional, less high tech, creative field, there are also hundreds of permanent theatres and touring companies throughout the UK which can provide interesting and stimulating opportunities, even if the earnings may not always be high.

Useful Contacts

Journalism.co.uk: Print and online vacancies. 01273 384293; www.journalism.co.uk

Formula Won: Media recruitment. 020 7987 1422; www formula-won.co.uk

Jobs in the Arts and Entertainment: www.careers-guide.com/arts-jobs.htm

◼ PROFESSIONAL AND TRADE BODIES

Advice on the requirements of specific professions may also be obtained from their Professional Associations. This is a selection of the professional and trade bodies for Britain.

Professional Bodies

Association of Chartered Certified Accountants: 0141 582 2000; www.accaglobal.com

Booksellers Association: 020 7802 0802; www.booksellers.org.uk

British Hospitality Association: 020 7404 7744; www.bha.org.uk

British Medical Association: 020 7387 4499; www.bma.org.uk

British Veterinary Association: 020 7636 6541; www.bva.co.uk

Chartered Institute of Building: 01344 630700; www.ciob.org.uk

Chartered Institute of Marketing: 01628 427500; www.cim.co.uk

Chartered Society of Designers: 020 7357 8088; www.csd.org.uk

Civil Engineering Contractors Association: 020 7227 4620; www.ceca.co.uk

Confederation of British Industry: 020 7379 7400.; www.cbi.org.uk

Federation of Master Builders: 020 7242 7583; www.fmb.org.uk

Federation of Small Businesses: 01253 336000; www.fsb.org.uk

Freight Transport Association: 08717112222; www.fta.co.uk

General Teaching Council for England: 0870 010308; www.gtce.org.uk

General Teaching Council for Northern Ireland: 028 9033 3390; www.gtcni.org.uk

General Teaching Council for Scotland: 0131 314 6000; www.gtcs.org.uk

General Teaching Council for Wales: 029 2055 0350; www.gtcw.org.uk

Institute of Chartered Accountants in England and Wales: 020 7920 8100; www.icaew.co.uk

Institute of Chartered Accountants of Scotland: 0131 347 0100; www.icas.org.uk

Institute of Chartered Accountants in Ireland: 028 9032 1600; www.icai.ie

Law Society of England & Wales: 020 7242 1222; www.lawsociety.org.uk

Law Society of Northern Ireland: 028 9023 1614; www.lawsoc-ni.org

Law Society of Scotland: 0131 226 7411; www.lawscot.org.uk

National Farmers Union: 024 7685 8500; www.nfu.org.uk

Offshore Contractors' Association: 01224 326070; www.ocaonline.co.uk

Royal College of General Practitioners: 0845 456 4041; www.rcgp.org.uk

Royal College of Nursing: 020 7409 3333; www.rcn.org.uk

Association of Consultant Architects: 020 8325 1402; www.acarchitects.co.uk

Royal Institution of Chartered Surveyors: 0870 333 1600; www.rics.org.uk

Royal Pharmaceutical Society: 020 7735 9141; www.rpsgb.org.uk

Society of Indexers: 0114 244 9561; www.indexers.org.uk

Trade Unions

Workers in Britain have the right to belong to a trade union relevant to their particular line of work, and it is unlawful for employers to penalise individuals for being – or, indeed, for not being – trade union members. Trade unions exist to represent the rights of employees, to ensure they have the most favourable conditions of work and levels of pay, and that they are not treated unreasonably or unfairly by their employers. Trade union members may ask to be represented by their trade union in any grievance with their employers.

The umbrella organisation for trade unions in Britain is the Trades Union Congress (TUC), which in 2007 consisted of 62 unions with a combined membership of nearly 6.5 million people. The TUC helps its member unions to promote membership in new areas and industries and campaigns for rights at work for all employees, including part-time and temporary workers.

For certain trades and professions, those who have completed the required training and examinations will be entitled to join the association representing them. Such associations act in a similar way to trade unions, representing the rights and conditions of service of their members, as well as representing the profession as a whole at government level.

Many employers' associations are affiliated to the Confederation Of British Industry (CBI) which represents around 250,000 companies in Britain, and works to bring the problems of British business to the attention of the Government, which in turn consults it on relevant matters.

Trades Union Congress (TUC): 020 7636 4030; www.tuc.org.uk

These are some of the largest UK unions:

AMICUS: (Members include manufacturing, banking, NHS staff.) 020 7420 8900; www.amicustheunion.org

Associated Society of Locomotive Engineers and Firemen (ASLEF): 020 7317 8600; www.aslef.org.uk

Association of Teachers and Lecturers (ATL): 020 7930 6441; www.atl.org.uk

Communication Workers Union (CWU): 020 8971 7200; www.cwu.org

Educational Institute of Scotland (EIS): 0131 225 6244; www.eis.org.uk

GMB: Britain's General Union. 020 8947 3131; www.gmb.org.uk

Musicians' Union: 0202 7582 5566; www.musiciansunion.org.uk

National Association of Schoolmasters/Union of Women Teachers (NASUWT): 020 7420 9670; www.teachersunion.org.uk

National Union of Journalists (NUJ): 0120 7278 7916; www.nuj.org.uk

Prospect: Union of Engineers, Scientists, Managers, and Specialists; 020 7902 6600: www.prospect.org.uk

Transport and General Workers' Union (T&G): 020 7611 2500; www.tgwu.org.uk

Union of Construction, Allied Trades and Technicians (UCATT): 020 7622 2442; www.ucatt.org.uk
Union of Shop, Distributive and Allied Workers (USDAW): 0161 224 2804; www.usdaw.org.uk
UNISON: Public sector staff; 0845 355 0845; www.unison.org.uk

■ SKILLS AND QUALIFICATIONS

When moving to the UK to take up a job with a work permit, you must have proof that you have the skills and qualifications appropriate for that job. Although your qualifications may be fine for that kind of job in your home country, it cannot necessarily be assumed that they will be recognised in the UK, so you and your potential employer need to ascertain whether they are acceptable or whether further examinations or training periods need to be taken. Because there exists such a wide range of courses and diplomas, academic, professional and vocational, each qualification obtained in another country will be looked at on a case by case basis to see how it compares with those in the UK.

EEA Nationals

Within Europe, academic qualifications will be assessed through the auspices of the National Academic Recognition Information Centres (NARIC) which have been set up in all member states to co-ordinate the drawing up of certificates for the academic recognition of diplomas.

As far as professional and vocational training are concerned, the EU has passed directives to ensure that these qualifications, plus practical experience, gained in one member country are considered valid throughout the EEA. This is achieved through a system of compensatory measures to take into account the differences in length and content of the courses. As a general rule, this means that if your training was much shorter or the content of your course was very different to that required in the UK, you would be asked to pass an aptitude test or to undergo a period of supervised practice.

For a number of professions, training requirements in all member states have been harmonised, which means that your national qualifications should be recognised automatically in any other EU country, allowing you to practice there. These professions are doctors, general practitioners, dental practitioners, nurses, midwives, veterinary surgeons, architects, pharmacists, and lawyers.

Mutual recognition of other professional qualifications within the EU is also made in respect of 'regulated' professions (i.e. those whose practice is regulated by law, Government regulations, private chartered bodies or professional associations) which require the completion of a higher education course of at least three years, or the equivalent part-time duration, at a university or other higher education establishment. Any professional training required in addition to the education course should also have been completed.

In the UK, regulated professions include lawyers, accountants, engineers, teachers, surveyors, physiotherapists, chemists, technologists, geologists, psychologists, and shipbrokers. Where the education and training in the home country is at least one year shorter than that required in the UK, the professional organisation or authority regulating the profession may require additional practical experience of up to four years as a fully qualified professional. Where the content of the course was very different you may be required to take an aptitude test covering the main subjects not covered by your training. Alternatively, you may be required to follow a period of supervised practice of up to three years.

In the case of other qualifications and diplomas obtained in regulated professions, all member states must recognise these, together with professional experience in the home country, although aptitude tests and periods of supervised practice may be required.

For further details about professional qualifications, contact the relevant professional body in your own country or in the UK (see contact details below).

A number of jobs and trades are also recognised by EU member states, if the candidate can demonstrate professional experience elsewhere in the EU. In such cases, a Certificate of Experience can be issued by the home country showing that the individual has practical experience of between three and six years. These include self-employed work in the wholesale trade, in the manufacturing, processing, repair and construction industries, in providing food, drink or accommodation, in the wholesale coal trade, and in services relating to transport, travel agencies, storage and warehousing. Itinerant traders, insurance agents and brokers, hairdressers and those involved in various fishing, transport, post and telecommunications, recreational and community services can also be issued a Certificate of Experience.

Useful Websites

European Commission: Information about recognition and transparency of qualifications can be found at http://ec.europa.eu/education/policies/rec_qual/rec_qual_en.html

Europe Open for Professions: A website of the Department for Education & Skills (DfES) with information and guidance, plus lists and contact details of regulatory bodies. www.dfes.gov.uk/europeopen/index.shtml

Certificate of Experience: Information and advice plus online applications. There is a charge of £104.81 made. www.certex.org.uk

Nationals of Other Countries

There are no international standard agreements between the UK and countries outside Europe, so each case will be looked at and advice given on an individual basis. This service is provided to international students inquiring on their own behalf by the UK National Reference Point for Vocational Qualifications (NRP – www.uknrp.org.uk). Independent enquirers should forward a photocopy of their qualification certificate(s) together with transcript(s), a translation in English if necessary and a covering letter to NARIC. A Certificate of Comparability will be supplied where appropriate. There is a charge of £36 for this service; 0870 990 4088; www.uknrp.org.uk/pages/Services_for_Individuals_Seeking_Employment/comparability.asp

■ EMPLOYMENT REGULATIONS AND CONTRACTS

If you enter the UK as an employee, you may need a work permit in addition to your entry clearance or visa. There are, however a number of groups of people who do not need a permit to work in the UK.

Permit-Free Employment

EEA Nationals

Nationals of EEA countries (except for Bulgaria and Romania – see below) have the right to travel for the purposes of work between all member countries. They do not require any formal permission to enter the UK and there is no time limit put on their stay. Once here, they are free to stay to work or set up in business and do not need to apply for permission to do so at any time. However, if they wish, they may obtain a 'residence permit' from the Home Office as confirmation of their right of residence in the UK. It is not compulsory, but it is an official document which will prove the individual's identity and immigration status in the UK.

This is particularly useful if you wish to apply for permanent settlement in the UK. After four years, during which the applicant has been working or doing business for most of that time, an EU national may apply for permanent settlement. A residence permit can be useful proof that they are entitled to apply, but proof of continuous employment in the UK for four years may be sufficient to obtain settlement status.

I was contacted by a contract broker who asked if I was interested in working on a six month project at an international bank. I grabbed the chance to get some experience from working abroad.
Roberth Lindholm

Bulgarian or Romanian Nationals

Bulgarians and Romanians do not require leave to enter or reside in the UK. However, those wanting to work in the UK still need to obtain authorisation to work before starting any employment, unless they are exempt from doing so. Exemption is granted for the same employment categories as described below. In addition, they are exempt if they are coming to Britain under the Seasonal Agricultural Workers Scheme (SAWS) and they hold a valid work card issued by a SAWS operator.

Authorisation to work normally takes the form of an Accession Worker Card. The process for obtaining authorisation to work is in two stages:

- The UK employer first applies for approval of the employment under the work permit arrangements.
- The Bulgarian and Romanian national must then apply for an Accession Worker Card which remains valid for as long as he or she remains in the employment for which the card has been issued.
- There are some aspects of the standard work permit arrangements that are not relevant to Bulgarian or Romanian nationals. These include:
- Bulgarian and Romanian nationals are not subject to immigration control.
- UK employers are not required to inform the authorities of a Technical Change of Employment.
- There are no restrictions on them switching from one employment category into another employment category whilst in the UK (but if an individual changes jobs, their new employer must apply for another

letter of approval from Work Permits (UK) and the individual must apply for a new Accession Worker Card).

■ There are no restrictions on Bulgarian or Romanian nationals changing their status in the UK from a worker to a student, a self-employed person or a self-sufficient person.

Non-EEA Nationals

Commonwealth citizens over 17 and with a grandparent born in the UK are granted entry for a period of four years on arrival in the UK and do not need a work permit. This means that they can seek employment once they arrive.

In addition, there is no requirement for a work permit for those whose employment falls into one of the following categories:

■ A working holidaymaker or au pair.

■ A Minister of Religion, a missionary or a member of a religious order.

■ The representative of a firm with no representative in the UK.

■ A representative of an overseas newspaper, news agency or broadcasting organisation on long-term assignment to the UK.

■ A domestic worker of a member of the staff of a diplomatic or consular mission.

■ A domestic worker in a private household.

■ A teacher or language assistant coming to a UK school under an exchange scheme. A member of the operational ground staff of an overseas airline.

■ A postgraduate doctor or dentist coming for training.

■ A seasonal worker at an agricultural camp.

Work Permits

Work permits are issued by *Work Permits (UK)*, part of the Home Office, in relation to a specific individual and a particular job. Generally, work permits are only issued for jobs involving a high level of skill and experience for which no resident labour is available in the UK or elsewhere in the European Union. An exception may be made to enable overseas nationals to come to the UK for training or work experience.

Work permits are normally issued for a limited period of between six months and four years. The permit may be extended after this time if the employment continues. Permit holders may be allowed to settle in the UK once they have completed four years' continuous employment.

An individual cannot apply for a work permit on their own behalf. This has to be done by an employer in the UK who wants to employ you. Application forms are available from the *Immigration & Nationality Directorate:* 0870-606 7766. They can also be downloaded from www.workingintheuk.gov.uk.

Alternatively, you can apply via various private companies (see details of some below). They make an additional charge for this service, but they will advise and guide you through the application process. You cannot travel to the UK to start work before you have received the permits, so your intended employer should apply for a permit at least eight weeks before you are to start work – it normally takes between one and two months for an application to be processed. You will be refused admission to the country if you arrive to take up your employment without a valid work permit. If you are a 'visa national', as described in the *Residence and Entry Regulations* chapters, you will need a visa in addition to your work permit, and the visa will not be issued until you have your work permit.

Those people who are admitted as work permit holders are normally allowed to settle in the UK on completion of four years' continuous employment in that capacity.

There are other conditions a work permit holder must satisfy in order to be allowed to enter the UK. These include being able to maintain and accommodate themselves without recourse to public funds. Where a work permit is valid for twelve months or less the holder must demonstrate that they intend to leave at the end of the period of employment. As a work permit is only valid for one specific job, the holder must also show they have no intention to take any other job than that for which the permit has been issued.

> "The position in UK was with the same organisation I worked for in East Africa. I work for a charity specialising in the removal of the debris of war and am currently Desk Officer covering the Horn of Africa and the UK.
> Joe Rawal"

Full Work Permit

This is usually granted to employ high level executives and managers, or those with scarce technical skills, which are not readily available in the UK or EU. The job would normally be one that requires at least two years' post-qualification work experience in addition to a degree or a degree-level professional or technical qualification.

A work permit will only be granted if the employer is intending to pay the normal rate for the job in the UK. They are seldom granted for positions paying an annual salary of less than £20,000.

Usually the spouse of a work permit holder will be automatically granted leave to take up employment. This leave is not job-specific so the spouse may change jobs without an application to the Department for Education and Employment.

Permits for Entertainers, Sports People and Models

These have their own less stringent category of work permit because most people in this category work on an international level, and they therefore do not normally wish to make their permanent home in the UK. In some circumstances, particularly where they are entering the UK for six months or less, it may not be necessary to apply for a permit.

Keyworker Permits

These are granted to those who have language, cultural or culinary knowledge which is rare in the UK. They are often used for hotel or restaurant managers, head chefs, highly skilled waiting staff and senior hotel receptionists. Keyworker permits will not generally be granted nor extended for more than three years so they do not lead to permanent residence status.

Training Permits

These enable people from abroad to enter the UK for up to three years to receive on-the-job training which is not readily available to them in their own country and which will be of use there. Such training should normally lead to a recognised professional qualification or, in exceptional circumstances, to a valuable occupational skill.

Candidates for training permits must be between 18 and 54 years old and have the necessary educational or professional experience to benefit from the training. The training must be provided by the employer who applies for the training permit, it must be for a minimum of 30 hours per week and the wages must be at the normal rate for such training.

After the training is completed the individual must spend at least two years outside the UK before they are eligible for a full work permit.

Work Experience Scheme

This is similar to the training permit, but a permit under this scheme is normally granted for a maximum of one year. The candidate must be between 18 and 35 and have the necessary educational, professional or job experience to benefit from the work experience given. The employment must be surplus to the normal needs of the employer and only pocket money or a maintenance allowance can be paid.

Useful Contacts

Work Permits (UK): Application forms, information and guidance on making an application for a work permit; 0870 606 7766; www.workingintheuk.gov.uk.

UK Visas: Has useful summaries of the immigration regulations. www.ukvisas.gov.uk. There are a number of consultants who provide further information and personalised advice regarding work permits. Their websites have useful information including online assessments which will help you and your prospective employer decide whether you are likely to obtain a visa and/or a work permit in your circumstances.

Cooper Tuff Consultants: 0870 990 9480; fax 0870 990 9483; www.uk-immigration.co.uk

UK Work Permits Ltd: 0845 226 4030; www.uk-wp.com

Work Permit.com: 020 7842 0800; www.workpermit.com

Work Permit Consultants: 01825 762444; www.workpermit consultants.com

Training, Work Experience and Exchange Schemes

There are a number of training and work experience schemes open to foreign nationals with positions available within the UK. These are some of the major ones.

The British Universities North American Club (BUNAC) runs schemes for students to work temporarily in other countries; 020 7251 3472; www.bunac.org.uk. There are links to all relevant national websites from here.

The British Council offers opportunities for pupils, students, teachers, trainers, lecturers, and administrators in the UK education and training sectors, including short term posts for language assistants to work in schools in the UK; 0161 957 7755; www.britishcouncil.org/learning-ie-training-and-work-experience.htm.

The National Youth Agency provide opportunities to work with young people; 0116 242 7350; www.nya.org.uk.

The Civil Service offers vacation work for students in a number of its departments and agencies. Details of current opportunities are listed at www.careers.civil-service.gov.uk.

Useful Books and Websites

Your Gap Year: Susan Griffith: www.crimsonpublishing.co.uk

Gap Years for Growns Ups: Susan Griffith: www.crimsonpublishing.co.uk

Green Volunteers: Fabio Ausenda: www.crimsonpublishing.co.uk

Summer Jobs Worldwide: www.crimsonpublishing.co.uk

The International Directory of Voluntary Work: Victoria Pybus: www.crimson publishing.co.uk

Working in Tourism – The UK, Europe and Beyond: Verite Reily Collins: www.crimsonpublishing.co.uk

The Au Pair & Nanny's Guide to Working Abroad: Susan Griffith: www.crimsonpublishing.co.uk

About Jobs: Includes sections offering summer jobs, overseas jobs and resort jobs throughout the world. www.AboutJobs.com

Careers Europe: Provides plenty of advice about working in the UK. 01274 829600, www.careerseurope.co.uk

Hotel Jobs and Seasonal Vacancies: www.livein-jobs.co.uk

Hotel Jobs and Vacancies in the UK: www.hotel-jobs.co.uk

Accommodation

Any entrant to the UK, under any category, must be able to demonstrate they have adequate accommodation when they arrive and, in many cases, that they can support themselves without recourse to public funds. The exceptions to this latter condition are EEA nationals, who under a pan-

European agreement are usually eligible to claim state benefits if they are 'habitually resident' in the UK.

It should also be remembered, when applying for most jobs in the UK, that a permanent residence address is a prerequisite, so this must be a priority when considering a move to Britain.

Employment Contracts

Employers are required by law to give all employees taken on for periods of longer than one month a written statement of their main terms and conditions of employment. This must include the names of employee and employer, job title or brief job description, the date the employment begins, and the date it will end if it is for a fixed term. It must specify the amount of wages or salary plus the interval at which they are paid. It should also list the hours of work, amount of holiday entitlement and pensions entitlement. It should also include details of the employer's disciplinary rules and grievance procedures.

The written statement must be given to the employee within two months of starting work. If you think you are entitled to a written statement and have not been given one, you can refer the matter to an Employment Tribunal. These are legal bodies which deal with matters of employment law, redundancy, dismissal, contract disputes, sexual, racial and disability discrimination, and related areas of dispute which may arise in the workplace.

■ WORKING CULTURE AND ETIQUETTE

The Typical British Office

One of the most successful British TV comedies in recent years was *The Office*. Presented as a mock 'fly-on-the-wall' documentary, it strikes a chord with everybody who has ever worked in an office. We recognize the characters, the office politics, the daily routines. The series was so popular that, in addition to the series being sold to broadcasters in over 80 countries, including Australia, New Zealand and Hong Kong, there have also been versions made in the USA, Canada, France, and Germany. The fact that it goes over so well in all these places suggests that offices and office life are pretty similar world-wide.

But although every office is similar in some ways, whatever the product they market or service they provide, each one is also unique because what is important in an office is the people who work there and the ways they interact. So although there will be an official hierarchy, an official way to get the job done, there may also be an informal hierarchy and unofficial 'rules' which you can only discover for yourself.

Most modern British offices tend to be open plan, with desks grouped together for different functions within a large undivided space – although if you take a job in a long-established firm which still occupies its original offices, you may find a more old-fashioned style of small offices with just a few people in each. Each employee has his or her own desk which they work at every day. In larger organisations, different functions usually occupy separate offices – marketing, finance, human resources, and so on. It is rare for workers to sit within individual cubicles, although sometimes groups of desks may have movable screens placed round them in order to cut down on distractions and noise.

Heads of Department and Managers will probably have their own private office, perhaps with an outer office for their personal secretary or assistant (PA). In some organisations a PA may be 'shared' by two or more managers.

All British companies have to comply with equal opportunities legislation, which says that jobs should be awarded on merit only and that nobody should be prevented from doing a job simply because of their race, gender, sexual persuasion or disabilities. So you will find a mix of people of all colours and creeds in big city offices, with disabled people often working alongside the able-bodied. Women managers are common, and although in the past it may have been the case, it is not seen as something to be resented or to be ashamed of if a man is subordinate to a younger woman.

There are other types of office you may encounter. A fairly new phenomenon is hotdesking, also known as location independent working. In this system workers do not have their own desks but choose a different space to work in each day. This only works successfully where there is up-to-date flexible technology which allows an individual's telephone calls and working files to be accessible from all locations. It is a cost-saving option, however, in businesses where staff are out of the office on a regular basis.

If you take a job in a small business you may find yourself working from a home office – either teleworking from your own home or in an office within the business owner's home. This can cause some discomfort if you are made to feel you are transgressing their personal space – and even where this isn't the case, you would have to accept a much closer, less formal, relationship than would be possible in a larger organisation.

Office Hierarchy

Most British businesses are organised on a hierarchical basis following a pyramid structure, with the managing director or equivalent at the top, over the heads of departments or managers, who are in charge of their own teams of workers. In all there can be several layers of staff, each one acutely aware of his or her position in the schema and paid on the basis of that position.

This is a pattern set in the public sector, where organisations have a very rigid hierarchy with many levels within it. For example, in the Civil Service, there are five levels in the senior civil service, with another five grades below those. When you add in the fact that staff are automatically given predetermined annual increments in salary, which adds extra layers of seniority within each of the ten grades, it is easy to see how employees are acutely conscious of their position in the pecking order – and on the salary scale.

In private companies the pay levels may be less clear-cut, and pay rises may depend on individual negotiation. But even here there is likely to be a very sharp awareness on the part of all employees as to what their status is. This makes for a fairly competitive atmosphere, which may be good for productivity. However, it can lead to apathy on the part of somebody who has been passed over for promotion and feels they are never going to improve their position, so give up trying.

There may also be informal hierarchies within an office: the youngest recruit may be designated the 'tea boy/girl' responsible for making tea or coffee for all the other staff at regular intervals. Or the oldest, longest-standing, employee may have a measure of influence that younger, more recent, staff may not, even if officially they are higher up the promotion ladder. It doesn't do to get on the wrong side of such individuals as they can make life uncomfortable for you if you do not recognise their status.

Some more modern, younger organisations try hard to avoid becoming too hierarchical, believing that a more democratic, less rigid, structure works better. Regular meetings may involve all members of a team rather than just those higher up the salary scale, with everybody's opinions and expertise being equally valued. This can bring about far greater trust among the workforce which can do wonders for staff morale and therefore productivity.

Generally speaking, most offices today encourage a certain degree of informality. You will probably find in most cases that employees address their co-workers and often their supervisors by their first names.

You will be expected to dress smartly for work – for men this means a shirt and trousers, but not jeans, for women blouse and skirt or trousers and smart shoes rather than trainers, although less formality is more acceptable in some offices than in others. Watch what others are wearing and do the same yourself. Even where a formal business suit and tie is not required, 'smart casual' is generally the order of the day. On your first day in a new job it's always safest to go for the smartest, most formal, option – you can always dress more casually the next day if you feel over-dressed!

> I can't say that I have found that the British are any different from Swedes, although there might be more of a hierarchy at work. But apart from that all I have met so far have been nice and helpful.
> Roberth Lindholm

Business Hours

In a traditional business, normal office hours are between 9am and 5pm (9:00–17:00), Monday to Friday. Some finish early, at 4-4:30, on a Friday afternoon. New industries such as call centres or other telephone helplines may have longer working hours – from 8am to 8pm or even later, and operate at weekends too.

Most office workers have a working week of between 35 to 38 hours. If you are required to work over your normal hours, you may be paid for this at a higher overtime rate, although this is not always available to office workers. You may instead be given 'time off in lieu' of extra payment.

A lunch break of between half an hour and an hour is normal, plus a tea break morning and afternoon. Some companies have their own canteens or rest rooms where breaks can be taken, but by no means all. Many office workers go to local cafes for lunch or buy a sandwich and bring it back to eat at their desk or in a rest room.

Many companies operate a flexi-time system, particularly in offices. This allows employees to vary their hours of work, as long as they are present between certain hours, known as 'core time'. They may prefer to start earlier and finish earlier, and to take a shorter lunch break than normal.

Working Relationships

Most managers aim to establish good working relationships with their subordinates rather than adopting a domineering style. Teamwork is seen as important, and the leader of the team should provide support and encouragement.

This form of working encourages friendships to develop between colleagues, even at different levels in the hierarchy. This may lead on to socialising with them outside the workplace, starting perhaps by going to lunch with them, then for a drink after work. From here a more personal, less work-based friendship may develop, and you may invite them to your home to meet your family, and vice versa. This is all perfectly acceptable – indeed, employers like to see friendships among their staff, as long as this does not involve unfair treatment, as it makes for easier and hopefully more productive relationships at work.

> Making friends is of course a bit tricky when you move anywhere. It might be even more difficult when you move from one country to another. But I have good contact with a few of the other contractors at work and try to socialise as much as possible at work to get to know people.
> Roberth Lindholm

Socialising after Work

You may be invited to go out with your co-workers outside work, perhaps for a drink on the way home, or for an evening meal to celebrate somebody's birthday. Although you are not, of course, obliged to accept, it is a good way of bonding with your colleagues.

You may get involved in sporting activities with them – perhaps going to see a football or other sports game, or even playing yourself in a works team, whether in a formal league or for an informal kick-around at the weekend.

Another popular way of socialising with work colleagues is to have a dinner party at your home. In this case you would be expected to invite their partners and introduce them to your own.

Most companies will arrange some social events during the year, as it is deemed to be good for staff morale. This may take the form of a Christmas Party held on the firm's premises, or a Dinner and Dance held in a local hotel or similar. In the first case normally only employees would be invited, but in an event held outside the workplace partners would normally be invited too.

Some companies have a social committee who arrange a number of social events throughout the year, including such things as day trips to the races, theatre visits and so forth. You are not obliged to attend these if they are not your idea of fun.

Business Manners

The British set great store by politeness and this, above all, will be what you are judged on in your business dealings with them. They also steer clear of public displays of emotion or over-friendliness, especially when doing business.

A degree of formality is expected, at least until you get to know each other better. Shake hands on meeting, and wait to be introduced if appropriate, otherwise introduce yourself. When entering a room it is good form to allow or invite those of a higher rank, or women, to enter the room before you. You should keep a respectful distance from them – the British guard their personal space and will feel uncomfortable if you get too close to them. Make eye contact, but don't go to the extreme and 'eyeball' them.

It is considered bad form to ask personal questions about the other person's background, occupation or income.

Doing Business with the British

Business matters are conducted in a detached and objective manner, with facts and figures carrying far more sway than appeals to emotion, personal relationships or 'you scratch my back and I'll scratch yours'.

The British tend to feel uncomfortable in the face of direct questions, which fits with their natural reserve – they don't like to let their defences down, feeling this can put them at a disadvantage. So you may find that you are getting what appear to be evasive or ambiguous answers to your questions.

You need to pick up on the subtleties of conversation – a superior may disguise an instruction as a polite request. If you do not comply this will be bad for your future dealings with them.

Another aspect of this shows in the British tendency to use humour to avoid directness, which often takes the form of irony so you may not always be able to take what is said at face value. You need to be aware of tone of voice and facial expression as a guide to what is really meant.

Some UK businessmen of the 'old school', especially in traditional industries such as manufacturing and finance, would far rather deal with an older man and may display a certain prejudice against women or newly qualified young people. Although this should not prevent business being done, it may make the negotiations more difficult and protracted as the negotiator has to first overcome their resistance to someone who, in their eyes, does not have the length or breadth of experience to do business 'properly'. This should not be an issue in new businesses such as IT – indeed, here a younger person may be viewed as more capable than an older one.

Negotiating Practices

Public sector organisations are legally obliged to operate Compulsory Competitive Tendering (CCT) when offering contracts for the supply of goods and services, so there is little or no opportunity for face to face negotiating. Suppliers must submit a written tender which lays out all the terms, conditions and specification. The time allowed for pricing and submitting a tender is normally around four to six weeks. All tenders must be returned in unmarked envelopes on the same day at a specified time before being opened. The contract will be awarded to the supplier who quotes the best price for the conditions offered (not necessarily the cheapest price). Most other companies will also have well-established policies regarding the way things are done, so any proposal you make will be better received if it fits in with their normal practices. When negotiating it is essential to have all the relevant facts and figures at your fingertips – poor preparation can cost you a contract.

In Britain you should avoid aggressive techniques such as the 'hard sell' or denigrating another company's product or service. Equally, you should avoid sycophancy – the British find excessive praise or gushiness uncomfortable and insincere.

Although British businessmen tend to look for short-term results rather than long-range objectives, they are generally interested in long-term relationships rather than quick deals so try to gain their confidence and respect. They will favour a win/win approach from which both parties benefit mutually.

The British weapons of reserve, politeness, taciturnity and humour are all brought to bear in negotiations. You may find they are quiet and difficult to read early in the negotiations while they get your measure and make their assessment of your company and your proposal.

Be alert to understatement and irony – although tone of voice or facial expression may hint at what is really meant this is not always the case. Sometimes what is not said can be as important as what is said.

Humour can go down well – if you are talented at it. But this is a very difficult thing to judge if you are not very familiar with British culture. It is easy to put your foot in it by telling jokes which don't go down well. If you are unsure in this area, it is best to avoid it and stick to being straightforward and professional.

Decision-making can be a slow and systematic process and the senior executive in the position to make the final decision will not take kindly to having undue pressure put on him or her to rush out a decision. This can be counterproductive and lose you a contract.

There are few absolute taboos when negotiating in Britain – but remember that this is one of the least corrupt societies in the world, so trying to give your opposite number a monetary back-hander as an inducement is a definite no-no. However, it's acceptable to take him/her out for a drink or a meal and attempt to win their favour that way.

Punctuality

You will be expected to arrive punctually for any business meeting, although if you are no more than ten to fifteen minutes late, that should not be a problem. If you are unavoidably delayed you should do your utmost to get a message through explaining that you are going to be late.

Ideally, you should arrive early but not too early arrive too early – five to ten minutes before the appointed time is fine. Because traffic congestion is a problem in many parts of the UK, and because the public transport systems are not known for their punctuality, you should always allow yourself plenty of time to get to an appointment. This may mean you arrive far too early, but it is better to kill time elsewhere – go for a walk or to a coffee shop, perhaps – before arriving for the meeting.

Formality

The British are far less formal than they once were, but it is always best to err on the side of formality in the business sphere. When attending a business meeting, men are safest wearing a business suit, collared shirt and tie, while women won't go wrong if they too wear a formal suit, with either skirt or trousers.

Over-familiar behaviour such as back-slapping, hugging or kissing will not be well-received, neither will offensive language. Slang expressions are fine as long as they are used correctly – if you are at all unsure whether you are using them in an appropriate manner for the social situation it is best to avoid them altogether.

■ ASPECTS OF EMPLOYMENT

Working Practices

It is impossible to generalise about working practices throughout Britain because they vary from place to place and industry to industry. However, the reputation of the British as somewhat work-shy, whether justified or unjustified in the past, is now far from the truth. There is a very strong work ethic, particularly within white collar occupations, and long working hours, above and beyond contractual obligations, are the norm in many fields.

Connected with this, habitual lateness is frowned on, as is leaving work early, and is a justifiable reason for dismissal if carried to extremes. Long lunch hours too are generally disapproved of – although business lunches are part and parcel of certain executive positions. Flexi-time systems give workers control over when they work, within broad parameters, as long as they satisfy their contractual obligations of overall hours worked.

Factory and shift workers generally have far less leeway as regards arriving late for work and leaving early. Many of them have to 'clock on' and 'clock off' at the beginning and end of the shift, so their hours of work are electronically recorded.

Tradespeople, such as plumbers and builders, have long had the reputation of being unreliable, not turning up when they say they will and charging high prices for minimal work. This is something which sadly doesn't seem to have changed. Consequently, the good, reliable tradesman who charges reasonably is never short of work. Starting dates for construction work are notoriously fluid. On the whole, the reason for this is not that they are work-shy, but that they are extremely busy. They are reluctant to let any job go, so will agree to take on a project even at a time when they are busy on other jobs. They will get round to it eventually, but this is small comfort if you have a deadline to meet. However, on the plus side, if you have an emergency, they will deal with it quickly.

Traditionally, conservative formal dress – collar and tie for men, skirt or smart trousers for women – is expected in offices, although some companies, particularly within new industries such as IT, have loosened up in recent years and encourage more informal dress. Amongst the older age groups, however, such informality would tend to be frowned on. You are unlikely to be censured for dressing too smartly, whereas overly casual attire could affect your promotion prospects, even if your work is exemplary in other respects.

Generally, it is fine to address colleagues by their first names within the workplace, even where they are superior in position to yourself. Be guided by what others in the office say and do.

The UK-wide smoking ban means that smoking in the workplace is illegal. Smoking breaks these days can only be taken outside – it is not unusual to see office workers standing outside in the street, sometimes in the pouring rain, just to get their 'fag break'. There have been cases where non-smokers have complained that this means smokers are working for fewer hours than they. In an effort to combat this, without discriminating against smokers, businesses such as Tower Hamlets Council in London have officially recognized smoking breaks – but say these have to be taken in smokers' own time, by extending their working day.

Salaries

Most wages and salaries in Britain are paid monthly (12 times a year), or sometimes four weekly (13 times a year), with payments generally being paid directly into bank accounts. The main exception to this is at the lower end of the market, where manual labourers, shop and hotel workers and the like, as well as part-time workers, may be paid weekly, by cash. Casual labour may be paid cash in hand, which is a way some employers avoid certain aspects of employment legislation, so if you are offered this, make sure exactly what your safeguards are.

Salaries in the UK tend to be lower than those for equivalent jobs elsewhere in Europe and in the USA. Average wages and salaries vary quite significantly across the regions of the UK.

These figures are averaged out over the whole range of full-time employment, and there are wide variations between the upper and lower rates paid within each area depending on the job. For the UK as a whole, the top earners were health professionals with average weekly earnings of £1,059.30, and lowest were those in elementary administrative and service occupations, earning just £179.10. In 2006, graduate starting salaries

Average Gross Weekly Earnings 2006	
Region	£
UK	567.00
England	
North East	380.90
North West	408.90
Yorkshire and the Humber	392.10
East Midlands	403.90
West Midlands	406.30
East	425.50
London	618.70
South East	461.20
South West	398.00
Wales	388.40
Scotland	411.90
Northern Ireland	381.70

Figures from Annual Survey of Hours and Earnings 2006 (ASHE): www.statistics.gov.uk.

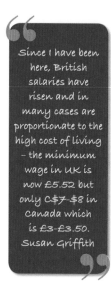

averaged £18,200 across the UK. Public sector workers in the capital are paid an allowance called 'London weighting' to offset the additional costs of living there.

Where a salary range is indicated in a job advertisement, it is negotiable on the basis of the applicant's previous experience. This is more commonly seen in jobs in the private sector. Public sector jobs, such as teaching, police, civil service and so forth, have set pay scales, with salaries paid at a set rate for a particular ranking of job with specified annual increments payable within that ranking. These pay scales are regularly renegotiated, and may be linked to the annual rate of inflation.

A National Minimum Wage came into force in the UK on 1st April 1999. It is adjusted annually and from October 2007 was set at £5.52 per hour for workers aged 22 or over; £4.60 per hour for workers aged 18-21, and £3.40 per hour for those aged 16 and 17.

Public Sector Salaries

In the UK, teachers are paid on different salary scales depending on the region in which they work. Teachers in London are paid on a separate salary scale, as are those in Scotland. All other teachers are paid similarly to those in England and Wales with a few minor variations. The entry point for individual teachers depending on their qualifications. In 2006, teachers in England and Wales earned £19,161-£33,249, with head teachers earning £33,249-£93,297. In London, these rates are £23,577-£52,266 and £40,527-£102,075 respectively.

Financial incentives for certain trainee teachers are also available. Maths and science postgraduate trainees may be eligible for a £9,000 bursary while they train and an additional £5,000 after they complete the teaching induction period. English, drama, design and technology, ICT, music, and religious education postgraduate trainees may be eligible for £9,000 during training and £2,500 after induction. A £6,000 bursary is available for other postgraduate trainees.

Staff working in higher education are paid on a single national payscale, first introduced in August 2006. There is a 51-point National Pay Spine which, in February 2007, ranged from £11,691-£49,607.

Basic rates of pay for police officers from April 2006 were £20,397-£32,025 for a constable, rising to £65,244-£68,961 for a chief superintendent. Chief constables received between £111,393 and £159,135 depending on the police force area they controlled.

General Practitioners, dentists, optometrists, and pharmacists are self-employed and work for the NHS under contract.

Benefits and Perks

The value of employment packages, especially in the higher paid and executive sectors, is often augmented by additional benefits, often called

A sample of jobs advertised on Recruitment UK, March 2007		
Location	**Job title**	**Salary**
London	IT Support and Systems Developer	£23,000
Manchester	Sous Chef	£21,000-£22,000
Cardiff	Internal Auditor	£16,000-£25,000
Edinburgh	Field Service Engineer	£15,000-£18,000
Ipswich	Personal Injury Paralegal	£15,000-£25,000
Aberdeen	Health and Safety Consultant	£27,000-£31,000
Belfast	Telesales Executive	£14,000-£16,000

Average NHS Salaries 2006	
Consultant	£57,944-£94,706
Senior Registrar	£33,325-£43,931
Registrar	£28,930-£35,092
Senior House Officer	£25,882-£36,292
GP	£50,000-£76,000
Registered nurse	From £19,166

'perks of the job'. These include such things as the provision of a company car for the sole use of the employee, or where this is not available, the payment of car allowance against travel made in one's own car; other expenses incurred in connection with the job may also be payable; private health insurance is sometimes offered as part of a salary and benefits package; where appropriate, a mobile phone or laptop may be provided; annual bonuses may be paid, either as a matter of course or on the basis of performance; commission is commonly payable in sales jobs depending on the numbers of new customers secured; in recent years, companies have begun offering share options to employees as part of a benefits package, occupations such as nursing and hotel work may include live-in accommodation, either free or at a subsidised rent.

These benefits and perks are usually taxable, although lump sum bonuses may be payable tax-free.

Working Hours, Overtime and Holidays

The hours worked by employees is regulated by the Working Time Regulations which came into force in October 1998. There is a limit of an average of 48 hours that a worker can be required to work per week (although they can work longer if they wish to). Nightworkers can only be required to work up to an average of eight hours in every 24, and should receive free health assessments to ensure night working is not affecting their well-being. Workers also have rights to 11 hours rest each day, a day off each week, an in-work rest break if the working day is longer than six hours, and four weeks paid leave per year.

Young workers (those above the minimum school leaving age but below 18) have enhanced rights, including the right to two days off each week and longer statutory periods of rest. Of course, employers can provide better conditions than these if they wish, and in many cases they do. Working hours vary depending on the type of industry as well as on individual employers and one's position in the company. In manufacturing industries the average working week is around 37.5 to 40 hours per week, while office workers are more likely to work between 35 to 38 hours per week. Traditionally, some employees in hospitals, security, catering and hotels have worked far longer hours, but the working time regulations have improved the conditions under which such people work.

Employees may find that their contract entitles them to five weeks' annual leave or more, although four weeks is the norm. During annual leave, the employee should be paid at their normal rate; where their normal hours include a regular amount of overtime, it may be that there is a requirement on the employer to pay them during holidays at their normal pay, which takes account of their average earnings where these generally include overtime.

The rules regarding overtime should be laid out in the contract of employment (see below). In general, working hours are a matter of agreement between employers and employees and their representatives, such as trade unions. Anything worked over these hours by blue-collar (e.g. factory or manual) workers would be paid as overtime, usually higher than the normal hourly rate, typically at time and a half or double time. In white collar jobs (e.g. office or executive) overtime may be compensated for by time off in lieu of the extra hours worked. This extra time off may be saved up and taken as a period of a day or more, depending on local agreements.

Many companies operate a flexi-time system, particularly in offices. This allows employees to vary their hours of work, as long as they are present between certain hours, known as 'core time'. They may prefer to start earlier and finish earlier, and to take a shorter lunch break than normal (although a minimum 30 minute lunch break is usually specified for legal reasons). With flexi-time, workers may find themselves able to avoid the worst of the rush hour, or to build up extra days off by working longer days.

Termination of Employment

The written statement must state the entitlement of the employer and the employee to notice of termination of employment. The length of notice an employer must give depends on the length of time the employee has been continuously working for them. Normally, one month to two years' service requires one week's notice of dismissal; two years to 12 years' service requires 1 week's notice for each complete year; more than 12 years' service requires 12 weeks' notice. Sometimes a longer period may have been agreed in the contact of employment, in which case the longer period applies.

However, the employer needs to give a good reason for terminating the employment, it cannot just be on a whim. If the sacked employee feels they have been treated unjustly, they can take the matter to an employment tribunal which will make investigations and decide whether it is a case of unfair dismissal. For a dismissal to be fair, it must be because the employee is unable or unqualified to do the job, or that their conduct is unacceptable (such as a poor attendance record, for example) or that a legal requirement prevents them continuing to do the job (such as where a driver loses his or her licence) or because of redundancy (see below).

There are certain types of dismissal that are deemed to be automatically unfair. These include dismissal on the grounds of being – or not being – a trade union member, being pregnant or taking maternity leave, or for reasons relating to the national minimum wage or relating to the working time regulations.

Where an employment tribunal decides that an unfair dismissal has taken place, they may order the employer to re-employ the person, but more usually will order the employer to pay compensation to the individual.

Where notice of termination of employment has been given, the employee should be paid at their normal rate during the notice period, even if they are away on sick, holiday or maternity leave, or if they are willing to work but none is provided. If the correct notice is not given, the employee may seek damages from an employment tribunal or a civil court.

Redundancy

Where employees lose their jobs because the employer needs to cut jobs, move the place of work, or close down completely, they may be entitled to a lump sum payment called redundancy pay. Normally, the worker should have been continuously employed by that employer for two years or more to be entitled to redundancy pay. The amount payable is calculated on the worker's age, period of employment and weekly pay. If an employee does not receive redundancy pay to which they think they are entitled, the matter may be referred to an employment tribunal.

Rights of Part-time, Temporary and Seasonal Workers

In July 2000, the UK Government introduced new rights for part-time workers. The new regulations were designed to ensure that part-time workers are not treated less favourably than their full-time counterparts. Part-timers are entitled to the same hourly rate of pay, the same access to company pension schemes, the same entitlements to annual, maternity and parental leave on a pro rata basis, the same entitlement to sick pay and equal access to training as full-time workers in comparable jobs.

The Working Time Regulations and National Minimum Wage relate also to temporary and seasonal workers, and employers are also legally required to deduct tax and National Insurance from their wages, as well as making their part of the NI contribution. However, because of the administration and costs involved, many employers who want casual workers will avoid this legislation by paying strictly 'cash in hand'. In this case, the workers' employment rights are unlikely to be protected and there will probably not be any redress to an employment tribunal.

Short term casual work is just one form of temporary work. Jobs are often advertised on fixed term contracts, maybe because it is genuinely a project which will only last six months, or two years, or whatever. Sometimes jobs will be advertised in the form of 'six month contract in the first instance' which implies there is the likelihood of extending the contract at the end of that period. This gives both employer and employee the option of withdrawing easily after the first 'trial period'. In such cases, it is almost certain that the full letter of the employment laws will be complied with.

There is also a constant need for temporary staff to cover for staff absences caused by holidays, long term sickness or maternity leave. Many workers prefer to 'temp' in this way, moving from company to company for a few days or weeks at a time. Depending on their experience, temp rates can be good. There are employment agencies which specialise in finding and supplying temporary workers at short notice.

Teleworking

Computers and the internet now allow employees to perform many of their duties from home or elsewhere, away from the central workplace, a process called teleworking. In 1994, the European Commission set a target of ten million teleworkers in Europe by 2000. By October 2002 there were 20 million, with one in ten people working from home more than once a week. Only 2% worked from home on a full time basis. Although telework is more widespread in certain sectors, like telecommunications, it is estimated now that 6% of European workers telework for at least

10% of their working time. However, the potential is far higher, with two thirds of people of working age interested in teleworking.

The UK is less geared up to teleworking than some other European countries, but even so there is a significant movement in that direction. In 2005, 2.4 million people were teleworking to one degree or another. This was an increase of over 150% since 1997. Of these, 1.8 million worked mainly in different places, using their home as a base, with only 0.6 million of these working mainly in their own home. Nearly two thirds of teleworkers are self-employed – around 41% of self-employed people were teleworking in spring 2005.

Where companies allow their employees to telework in full or part, they tend to be larger companies with 250 employees or more. It is an interesting feature that teleworkers work longer hours than other workers. Almost half of regular teleworkers report an actual working week of more than ten hours longer than that specified in their contract of work, compared to only 10% of other workers.

The picture varies throughout Britain with, paradoxically, the biggest opportunities for teleworking as an employee in the main centres of population – rather than in rural areas. However, there are significantly higher numbers of self-employed teleworkers, often one-man businesses, working from home offices in such areas. (For more on this see *Starting A Business*.)

Teleworking Resources

The Telework Association claims to be Europe's largest organisation dedicated to the promotion of all forms of teleworking, with a membership of over 7,000 people and organizations. Membership starts at £34.50 per year. They also publish *The Teleworking Handbook*; 0800 616008; Buy online at £26, or sent free to members. www.tca.org.uk.

For further information on teleworking, see the following websites:
Gil Gordon Telecommuting: www.gilgordon.com
Homeworking Information: www.homeworking.com

Women in Work

In 2005, 70% of women were working, compared to 79% of men. Despite a growth in numbers of women in work every year, and although equal pay legislation was introduced in 1970, women in Britain earn only 83% of men's average hourly earnings.

This is partly due to differences in types of work undertaken and working patterns of women and men. The majority of part-time workers are women, and generally in low paid jobs. Of the working population, 42% of women and only 9% of men work part-time, while 2,750,000 women (81%) work in administrative and secretarial jobs, compared with 653,000 men.

There is a huge pay gap of 41% between the hourly rates of part-time women workers and full-time male workers, and this is where the main gender discrimination comes in – because women's traditional responsibilities of caring for the home and family very often prevent them working full-time, this means there is structural discrimination against them, as there are so few higher paying jobs available on a part-time basis.

The Sex Discrimination Act, introduced in 1975, makes sex discrimination in employment unlawful, but there is still notable segregation in occupational areas between men and women. This, of course, is partly due to women's aspirations and proclivities, plus social attitudes about the 'right' sort of jobs for women. In the UK, attitudes about 'women's work' and 'men's work' are still strong. Women predominate in the public administration and health sectors, distribution, hotels and catering. Men still dominate as managers in all sectors and in traditional industries such as construction, transport, motor trade, energy and water supply.

Maternity Benefits and Parental Leave

Expectant mothers may take up to 39 weeks' paid maternity leave, regardless of their length of service with their current employer. They may be able to take another 26 weeks of additional maternity leave if they have completed 26 weeks continuous service with their employer by the beginning of the fourteenth week before their expected week of childbirth. Additional maternity leave is usually unpaid, but some companies will contribute.

Maternity leave can be taken from any time between the 11th week before the baby is due and the day following the birth. Statutory Maternity Pay (SMP) is paid at 90% of the mother's average weekly earnings for the first six weeks, and after that at standard rate, or 90% of average weekly earnings, whichever is lower. From April 2006 standard rate is £108.85.

A father has the right to two weeks' paid paternity leave as long as he has worked for his employer for 26 weeks by the fifteenth week before the baby is due and earns more than £79 a week. Paternity leave can be taken from the date of birth or up to eight weeks from the birth.

Fathers will get Statutory Paternity Pay (SPP) at £108.85 a week or 90% of their average weekly earnings if this is less.

Useful Contacts

Women and Equality Unit: 020 7944 4400 (8:30am-5.30pm Mon-Fri); www.womenandequalityunit.gov.uk
Equal Opportunities Commission (GB): 0845 601 5901 (Monday to Friday, 9am to 5pm); www.eoc.org.uk

Equality Commission for Northern Ireland: 028 9089 0890; www.equalityni.org

National Day Nurseries Association (NDNA): 0870 774 4244; www.ndna.org.uk

The Pre-school Learning Alliance: 020 7833 0991; www.pre-school. org.uk

Wales Pre-school Playgroups Association: 01686 624573; www.walesppa.org

Scottish Pre-school Play Association: 0141 221 4148; www.sppa.org.uk

Northern Ireland Pre-school Playgroups Association: 028 9066 2825; www.nippa.org

National Childminding Association (England and Wales): 0845 880 0044; www.ncma.org.uk

Scottish Childminding Association: 01786 449063; www.childminding.org

Northern Ireland Childminding Association: 028 9181 1015; www.nicma.org

■ INDUSTRY OVERVIEW

The strongest performing sector in the UK economy today is business and financial services, accounting for over one third of economic output. It is more than double the size of the manufacturing sector, while Information and Communication Technologies contribute 6.4% to national output and agriculture less than 1%.

Although the manufacturing industry is just a fraction of the size it once was, it is still very important to the economy. It accounts for over half of UK exports, and undertakes 75% of all business research and development. It employs about 3.5 million people and many more indirectly through the supply chain and service industries. The production of food, beverages and tobacco is one of the UK's largest manufacturing sectors.

The number of businesses in the UK is on the increase, with 1.64 million in 2006. The growth is partly accounted for by new business start ups, so consequently there are an increasing proportion of small businesses. Approximately 29% of companies are in property and business services, while 9% are in the manufacturing sector.

Agriculture is now one of the smallest sectors in the UK economy and most businesses within the sector are fairly small with 85% having a turnover of less than £250,000.

Higher education is a highly competitive market, especially as far as attracting overseas students is concerned. These make a big contribution to the wider economy, bringing an estimated £3 billion both through tuition fee income and through spending on goods and services from overseas students residing in Britain.

Since the 1960s there has been a significant transformation of the British economy. There have been two main strands to this change: new industries based on modern technologies have been created, with the traditional heavy industries declining in importance; and, following the trend of other western industrialised nations, the service sector has become an increasingly dominant part of the economy.

Output per head measured by gross value added (GVA) has increased significantly in recent years, with a nationwide rise of over 50% in the last decade. Although all regions have shown increased output over this time, there are significant variations between the regions, with Wales in bottom position and London top by a wide margin.

■ REGIONAL EMPLOYMENT GUIDE

London and the South East

Enterprise & Development Agencies

Capital Enterprise: 020 7300 7252; www.capitalenterprise.org
South East Association of Enterprise Agencies (SEALEA): 01474 327118. www.businessnorthkent.co.uk
London Development Agency: 020 7593 9000; www.lda.gov.uk
South East England Development Agency: 01483 484200; www.seeda.co.uk

This is a region of great contrasts as far as the employment scene is concerned. The regional output is the highest of all the UK regions, and yet London also has the highest unemployment rate and the highest proportion of people economically inactive and/or unemployed. This arises because there are some very wealthy, productive areas, pre-eminently the business area of the City, with not many miles away some of the most deprived areas of the country in the east of London.

In the wider south east region, the inner core which rings London is the wealthiest part, while the rural and coastal areas under-perform in comparison.

The service industries are the biggest contributor to the region's wealth, with real estate, renting and business activities producing over a third of output, and financial services another 17%. With the large shopping centres of London at its core, it's not surprising that wholesale and retail businesses are also big employees, with manufacturing less important to the region.

There is plenty of employment, although not generally highly paid, in the many hotels and restaurants which are essential to the tourism sector. London is one of the world's tourist cities, and the south coast is a popular area for holidays too, so this is a big employer overall.

The Olympic Games will be held in London in 2012, and this is creating a huge demand for extra jobs, especially in the construction industry where it is estimated around 60,000 'person years' (ie one person employed for a year) will be required between now and 2012. In addition, a further 40,000 jobs will be needed to stage the games and in additional roles within the leisure and tourism industries to cater for the influx of visitors.

One of the biggest problems for employment in the region, particularly in London, is the high cost of housing, both to buy and to rent. Many key workers in the public sector (e.g teachers and nurses) cannot afford to live close to their work unless there is special low cost housing provided, and consequently they have to commute into the capital, which may bring down accommodation costs but of course adds to the transport bill. Employees in the public sector in London are paid an allowance called London weighting to offset the higher cost of living, and private companies too generally pay comparatively higher wages than elsewhere in the country.

There may be opportunities to work remotely (telework) using ICT, which has the potential to improve work-life balance and cut down on travelling costs, as well as helping to manage the serious traffic congestion in London. If applying for a job, where appropriate it is worth asking whether you could work for part of the time from home. The Regional Economic Strategy for the south east has made a commitment to increasing the proportion of teleworking so companies should hopefully take this on board.

The South West

Enterprise and Development Agencies
South West Regional Association of Enterprise Agencies: 01793 428314; www.gwe.uk.com
South West of England Regional Development Agency: 01392 214747; www.southwestrda.org.uk
There has been an improvement in the economic picture in the south west over recent years, with parts of the region having growth rates higher than the UK as a whole. Unemployment has been decreasing and has stayed at a level lower than the English average for several years. There is, however, a big difference in employment prospects in different parts of the region, with the south and west of the region having higher unemployment.

As in other parts of the country, real estate, renting and business activities are the highest generators of wealth, followed by manufacturing, then wholesale and retail. As a mainly rural area, agriculture generates a significant portion of the region's wealth as measured by GVA (Gross Value Added).

The main sources of employment are:

- Public administration, education and health (28%).
- Distribution, hotels and restaurants (22%).
- Banking, finance and insurance-related industries (14%).
- Manufacturing (13%).

As is also common throughout the UK, there is an ongoing change in the structure of the local economy, with recent substantial growth in the business and financial services sector, and multimedia, electronic and hi-tech industries.

The region is a major centre of bio-medical research. This sector employs around 15,000 people in 500 companies and the demand for workers is still growing.

The South West accounts for over 20% of domestic tourism and 8% of overseas trips to England. As a result, employment within the tourist industry is important to the local economy, but it also means that there is a high proportion of part-time and seasonal working. Overall more than 10,000 businesses are involved either directly or indirectly in tourism, and the sector supports around 225,000 jobs.

ICT is one of the largest sectors in the region. It has grown about 10% in the last ten years, and continues to grow, currently employing around 70,000 people.

Although engineering has suffered a decline across the UK, it is still significant in the South West, especially in the areas of aerospace, automotive and measuring instruments and medical devices.

Pay levels vary quite widely in different parts of the region, a reflection of the different jobs available in the urban and rural areas. For full-time employees, the median gross annual pay is around £22,000, below the English median of £24,000. However, this encompasses a rate of £16,600 in the Torridge District Council area (in Devon) and £27,000 in South Gloucestershire.

The East

Enterprise and Development Agencies

Eastern Association of Enterprise Agencies: 01206 548833; www.colbea.co.uk

East of England Development Agency: 01223 713900; www.eeda.org.uk

The East of England is renowned as an 'ideas and innovation powerhouse', thanks in part to the presence of Cambridge University in the region. Research and development expenditure contributes more to this regional economy than to any other in Britain, and the share of its workforce engaged in research and development is well above the UK average. It appears among the top ten regions of Europe for innovation according to EU figures.

Cambridge University is at the heart of a cluster of biotechnology and information and communications technology (ICT) businesses, which is enhanced by close connections with London and Oxford. There are significant clusters of business activity in other sub-regions, including telecoms in Suffolk, biosciences and financial services in the Norwich area, and chemicals and pharmaceuticals in Hertfordshire, Bedfordshire and Essex.

It is no coincidence, then, that a recent survey discovered that young people and graduates between 18 and 24 are more likely to set up their own businesses than in other regions – 7.8% of them, compared with 5.7% across the UK. Women too show a greater entrepreneurial spirit here than elsewhere with the number of female-run businesses on the rise – although this may partly be their response to the fact that there is a bigger than average gap between male and female earnings among employees in the region.

Economic migrants are attracted to the region, with 80,000 migrants currently registered to work in the East of England. A project is currently being launched to address the needs of this group and there will soon be available a pre-arrival information pack and DVD plus a specialised website for migrant workers. Some concerns have been raised that migrants are often treated unequally, with their skills being under utilised. It is hoped that the new project will help to address these issues.

Although there is a below average rate of unemployment across the area, there are concentrations of residents claiming social security benefits in certain areas, most of these in the northern periphery.

Because of its proximity to London and the South East, there is a significant number of people who live in the East, taking advantage of comparatively lower house prices, and commute out of the region for work.

Midlands

Enterprise and Development Agencies
CES Central Enterprise Solutions: 01283 537151;
www.enterprisesupport.org
Advantage West Midlands: 0121 380 3500; www.advantagewm.co.uk
East Midlands Development Agency: 0115 988 8300; www.emda.org.uk
The Midlands region has traditionally been strong in manufacturing and this is still an important sector, being second only to the service sector. Manufacturing employs over 20% of the workforce, but this is far smaller than it once was and it continues to fall. In comparison, the service sector employs nearly 70% of the working population.

It is the business services sector which is predicted to grow the most rapidly – by as much as 30% over the next seven years. Currently there is in the west of the region the largest concentration of professional firms outside London.

Traditional manufacturing strengths include aerospace, advanced engineering and polymers, automotive and motorsport industries. Although the UK car industry is just a tiny proportion of what it once was, Coventry and other Midlands towns still manufacture car parts and associated items while local expertise in engineering has been used to diversify into other areas

New technologies are becoming increasingly important, and both the medical and media sectors are growing.

The East Midlands economy is not as thriving as the West Midlands, partly due to a lower skills base. Although employment levels are high, there is a high proportion of low-paid, unskilled jobs, and local people do not have the skills very often to improve their employment prospects. Small and medium-sized enterprises (SMEs) make an important contribution to the economy here, employing 1.4 million of the total 2 million workforce. However, they are hampered when they want to improve and expand, because they face acute shortages of skilled people.

In addition, there are still areas in the region where there are high levels of worklessness and acute deprivation.

This is quite a contrast with the West Midlands. Here they are making positive efforts to diversify the region's business base by embracing hi-tech, high-skill industries. These are concentrated in three 'High Technology Corridors', geographical areas that have clusters of certain types of new, technology-led businesses plus the infrastructure to support them.

- The Central Technology Belt runs from central Birmingham to north Worcestershire, and specialises in medical sciences, materials engineering and environmental technologies.

- The Coventry, Solihull, Warwickshire Triangle is an area of high-technology transport, ICT and design businesses.

- The Wolverhampton, Telford Technology Corridor focuses on encouraging innovation, stimulating enterprise, exploiting knowledge and developing technology in areas including IT, building technologies and creative industries.

- New businesses in these developing areas are assisted by institutions such as the Polymer and Advanced Engineering Cluster Centres, the Creative Industries Centre at the Wolverhampton Science Park, the IT Futures Centre, the e-Innovation Centre and the Institute of Innovation and Enterprise. For full details of these, see Advantage West Midlands (contact details above).

North

Enterprise and Development Agencies

North West Enterprise Agencies Ltd: 01772 422242; www.bvg.org.uk
North West Development Agency: 01925 400100; www.nwda.co.uk
One North East: 0191 229 6200; www.onenortheast.co.uk
Yorkshire Forward: 0113 394 9600; www.yorkshire-forward.com

Historically, the north of England has underperformed economically when compared with the south, and this is still the case today. Manufacturing has always been important to the region and remains so, despite the decline in certain sectors of the industry in recent years. In fact, in Yorkshire and Humberside manufacturing is actually predicted to grow by over 12% in the next ten years, which is in direct opposition to the situation in the rest of the country. However, there is a change in the type of manufacturing undertaken with a move away from more routine, traditional industries which are being affected by competition from emerging world markets, into more innovative, higher value-added products such as chemicals and pharmaceuticals. The country's largest concentration of food research and production businesses are in the region.

Along with everywhere else in the UK, the service sector is the biggest employer by a long way. Leeds is the largest financial and business services centre in the UK outside London, employing around 111,000 people. The other cities of the north are together home to around three quarters of the UK's biggest companies, and many overseas-owned companies. The public sector, including public administration, teaching and healthcare are big employers.

The North West and North East tend to be less economically productive than the other regions, with lower average wages and comparatively higher levels of economic inactivity. Although there has been employment growth in recent years, much of this is in low-waged activity. This is to be expected in such a rural part of the country. The highest wages are found in the urban centres, and even these fall below national averages, although it should be noted that the costs of living, in particular the price of buying or renting property, are lower here, taking up a smaller proportion of take-home pay.

With much of England's most beautiful natural areas in the north – there are several national parks in the region not to mention other areas with environmental designations – tourism is a very important sector, bringing millions of pounds to the region each year and providing both seasonal and year-round jobs.

Newer industries are at least as important in the north as elsewhere, being used to modernise the economic base and replace moribund industries. It has one of the fastest growing IT sectors in the UK and has attracted some major ICT companies, including Brother, IBM, Hewlett Packard, Siemens, ICL/Fujitsu, and Sun Micro Systems.

A number of hi-tech clusters have been encouraged to grow:

■ Science City, centred on the University of York, is a world-class cluster of hi-tech businesses, both start-ups and longer established firms.

■ Bioscience York has been growing for ten years and now contains 54 companies and 3,700 life scientists.

■ Sheffield is home to a major cluster of market-leading creative, digital media and ICT businesses including e-learning services, games, animation, film and TV, video, sound, radio, and photography businesses.

Wales

Enterprise and Development Agency

Department of Enterprise, Innovation and Networks: 0845 010 3300; http://new.wales.gov.uk/topics/businessandeconomy

Wales has historically been the poorest nation of Great Britain, with both England and Scotland producing a greater share of its per capita wealth. However, since devolution in 1999, Wales has improved its comparative economic standing considerably, although it still falls behind its larger neighbours. GVA per capita now is very similar to that of Northern Ireland and the North East of England. Employment has been increasing, unemployment falling, earnings rising and the economy growing strongly. At a time when the public sector is increasing proportionately across the UK, Wales is the only region where the private sector's share of total jobs has increased in the last seven years.

The traditional industries of Wales were manufacturing, mining and agriculture. All these have declined in recent years, although manufacturing and agri-food are still important sectors.

The most important sectors for continuing economic growth in Wales are:

■ Automotive
■ Aerospace
■ Agri-food
■ High technology
■ Pharmaceuticals/bio-chemicals
■ Financial services
■ Creative industries
■ Construction
■ Hospitality, leisure and tourism
■ Social care

The Welsh Assembly is actively encouraging the development of new businesses and investment in research and development is increasing, as are business start-up rates. They have succeeded in attracting a few large, high profile employers – among them Airbus – to do business in Wales, and the knock-on effects of business clusters that form around them have been significant in improving levels of investment and employment.

The overall figures mask to some degree the fact that employment and average earnings levels vary considerably across Wales, with the east of the country performing better than the west and mid-Wales. While the employment rate for Wales as a whole is slightly below that of the UK, in north east Wales it is well above the UK average.

In common with other parts of Britain, technology-driven companies and professional services firms are important, and particularly so in Cardiff, Swansea and the north east. The agri-food and tourism sectors are proportionally larger in mid and west Wales.

Although all areas are experiencing high employment, there is a wide disparity in earnings levels, largely to do with the types of jobs available. However, in places such as Cardiff, where earnings are high, the cost of living too is commensurately higher than in low-earning areas such as Powys, so disposable income does not vary as much as bald earnings figures might suggest.

There has been substantial regeneration of the largest cities in Wales, especially Cardiff and Swansea, and major companies have helped to stimulate technological development and innovation. Important among these are the growth of the aerospace complex around Broughton, Unilever establishing its European IT headquarters in Ewloe, and the establishment of the new Institute of Life Sciences in Swansea, backed by IBM.

Two other new research and development institutions are The Centre for Advanced Software Technology in Bangor and ECM2 in Port Talbot, a centre for manufacturing research and development.

Scotland

Enterprise and Development Agency
Scottish Enterprise: 0141 228 2000; www.scottish-enterprise.com
Highlands and Islands Enterprise: 01463 234171; www.hie.co.uk
The public sector accounts for nearly 24% of employment in Scotland, within which the local councils, hospitals and universities are very important.

Tourism provides around 8% of jobs in Scotland as a whole, and is particularly significant in the Highlands and Islands where other sectors perform less strongly than in the central belt.

Edinburgh is the capital city and seat of government of Scotland. Service industries, in particular those in the professional, scientific and financial sectors, dominate the economy, with the Scottish parliament creating many jobs. It is the second largest financial and administrative centre in the UK after London.

The surviving manufacturing sector is still important, especially in the areas of electrical and electronics engineering; paper, printing and publishing; and food and drink. Biotechnology, software and creative industries such as TV and film make a major contribution to the region's considerable economic wealth.

Glasgow is Scotland's largest city. Its economy too is dominated by the service sector, particularly in the areas of finance and banking, public administration, education, healthcare, hotels and tourism, and business services. The knowledge-based industries such as e-commerce technology, computing and science are a growth area in the city.

Moves are being made to strengthen links between Edinburgh and Glasgow, only 50 miles apart, to produce a 'metro region' able to exploit the strengths of both and benefit from economies of scale.

Perth, right in the heart of Scotland, is one of its most fertile areas, hence agriculture, food and drink are important to the local economy.

Scotland's fourth city, Dundee, has traditionally been summed up in the phrase 'jute, jam and journalism'. Today, although the textile industry has declined, the main industries in the city still include textiles, printing and food processing, together with engineering, computers and other electronic industries, including computer games development. Dundee University excels in Life Sciences, and is a high calibre cancer-research centre, attracting biotechnology companies to the city. The Scottish Crop Research Institute here carries out research into genetic modification of foods.

Aberdeen, the 'oil capital of Europe', owes its prosperity to North Sea oil and gas which have attracted many international companies to the city, directly and indirectly linked with the oil industry. Traditional activities including fishing, agriculture, textiles, and papermaking are still important to the city's economy. New hi-tech businesses, including software development, are growing.

Inverness is a very important retail, business and medical centre for those living in the Highland region. The biggest employers are public sector administration and services, light engineering, technology and electronics, oil platform construction, food processing, timber, printing, and tourism.

> I settled into work immediately and found a place to live without too many problems. The pace of life in Edinburgh is unlike that in other capital cities, but gives access to far greater amenities. Living and working here is easy to do – plenty of jobs and accommodation available if you look at the right time of year (avoid festivals and start of terms).
>
> Bob Grayson

Over one quarter of employment in the Highland region is in distribution, hotels and catering, with a further quarter in public administration, education and health. Fishing and agriculture also account for much employment.

The most important sectors of the Islands' economies are fishing, fish farming and processing, agriculture, and tourism. New sectors of potential growth are emerging, which include wind farming, renewable energies, teleworking and Gaelic broadcasting.

Northern Ireland

Enterprise and Development Agencies
Enterprise Northern Ireland: 028 7776 3555; www.enterpriseni.com
Invest Northern Ireland: 028 9023 9090; www.investni.com

Northern Ireland is the smallest economy of all the UK regions, only about two-thirds the size of NE England, the next smallest. However, on a GDP per capita basis Northern Ireland is performing very well with a higher rate than both NE England and Wales.

For many years, the economy was held back by sometimes violent conflict between Catholic and Protestant paramilitary organisations and the British Army, with the region receiving low levels of foreign investment due to the perception that it was little more than a warzone due to the fighting between the various terrorist factions. Since the 1990s this picture has changed dramatically, with the political situation being improved greatly since the long-awaited peace agreement which has finally brought some measure of stability.

The economy has also been boosted by the knock-on effect of the equally recent and rapid growth of the Republic of Ireland. In 2005 the Northern Ireland economy grew almost twice as fast as the UK as a whole, a feature which is expected to continue. The unemployment rate is around 4.5%, lower than the UK as a whole at 5.6%. When you consider that it stood at 17.2% in 1986, it is easy to see what a dramatic change has taken place over the last twenty years.

The main industries in Northern Ireland are in the manufacturing sector, including machinery and equipment, electronics and textiles – especially the production of the world-renowned quality Irish linens. Aerospace and shipbuilding are also important. As in other parts of the UK, some of these traditional industries are showing a decline, with more modern industries such as chemicals and engineering increasing their share of manufacturing output. Since the Good Friday Agreement, tourism to the province has increased and it makes an important contribution to the employment scene.

Belfast is in the process of undergoing a complete regeneration and face-lift, centred on redevelopment of the shipyard close to the city airport. It has a place in history, being the yard where the Titanic was built, and is being remodelled for the 21st century as the largest (185 acres) mixed-use waterside development in Europe, appropriately enough called Titanic Quarter.

United Kingdom's 20 Biggest Private Companies 2006		
Rank	Company	Activity
1	Gala Coral	Betting and Gaming Operator
2	John Lewis Partnership	Retailer
3	Somerfield	Supermarket Operator
4	Palmer and Harvey	Food Wholesaler
5	Ineos Group	Chemicals Maker
6	Booker	Cash and Carry Operator
7	Stemcor	Steel Trader
8	Littlewoods Shop Direct	Home Shopping Retailer
9	John Swire and Sons	Conglomerate
10	Caudwell Holdings	Mobile Phone Retailer
11	SCH Group	IT Infrastructure Integrator
12	Laing O'Rourke	Construction Contractor
13	Grampian Country Food	Food Producer
14	Arcadia Group	Fashion Retailer
16	Virgin Atlantic	Airline and Tour Operator
17	Brakes	Food Distributor
18	TI Automotive	Car Part Maker
19	Iceland	Frozen Food Retailer
20	Vetco International	Oilfield Services Provider

Source: Fast Track Top Track 100. For the full list, see www.fasttrack.co.uk.

Several big multinational companies have already taken up office space in the area, including Microsoft and Citigroup, attracted by the lowest house prices and office rents in the UK. This is a situation which may not last, however – house prices are rising rapidly as a result of Northern Ireland's booming economy.

◼ DIRECTORY OF MAJOR EMPLOYERS

Public Services

Some of the largest employers throughout Britain are found in the public service sector.

Government

Civil Service: 020 7276 1234; www.civil-service.gov.uk
National Assembly for Wales: 0845 010 5500 www.wales.gov.uk
Scottish Executive: 0131 556 8400 or 08457 741741;
www.scotland.gov.uk
Northern Ireland Executive: 027 9052 0700; www.northern
ireland.gov.uk

Local Councils

Links to all local authority websites are at www.direct.gov.uk/en/Dl1/
Directories/Localcouncils/index.htm
Police Service: www.police.uk/recruitment.asp

Judicial System

Her Majesty's Courts Service: 020 7189 2000 or 0845 456 8770;
www.hmcourts-service.gov.uk
Crown Prosecution Service: 020 7796 8000; www.cps.gov.uk
Scottish Court Service: 0131 229 9200; www.scotcourts.gov.uk
Crown Office and Procurator Fiscal Service: 0131 226 2626;
www.crownoffice.gov.uk
Northern Ireland Court Service: 028 9032 8594; www.courtsni.gov.uk
Public Prosecutions Service (N.I): 028 9054 2444; www.cjsni.gov.uk

National Health Service

England: www.nhs.uk
Scotland: www.show.scot.nhs.uk
Wales: www.wales.nhs.uk
Northern Ireland: www.healthandcareni.co.uk
Universities: Links to all university websites are at www.ucas.ac.uk

Tourist Boards

Enjoy England: 020 8846 9000; www.enjoyengland.com
Visit Wales: 08708 300306; ww.visitwales.co.uk
Visit Scotland: 01463 716996; www.visitscotland.com
Northern Ireland Tourist Board: 028 9024 6609;
www.discovernorthernireland.com.

Other

The Post Office: 08457 223344; www.postoffice.co.uk
English Heritage: 0870 333 1181; www.english-heritage.org.uk
Welsh Historic Monuments: 01443 336000; www.cadw.wales.gov.uk
Scottish Natural Heritage: 01463 725000; www.snh.org.uk
Historic Scotland: 0131 668 8600; www.historic-scotland.gov.uk
Environment and Heritage Service Northern Ireland: 028 9054 3145;
www.ehsni.gov.uk

Northern Ireland Water Service: 08457 440088; www.waterni.gov.uk
Scottish Water: 0845 601 8855; www.scottishwater.co.uk

Retail and Wholesale

Agnew Group: 028 9034 2411; www.agnewcars.com. Car dealer
Alliance Boots: 0115 950 6111; www.allianceboots.com. Pharmacy, health and beauty.
Arcadia Group: 0113 380 6623; www.arcadiagroup.co.uk. Fashion chains including Burton, Wallis, Topshop, and Miss Selfridge.
Arnold Clark Automobiles: 0845 600 3775; www.arnoldclark.co.uk. Vehicle retail.
Booker: 01933 371000; www.booker-plc.com. Cash and carry wholesalers.
Brakes: 0845 606 9090; www.brake.co.uk. Catering food wholesaler/ distributor
Capper and Co: 01444 233238; Grocery wholesaler and retailer.
Caudwell Holdings: 01270 412020; www.caudwell.com. Mobile phone retail.
DSGi: 0870 850 3333; www.dsgiplc.com. Electrical goods inc. Dixons.
Henderson Group: 028 9034 2733; www.henderson-group.com. Food wholesaler.
Iceland: 01244 842842; www.iceland.co.uk. Frozen foods.
John Lewis Partnership: 08456 049 049; www.johnlewis.com. Department stores.
John Menzies: 0131 225 8555; www.johnmenziesplc.com. Books and newspaper distribution and sales.
Kingfisher: 020 7372 8008; www.kingfisher.co.uk. Home improvement chain stores.
Kwik-Fit: 0800 222111; www.kwik-fit.co.uk. Motor parts.
Littlewoods Shop Direct: 08457 888222; www.lwsdg.co.uk. Home shopping.
Marks & Spencer: 0845 302 1234; www.marks-and-spencer.com. Clothes, foods and household.
Palmer and Harvey Group: 01273 222100; www.palmerharvey.co.uk. Food wholesaler.
J. Sainsbury: 020 7695 6000; www.j-sainsbury.co.uk. Supermarkets.
W.H. Smith: 01793 616161; www.whsmith.co.uk. Stationery and books.
Somerfield: 0117 935 9359; www.somerfield.plc.uk. Supermarkets.
SHS Group: 028 045 4647; www.shs-group.co.uk. Grocery.
Tesco: 0800 505555; www.tesco.com. Supermarkets.

Hotel, Bar and Restaurant Chains

Hilton Hotels Corporation: 020 7856 8000; www.hiltonworldwide.com. Hotels.
Scottish and Newcastle: 0131 203 2000; www.scottish-newcastle.com. Hotels, motels, bars, and restaurants.
Whitbread: 020 7606 4455; www.whitbread.co.uk. Pubs and restaurants.

Leisure

Bourne Leisure Holdings: 0870 165 0154; www.havenholidayhomes.co.uk.
Gala Coral: 0208 591 5151; www.galacoral.co.uk. Betting and gaming.
Odeon and UCI Cinema Group: 0800 88 89 50; www.odeon.co.uk. Cinemas.

Manufacturing and Production

British Polythene Industries: 01475 501000; www.bpipoly.com. Plastics manufacture.
Coats: 01325 394394; www.coatscrafts.co.uk. Needlecraft products.
Diageo: 020 7927 5200; www.diageo.com. Alcoholic drinks.
Imperial Chemicals Industry (ICI): 020 7009 5000; www.ici.com. Paints, adhesives and specialty products.
Norbord: 01786 812921; www.norbord.com. Wood-based laminates, veneers, flooring, etc.
Ethicon: 0131 453 5555; www.ethicon.com. Medical and pharmaceutical products.
Foyle Food Group: 028 7186 0691; www.foylefoodgroup.com. Meat producer.
Grampian Country Food Group: 0113 386 5000; www.gcfg.com. Meat and poultry production and processing.
Ineos Group: 02380 287043; www.ineos.com. Chemicals.
JCB: 0800 581761; www.jcb.co.uk. Construction equipment.
Linpac Group: 0121 607 6700; www.weir.co.uk. Packaging.
Lucite International: 0870 240 4620; www.lucite.com. Acrylic-based products.
TI Automotive: 01865 871883; www.tiauto.com. Car part maker.
Unilever: 020 7822 5252; www.unilever.co.uk. Food, household, beauty products.

Computers, IT and Electronics

Cisco Systems: 020 8824 1000; www.cisco.com/uk. Networking for the internet.

Ericsson: 01483 303666; www.ericsson.com. Mobile communications technology.

IBM UK: 023 9256 1000; www.ibm.com/uk. IT products.

Motorola: 01506 473300; www.motorola.com. Wireless, broadband and automotive communications technologies.

SCH Group: 01794 830377; www.schgroup.com. IT infrastructure integrator.

THUS: 0800 027 5848; www.thus.co.uk. Telecommunications, call centres.

Westcoast: 0118 912 6000; www.westcoast.co.uk. IT product distributor.

Finance and Banking

High Street Banks

Bank of Scotland: www.bankofscotland.co.uk.

Barclays: 0845 677 0002; www.barclays.co.uk.

First Trust Bank: 028 9032 5599; www.aibgroup.com.

HSBC: 0800 032 4738; www.hsbc.co.uk.

Lloyds TSB: 0845 300 0000; www.lloydstsb.com.

NatWest: 0800 015 4212; www.natwest.com.

Northern Bank: 028 9024 5277; www.northernbank.co.uk.

Royal Bank of Scotland: www.rbs.co.uk

Other Finance

JPMorgan: 0800 204020; www.jpmorgan.com. Banking and asset management.

Prudential: 0800 000000; www.pru.co.uk. Insurance and financial services.

Scottish Widows: 0845 608 0371; www.scottishwidows.co.uk. Insurance, pensions and investments.

Standard Life: 0131 245 9944; www.standardlife.co.uk. Insurance.

Construction and Engineering

Airbus UK: 01179 693831; www.airbus.com.

Barratt Construction: 01923 297311; www.barratthomes.co.uk. House-building.

Boeing UK: 020 7930 5000: www.boeing.co.uk. Aerospace and defence systems.

British Aerospace: 01252 373232; www.baesystems.com. Defence and aerospace systems.

David McLean Holdings: 01244 283591; www.davidmclean.co.uk. Building contractor.

Lagan Group: 028 9026 1000; www.lagangroup.co.uk. Construction and civil engineering.

Laing O'Rourke: 01322 296200; www.laingorourke.com. Large scale construction projects.

The Miller Group: 0870 336 5000; www.miller.co.uk. General construction, property development and civil engineering.
Persimmon Homes: 01904 642199; www.persimmonhomes.com. House-building.
Redrow Homes: 01628 539703; www.redrow.co.uk. House-building.

Fuel and Energy

British Gas: 0845 600 6113; www.house.co.uk. Gas and electricity supplier.
npower: 0800 316 2604; www.npower.com. Gas and electricity supplier.
Powergen: 0800 052 0346; www.powergen.co.uk. Gas and electricity supplier.
Scottish Power: 0800 027 5812; www.theenergypeople.com. Gas and electricity supplier.
Scottish and Southern Energy: 0173 456000; www.scottish-southern.co.uk. Gas and electricity supplier.
AEA Group: 0870 190 1900; www.aeat.co.uk. Energy and environment consultancy.
Abbot Group: 01224 299600; www.abbotgroup.com. Oil and gas industry drilling services.
BP Oil: 020 7496 4000; www.bp.com. Oil exploration and supply.
British Energy: 01452 652222; www.british-energy.co.uk. Electricity producer.
John Wood Group: 01224 851000; www.woodgroup.com. Energy services.
Shell UK Exploration & Production: 0845 600 1819; www.shell.com. Oil exploration and supply.
Vetco: 020 7845 8800; www.vetco.com. Oilfield services provider.

Communications

British Telecom (BT): Freefone 0800 800150; www.bt.com. National telephone network.
Orange Mobile Phone Service: 0800 079 2000; www.orange.co.uk. Mobile phone network.
Vodafone Mobile Phone Service: 0808 040 8408; www.vodafone.co.uk. Mobile phone network.

Media

British Broadcasting Corporation (BBC): 08700 100222; www.bbc.co.uk. Non-commercial television and radio.
British Sky Broadcasting Ltd: 08705 800874; www.sky.com. Satellite television.
Channel 4: 0845 076 0191; www.channel4.com. Commercial television.

Channel 5: 0207 421 7270; www.channel5.co.uk. Commercial television.
Independent Television (ITV): 0870 600 6766; www.itv.com.
Commercial television.
Independent Television News (ITN): 020 7833 3000; www.itn.co.uk.
Television news.
Virgin Media: 0845 840 7777; www.virginmedia.com. Cable TV and
internet.
Johnston Press: 0131 225 3361; www.johnstonpress.co.uk. Local
newspaper publishing.
News International: 0207 782 6000; www.newsint.co.uk. National
newspapers.
Northcliffe Media: 020 7938 6000; www.thisisnorthcliffe.co.uk. Regional
newspaper publishing.
D.C Thomson & Co: 01382 223131; www.dcthomson.co.uk. Newspaper
and magazine publishing.

Transport

Ballyvesey Holdings: 028 9084 9321; www.ballyveseyholdings.com.
Transport services provider.
British Airports Authority (BAA): 020 7834 9449; www.baa.co.uk.
Airport management.
British Airways: 0870 850 9850; www.britishairways.com. Domestic and
international flights.
easyJet: 020 7241 9000; www.easyjet.com. Domestic and international
flights.
London Underground: 020 222 1234; www.tfl.gov.uk/tube.
National Express Coaches: 08705 808080; www.nationalexpress.com.
Network Rail: 020 7557 8000; www.networkrail.co.uk. Rail infrastructure.
Stagecoach: 01738 442111; www.stagecoachbus.com. Bus and coach
services.
Strathclyde Passenger Transport: 0141 332 6811; www.spt.co.uk.
Public transport services in the Glasgow area.
Translink: 028 9089 9400; www.translink.co.uk. Public transport provider
Northern Ireland.
UK Rail Companies: www.rail.co.uk/ukrail/railcomp/towelcm.htm. Links
to most UK rail companies.
Virgin Atlantic: 01293 562345; www.virgin-atlantic.com. Airline and tour
operator.

Science and Biotechnology

Acambis: 01223 275300; www.acambis.com. Vaccine development.
Agri-Food and Biosciences Institute (AFBI): 028 9025 5689; www.
afbini.gov.uk. Research in agriculture, food, animal health, environment,
and biosciences.

Antisoma: 020 8799 8200; www.antisoma.com. Cancer treatments.
Cambridge Antibody Technology: 0122 471471; www.
cambridgeantibody.com. Human monoclonal antibody therapeutics.
Cancer Research Technology: 020 7269 3640; www.cancertechnology.
com.
Protherics: 020 7246 9950; www.protherics.com. Critical care
pharmaceuticals.
Roslin Institute: 0131 527 4200; www.roslin.ac.uk. Animal genetics and
development.
Rowett Research Institute: 01224 712751; www.rowett.ac.uk. Research
into human nutrition.
Scottish Crop Research Institute: 01382 562731; www.scri.sari.ac.uk.
Crop research, including genetic modification.
Vernalis: 0118 977 3133; www.vernalis.com. Neurology and central
nervous system disorder treatments.

Miscellaneous

John Swire and Sons: 020 7630 0353; www.swire.com. Conglomerate.
PHS: 02920 851000; www.phs.co.uk. Office services provider.
Stemcor: 020 7775 3600; www.stemcor.com. Steel trader.

Online Company Directories

The following websites include searchable databases of companies based
in a geographical area or a particular field of business.
1st Directory: www.1stdirectory.com.
All Jobs: www.alljobsuk.com.
Business Directory UK: www.business-directory-uk.co.uk.
Companies House: www.companieshouse.gov.uk. Database of all UK
companies.
London Biotechnology Network: 0207 665 1500; www.
londonbiotechnology.co.uk
London Stock Exchange: www.londonstockexchange.com.
Scottish Oil and Gas Industries: www.oilandgas.co.uk.
UK Technology, Innovation and Growth Awards: http://etf.
cnetnetworks.co.uk/ig07/showcase-companies.htm.
UK Networks Directory: www.entrepreneurs.gov.uk/directory.cfm

Useful Publications and Websites

Writers' & Artists' Yearbook: published annually by A&C Black (London).
The Writer's Handbook: published annually by Macmillan (London).
Both the above list UK publishers and other media companies together
with contact details of newspapers and magazines.
Fast track: www.fasttrack.co.uk. League tables of top UK companies.
EURES (European Employment Services): http://europa.eu.int/eures.
British Employment Law: www.emplaw.co.uk.

■ STARTING A BUSINESS

The numbers of new businesses started in the UK has been rising steadily in recent years and there are signs that the rate will increase in coming years. In the first six months of 2004, for example, 288,000 new UK businesses were started, almost 25% up on the same period in 2003, when there were 233,000. It was the highest level recorded since figures were first kept in 1988.

At the regional level, London had the highest number of business start-ups – with London local authorities taking the top eight positions.The South West was the next most entrepreneurial region. Leisure, business and professional services, hotel and catering have all seen high numbers of start-ups in the past decade.

This is a reflection of large rises in people becoming self-employed to boost their income or achieve a change in lifestyle. The strength of the economy has been pivotal in providing greater opportunities for individuals to set up in business. There has also been a positive government effort to encourage entrepreneurial activity, and there are a number of agencies and websites offering assistance and advice to new business-owners.

Not all these businesses succeed, of course – many new businesses founder fairly quickly. Across the UK there is about a 70% success rate, measured on the numbers of new businesses still trading after three years.

In rural areas especially, where the chance of finding a traditional nine to five job is limited, many people start their own businesses, sometimes supplemented by a number of short-term, seasonal or part-time jobs. There are an increasing number of very small businesses in rural areas, many of them designed to start and stay small and local, others with the potential to grow into far larger companies.

New technology has created far more opportunities for entrepreneurs to set up small businesses. With no more than a computer and a website, you can set up and carry on an e-commerce business from the

> Stuart was involved in a new start company based in Livingston and would work part time for them and part time for our own company still doing system architecture work. I would build up an accountancy business gaining local clients and doing some telephone support work for my replacement at my previous employer's offices. We also planned to buy a small croft to grow vegetables, keep a few chickens, and maybe a couple of pigs.
>
> Sandy Nairn

most remote areas. In the publishing industry, more and more functions are being carried out remotely by freelance writers, editors and indexers. Copy is produced and sent electronically with no need for long, expensive trips to a publisher based in London or Glasgow – or indeed, New York or Lausanne.

The tourism industry presents plenty of opportunity for small businesses. Foreign and domestic visitors all need accommodation, food and drink, and 'things to do' during their holidays. And they all want to spend money on good value products and services.

Businesses which are less likely to do well in remote rural areas are those which incur expensive transport costs. Traditional agriculture is becoming hardly viable in many remote areas, although with some imagination and the willingness to try something new, there are markets to be tapped in this area too. With concerns about the genetic modification of foods being much in the news, small-scale organic farms and market gardens are finding new customers among catering businesses and residents looking for good quality, local produce.

Residence Regulations

EU nationals have the right to move to the UK to set up in business, to buy an existing business or to provide services without any restrictions, and do not need a visa.

Businessmen and self-employed persons from other countries are free to visit the UK and transact business during their stay (as long as they have the necessary visa and/or entry clearance). Those who want to come permanently to the UK to set themselves up in business or self-employment, or to join as a partner or take over an existing business, must satisfy certain requirements. Most importantly, they must bring at least £200,000 of their own money to invest in the business and they must show that the business will create new, paid full-time employment for at least two people who are already settled in the UK. For further details see the section *Residence and Entry Regulations for Non-EU Nationals*.

> For a few years we augmented our pensions by offering bed and breakfast in our home – at which we were so successful that when [my wife] Pam reached 60 and chose to give up the B&B, we found several previous guests still insisted on coming each year, even though we were no longer advertising accommodation. They had by then become friends, and it was difficult to say no to the extra money, so we continued to have paying guests for several weeks every summer.
> Tony Shinkins

Planning Permission

If your business is to run from a property which needs conversion or alterations for the purpose, you will need to investigate the planning implications. Unless the property was previously used for the same purpose, you will have to apply to the planning department of the local council for permission for 'change of use'. Where the business is open to members of the public they will take into account such things as parking provision and health and safety considerations. In the end, it may be that you are simply not allowed to run that sort of business from the premises you have in mind. So it is wise to do your research first – ideally before you've even bought the property. Planning department officials will advise you on the chances of obtaining planning permission.

Buying an Existing Business

One way of avoiding planning problems and the pitfalls of starting a business completely from scratch, is to buy an existing business. This affords the obvious benefits of being able to walk into a business and take up where the previous owner left off. However, it is advisable to do some research locally to discover why the business is being sold, and how long it has been on the market. If it didn't do well, you need to work out whether you could make a go of a similar business in the same place. The viability of the business is generally reflected in the price asked, of course – a thriving business with 'a genuine reason for sale' is likely to cost you far more than one which has been struggling to make a profit.

Buying a franchise is another way into business, which takes some of the risk out of setting up on your own. Franchises have the advantage of offering, in most cases, a tried and tested name and product, training and back-up support. The pros and cons of franchises are discussed further below.

Finding Premises or an Existing Business

Properties suitable for conversion into business premises, as well as existing businesses, can be found for sale and to rent from the same sources as domestic properties. Estate Agents usually have commercial properties on their books. Details can be obtained from their websites. See *Setting Up Home* for a full list of contacts.

Local newspapers also advertise businesses and business properties. *Daltons Business* has a database of businesses for sale across the UK at www.daltonsbusiness.com.

Cost of Buying a Business

When considering businesses for sale or to lease, the price asked will depend on a number of factors. Bear in mind that some are sold simply as premises, previously used for a certain purpose, while others are selling the entire business, together with fixtures and fittings, stock and 'goodwill'

Sample Businesses For Sale In Britain March 2007		
Type	**Area**	**Price**
Internet Café with flat	Greater London	£69,000 (leasehold) £545,000 (freehold)
Plumbing and Drainage Services	Devon	£20,000 (franchise business)
Grocery Store	West Midlands	£150,000 (leasehold) £450,000 (freehold)
Bed and Breakfast	Kent	£465,000 (freehold)
Newsagent/Off Licence	Lancashire	£249,995 (freehold) with accommodation
Fast Food Takeaway with accommodation	Essex	£60,000 (leasehold) £260,000 (freehold)
Designer Jewellery Studio	Cornwall	£85,000 (leasehold)
Residential Village Inn	Wales	£50,000 (leasehold) £395,000 (freehold)
Tearoom and MOT Workshop	Scotland	£300,000 (freehold)
Kitchen Design/Manufacture	N. Ireland	£55,000 (leasehold)

– i.e. you are paying an element for the existing customer base that hopefully will continue to patronise the business after it changes hands. Location is, of course, another important element of the asking price.

Always try to ascertain how long the property has been for sale, as this is generally a good guide to whether the price being asked is reasonable or not. If it has been on the market for at least a year it is generally worth making an initial offer below the asking price. Where they are selling a business as a going concern, the vendors should make copies of previous accounts available to you. If they will not, or say they have none available, it is wise to be cautious – it may not be such a thriving business as they imply. There are few regulations in relation to bed and breakfast providers, so it is rare to find that such businesses maintain full accounts.

Prices of Business Premises

Prices of business premises vary greatly depending on location. Generally, the closer to centres of population, the more expensive the property.

Procedures Involved in Starting a Business

People who work for themselves on their own or in partnership with one or more people are classified as self-employed. You must inform Her Majesty's Revenue and Customs (HMRC) if you are self-employed. If your

> Don't forget to register with the Department of Revenue and Customs as self-employed. All you need to do is call 0845 915 4515 with your business plan and NI number to hand. They will take all the details and send you out a letter confirming your status with your all-important individual reference number. Don't lose this letter whatever you do! This number is the holy grail of all your business information when it comes to applying for funding.
>
> Dionne Rennie

taxable turnover (total sales) is more than £64,000 in a 12-month period, you must also register for value added tax (VAT) with Customs and Excise. The VAT registration threshold is usually increased each year.

To register as self-employed, call the Self-Employment Registration Helpline on 0845-915 4515. Or you can download form CWF1 from their website and post it to National Insurance Contributions Office, Central Agent Authorisation Team, Longbenton, Newcastle upon Tyne NE98 1ZZ, or take it to any HM Revenue & Customs office. www.hmrc.gov.uk.

You can register for VAT online at www.hmrc.gov.uk. For general registration queries contact the National Advice Service on 0845 010 9000.

There is a simple guide to *Starting Up In Business* on the HMRC website which explains the legal processes required.

Business Structures

There are a number of different structures you can adopt for a business, which vary in the number and type of regulations the owner is required to observe.

Sole Trader

The simplest form of business. As its name suggests, this is a 'one-man' or 'one-woman' business. There is no need to register it with anybody, other than notifying the Inland Revenue that you are self-employed. You will be liable to pay National Insurance contributions unless your earnings are very low, in which case you may be able to elect not to pay contributions until your earnings reach the statutory level.

There is risk involved if the business should fail, because a sole trader is personally liable for all debts, which means he or she could lose all their assets, including their house.

Records of all income and outgoings should be kept, together with relevant receipts, because these details must be entered on the self-assessment tax return, sent each year in April. This asks for the information required to calculate income tax and capital gains tax for the year. Once the form is completed, it is returned to the Inland Revenue, who will calculate the tax owed if they receive it before 30th September. Alternatively, the business owner or their accountant can calculate the tax bill, in which case it must be returned by 31st January. There is no requirement to send receipts with the tax return, but the tax office may ask to see them to check the submitted figures.

If a sole trader trades under a name other than that of the owner, the owner's name and address must legally be displayed at the business premises and on stationery.

Partnership

Where two or more people run a business together, they may set up a partnership. Partners can set up a business as informally as a sole trader, but this may not be advisable. Even the best of friends or colleagues who work well together might have disagreements once entering business, and this could lead to disputes in the future unless financial arrangements regarding the business are clearly laid out in the first place. For this reason, a formal deed of partnership, drawn up by a solicitor, should be considered, although it is not mandatory.

A self-assessment tax return is completed in April by each of the partners. The tax bill for each is calculated as if their share of the partnership is a profit that they have made on their own.

If a partnership is trading under a name other than that of the owners, their names and addresses should be displayed. Partners are each personally liable for all the debts of the business should it fail.

Company

Setting up a company is a far more complicated procedure than starting a business in the ways listed above. It may not be necessary or worthwhile to turn it into such a formal and highly regulated structure, at least in the early days when the business is small and still finding its feet. Company officers have wide responsibilities and obligations in law, so it is a good idea to take advice from a solicitor or an accountant as to whether an incorporated company is the best way to run your business.

One of the biggest advantages of a company is that, in most cases, a director's or member's liability for debts is limited, so personal assets are not at risk if the company is wound up.

There are four main types of company:

- **Private company limited by shares.** Members' liability is limited to the amount unpaid on shares they hold.
- **Private company limited by guarantee.** Members' liability is limited to the amount they have agreed to contribute to the company's assets if it is wound up.
- **Private unlimited company.** There is no limit to the member's liability.
- **Public limited company (PLC).** The company's shares may be offered for sale to the general public and members' liability is limited to the amount unpaid on shares held by them.

> I was amazed how quick and easy it was [to form a company].
> I simply filled in a number of online forms, giving details of the
> business, the directors – there were to be three of us, myself, my son
> and my best friend – and the shareholders. We three were also the
> only shareholders, with me holding 50% and the other two holding
> 25% each. I named myself as Company Secretary, although that is
> a role my accountant will later be taking on for me. I received my
> Certificate of Incorporation and Memorandum and Articles through
> the post the following day – and it all cost me just £37.
> Sally Hargreaves

Companies in Great Britain are registered at Companies House in London, while those in Northern Ireland are registered via the NI Department of Enterprise, Trade and Investment (DETI).

Briefly, a private company must have a minimum of one director and a company secretary, while a public company must have at least two directors and a formally qualified company secretary. The business of the company and the way it will be run is laid out in a memorandum and articles of association. These itemise such matters as the minimum and maximum number of directors it should have, how many of these constitute a quorum at meetings and the procedure should the company be wound up at any time. Companies are legally obliged to hold regular, minuted meetings for members, and to deliver full annual accounts and an annual return to Companies House. The names, addresses and occupations of all directors must be notified to Companies House, and any changes must be notified immediately. These details are available for public inspection by anyone who asks.

There are minor differences in the rules and regulations regarding companies registered in England, Scotland and Wales. Your company will automatically be registered in the appropriate country. The process of formation and fees are different but broadly similar in Northern Ireland.

It is possible to buy ready-made companies from company formation agents, and company registration agents will help with the work involved in forming a new company. For a small fee (£30–£40 for 'same day formation' and even less if you are prepared to wait a little longer) you can complete online forms and they will send you your incorporation documents through the post.

Useful Contacts

Smart Company Formations: 0800 8030818; www.smartcompany formations.co.uk
UKPLC: 0870 486 6000; www.ukplc.net
Coddan: 0207 637 3881; www.ukincorp.co.uk

Alternatively, you can incorporate a company yourself by sending the following to Companies House:

- **A memorandum of association** including the company's name, the address of the registered office, and what the company will do (its object). This may be stated as simply as 'to carry on business as a general commercial company'.
- **Articles of association** which set out the rules to follow for running the company's internal affairs.
- **Form 10,** listing personal details of the company's directors and secretary.
- **Form 12,** a statutory decollation of compliance with all the legal requirements relating to the incorporation of a company.
- **A registration fee** of £20. (A premium 'same-day service' is also available at £50 which guarantees incorporation on the same day documents are received at Companies House offices as long as they are hand delivered before 3pm.)

A similar process applies for Northern Ireland incorporations. For full details see Companies Registry on the DETI website.

Useful Contacts
Companies House: 0870 3333 636; www.companieshouse.gov.uk
Companies Registry (N.I.): 0845 604 8888; www.detini.gov.uk

Franchise
The full term for this way of doing business is 'business format franchising'. It is the granting of a licence by one person (the franchisor) to another (the franchisee) which entitles the franchisee to trade under the trade mark or trade name of the franchisor and to make use of an entire package, comprising all the elements necessary to establish a previously untrained person in the business and to run it with assistance of a predetermined basis.

The franchisor receives an initial fee from the franchisee, payable at the outset. This is followed by on-going management service fees, usually based on a percentage of annual turnover or mark-ups on supplies. The franchisor has an obligation to support the franchise network with training, product development, advertising, promotional activities, and management services.

A formal contract must be made between franchisor and franchisee, and legal advice is essential. It is also strongly recommended that any franchise you consider should be run by a member of the *British Franchise Association:* 01491-578050; www.thebfa.org. They are the regulatory body for franchising in the UK.

> There's quite a lot of funding available and your advisor will be
> able to point you in the right direction. If you're under 30, like me,
> then the world's your oyster as there are quite a few grants just
> an application form away. The most important thing to remember
> about these forms is to check and double check you've filled them in
> correctly, you don't want your money disappearing into someone
> else's bank account! It can take a while to get your funding, so be
> patient but don't be afraid to call for regular updates.
>
> Dionne Rennie

Sources of Finance

There are a number of sources of funding to assist with the formation
or expansion of a business, although unless you have some personal
capital to invest, whether from your savings or through financial help from
friends and relatives, you may find it difficult to lever further funds from
external sources. Broadly, the formal sources of finance are banks, venture
capitalists and the public sector. As part of the move to encourage the
formation of businesses of all sizes in Britain, a variety of public bodies
have funds available to assist new businesses to get off the ground and to
develop or expand existing businesses.

Enterprise Agencies

There is a network of these bodies throughout the UK, going by different
names – in England most of them are known as Local Enterprise Agencies
(LEAs), while the Scottish equivalent are Local Enterprise Companies (LECs).
They are funded by a mixture of government and private sponsorship
and exist to help businesses, in particular new small businesses, through
offering advice, training and information. Their remit is to promote economic
regeneration through the formation and growth of small firms. Different
services are offered by different LEAs and LECs, so visit their individual
websites for details of what is available in your area.

A similar role is performed by Enterprise Northern Ireland, and in Wales
by the Department for Enterprise, Innovation and Networks.

In addition there are national development and investment agencies
which tend to concentrate on bigger, longer-established firms, and also
work to attract foreign companies to set up subsidiaries and/or do business
in the UK.

These bodies do offer some finance for new businesses, in the form of
grants and loans under a variety of schemes. It is not always clear from
their websites exactly what forms of finance might be available – but just
because you can't find a specific reference to them it does not mean there

may not be funding available for you. It is always worth contacting them by telephone to ask what assistance they can give. They tend to prefer to work on a face to face basis as their own funding from government is dependent on tangible results – ie numbers of businesses created in their areas – so they are generally eager to help.

Business Link is a government guide to all aspects of starting a business plus sources of further advice and financial assistance. The website (details below) includes the Grants and Support Directory, a database containing details of grant and support schemes from central and local government as well as private organisations.

The Scottish Executive administers Regional Selective Assistance, a national grant aimed at encouraging investment and job creation mainly in the areas of Scotland designated for regional aid in Assisted Areas, as specified by the European Commission. In addition, support may be available to SMEs in other designated areas. Businesses of all sizes can apply for RSA, whether they are Scottish-owned or owned or headquartered outside Scotland.

Useful Contacts

Business Link: 0845 6009 006; www.businesslink.gov.uk

England

National Federation of Enterprise Agencies: 01234 831623; www.nfea.com
Regional Development Agencies: 020 7222 8180; www.englandsrdas.com
UK Trade & Investment: 020 7215 8000; www.ukinvest.gov.uk

Wales

International Business Wales: 01443 845500; www.walestrade.com
Department of Enterprise, Innovation and Networks: 0845 010 3300; http://new.wales.gov.uk/about/departments/dein/?lang=en

Scotland

Business Gateway: 0845-609 6611; www.bgateway.com
Scottish Development International: 0141-228 2828; www.sdi.co.uk
Scottish Enterprise: 0141-228 2000 or 0845-607 8787; www.scottish-enterprise.com
Scottish Executive Regional Selective Assistance: 0141-242 5676/5481; www.rsascotland.gov.uk
Highlands and Islands Enterprise: 01463-234171; www.hie.co.uk

Northern Ireland

Enterprise Northern Ireland: 028 7776 3555; www.enterpriseni.com
Invest Northern Ireland: 028 9023 9090; www.investni.com
NI Business Info: 0800 027 0639; www.nibusinessinfo.co.uk

Local Councils

Local councils may have their own financial packages to assist in the improvement of properties and the creation and expansion of businesses. Generally these would be administered by the Economic Development Department or the local equivalent. (Department names vary between councils, so the best thing is to enquire via the switchboard or reception as to who would deal with your particular enquiry.) See the full list of local councils in *About Britain*.

Loan Finance

Most new businesses which receive external finance get it mainly in the form of loans, usually from the banks. Loans account for 40% of total external funding for new businesses.

Loans are available at competitive rates from some other sources. For example, *The Prince's Trust* offers loans to 18-30s who have a viable business idea.

Whether you can obtain a loan from any of these will depend on the quality of your business plan, the amount of revenue your business will generate, the security you can provide and your own personal credibility. As the main concern of any lender will be your ability to repay the loan and meet the interest charges, your main concern must be to convince them you are a 'safe bet'.

Those businesses which apply for, and receive, a loan are in the minority. In fact, fewer than 30% depend on loans, either because they do not wish to take on the risks and costs involved, or they are unable to raise external finance. It is very often those which do rely on this sort of financial assistance that get into trouble, so you need to think carefully about whether you actually need a loan or can manage without.

Useful Contacts

Finance Wales: 029 2033 8100; www.financewales.co.uk
Prince's Trust: 0800 842842; www.princes-trust.org.uk

Equity Capital

This is the core capital of the business, which helps to set it up in the first place and keep it going. If you have a good equity base it can help to unlock other funds such as loans or grants. You may have enough capital for this purpose from personal and informal sources. If not, there are other sources of equity capital, but they are not easy to obtain, and may involve you in losing some control over your running of the business.

Private individuals, venture capitalists and the public sector may inject funds if you can convince them your business is a sure-fire winner. However, their risks are high, so they will generally expect a high return. Where a substantial up-front investment is required, banks may be unable to finance such a project due to lack of security or cashflow – the high street banks are not in the business of risk-taking, which is perhaps why so few new businesses obtain funding from this source. Venture capitalists are professional investors looking for a good return on their money, and will therefore only back businesses capable of earning significant financial returns. Many of them avoid start-up businesses, seeing them as too big a risk and instead concentrate on developing existing businesses with a strong track record.

Useful Contacts

British Business Angels Association: 0207 089 2305; www.bbaa.org.uk
The British Venture Capital Association: 020 7025 2950; www.bvca.co.uk
Scottish Equity Partners: 0141 273 4000; www.sep.co.uk
Small Business Service: 0207 215 5000; www.sbs.gov.uk

Ideas for New Businesses

Freelancing

There is a wide range of work you can do from home, making use of new technology to find and keep in contact with clients. Such occupations as writing, editing, proof-reading, data input, indexing, translating, technical authoring, abstracting, distance teaching, graphics, illustration, web design, programming, and music composition can all be carried out successfully by individuals working from their own homes. This way of working has the advantage that you can adjust your working hours and work-rate to suit your own situation, either working full time or fitting the work around your other commitments as a part-time source of income.

If you have talents in these areas but are not formally trained in them, there are distance learning courses you can take from home, or face-to-face day and residential courses available in all manner of creative fields. Some courses allow you to work towards a formal qualification or diploma, others focus on assisting you to find markets for your work and launch you on the freelance path.

Courses

Eston Training: 01224 311992; www.estontrg.com. Technical authorship.
Chapterhouse: 01392 499488; www.chapterhousepublishing.co.uk. Copy-editing and proofreading.
College of Technical Authorship: 0161 437 4235; www.coltecha.u-net. com. Technical authorship.
Institute of Copywriting: 01934 713563; www.inst.org/copy. Copywriting.
The Society of Freelance Editors and Proofreaders: 020 7736 3278; www.sfep.org.uk. Copy-editing and proofreading.
The Society of Indexers: 0114 244 9561; www.indexers.org.uk. Indexing.

The Writers Bureau: 0845 345 5995 or 0161 228 2362; www.
writersbureau.com. Creative writing and journalism.
Hot Courses: www.hotcourses.com. Database of full time, part time and
evening classes in Britain.

Franchises

Franchising is a technique used by a variety of businesses in retailing,
business services, domestic services, car repairs, and fast food. This is one
of the fastest-growing areas for new businesses in the UK, which has come
relatively late to the technique compared with the USA.

The main advantages of franchising are that the business concept
and name is already established and works well, and that the franchisor
offers a complete package of support including advertising, training,
assistance to launch the business, and instructions about its day to day
running.

The disadvantages are that they require quite a large amount of capital
to begin with and that you do not have total control over your business.
If the franchisor gets into difficulty this can affect you through no fault of
your own. Generally, franchise agreements involve up-front support for the
initial period, with this support reducing after the initial period, however
the fees and royalties you pay to the franchisor continue for the full length
of the franchise agreement. This can mean that the returns on the business
are not as good as the returns you would get on a totally autonomous
business.

Franchises for sale can be found advertised alongside other businesses
for sale in newspapers and estate agents' publications.

British Franchise Association: 0870 161 4000 | www.british-franchise.
org.uk

Business Ideas

- **Tourism:** accommodation, sightseeing tours, provision of outdoor
  activities, painting/photography holidays, ancestry research.
- **Food and drink:** cafe, restaurant, hotel, bar, specialist food
  production.
- **Retail:** arts and crafts shop, specialist food shop, general store, post
  office, antiques, shop, bookshop.
- **Computer services:** hardware and software design, website design,
  support and repairs for home and business computer users.
- **Alternative therapies:** aromatherapy, psychotherapy, chiropractic,
  massage, yoga.
- **Trades:** builder, plumber, hairdresser, gardener, decorator, odd
  jobs.

- **Freelancing:** writing, editing, proofreading, data input, indexing, translating, technical authoring, abstracting, distance teaching, graphics, illustration, web design, programming, music composition.
- **Innovation and Technology:** new inventions; development of new products; research and development.
- **Manufacturing and Production:** new products, new brands, new techniques.
- **Property Services:** estate agency, managing holiday properties, lettings agency, relocation agency.
- **Financial Services:** accountancy, taxation.
- **Audio/Visual:** photography, videography, producing CDs and DVDs.
- **Animals:** kennels and catteries, horse riding school or trekking centre, alternative therapies for animals.
- **Music:** recording, composing, playing or singing at pubs, hotels, dances, weddings, running a recording studio, record label.
- **E-commerce:** buying and selling through internet auctions, travel site, weddings agency, marketing your business.
- **Consultancy:** providing professional advice in your sphere of expertise.
- **Exporting:** supplying typically British products to the folks back home.

Opening a Subsidiary

UK central Government and the devolved regional governments are all eager to tempt international businesses to expand into Britain. They will provide plenty of free advice and assistance, and also have various financial incentives available, in the form of grants and loans and tax breaks. In addition there are many private companies eager to invest in new businesses. There are more venture capitalists in the UK than in the rest of Europe, in addition to the commercial banks, companies and investment trusts. Some of these specialise in investing in new companies and all will provide finance for start-ups and expansions if you can persuade them you are a viable prospect.

The London Stock Exchange is a source of funding for businesses wishing to grow. The full-listing, main market is for established companies looking for £200 million or more, while for small, young and fast-growing companies, AIM is a quick, uncomplicated route to funding in the £5-200 million range. Full details of how to trade in these two markets can be found on the Stock Exchange website (see below).

You should not find any institutional barriers to setting up in Britain as a foreign business, because UK competition law is designed to ensure that all businesses have free access to the UK market place. Because the UK is part of the European Union, EU law may also have an effect, so it is important to understand the issues. If you feel your rights have been infringed or are concerned about any aspect of UK and EU competition law, a useful resource is the Competition Pro Bono Scheme. This is open to all individuals and businesses requiring advice, regardless of their location. Under the scheme, expert competition lawyers provide up to two hours free legal advice on the possible impact of UK, and European Union, competition rules on business activities within the UK.

UK Trade and Investment, part of the Department of Trade and Industry (DTI) provide free advice and assistance to companies. They will help you find business sites in the UK which best suit your needs, assign experts to assist you in setting up your business, provide facts and figures and analysis so you can make informed judgements. They will also give you ongoing support to help you access new markets and continue to grow your business. Advice about local labour markets, levels of employment, the costs of leasing or buying property, and the legal and taxation requirements of doing business in the UK are all essential details to investigate before embarking on this step.

UK Trade and Investment give a great deal on information on their website, including case studies of companies which have set up in the UK as well as plenty of practical advice and facts and figures. This is the best place to start when considering setting up a subsidiary in the UK. More advice and assistance is available if you contact them direct.

In addition to assistance available via the London-based UK Trade and Investment, each of the countries of the UK offer their own packages to attract international business to relocate in their regions.

Although many foreign businesses automatically think of London and the south east when looking to relocate in the UK, you may find you can benefit from lower costs by setting up in a less 'obvious' region where the costs of property and general living costs are lower. You may also find a larger pool of potential employees prepared to work for lower wages in these areas.

Certain regions too have extra incentives to offer by virtue of being themselves given additional support by the EU because of their economic status. In Scotland, for example, if you set up in specific localities you may be eligible for Regional Selective Assistance.

Programmes and Contacts

Competition Pro-Bono Scheme: 0207 929 5601; www.probonogroup. org.uk/competition. Advice on competition law.

Global Entrepreneurs Programme: 020 7215 8349; www. entrepreneurs.gov.uk. Finance and funding available for businesses in IT or life sciences sectors.

International Business Partnering Opportunities (IBPO)
Scotland: 0845 607 8787 or 0141 228 2000; http://ibo.

scottishdevelopmentinternational.com/se_home.aspx. A web-based system to link you with potential business partners based in Scotland.
International Business Wales: 01443 845500; www.ibwales.com. Location and business advice, support and funding available.
Locate in Northern Ireland: 028 9023 9090; www.investni.com. Business incentive packages and financial assistance.
London Stock Exchange: www.londonstockexchange.com. Source of funding for established and new companies.
Scottish Development International: 0141 228 2828; www.sdi.co.uk. Grants, tax credits and financial incentives available.
Scottish Executive Regional Selective Assistance: 0141 242 5676/5481; www.rsascotland.gov.uk. Projects involving relatively low levels of capital investment can receive grants calculated against the first two years' salary costs of new project jobs.
UK Trade & Investment: 020 7215 8000; (For telephone numbers of Global Offices see the website) www.ukinvest.gov.uk/gateway/index. html. Grow your international business in the UK.

◼ RUNNING A BUSINESS

Taxation

If you are running a company you must pay corporation tax on company profits, at a rate depending on the amount of profit made. Capital expenditure, expenses and outgoings of the company can be offset against tax payable. Capital allowances against tax are made on items purchased for the company such as machinery and plant, cars, industrial

Corporation Tax Rates 2007-08		
Small Companies Rate	**20%**	**£0 – £300,000**
Main rate	30%	£300,001 – £1,500,00

In the March 2007 budget the Chancellor of the Exchequer announced that the main rate of corporation tax would fall to 28% in April 2008.

Capital Gains Tax Allowances And Rates 2007-08		
Annual Exempt Amount	**£9,200**	
Taxable income	**Rate**	
0-£2,230	10%	Starting rate
£2,231 – £34,600	22%	Basic rate
Over £34,600	40%	Higher rate

and agricultural buildings, scientific research, and information and communication technology equipment.

Sole traders and partners pay income tax on a sliding scale as detailed in *Daily Life*. Tax liability for each tax year is calculated on the basis of information provided on the self-assessment tax return. Outgoings, expenses and purchases of capital equipment and other supplies for the business may be offset against the tax bill, so it is important to keep records of all outgoings and enter these on the tax return. If you work from home, you can claim a percentage of the costs of running your home against tax. The Inland Revenue will accept your estimation of the proportion of your electricity, gas, telephone, and house insurance costs which should be put down to your business, as long as you are reasonable about it: while they might be happy with an estimate of 20% of costs, they are likely to look very closely at your actual expenses if you claim 90%.

Company cars are taxable, with an employee paying tax on a percentage of the list price of the car each year, depending on the business mileage per annum and the age of the car. If the employer provides free fuel this will be taxed based on the car's engine size and whether it is petrol or diesel powered. Employers are also liable to pay National Insurance Contributions on these benefits. The use of cleaner, more fuel efficient cars is rewarded by lower rates. Full details at www.hmrc.gov. uk/cars/index.htm.

Capital Gains Tax (CGT) is payable on profits made from selling land, property or businesses, other than one's own dwelling house. There is an exempt amount of profit you are allowed to make each year before tax is due. The amount chargeable to CGT is added on to the top of income liable to income tax at three rates. If profits made are invested in another business, capital gains tax may be 'rolled over' and not become due until that business is disposed of.

If your business turnover (i.e. taxable supplies to customers) exceeds a certain amount you must register for value added tax (VAT) with Customs and Excise. In 2007 this amount stands at £64,000, but it is reviewed annually. You must register if at the end of any month the total value of the taxable supplies you have made in the past 12 months or less is more than £64,000, or if at any time you expect that your annual turnover will exceed that amount in the next 30 days.

If your turnover is less than this, and you supply goods and services which are not exempt from VAT, you may choose to register if you wish. This may be to your benefit, because it means you can claim back VAT you have paid out on purchases. However, advice should be taken on this from an accountant or tax adviser. If you run a company which is registered for VAT, only the company is liable, but if you are a sole trader or partnership and you register for VAT, it is the individual who is liable. This means that, if you have more than one source of income you are liable for VAT on all your business activities, even those which do not exceed the VAT threshold and this could work to your disadvantage.

Employing Staff

If you employ somebody in your business, you must tell your Tax Office. They will send you a *New Employee's Starter Pack* which contains all the instructions, tables and forms you will need.

You must deduct tax and Class 1 National Insurance contributions from the pay of your employees under the Pay As You Earn (PAYE) scheme. It is the employer's responsibility to work out the tax and NI due each pay day and pay it over to the Inland Revenue Accounts Office each month. You must tell your Tax Office at the end of each tax year how much each employee has earned and how much tax and NI contributions you have deducted, and give each employee a statement showing these details.

Employers also have a number of responsibilities to their employees under employment legislation, regarding such things as contracts of employment, working hours, conditions of working, health and safety, and sexual and racial equality of opportunity. For fuller details of these, see *Employment*. The Department of Trade and Industry website contains advice and information on these aspects of employment. www.dti.gov.uk.

HMRC Enquiries

HM Revenue and Customs deal with tax and National Insurance and have all the information you need on their website. If you have any further queries, they have a range of telephone helplines and email contacts. Full details at www.hmrc.gov.uk/menus/contactus.shtm.

Rates

Businesses pay business or non-domestic rates to the local authority based on the rateable value of the property which is determined by the Assessor for the local authority area.

If you work from a room in your home, it is possible to class your office as business premises, paying non-domestic rates on that amount,

> Paying employees: has to be done every month, and there is a series of calculations to go through. Although there are step by step instructions these seem unnecessarily complicated, although I have got quicker at it with practice. I considered buying an automated payroll package I could use on my computer but it seemed too much of an expense or just two employees.
> Sally Hargreaves

although you are still liable for council tax on the rest of the property. If your office is distinct from the rest of the house, this might be feasible, and would allow you to claim the whole of any expenses relating to that portion of the property. However, you would be liable to pay business insurance in that case, and if you ever sold your house you would also be subject to capital gains tax on a proportion of the sale price. In most cases it is probably best to claim just a proportion of allowable household bills against your business, as described in *Taxation*. An accountant or tax advisor will be able to give you advice on the best arrangement in your personal circumstances.

 Valuation Office Agency: 0845 602 1507 | www.voa.gov.uk

Insurance

Insurance for most types of small to medium sized businesses is available from the main insurance companies. If you need specialist insurance for your particular business, an insurance broker should be able to source a company giving the cover you need at a competitive price. Insurance for self-catering cottages is one area which some companies are wary about providing, presumably because they are perceived as being a bad risk. Other companies, such as Pearl Insurance, may insure a holiday property as long as you take out the insurance on your own dwelling house with them. There are some companies which offer policies specifically for holiday properties, but ensure that the cover is sufficient and that the company is reputable – as a holiday cottage owner you are likely to be direct-mailed by obscure companies offering cover. As a general rule of thumb, the better known companies are probably a safer bet as far as the business owner is concerned. If your letting property is close by your own house you may find that the insurance premiums are lower than if you live a distance away so cannot easily keep your eye on the property. If you offer bed and breakfast in your own house you may be required to take out business insurance, as a normal domestic policy probably would not cover you in the event of a claim.

Apart from insurance cover for buildings and contents, you can cover your business for a range of other eventualities, including business interruption, employer's, public and product liability, stock and goods in transit, personal accident and sickness, and insurance for commercial vehicles.

Insurance Companies

British Insurance Brokers Association: 0901 814 0015;
www.biba.org.uk
AXA Insurance: 0845 300 0678; www.axa.co.uk

Royal & Sun Alliance: 01403 232323; www.royalsunalliance.com
Zurich UK Commercial: www.zurich.co.uk/Commercial/Home/
introduction.htm

Data Protection

If you keep computer records of names and addresses and other personal data regarding people you employ and do business with, you may be required to notify the Data Protection Commissioner. If you are classed as a data controller who is processing personal data you must notify unless you are exempt. Exemptions may be allowed for some not-for-profit organisations; if you are processing personal data for personal, family or household affairs; if you only process personal data for the maintenance of a public register; or if you only process personal data within your own business for the purpose of staff administration, advertising, marketing and public relations, accounts, and records.

If you are required to notify, you are legally obliged to ensure any data you hold on computer is up to date and accurate. Individuals have the right to examine those records, and fines or compensation may prove to be payable if the information is incorrect. Failure to notify where required is a criminal offence. If you keep only manual records, there is no requirement to notify.

Further details can be found on the Information Commissioner's Office website, which also includes an easy to use self-assessment section which helps you to identify whether you need to notify. If you are required to do so, you can complete a form online or phone the notification helpline 01625-545740. Notification must be accompanied by a fee of £35 for the first year, and a continuation fee of £35 must be paid annually.

 Information Commissioner's Office: 08456 306060 | www.ico.gov.uk

The Euro

Although at the time of writing Britain has not yet adopted the Euro, the single European currency introduced on 1 January 1999, it may well happen in the long run. Until the UK joins the European Monetary Union (EMU) the euro will be a foreign currency in the UK and will not be legal tender. This means that UK businesses will not have to accept it unless they agree to. However, businesses may use it in their transactions with member states within EMU if they wish to.

The single currency is already directly affecting many UK-based businesses, particularly those which buy and sell products throughout Europe. Those exporting into the euro zone have at times found a competitive disadvantage because of the relatively strong pound. Some have therefore begun to trade directly in euros. This has implications for their accounting systems, which need to handle the euro. Most UK retail banks offer euro accounts for businesses which require them.

The sorts of businesses most affected by the euro, even before the UK joins, are exporters and importers, multinational firms, UK firms in supply chains headed by multinational companies, and wholesale financial markets.

 Euro Information: www.euro.gov.uk

Accountancy Advice

A good accountant can help you to order your business affairs most efficiently, and can prepare your tax return on the basis of information you supply. The amount of tax they may be able to save you is usually well worth what they would charge in fees.

Qualified accountants will be members of the Institute of Chartered Accountants or the Association of Chartered Certified Accountants (ACCA). Useful Contacts

Association of Chartered Certified Accountants: 0141 582 2000; www.accaglobal.com

Institute of Chartered Accountants in England and Wales: 020 7920 8100; www.icaew.co.uk

Institute of Chartered Accountants of Scotland: 0131 347 0100; www.icas.org.uk

Institute of Chartered Accountants in Ireland: 028 9032 1600; www.icai.ie

Tax Advice

Specialist and general tax advice can be obtained from chartered tax advisers. Details of CTAs in your area can be obtained from their governing body.

 Chartered Institute of Taxation: 0207235 9381 | www.tax.org.uk

Legal Advice

Any contracts relating to your business should be drawn up or vetted by a qualified solicitor, and any purchase of property must be handled by a solicitor. All solicitors in the UK must be members of the relevant law society.

Law Society of England & Wales: 020 7242 1222; www.lawsociety.org.uk

Law Society of Northern Ireland: 028 9023 1614; www.lawsoc-ni.org

Law Society of Scotland: 0131 226 7411; www.lawscot.org.uk

Other Sources of Advice and Assistance

In addition to the contacts given during the course of this chapter, there are a number of other sources of support for those who are running or wish to start a business.

Chambers of Commerce throughout Britain represent business people in their local area. For details of your local branch contact:

British Chambers of Commerce: 020 7654 5800; www.chamberonline.co.uk

Northern Ireland Chamber of Commerce & Industry: 028 9024 4113; www.nicci.co.uk

Relocation Agencies can assist companies to find premises for their businesses and homes for their staff to rent or buy when moving to Britain. *The Association of Relocation Professionals* (ARP) can provide a full list of their members. PO Box 189, Diss IP22 1PE; 08700 737475; www.relocationagents.com

Small Business Associations throughout Britain represent the interests of local businesses. *Federation of Small Businesses:* 01253 336000; www.fsb.org.uk

Crimson Business publish a range of print and online information for entrepreneurs, including *Growing Business* magazine and *The Startups Guide to Starting a Business* 020-8334 1600 | www.crimsonbusiness.co.uk

■ TAXATION, PENSIONS AND NATIONAL INSURANCE

Whether or not you are liable to pay taxes in the UK depends on whether you are classified as 'resident' or 'ordinarily resident' in the country. To be classified as resident in a particular year you must normally be physically present in the UK for 183 days (6 months) or more in the tax year, which runs from 6th April to 5th April. It does not matter whether you have been in the UK continuously for this period or whether you have come and gone in the meantime, as long as the total count of days is 183 or more. In certain cases, where you visit the UK regularly over a number of years, you may be classed as resident even if you have been in the UK for less than 183 days. The rules are laid out in the Inland Revenue leaflet IR20, *Residents and non-residents – liability to tax in the United Kingdom.*

Ordinarily resident means that you are resident in the UK year after year. You may be resident but not ordinarily resident for a tax year if you normally live outside the UK but are in the country for more than 183 days in one particular year. On the other hand, you may be ordinarily resident but not resident for a tax year if you usually live in

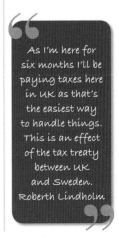

> As I'm here for six months I'll be paying taxes here in UK as that's the easiest way to handle things. This is an effect of the tax treaty between UK and Sweden.
> Roberth Lindholm

the UK and have gone abroad for a long holiday and do not set foot in the UK during that year.

In addition, the Inland Revenue use the concept of 'domicile' to determine tax liability. There are many factors which affect your domicile, but broadly speaking you are domiciled in the country where you have your permanent home. Domicile is distinct from nationality or residence and you can only have one domicile at a given time.

Income Tax

Residents of the UK are liable to pay income tax on earned income and, with a few exceptions, on unearned income. Income tax on investments is usually deducted at source, interest being paid net of tax, although those who are non-taxpayers due to their low earnings may fill out a tax exemption form which allows them to receive the gross interest on investments. If you are not ordinarily resident in the UK you can apply to have the interest paid without deduction of tax. Ask your bank or building society for a declaration form R105. You are still liable to tax on the interest, but you may be exempted or qualify for tax relief during years or part years where you are not resident in the UK.

Income tax on earned income is paid in two ways: for employees, under a system called PAYE (Pay As You Earn), and for the self-employed by a system of self assessment. With PAYE, income tax is deducted at source from your gross pay, so the employer will pay your salary with the income tax already deducted. The amount of tax payable is determined by

Tax allowances and rates			
Taxable income (07-08)	**Rate (2007-08)**	**Rate (2008-09)***	
0-£2,230	10%	n/a	Starting rate
£2,231 – £34,600	22%	20%	Basic rate
over £34,600	40%	40%	Higher rate
Age		**Personal Allowance (2007-08)**	
up to 65		£5,225	
65 -74		£7,550	
75 and over		£7,690	

In the March 2007 Budget the Chancellor of the Exchequer announced that from April 2008 the 10% starting tax rate would be abolished and the basic rate would be cut to 20%. The levels of taxable income in that year may be different from those shown above.

a tax code which you are assigned by the Inland Revenue based on your personal circumstances.

With self assessment, you are sent a tax form at the end of the tax year on which you itemise all your earned and unearned income for that year, and either send it to the tax office for the tax payable to be calculated, or calculate it yourself on the basis of rules given. Tax is payable 'on account' in two lumps, due on 31st January in the tax year and 31st July following the tax year, each normally equal to one half of the previous year's tax liability. Any over or underpayments for the year are settled by 31st January in the following year. Self assessment tax returns may be filed over the internet. They offer various discounts on tax due for filing the return in this way and for paying tax due electronically.

All tax payers are allowed a 'personal allowance', an amount they are allowed to earn before starting to pay tax. Personal allowances and tax rates for the following year are announced in March each year in the UK Government budget.

National Insurance

National Insurance (NI), known as social security in other countries, is mandatory for most working people between 16 and 65. Paying regular NI contributions entitles you to state benefits including the state retirement pension, unemployment benefit, sickness benefit, maternity allowance, and so forth. The rules are complicated – you have to have paid the right number of contributions at the right rate at the right time to qualify for these benefits. If there is a 'gap' in your contributions at any time – due to periods of unemployment, say, when you did not claim benefit – you may find that you are not entitled to a full pension. This is a position that many women in particular find themselves in if, for instance, they have taken a few years out of work to have a family.

Anybody who comes to Britain to work should apply for a National Insurance number from their local Department of Social Security (DSS) office. This personal NI number is stamped on a plastic card and stays the same for life, so must be kept safe. To apply for a National Insurance number you need to call 0845 600 0643 to set up an appointment for an in-person interview in which your identity and right to work will be checked. You will be sent a letter with the details of where and when your appointment will be, and a list of official documentation you need to bring such as passport, proof of address, employment contract or proof you have registered with an employment agency.

 For more National insurance information go to http://www.dwp.gov.uk/lifeevent/benefits/ni_number.asp#where

Contributions paid depend on the level of earnings and whether you are employed or self-employed. Those who are self-employed pay their own contributions while employees have their contributions deducted at source, and their employers also have to pay a contribution for each of their employees. Basically, contributions are calculated as a percentage of salary and are paid on earnings between £87 and £670 per week. These are the figures for tax year 2007-08 – they are usually adjusted in the March budget of each year, to take effect from 6th April following, i.e. the new tax year. In 2007-08 the basic employee's contribution is 11% of their income between £100 and £670 per week, and 1% above £670 per week. The employer's contribution is 12.8% on earnings above £100 per week.

For the self-employed, the basic contribution is £2.20 per week (Class 2 contribution), although you can choose to pay a higher voluntary contribution of £7.80 (Class 3) which will give enhanced benefits. In addition, the higher-earning self-employed must pay Class 4 contributions of 8% of any profits between £5,225 and £34,840 per year, and then 1% of profits above £34,840 per year.

However, there are different categories of contribution where you may choose to pay reduced rates: married women, for instance, have this option, and the self-employed with earnings below £4,635 are exempt.

If you are not working because you are in full-time education, are on an approved training course, you have taken early retirement or are claiming unemployment, sickness, maternity or invalidity benefit, you will receive NI credits to ensure your contribution record is unbroken during that period. If you are at home looking after children or a sick, elderly or disabled person you may be eligible for Home Responsibilities Protection which helps to keep your pension rights although you are not working.

Value Added Tax

Value Added Tax (VAT) is payable on most goods and services, at a standard rate of 17.5%. There are some exceptions to this: certain categories of goods and services carry VAT at a lower rate, some are zero-rated, others are exempt. Domestic fuels for heating and lighting carry a rate of 5%, while children's clothes and footwear, books, magazines and newspapers, and most foods, are zero-rated. Sales and lettings of land and buildings are completely exempt of VAT, as is insurance, the provision of credit, and the services of doctors, dentists and opticians.

A company or a self-employed person with an annual turnover of more than £64,000 must be registered for VAT. Those with a lower turnover can choose to be VAT registered. A business which makes only VAT exempt items cannot register for VAT, but one making zero-rated items can. The VAT charged on goods and services used in setting up or running your business can be reclaimed, subject to certain conditions. It is a person rather than a business which is registered for VAT, so registration covers all business activities of the registered person.

There are high penalties for failing to register for VAT or making a false declaration, and the Customs and Excise are renowned for making stringent checks. Publications and leaflets explaining the regulations regarding VAT are available from VAT offices or from the Customs and Excise website at www.hmce.gov.uk.

Council Tax

All people living in Great Britain must pay council tax, and in Northern Ireland they pay rates, both of which are based on the value of their dwelling. For further details see the section on Council Tax in *Setting Up Home*. Businesses must pay non-domestic, or business, rates to pay for local services. Further details on these can be found in *Starting A Business*.

Other Taxes

- **Corporation tax** is payable on company profits, at varying rates depending on levels of profit. See *Starting A Business* for further details.

- **Capital gains tax** is payable on profits made from selling land, property or businesses (other than one's own dwelling house). The tax is payable on any increase in an asset's value during the period while you have owned it. Any profit made on the transaction over the exempt allowance of £9,200 (in 2007-08) is added onto the top of income liable to income tax for individuals and is charged to CGT below the starting rate limit at 10%, between the starting rate and basic rate limits at 20%, and above the basic rate limit at 40%. (See above for income tax rates.) If profits made are invested in another business, however, capital gains tax may not be payable.

- **Inheritance tax** (death duty) is payable at 40% on estates with a value of above £300,000. Although this used to affect very few people, over recent years the rates have not kept pace with house price inflation and it is estimated that now around 20% of British residents would be liable to the tax on their death.

Further Information

HM Revenue & Customs produces a whole range of leaflets on UK tax matters, available free of charge on request. Most leaflets are downloadable from the website or can be ordered from the relevant telephone orderline.

If you have any queries on your tax position, you should contact your local Tax Office. The address will be listed in the phone book. Alternatively, there are telephone helplines to deal with queries about National Insurance, tax or VAT, These are listed in the phone book under HM Revenue & Customs or can be found on the website. They will ask for your NI number when you call.

 HM Revenue & Customs: www.hmrc.gov.uk

Investment Income

This refers to any income which is not a pension and is not earned by you as an employee, from carrying on your profession or from running your own business. It includes interest from bank and building society accounts, dividends on shares, interest on stocks and rental income (unless your business amounts to a trade).

If you are resident in the UK you will normally pay UK tax on all your investment income, wherever in the world it arises.

However, if you are resident but not domiciled in the UK, or resident but not ordinarily resident in the UK and a British or Commonwealth citizen, or a citizen of the Republic of Ireland, you are liable to UK tax only on the amount of your overseas investment income which is 'remitted' to the UK: this means if it is paid in the UK or brought to the UK in any way.

If you are not resident in the UK, you are only charged UK tax on investment income arising in the UK. If you are a resident of a country with which the UK has a double taxation agreement you may be able to claim exemption or partial relief from UK tax on investment income.

Any profits you make from letting property in the UK are taxable there, even if you cease to be resident in the UK.

There are certain UK Government securities known as 'Free of Tax to Residents Abroad' (FOTRA) securities which are free of UK tax to people who are not ordinarily resident in the UK. For a list of eligible FOTRA securities, see www.hmrc.gov.uk/cnr/fotra_sec.htm.

Capital Gains Tax

For an explanation of the basic rules on capital gains tax, please see *Taxation* in the section on *Daily Life*. If you are resident or ordinarily resident in the UK, you may be liable to capital gains tax on disposing of assets situated anywhere in the world. However, where you are a resident of a country which has a double taxation agreement with the UK you may be exempt from capital gains tax in the UK.

Sources of Information

Information on all these matters, in more detail, is given in the Inland Revenue booklet IR20 *Residents and Non-residents – Liability to Tax in the United Kingdom.* A number of other leaflets are available free of charge, most of which can be downloaded from the Inland Revenue website: www.hmrc.gov.uk/leaflets/index.htm.

If you have any queries on your tax position, you can contact your local Tax Office. The address is listed in the phone book under 'HM Revenue & Customs'.

It is sensible to consult a tax advisor or accountant who can work out the most tax- efficient way of managing your affairs. Any advisor you consult should be a member of the *Chartered Institute of Taxation (CIOT)*: 020-7235 9381; www.tax.org.uk.

Pensions

Many companies operate employee pension schemes. There is no obligation on employees to belong to such schemes, although generally they offer a better deal than a personal pension plan, especially for an employee who stays with the same company until retirement. When you change jobs, it may be possible to transfer the contributions made so far to another company scheme, or to a personal pension. In some cases, only the employer pays contributions to the pension fund in respect of employees, in which case it is termed a non-contributory scheme. More often both employer and employee make contributions, with on average employees paying around 4% of their gross salary into a company pension fund, while employers make contributions of around 8 or 9%.

Where employers do not provide an employee pension scheme, they may be legally obliged to provide access to a government-approved 'stakeholder pension'. Using their own money, together with tax relief and investment returns, employees can buy a pension which will give them a regular income for life when they retire. Stakeholder pension schemes are low-charge pensions meant for people who do not have access to an occupational pension or a good-value personal pension. There are a few exceptions to the requirement on employers to provide access to stakeholder pensions, mainly where very small companies are concerned.

 For further details see The Pension Service website. www.pensionservice. gov.uk.

Time Off

PUBLIC HOLIDAYS

Statutory public holidays are called 'bank holidays' for obvious reasons. Traditionally, many shops and services is addition to the banks were also closed on these days. However, in line with the general lengthening of shop opening hours over recent years, retail outlets now tend to stay open on bank holidays, because it is, of course, an ideal time to attract all those customers who would normally be at work. Nowadays, far from Christmas and Easter and other bank holidays being a time when shops are closed, they are more likely to be a time of seasonal special offers and sales although certain days such as Christmas day does of course see all shops shut.

Post offices, schools, offices and workplaces, apart from essential services, are usually closed on bank holidays. Where people are obliged to work they are generally paid at a higher than normal rate for those days and are also entitled to time off on another day to compensate.

Bank holidays are normally on a Monday, although those associated with religious or secular occasions, such as Christmas and New Year, may fall on different days of the week.

Public Holidays	
New Year's Day	1 January (E,W,S,NI)
New Year Bank Holiday	2 January (S)
St Patrick's Day	19 March (NI)
Good Friday	Varies (early–mid April) (E,W,S,NI)
Easter Monday	Monday following Good Friday (E,W,S,NI)
May Day	First Monday in May (E,W,S,NI)
Spring Bank Holiday	Last Monday in May (E,W,S,NI)
Battle of the Boyne	12 July (NI)
August Bank Holiday	First Monday in August (S) Last Monday in August (E,W,NI)
Christmas Day	25 December (E,W,S,NI)
Boxing Day	26 December (E,W,S,NI)

E = England; W = Wales; S = Scotland; NI = Northern Ireland

MEDIA

Britain is media mad. There are over 1,000 daily, Sunday and weekly national, regional and local newspapers published, around 8,000 general interest magazines and 4,000 trade and technical publications. In addition, there are many specialist or local magazines and newspapers with a small but loyal readership.

In addition to its publications, there are also a plethora of radio stations, national, regional and local. Until recent years, the number of TV stations was tiny in comparison, with just five channels transmitting nationwide but this has now charged with literally hundreds of TV stations now accessible via satellite and cable.

Television

In the UK as a whole, 99% of homes have at least one TV set and over 60% have two or more. Britain watches more television than any other European country, average viewing being estimated at around 25 hours a week. Just under 72% of UK households have changed to digital TV as it offers more choice and better reception, particularly in remote or mountainous areas. Analogue TV is going to be 'switched off' in the next few years, starting with southern Scotland in 2008, and with the rest of the UK scheduled to follow, region by region, the whole process to be completed by 2012. It will be necessary for all homes to have digital TV by then.

The British Broadcasting Corporation has two main TV stations: BBC1 and BBC2. There are three Independent channels, ITV1, Channel 4 and Channel 5, which get their revenue from advertising. In addition to these there are hundreds of other channels, available through satellite and cable.

Although programming on the main channels is broadly the same across Britain, there are regional variations. The BBC in Scotland offers Gaelic programmes and local news programmes in all regions of the UK, while in Wales there is a dedicated Welsh language channel, S4C. Independent Television (ITV) has regional companies across the UK which, in addition to showing UK-wide programmes, also have regionally specific transmissions.

The main provider of satellite TV is Sky. In addition to its own channels, it also broadcasts a number of joint-venture channels and distributes other channels for third parties. Cable TV companies provide programming via underground cables, often in conjunction with telephone services. Subscribers to these services generally pay a monthly fee, but the Government has made a commitment to provide free to view TV via satellite, cable or broadband once the analogue signal is switched off. It is likely that the householder will still have to pay for the satellite dish or broadband installation.

Satellite TV is received through an external satellite dish fixed to your house and a box connected to your TV. Installation is usually free if you take out a subscription to the provider, such as Sky, or you can purchase a box and pay for it and installation without taking out a Sky subscription, in which case the box and installation is around £200.

Subscribers pay a monthly charge for satellite reception, which varies depending on the number of channels they wish to access and whether they choose a standard or digital box and service. Sky digital subscription has packages from £13.50 to £60 per month.

The cheapest way of receiving digital TV is through Freeview. This involves buying a set-top box, for which prices start around at £30. The number of digital channels available through Freeview is limited compared to satellite and cable because of technical reasons to do with the limited bandwidth available, but it still offers far more choice than traditional analogue broadcasting.

Digital TV, however it is received, provides up to 200 TV channels, which include the terrestrial channels as well as specialised film channels, sports channels, children's channels, and music channels as well as other restricted interest channels, such as Gaelic programming and channels in other minority languages to cater for such groups as immigrants from India and Pakistan. In addition there are a growing number of interactive shopping channels. There are some 'pay per view' broadcasts, usually large sporting events or box-office movies, where the broadcast can be only received and decoded in return for a one-off payment. Major radio stations can also be received through your digital TV set.

Television Companies

BBC Television: 08700 100222; www.bbc.co.uk
Independent Television (ITV): 0870 600 6766; www.itv.com
Channel 5: 0207 421 7270; www.channel5.co.uk
Channel 4: 0845 076 0191; www.channel4.com
Sky: 08705 800874; www.sky.com
Virgin Media: 0845 840 7777; www.virginmedia.com

Radio

UK domestic radio services are broadcast across three bands: FM (also called VHF); medium wave (or AM) and long wave.

The BBC has five nationwide stations. Radio 1 broadcasts pop music; Radio 2 provides a mix of easy listening music and relaxed discussion; Radio 3 is good for classical music and serious drama; Radio 4 broadcasts drama, documentaries, comedy, quiz shows and general interest programmes; Radio 5 broadcasts live sport and news. In addition, there are regional BBC radio stations in Scotland, Wales and Northern Ireland, including programming in Gaelic and Welsh. The BBC World Service broadcasts globally in 44 languages, including English. The three main national commercial radio stations are Classic FM, TalkSport and Virgin Radio. In addition there are numerous local independent stations.

While the main stations can still be picked up on a traditional radio set, many radio stations now also transmit digitally and some can only be

Frequencies of BBC Radio stations	
Radio 1	97.6-99.8 FM
Radio 2	88-90.2 FM
Radio 3	90.2-92.4 FM
Radio 4	94.6-96.1 FM, 103.5-105 FM, 1449 AM
Radio 5 Live	693/909 AM
Radio Wales	94.6-95.9 FM
Radio Scotland	92-95 FM
Radio Ulster	92-95 FM

received through a digital (DAB) set. Many can also be received through satellite, cable or the Internet.

Newspapers

Throughout Britain there is a wide choice of national, regional and local daily and weekly newspapers available. In addition, in remote rural areas, which the regional papers tend not to cover in depth, there are many small local papers, often produced on a voluntary basis, usually weekly, fortnightly or monthly.

The national newspapers, which are all produced in London although they purportedly cover events throughout the UK, tend to be Anglo-centric, concentrating on English events unless there are really big stories relating to other parts of the UK. There are some special editions of the biggest ones produced in Scotland. There are a few regional newspapers produced in Wales, Scotland and Northern Ireland.

Newspapers are divided into the 'broadsheet' and 'tabloid' press, the first serious and aimed at a highly educated readership, the second group gossipy and sensationalist.

Weekend newspapers are far more than just another edition of the daily papers. They are large and stuffed with supplements, often in colour, on all sorts of subjects, such as Lifestyle, Arts and Culture, Property, Sports, Business – so extensive they require a concerted effort to get through them in their entirety on Sunday.

Main British Newspapers
National Papers
Daily Papers
- The Times
- The Independent
- Daily Telegraph
- The Guardian

> " I think [the radio is] mostly excellent. I watch less and less TV (not sure why) but enjoy the news coverage, which is vastly superior to the equivalent in North America.
> Sue Griffith "

- Daily Mail
- Daily Mirror
- Express
- The SunDaily Star

Sunday Papers

- Sunday Times
- The Independent on Sunday
- Mail on Sunday
- The Observer
- The People
- Sunday Express
- Sunday Mail
- Sunday Mirror

> There are plenty [of newspapers] to choose from, but a lot also have too much exposure to sex that can be harmful for growing kids.
>
> Joe Rawal

UK newspapers are usually financially independent of any political party, but most adopt a political stance in their editorial content. Traditionally the British have bought more newspapers than any other country in Europe, but their circulation figures are dropping dramatically as there is increased competition from television and the internet. One of the biggest sources of news online is now the BBC. To fight back, all the big newspapers are using new media, with websites containing online versions of the newspaper, and other gimmicks such as podcasts, blogs and news services to mobile phones.

Magazines

There are thousands of magazines, on all sorts of subjects, for sale in the UK, available from newsagents or by subscription. Most of them also have their own websites, some just as a medium for advertising and selling subscriptions, while others include at least part of their editorial content online. In most parts of the country newsagents will deliver newspapers and magazines to your door for a small weekly charge.

 British Newspapers and News Online: www.wrx.zen.co.uk
Media UK: www.mediauk.com

Books and Bookshops

There are around 125,000 new books published every year in the UK. The top selling books are almost exclusively a mix of popular 'genre' fiction by big name authors and non-fiction books such as cookery books, horoscopes, biographies and TV or cinema tie-ins. Around 50% of these are written by British authors, 40% by Americans, with fewer than 10% from elsewhere.

VAT is not charged on books in the UK, although the spectre of adding the tax to their cover price is regularly raised. So far, the threat has been fought off. Despite this, books are comparatively expensive in the UK. Traditionally, mass market books were produced in expensive hardback format first, with a cheaper paperback edition following a year or so later. However, today much popular fiction is produced directly in paperback.

◣ SPORT

A wide variety of sport is played in Britain. Over 50% of the population regularly participate in some form of sport. There are many more armchair sportsmen and women who watch sport, whether on the TV in the comfort of their own home or by visiting sporting events in person.

Participation in Sport	
Most popular	**Percentage**
Walking	46
Swimming	35
Keep fit/yoga	22
Cycling	19
Billiards, snooker and pool	17

Football (soccer), rugby and cricket are among the most popular team sports, in terms of participators and spectators. Golf too is popular, especially in Scotland (the historic home of the game), which has many superb courses throughout the country, from the high status historical courses such as St Andrews to small courses in beautiful settings in the Highlands.

Outdoor pursuits such as walking, climbing, cycling and skiing are popular in the more mountainous and wilder parts of Britain Highlands, attracting people from all over the world to face the challenges of the terrain.

Leisure Centres run by local authorities provide a range of facilities for different sporting activities, such as squash, tennis, badminton, swimming, exercise classes, indoor and outdoor football pitches and gyms.

 UK Sport: 020 7211 5100 | www.uksport.gov.uk

ENTERTAINMENT AND CULTURE

Whether your preference is for traditional cultural pastimes or for modern entertainment, all groups are catered for. Eating and/or drinking out, going to the cinema or theatre, visiting museums or historical monuments, music and dancing, and playing or watching sports are all popular pastimes in Britain.

Cinema

Cinema is popular, with most reasonable sized towns having their own cinema, and cities having large multiplex cinemas with half a dozen films or more showing on different screens. For true film buffs there are also specialist cinemas showing classic and 'art' films.

Theatre, Opera and Ballet

There is a thriving arts scene throughout Britain. There is an Arts Council for each of the four countries of Britain which funds arts organisations and artists using public money received from the Government and the National Lottery Fund. There are local and national companies performing at venues large and small, in drama, opera, ballet, and many other art forms.

England, Wales and Scotland each have their own national opera and ballet companies, putting on regular performances at different venues. Just about every town of any size in the UK has at least one theatre, larger ones may have several. London alone has 100 theatres, 50 of those in the West End. There is a wide variety of live performances on offer, including classical drama, Shakespeare, modern comedies, stand-up comedians, musicals, experimental works, and traditional pantomimes at Christmas, to name but a few of the things you could see.

There are many touring companies in all these areas, from the UK and all over the world, who perform in a variety of venues around the UK, from large city theatres, to tiny community halls in remote villages.

Music and Dancing

Each of the four countries of the UK has a rich heritage of traditional music, singing and dancing. The feisean movement in Scotland and Ireland aims to keep traditional music and the Gaelic language alive, by running classes and residential courses where children and adults can learn and improve their skills in traditional Celtic instruments and Gaelic singing.

The Mod is a Gaelic music festival where singers and musicians compete for honours in various categories. It is held every year at local, regional and national levels in Scotland.

'Comhaltas' is an Irish organisation which runs similar classes and competitions throughout Ireland. Irish step dancing is thriving in its home country with classes available for all age groups.

The National Eisteddfod of Wales is an annual festival where the Welsh language and culture is celebrated. England too has a thriving folk scene, with traditional dance and song attracting a large following.

Classical and popular music are also popular throughout Britain. From full orchestras to solo singer-songwriters, and every style of music between, you can find regular performances and concerts in a huge number of venues, from the smallest pub to the largest football stadium.

There are a huge number of music and arts festivals throughout Britain every year, from the biggest and most famous of all, the Edinburgh International Festival and the Glastonbury music festival, to small local ones. There are festivals for just about every aspect of the arts, including literature and books, drama, comedy, dance, rock and pop music, opera, the list goes on.

Useful Contacts

An Comunn Gàidhealach: 01463 231226; www.ancomunn.co.uk
Fèisean Nan Gàidheal: 01478 613355; www.feisean.org
National Eisteddfod of Wales: 0845 120 9555; www.eisteddfod.org.uk
Comhaltas: +3531 2800 295; www.comhaltas.com
English Folk Dance and Song Society: 020 7485 2206; www.efdss.org
Association of British Orchestras: 020 7287 0333; www.abo.org.uk
UK What's On Guide: www.ukwhatsonguide.co.uk
London Theatre Guide: www.londontheatre.co.uk
Arts Council of Northern Ireland: 028 9038 5200;
www.artscouncil-ni.org
Arts Council England: 0845 300 6200; www.artscouncil.org.uk
Scottish Arts Council: 0131 240 2444; www.scottisharts.org.uk
Arts Council Wales: 029 2037 6500; www.artswales.org.uk
British Arts Festivals Association: 020 7240 4532;
www.artsfestivals.co.uk
Efestivals: www.efestivals.co.uk

Museums, Galleries and Historical Monuments

There are around 6,400 visitor attractions in Britain, and many of them celebrate the history and heritage of the country. London and the other cities of the UK, of course, are full of historical buildings, art galleries, museums and the like, but each town of any size and many villages have their own historic buildings and museums, displaying historical and social artefacts from the area. There are castles around practically every corner – the history fan has no shortage of places to visit.

There are many historic buildings and monuments open to the public, many of these under the guardianship of bodies such as the National Trust and the National Trust for Scotland, English Heritage and Historic Scotland.

National Trust: 0870 458 4000; www.nationaltrust.org.uk
National Trust for Scotland: 0131 243 9300; www.nts.org.uk
English Heritage: 0870 333 1181; www.english-heritage.org.uk
Historic Scotland: 0131 668 8600; www.historic-scotland.gov.uk
Guide to Museums and Art Galleries: www.tourist-information-uk.com/museums-art-galleries.htm

> There is great attention paid to the arts here, one is never at a loss for something wonderful to do whether it be a jazz show, a quick stop by the Gallery of Modern Art or a show at the Royal Concert Hall.
> Amy Burns

Gambling

The British love a flutter. Bookmakers, found in high streets throughout the country and now on the internet, will take bets on just about anything from horse races to whether snow will fall at Christmas. Bingo is popular, particularly among women, and the national lottery (Lotto) is a national obsession. There are two major national draws each week on Wednesdays and Saturdays, with a jackpot prize generally between four and eight million pounds; if the jackpot is not won, the prize rolls over to succeeding weeks with the jackpot accumulating until it is won, sometimes reaching over twenty million pounds, causing a ticket-buying flurry! There are also various other smaller draws including a daily one.

Scratch cards, on sale in newsagents at £1 each, promise instant cash prizes ranging from a few pounds to a fortune – and people spend a small fortune on them.

Gambling for large stakes can only take place in a casino licensed for the purpose by the Gaming Board. Gambling in public houses and bars is not permitted other than for small stakes. Bets cannot be taken in such premises.

Fashion

Britain exerts a quietly understated yet significant role in the world of fashion. From the miniskirts and pixie boots of 'swinging' 1960s London and designers like Mary Quant, to the avant garde work of Vivienne Westwood to current favourite Stella McCartney, the UK fashion industry has been at the forefront of trend setting for half a century.

This is hardly surprising given the background to the UK fashion industry. Rooted in the days of the industrial revolution back in the 1800s, the fashion and textiles trade has grown from the traditional cluster of gentlemen's outfitters in Savile Row, London (which is still a great, albeit expensive, location for a tailor-made suit) to a massive culture – many UK universities offer excellent fashion and textile design courses and these have spawned some truly great works of art.

For the average Brit, most of the outfits paraded on the runway are well out of range, but retailers are wise to the whims of the fashion industry, and also to the fact that fashions are closely followed and aped through glossy consumer magazines, so they are often quick to produce budget versions of leading designers' work.

For an interactive tour of British fashion as it has evolved over the last 200 years, visit the Victoria and Albert Museum in London and the Museum of Costume in the city of Bath in south west England.

About Britain

■ THE PEOPLE
National Characteristics

It is difficult to talk about the British character type – simply because people from the four countries of the UK have different national characteristics. In fact, probably one of the few traits which is common to them all in the mass is that none of them like to be lumped in with the others. Those residents of the UK who describe themselves as British are in the minority – generally they prefer to describe themselves as English, Welsh, Scottish, and Irish respectively. And it is usually residents of the other countries of the UK who are the quickest to ascribe the more negative traits to their closest neighbours. This, however, is usually done in humorous vein – one of the characteristics common to all parts of the UK is the British sense of humour, for which they are renowned. This humour often takes the form of self-deprecation about themselves as a nation. On the whole, the British tend not to take themselves too seriously.

It can be difficult sometimes for a foreigner to realise when a Brit is joking. They tend to use 'deadpan' humour, employing irony and word play, and it requires a keen grasp of the English language sometimes to realise when what is being said is expected to be taken as a joke, rather than at face value. Because tone of voice, facial expression and context give the clue to whether they are joking or not, there is room for misunderstanding if your grasp of the language is not too good.

The English have a reputation for being reserved and aloof – not actively unfriendly,

> I have always felt at home with the British sense of humour (= irony) and miss it when I have been back in Canada or travelling abroad for extended periods.
> Susan Griffith

but not ready to instantly go out of their way to be helpful or welcoming. This is probably true, up to a point, but you will find that northerners pride themselves on being warmer and friendlier than their southern neighbours, while the Scots and the Irish would claim they are more welcoming than the northern English. Generally in the more crowded, busier, urban areas, where the pace of life is faster and people tend to work longer hours and have more stressful jobs, people will be less ready to go out of their way to welcome you than in the rural areas where there is more space and time to get to know new people. And even here, most people will be sensitive to the feelings of newcomers – they would not wish to intrude if you want to 'keep yourself to yourself', so they may wait for you to approach them and introduce yourself, or get involved in local events, before they attempt to get to know you better.

About Britain

The class system is another subtlety of British life that foreign visitors can find difficult to grasp. This is because it is not always obvious exactly where in the social scale somebody fits, unless you can pick up certain cues in their accent, the way they dress, or know about their background. Although the class system is less important than it once was, it still holds sway in certain areas of life. Where somebody went to school and university counts for a great deal when going for a job, especially within certain professions, such as the law. Although there are equality laws which aim to prevent this sort of privilege being taken into account, it is so much a part of the British psyche – one of the first things people do when they meet somebody new, without even being conscious of it, is to pigeon-hole them within a certain social sphere – that it is almost impossible to eradicate. An advantage a foreigner has in this respect is that being brought up in another country means that it is difficult to be pigeon-holed in the same way.

The British have a reputation for being unemotional and lacking in passion. This is a remnant from the days when an English gentleman was expected to have a 'stiff upper lip' and not to show his emotions in public. What he does behind closed doors is a different matter! Again this is something more noticeable amongst the English, which maybe stems from their Anglo-Saxon heritage. The Celts in Wales, Scotland and Ireland tend to be far more volatile and passionate. In all of these countries, anyway, this is something which is changing. Nowadays it is far less frowned upon to show your emotions in public, and where once even the closest friends – men especially – would greet each other with a handshake and would rarely touch each other, today women will greet

> When I first arrived, I did find the British bizarrely private, e.g. they seldom struck up conversations on trains, but now I have converted to thinking that that is preferable. Am now so used to the restrained service that you tend to get in shops and pubs that I feel slightly disapproving of the over-the-top (and often false) friendliness of shop and restaurant staff in North America.
> Sue Hardie

others (men or women) with a kiss on the cheek and male friends may even hug each other.

An area where the British male has long shown his emotions is when watching, or taking part in sports, which are very popular everywhere, with both males and females. Competition between the four nations of the UK is nowhere seen more obviously than on the rugby field, rugby being one of the few sports in which England, Wales, Scotland, and Ireland all participate at an equal level of excellence.

The British are a nation of animal-lovers. Dogs and cats are the most popular pets, some people having several of each.

Like people everywhere, the British are riddled with contradictions: it is one of the most democratic nations in the world, yet the class system still exerts an influence; most people would claim not to be racist, but there is undeniably racism to be found; women have equal rights with men, enshrined in law, yet they (and ethnic minorities) are under-represented in high status jobs and their average earnings are lower for equivalent jobs. So don't always believe what you are told by people – the best way to find out about the national character is to watch how they act, and take what they claim to do with a pinch of salt!

Attitudes

The British are generally liberal and tolerant, and there are plenty of laws in place to ensure that people are not discriminated against either at work or in the wider social

sphere. Equal opportunities legislation says that everybody should have an equal chance of applying for a job, and that the job should be given to the person best qualified to do it, regardless of their race, gender, sexual persuasion or disabilities.

Women work alongside men and, although there are still 'glass ceilings' in existence which mean they may have a harder time progressing to the top jobs, changing attitudes backed by strong anti-discrimination legislation mean this is changing year on year.

Marriage has shown a steady decline over the years, although there have been minor fluctuations from time to time. There were 283,730 weddings in the UK in 2005, a fall of nearly 10% compared with 2004. There has been a long-term decline from the peak number of 480,285 marriages in 1972.

Between 2004 and 2005, the number of divorces granted in the UK decreased by 7% to 155,052, from 167,138. This is the lowest number of divorces since 2000, and the first annual decrease since 1999/2000. This is 14% lower than the highest number of divorces which peaked in 1993 (180,018). It is to be expected that the divorce rate will continue to fall, as the number of marriages overall declines. There are a large number of couples who now choose to cohabit without marrying, and of course the divorce rates do not include the numbers of cohabiting couples whose relationships break down.

Generally, there is no great stigma now attached to unmarried couples living together, even when they have children. However, greater prejudice may well be encountered in the rural areas, particularly those where the church still retains a strong hold. Social attitudes in these areas are behind the times and, if you go from the south of England, say, to the Scottish Highlands, it can feel as if you have stepped back in time ten or twenty years. However, the natural courtesy of the local people would

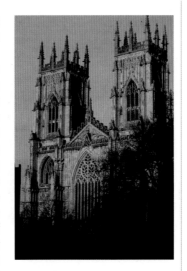

generally prevent them from showing disapproval to your face – although what they say behind your back might be a different matter!

Although gay and lesbian relationships are still looked at askance by many, social attitudes are changing in this area too, as is demonstrated by the fact that from 21st December 2005 it became legal for same-sex couples to seal their mutual love and long-term commitment in a civil partnership ceremony. In addition to allowing them to make a public statement about their relationship, this also affords them similar legal rights to heterosexual married couples in relation to social security benefits, inheritance rights and the like.

There were 15,672 civil partnerships formed in the UK between December 2005 and the end of September 2006. A total of 14,084 partnerships took place in England with 537 in Wales, 942 in Scotland and 109 in Northern Ireland. It is not clear yet how many civil partnerships will take place per year in the future – doubtless fewer than these first figures imply. They will be high because so-called gay weddings have not previously been possible.

England has more of a problem with racial intolerance than the other three nations, simply because there is a much higher number of immigrants in England compared with Wales, Scotland and Northern Ireland. The Race Relations Act of 1976 made racism illegal, and the Commission for Racial Equality works towards the elimination of discrimination and promotes equality of opportunity and good relations between different racial groups.

There has always been a fairly vociferous minority in the UK who think that immigration should be restricted, claiming that immigrants are taking jobs and homes which should go to indigenous British citizens. Although

The Art of Queuing

Wherever you go, whatever you do in the UK, if there are other people wanting to do the same thing, you will form an orderly queue (wait in line). Waiting for a bus, going to the cinema, waiting to be served in a shop – always you are expected to join the end of the queue until it is your turn. Queue-jumping is frowned upon. If you push to the front you will upset everybody else there, you will hear muttering, somebody might even say something to you... but this is unlikely, because of another cultural trait; politeness

this is not something which is borne out by the facts – the UK currently has a very high level of employment, with shortages of workers in some areas, which are being filled in many cases by workers from overseas.

Recent large influxes of people from the new EU countries, together with suspicion of the Muslim community after al-Qaida terrorist attacks

in London and elsewhere, have increased the level of resentment of immigrants among some people, and put the whole issue of multiculturalism at the top of the news agenda. However, this does not seem to be discouraging foreigners from heading for Britain, as it still has a reputation as one of the most tolerant societies in the world to live in.

British Culture

There are certain aspects of life in the UK which are quintessentially 'British' and sum up the atmosphere of the nation, particularly for the foreign visitor. Here is a selection of some of the most persistent and universal through the four countries.

Politeness

The British conduct themselves politely and patiently when out in public. They say 'please' and 'thank you' and are affronted when others don't do the same. They tend not to complain in shops and restaurants, even when it is justified, as it would be felt to be impolite. The average Brit doesn't like to 'make a fuss' and is embarrassed when others do.

Tea

Tea is the national drink, and people will have a 'nice cup of tea' at any hour of the day or night. If you visit them in their homes, or attend a meeting or an interview, at some time you are likely to be offered a cup of tea. Although coffee is also offered, and many Brits drink it as a change from tea, coffee does not have the same feeling of 'Britishness' as does tea. It is always drunk hot (none of your iced tea nonsense!) usually with milk, often with sugar. If asked 'how do you take your tea?' you should explain whether you want milk or sugar, and how much of each.

Pubs

When they are not at home drinking tea, you are quite likely to find the average Brit in a pub (short for public house). Once this would only have been at lunchtime or in the evening, but now licensing laws have been relaxed so pubs stay open for much longer hours. The classic pub drink is beer, but you will find a huge array of wines, spirits and other alcoholic drinks to choose from.

Pubs are great social centres and most people will regularly visit their nearest pub (the 'local') to meet – and make – friends.

Sport

The British love sport, playing it or watching it (either live or on television) and, most important of all, commenting on it. Everybody has an opinion on how well (or usually how badly, when it comes to discussions in the pub) their local or national team has done. The year is marked by the various sporting seasons – football and rugby in the winter, cricket, athletics and tennis (especially Wimbledon) in the summer.

The Royal Family

The ultimate in Britishness, the Royal Family probably means more to the foreigner than to the average Brit. Although families may make sightseeing trips up to London to visit Buckingham Palace, or to see the Changing of the Guard or the Trooping of the Colours, and although people are mildly interested to read about them in the papers, nowadays the Queen and her family do not impinge greatly on the British consciousness.

Manners and Customs

Generally, the British are prepared to forgive foreign visitors for the odd faux pas – the one thing which will really irritate them and make them less likely to be tolerant of any mistakes you make, is if you are not polite. Overall, Britons are very polite. You will find that they say 'please' and

'thank you' in all social situations, even when they are not always being treated as well as they might be.

- Always say 'please' when asking for anything, and 'thank you' when being given something, or being told information.
- If you don't understand, or have made a mistake, say 'I'm sorry' and if you need to interrupt somebody or wish them to move out of your way, say 'excuse me'.
- There are a few rules of behaviour which you should also adhere to:
- Don't queue-jump: always join the back of a queue and wait your turn to be served.
- Shake hands and say 'pleased to meet you', or 'how are you' on being introduced to someone.
- Other greetings to use are: 'Good morning/afternoon/evening' (formal or to someone you don't know very well). 'Hello' or 'Hi' (informal to your friends).
- It is acceptable to kiss a woman friend on one cheek when you meet.
- Be punctual – don't keep people waiting when you have an appointment or an invitation. If you are unavoidably delayed, try to call and let them know.
- Don't spit or stare at people in public.

- Don't swear in the presence of ladies – if you do so inadvertently, apologise for it.
- Don't ask personal questions such as 'How much do you earn?' or 'How old are you?'.
- Observe good table manners and don't speak with your mouth full.

If you follow this advice you won't go far wrong: you will be seen as an agreeable person and therefore forgiven for the odd mistake.

Gift-Giving

If you have been invited to someone's home in the evening, for a drink or a meal, although not necessarily expected, it is a nice touch to bring a gift for your hosts: a bottle of wine, box of chocolates or bunch of flowers are all acceptable. If you have been invited for morning coffee or afternoon tea, however, a gift is not appropriate.

It is normal to take a small gift if visiting someone in hospital – some fruit, sweets (candy) or a bunch of flowers are all traditional in these circumstances.

If you have been invited to a birthday party or a wedding you should normally give an appropriate gift, unless you have been expressly asked not to.

▌ GEOGRAPHICAL INFORMATION

Great Britain comprises the countries of England, Scotland and Wales, with the province of Northern Ireland located in the north-eastern part of the smaller island of Ireland situated to the west. Southern Ireland, or Eire, has been a republic since 1949.

The Isle of Man and the Channel Islands are Crown Dependencies, and as such have their own systems of government, administration and taxation. Due to lack of space they cannot be discussed in any detail in this book.

England is by far the largest country within the UK, making up around 54% of the landmass. It is also the most populous and the wealthiest. Part of the reason for its greater density of population is that the terrain is far flatter than the other parts, with a milder climate, and has thus historically afforded an easier life to the peoples living there. The less productive areas of Scotland and Wales take up 32% and 8.5%. Northern Ireland makes up the remaining 5.8% of its area.

Topography

The island of Great Britain is divided into a lowland region, running roughly from the River Exe on the south-west coast to the River Tees on the north-east coast; and a highland region which includes Wales and Scotland. The Lake District in the north west falls into the highland region, and it is here that the highest English mountain, Scafell Pike, is found. However, compared with Wales and Scotland, this is relatively tame countryside – although beautiful and a favourite tourist destination. Scotland has 284 mountains over 3,000 feet (914 m) high (known as 'Munros'); tiny Wales has 14, known collectively as the Welsh 3,000s; whereas England has just seven. Equally, England's largest inland body of water, Lake Windermere (the main draw for tourists to the Lake District) is dwarfed by the largest in Northern Ireland and Scotland.

England has two ranges of mountains: the Cumbrian Mountains, which include the Lake District, and the Pennine Chain which runs south-north for 160 miles (260 km) from the midlands almost to the Scottish border. For obvious reasons it is sometimes called 'the backbone of England'.

The lowland zone of England is characterised by its grassy rolling plains which are far more fertile and better for farming than the harsher highland zone. The lowest-lying region of the country is East Anglia. The Fens, a large area of marshland in Cambridgeshire, is in parts 13 feet (4m) below sea level. In south east England there are the Cotswolds and Chilterns, two ranges of hills rising from the Thames Valley, which together are designated an area of outstanding natural beauty. They are renowned for their many attractive small towns and villages which are popular as country retreats for commuters to London.

Wales is mountainous throughout apart from a thin strip of lowland which runs along the coast and taking in the island of Anglesey, situated off the north-west coast and separated from the mainland by the Menai Strait, a strip of water varying in width along its 15-mile (24 km) length between 200 yards (180 m) and 2 miles (3 km).

In the north of Wales, the mountainous region of the Snowdonia national park includes Snowdon, the country's highest mountain. In central Wales are the Cambrian Mountains, and in the south are the Brecon Beacons, a range of lower, less rugged mountains. The flatter south-eastern corner of Wales is sometimes considered an extension of the lowland zone of Britain. It is here that the largest towns, cities and industrial regions are found. Coal mining just to the north of this area was especially important to the Welsh economy in the past, although today the industry is a fraction of its former size.

Scotland comprises the mainland and many islands including the Hebrides and the Orkney and Shetlands isles. Mainland Scotland is divided into three topographical regions: the southern uplands, bordering England; the central lowlands formed by the valleys of the Clyde, the Forth and the Tay; and the northern Highlands, which are themselves divided into a northern and southern system by the Great Glen, a major geological fault running between Inverness and Fort William. The Grampian Mountains cover the southern Highland area and include the Cairngorm Mountains in the east and Ben Nevis, the highest mountain in the British Isles (4406 ft /1,343m) in the west.

The western coast is characterised by its islands and sea lochs. The longest is Loch Fyne at 42 miles (26 km) long. The largest inland loch is Loch Lomond at 27.46 square miles (71.12 sq km), while the longest and deepest is Loch Ness at 24 miles (38 km) long and 800 feet (244 m) deep.

Northern Ireland has two striking geographical features: in the centre of the province is Lough Neagh, which covers an impressive 151 square miles (392 km²), making it the largest freshwater lake in the British Isles, and the third largest lake in Western Europe. On the north Antrim coast the Giant's Causeway is an area of 40,000 interlocking basalt columns resulting from a volcanic eruption, forming natural 'stepping stones' which disappear under the sea. The highest of them are 36 feet (12m) high.

Northern Ireland's most mountainous area is the Sperrin Mountains in the central region. They are not particularly high, with the highest mountain in the province, Slieve Donard, reaching 2,782 feet (848 m). There are extensive river and lake systems throughout the province, with fertile lowlands in the river valleys.

Population

In July 2006 the estimated UK population was 60.609 million making it the third largest country in the EU (after Germany and France) and the

Britain's Geography: Facts And Figures

Total area of the UK: 94,525 sq miles/244,820 sq km.

Area of England: 50,351 sq miles/130,410 sq km.

Area of Wales: 8,020 sq miles/20,760 sq km.

Area of Scotland: 30,420 sq miles/78,790 sq km.

Area of N. Ireland: 5,470 sq miles/14,160 sq km.

Inland water area: 1,247 sq miles/3,230 sq km.

Coastline: 7,723 miles/12,429 km

Highest mountains: Scafell Pike (England) 3,208 ft/978 m; Snowdon (Wales) 3,560 ft/1,085 m; Ben Nevis (Scotland) 4406 ft/1343 m; Slieve Donard (N. Ireland) 2,786 ft/849 m.

Largest inland bodies of water: Lough Neave (N. Ireland) 150 sq miles/388 sq km; Loch Lomond (Scotland) 27.46 sq miles/71.12 sq km; Lake Windermere (England) 5.69 sq miles/14.73 sq km; Lake Vyrnwy (Wales) 3.18 sq miles/8.24 sqkm.

Islands: there are about 1,000 islands and islets in total; over 700 of these in Scotland.

Largest island: Skye (Scotland) 643 sq miles/1648 sq km.

21st largest in the world. At 243 people per square kilometre, the UK's population density is one of the highest in the world. However, this figure is somewhat misleading because there are huge variations between areas. About one quarter of the population lives in the south east of England, and an estimated 7,517,700 live in London, giving the city a population density of 3,172 people per square kilometre, while Greater London's density is a massive 4,761 per square kilometre. At the other extreme, the Highlands of Scotland have a population density of just eight people per square kilometre.

Scotland covers around one third of the area of the United Kingdom, but at just over five million, its population is only one twelfth of the total UK population. The bulk of the population is concentrated in the Central Belt, which includes Scotland's two largest cities: Edinburgh, the capital, has a population of around 448,000, while Glasgow is much larger at 577,000. The unevenness of distribution of the population is pointed up by the remarkable fact that 90% of the population live within one hour's drive of Perth.

The United Kingdom's population is on the increase, with a growth of 7.7% since 1971. In recent years the rate of growth has increased in all the constituent nations, a significant proportion due to higher immigration. The long-term picture for Scotland is uncertain: although it has in the last three years shown good signs of halting an ongoing decline, the trend is for the population to fall.

> Because of the very high density of population in many parts of the UK, you have to work hard to find uncrowded places but it is usually worth the effort. I prefer a peopled landscape to great wildernesses in any case.
> Sue Hardie

> " I cannot pretend that the weather is something that has not taken some 'getting used to'. Compared with Alabama, which enjoys extremely sultry summers and generally mild winters, the average temperatures here have kept me bundled up in sweaters and jackets and constantly going over just to make sure the thermostat isn't 'broken'. It rains much more frequently here, so I've had to get used to that... but all in all, I've taken it in stride and it is nothing that has disturbed me so terribly that I have locked myself indoors, refusing to come out. I've just accepted it as part of my new surroundings and don't really mind it, so much. Not to mention, when the weather is beautiful, it is absolutely stunning, I love it.
> Amy Burns "

Wales and Northern Ireland are the smallest nations of the UK, with far lower population densities than England. Unlike Scotland, their populations have seen a slow but steady increase over recent years and are predicted to continue growing.

Climate

If there's one thing which brings the British together, it's the climate. It is widely believed that the weather is a constant topic of conversation – and to a certain extent that is true. The reason is that it is so changeable that you can never be certain what it is going to do next! Sometimes it feels as though there have been all four seasons in one day.

Britain is well known for having a lot of rain, but there are actually wide variations in the average amounts which fall in different parts of the country. In England the driest parts are the south and east, with some areas having less than 700mm a year. In contrast, the Lake District has over 2,000mm a year. In fact, although most people believe that Scotland has far and away the greatest rainfall of all the countries of the UK, the Highlands actually have a comparable rainfall to that of the English Lake District, the Welsh Mountains and Cornwall, while Edinburgh's rainfall is similar to London's. Generally speaking, the flatter areas and the eastern coastal areas experience lower rainfall than the higher western areas.

With prevailing south-westerly winds across the UK, weather systems tend to come in from the west, which is one reason for the higher rainfall in those areas. The west coast is also warmer than the east, due to the Gulf Stream, a warm current which keeps the Atlantic and the Irish Sea at higher temperatures year round, compared with the colder North Sea.

As well as differences in total amounts of rain falling over the year, there is a great variation in the time of year and the number of days in the year when it falls, depending on local topography. For example,

> [There are] no extremes, which is not as interesting as the Canadian climate but much easier to manage. It goes without saying that the weather is often disappointing, but I love the way that Brits carry on regardless, and hold many outdoor events over the summer (folk music festivals, barbecues, Shakespeare plays) and stoically carry on if the weather is inclement.
>
> Susan Griffith

on the south coast January has about twice as much rain as July, while the western, northern and eastern coasts tend to be driest in spring and wettest in autumn. And inland, parts of the Midlands see their maximum rainfall in summer. On average, it rains about one day in three in England, around 175 days per year in the coastal areas near Edinburgh, and over 250 days per year in the West Highlands. However, in all these places, long dry spells are not uncommon.

It doesn't rain all the time – it just seems that way sometimes! Britain also gets its fair share of sunshine. The sunniest parts are the south coast of England, with Wales, Scotland and Northern Ireland all cloudier due to the higher terrain. But again there is great variation, with the sunniest parts of Scotland – Angus, Fife, the Lothians, Ayrshire, and Dumfries and Galloway – averaging over 1,400 hours of sunshine per year, compared with 1,750 hours on the south coast. Whereas the average for sunshine in the Scottish Highlands, at less than 1,100 hours per year, is marginally higher than the mountainous areas of England, which enjoy fewer than 1,000 hours per year.

Because of its latitude, winter days in Scotland are short, but this is more than compensated for by the long days of summer. On the longest days of the year, the north of Scotland does not go completely dark, experiencing an extended twilight.

Gusting high winds can cause damage to property, particularly during the winter months. These can occur anywhere in the UK, although the frequency of strong winds is higher in Scotland because many Atlantic depressions pass over. Throughout the UK the windiest areas are in the north and west.

Although Wales and Scotland are generally cloudier than England, because of far lower pollution levels they both enjoy good visibility. Poor visibility on the east coast of Scotland and in the northern isles during April to September is frequently caused by fog coming in off the North Sea, known locally as *haar*. Hill fog is a regular occurrence in all upland areas, and hill walkers should always be careful for that reason.

Snow is comparatively rare at sea level, increasing with altitude wherever in Britain you may be. Other than on the highest mountains,

UK Climate Figures 2006					
Region	Max temp	Min temp	Mean temp	Sunshine	Rainfall
	[°C]	[°C]	[°C]	[hours]	[mm]
UK	13.4	6.1	9.7	1507.3	1176.3
England	14.4	6.8	10.6	1637.8	851.5
Wales	13.4	6.5	9.9	1534.4	1419.7
Scotland	11.7	4.9	8.3	1300.5	1651.5
N. Ireland	13.3	6.0	9.6	1408.5	1156.0

> Be prepared for long periods of very dull weather, especially if you come from very sunny climates!
>
> Joe Rawal

snow rarely lies for more than a few days at a time. Scotland sees more snow than the other countries, but even here, although snow may lie for months on the mountains of the north east of Scotland, the west coast, due to the influence of the Gulf Stream, has comparatively mild and wet winters with snow rarely lying on low ground for more than a couple of days at a time.

England experiences overall the highest average temperatures, followed by Wales, Northern Ireland, then Scotland, which is generally between two and three degrees colder than the south of England.

Extremes

- **Highest temp:** 38.5°C at Brogdale, Kent on 10/08/2003.
- **Lowest temp:** -27.2°C at Braemar, Aberdeenshire on 11/02/1895 and 10/01/1982.
- **Maximum sunshine in a month:** 383.9 hours at Eastbourne, East Sussex in July 1911.
- **Minimum sunshine in a month:** 0.0 hours at Westminster, London in December 1890.
- **Maximum rainfall in a day:** 279 mm at Martinstown, Dorset on 18/07/1955
- **Highest gust of wind:** 150 knots (173 m.p.h). Cairngorm, Highland Region on 20/03/1986.

Figures from the Met Office, www.metoffice.gov.uk

◼ REGIONAL GUIDE

The United Kingdom has a fairly complicated system of regional divisions. The main ones are obviously the four distinct countries: England, Wales, Scotland, and Northern Ireland. However, within these, Britain has for centuries been divided into much smaller geographical divisions known as counties. Until relatively recently there were 86 counties in Great Britain, plus another six in Northern Ireland. The majority of the 39 counties in England pre-date the Norman Conquest in 1066, while the 13 counties of Wales were fixed by statute in 1539. The 37 counties of Scotland and those in Northern Ireland are equally ancient. The counties were traditionally important divisions as far as administration, government and the legal system were concerned. However in the last forty years there have been successive local government reforms, which have introduced new divisions that do not always follow the boundaries, nor the names, of the historic counties.

As a result of these changes, one finds that the regions covered by large public organisations do not necessarily follow the same regional boundaries. So, for example, the local councils, police forces, health boards, and tourist board regions overlap each other in many places.

In the following sections, therefore, an attempt has been made to focus on common-sense divisions which take into account these variations. Wales, Scotland and Northern Ireland are each small enough to be dealt with as a whole. England is divided into nine Government Office Regions (GORs) which, in combination with various Government departments, are intended to work together with local people and organisations to improve prosperity and quality of life in their areas. The regions used in the discussion which follows are either contiguous with the GORs or are combinations of two or more as follows:

A list of local councils can be found at the end of this chapter. The local council websites are a useful source of further information about living in the area, but these vary greatly from one area to another. Some concentrate solely on practical administrative subjects, listing services and so forth, while others have given themselves a much wider remit and contain far more information on the history and daily lifestyle of their region. Some towns have their own local websites, another important source of information about the culture and lifestyle you could expect. It is always worth searching on the internet for other websites about specific areas – there is a wealth of information on the net, with updates and new websites regularly appearing.

England

London and the South East

- **Major Towns:** London, Brighton, Southampton, Portsmouth, Canterbury, Oxford.
- **Main Airports:** London Heathrow, London Gatwick.
- **Regional Information – London:** Government Office for London: www.gos.gov.uk/gol

MAP**OF**BRITAIN NORTH ↑

NORTH
SEA

BRITAIN

NORWAY

NETHERLANDS
○ Amsterdam
BELGIUM
GERMANY
○ Paris
FRANCE

Shetland
Islands

Foula

Fair Isle

NORTH
SEA

Orkney
Islands

Lewis

Outer
Hebrides
St. Kilda
North Uist

Skye

Inverness ○

SCOTLAND

Aberdeen ○

South Uist

Barra

Rum

Cdl

Tiree

Mull

Dundee ○

Islay

Glasgow ○

Edinburgh ○

Holy
Island

Tory
Island

Rathlin
Island

Arran

NORTH
EAST

Aran
Island

Londonderry ○

NORTHERN
IRELAND

Belfast ○

Carlisle ○

Newcastle
uponTyne

NORTH
WEST

Isle of
Man

Walney
Island

YORKSHIRE &
THE HUMBER

York ○

Hull ○

Aran
Islands

IRISH
SEA

Liverpool ○
Manchester ○

ATLANTIC
OCEAN

Gt. Blaslet
Island

Bangor ○

Nottingham ○

Norwich ○

Birmingham ○

EAST
MIDLANDS

EAST OF ENGLAND

WALES

WEST
MIDLANDS

○ Cambridge

Cardiff ○

Bristol ○

○ Oxford

LONDON

CELTIC
SEA

Lundy

SOUTH EAST

SOUTH WEST

Portsmouth ○

Plymouth ○

Isle of
Wight

Isle of
Scilly

London

Cornwall

Wales

Scotland

North England

Northern ireland

- **Regional Information – South East:** Government Office for the South East: www.gos.gov.uk/gose
- **Tourist Information – London:** www.enjoyengland.com/where/destinations/london/dg.aspx
- **Tourist Information – South East England:** www.enjoyengland.com/where/destinations/south-east/dg.aspx
- **National Parks:** New Forest.
- **UNESCO World Heritage Sites:** Blenheim Palace; Canterbury Cathedral, St Augustine's Abbey and St Martin's Church; Maritime Greenwich; Royal Botanic Gardens, Kew; Tower of London; Westminster Palace, Westminster Abbey and St Margaret's Church.

This is the most prosperous region of Britain, although within it there are areas which fall significantly below the national average for per capita Gross Value Added (GVA), which measures the contribution to the economy of each individual, notably the eastern part of outer London and the coastal fringe.

Region (as used in this book)	Government Office Region
England	
South West	South West
London and the South East	London
	South East
East	East of England
Midlands	West Midland
	East Midlands
North	Yorkshire and the Humber
	North West
	North East
Wales	
Scotland	
Northern Ireland	

> I was 25 when I moved here, and single, so travelling, finding accommodation and generally getting settled wasn't a big deal for me like it would be if I'd had a family. There are lots of Kiwis in England, especially in London, and I already had friends here so I had an established network of people who could help me as soon as I got here. In fact, I lodged with a friend in London for about six months before getting myself properly established, which was a great help.
>
> John Livesey

London, England's capital city, has over seven million residents and is the biggest city in Britain and in Europe. It is also the most densely populated area of Britain, and has in addition to cope with a huge influx of workers and visitors every day. This means that traffic congestion is a constant problem, which has been alleviated somewhat by a congestion charge of eight pounds per day levied on people driving into designated areas of London. For more details see www.cclondon.com.

There is a big racial mix in this region, with people of over 270 nationalities making their homes here, and over 250 languages spoken. The biggest concentration of people from ethnic backgrounds is found in the London area, but many workers find London prices make it impossible for them to live within the metropolitan area, so there is a large number of commuters who live within the wider south east region and travel to the capital for work every day. This means that the ethnic and cultural mix throughout the region is very diverse.

The prosperity of the south east region is helped greatly by the presence of London at its heart. The belt around London is the wealthiest part with the coastal areas being comparatively poorer. However, these coastal areas boast some of the most beautiful countryside in Britain, and with less congestion and traffic pollution many of London's wealthier residents choose to live on the south coast and commute in for work, or they have a second home there so they can escape the city at weekends.

> I had spent a summer at an international summer school a few years before and instantly loved the UK and Oxford in particular.
>
> Sue Griffith

In addition to London itself, which is one of the world's most historic cities, with famous attractions such as Buckingham Palace, the Houses of Parliament and Westminster Abbey, there are many other venerable towns within the region, including the ancient university city of Oxford; Windsor and Eton, famous for the castle and the college respectively; and the cathedral cities of Canterbury, Winchester and Chichester, all of which have had important roles to play during Britain's long history.

The south coast is full of seaside towns where traditionally British families would take their summer holidays. Although the British seaside holiday has become less popular as worldwide travel – to places with more reliable summer sunshine – has become cheaper and more accessible, day trips to the south coast are still popular and any sunny weekend in the summer is likely to see an exodus from the more built-up areas of the region.

Brighton is the largest of these seaside resorts, and has long had a reputation for glamour and flamboyance. Today it has a cosmopolitan feel, with a vibrant nightlife and unique shops to be found in the 17th-century 'Brighton lanes'.

Despite being the most built-up area of Britain, there is plenty of countryside to enjoy. There are the chalk hills of the north and south downs which include the famous white cliffs of Dover; the orchards and flowers of Kent, known as the 'Garden of England'; and the ancient New Forest which has changed little since William the Conqueror gave it special protection nearly 1,000 years ago. The River Thames winds through London and the west of the region, its banks lined with attractive towns and villages.

Britain has a long maritime tradition, and fishing, merchant shipping and naval connections can be found in towns along the south coast. Portsmouth was a significant naval port for centuries and is still a major Royal Navy dockyard and base.

South West

- **Major Towns:** Bristol, Plymouth, Exeter, Gloucester, Bournemouth, Bath.
- **Main Airports:** Bristol.
- **Regional Information:** Government Office for the South West: www.gos.gov.uk/gosw
- **Tourist Information:** South West England: www.enjoyengland.com/where/destinations/south-west/dg.aspx
- **National Parks:** Dartmoor; Exmoor.
- **UNESCO World Heritage Sites:** City of Bath; Cornwall and West Devon Mining Landscape; Stonehenge, Avebury and Associated Sites; Dorset and East Devon Coast.

The South West peninsula covers an area of 9,203 square miles (23,837 sq km) and is over 217 miles (350km) long, extending from the south western tip of Cornwall to the northern edge of Gloucestershire. The third side of its roughly triangular shape follows the eastern boundaries of Gloucestershire, Wiltshire and Dorset. It is a predominantly rural area with three-quarters of the land being used for agriculture. The south west is also an area of outstanding natural beauty and interest. The cliffs of the Dorset and East Devon Coast area contain a geological record of 185 million years of the earth's history during the Mesozoic Era and includes several fossil sites of such importance that the whole area has been listed as a World Heritage site. This, together with the many miles of safe sandy beaches, historic sites of interest including the city of Bath and the prehistoric standing

> I just love the rugged coastline, golden beaches and sense of space in Cornwall. And of course, as an Australian, the surfing attracts me too!
>
> Jo Penfold

stones of Stonehenge and Avebury, make the region very popular with tourists, both from home and abroad. Well over 20% of tourist trips within England are made to the region, giving it a higher share of the domestic holiday market than any other of the English regions.

Other places of interest in the region are medieval cathedral towns such as Salisbury, Gloucester and Wells, and the maritime town of Plymouth from where the Pilgrim Fathers and Sir Francis Drake sailed. In addition to its coastal delights, there are vast areas of natural beauty further inland, including the National Parks of Exmoor and Dartmoor; the ancient woodland of the Forest of Dean; and the gentle hills of the Cotswolds where picture postcard villages nestle, with many people still living in traditional thatched cottages.

Bristol is the region's largest city. Although it has some deprived inner-city areas which have seen unrest in recent years, it is seeing an improvement in its fortunes, as are many British cities, with a deliberate effort by the government and local authority to regenerate the run-down areas. The Harbourside is now a lively place with arts centres, bars and restaurants, and the Old City is full of historic and architectural interest.

Overall the region provides a high quality of life – it has the lowest population density of any region in England – and this has encouraged many people to move there. Between 1995 and 2005 it had one of the fastest growing populations of the English regions, mainly due to people moving into the rural areas. The population of the south west is predicted to grow by over three-quarters of a million people by 2028.

East

■ **Major Towns:** Peterborough, Chelmsford, St Albans, Norwich, Cambridge, Colchester.

Cornwall

Cornwall is a county with a fascinating history: smuggling was a major activity there for hundreds of years, while a more legal form of enterprise was the copper and tin mining industry which has left a dramatic mark on the scenery which has been recognized by the area's listing as a World Heritage site. There is a strong Celtic influence in Cornwall, and the ancient Cornish tongue is now officially recognized – it can be seen in evidence on local signs and a growing number of people are learning the language. Cornwall's beaches are popular with surfers, while St Ives has been a favourite with artists since the 19th century due to its unique light.

- **Main Airports:** London Stansted, Luton.
- **Regional Information:** Government Office for the East of England: www.gos.gov.uk/goeast
- **Tourist Information:** East of England: www.enjoyengland.com/where/destinations/east-of-england/index.aspx
- **National Parks:** Broads.

This is the lowest-lying area of Britain, located largely in the large, hump-shaped area called East Anglia. The large inlet on its northern coast, called 'the Wash', was once surrounded by a large expanse of marshland called the Fens. This area has now mostly been drained, leaving a network of waterways. The largest city in the region, Peterborough, is situated in the Fens and boasts a Norman cathedral and 2,000 acres of riverside parkland.

To the east is another area of wetlands known as the Norfolk and Suffolk Broads which is rich in wildlife and a favourite boating and tourist area. Great Yarmouth, a popular seaside resort in the Broads, was described by Charles Dickens as 'the finest place in the universe' and he used many of the town's characters and landmarks in his novel *David Copperfield*.

Although it has remote rural areas and a wealth of rare animal and plant species, with over 600 Sites of Special Scientific Interest, the region is easy to reach from London which borders it to the south.

There are many attractive historic towns in the region. Although Norwich tries to claim the crown as the regional capital, in truth there are around a dozen medium-sized towns and cities, with no major city acting as a regional focus. Norwich, with its cathedral and castle, has some of the finest medieval architecture in Europe, alongside some striking modern architecture.

Cambridge too has historic architecture in abundance, particularly within the university bounds. The River Cam winds through, the stretch behind the college buildings being known as 'the Backs', with its famous punts for hire (flat-bottomed boats) – the British version of a Venetian Gondola.

To the south the county of Essex borders London and is a popular place to live with commuters to the city, as well as being rich in history. Ipswich is England's oldest continuously settled Anglo-Saxon town and also has a rich maritime heritage – it has been a working port since the sixth century.

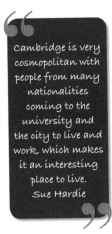

Cambridge is very cosmopolitan with people from many nationalities coming to the university and the city to live and work, which makes it an interesting place to live.
Sue Hardie

Midlands

- **Major Towns:** Birmingham, Coventry, Nottingham, Leicester, Derby.
- **Main Airports:** Birmingham, East Midlands.
- **Regional Information West Midlands:** Government Office for the West Midlands: www.gos.gov.uk/gowm
- **Regional Information East Midlands:** Government Office for the East Midlands: www.gos.gov.uk/goem

- **Tourist Information Heart of England:** www.enjoyengland.com/where/destinations/heart-of-england/index.aspx
- **Tourist Information East Midlands:** www.enjoyengland.com/where/destinations/east-midlands/index.aspx
- **National Parks:** Peak District.
- **UNESCO World Heritage Sites:** Derwent Valley Mills; Ironbridge Gorge.

The Midlands is a region of great diversity. Although this is the manufacturing heartland of the UK, there are also large tracts of rural and agricultural land. The birthplace of the Industrial Revolution, and once the centre of the British coal and textile industries, now there are few working collieries and mills. Much of the remaining industrial heritage generates more income from tourism than production. The region's two World Heritage Sites have been listed for their contribution to the history of technology.

At the heart of the nation's road and rail network, communications here are good, which makes the region attractive to businesses. With a population of just under 1,000,000, Birmingham is the UK's second largest city and a large proportion of the region's residents live in an area with Birmingham at its centre, and taking in Solihull, Coventry and the Black Country, an area which gained its name in the mid-19th century, as a result of the smoke from the many iron foundries and the dark spoil heaps from the collieries which littered the landscape. The largest proportion of black and ethnic minorities outside London live in this area.

In the East Midlands, the main towns are the so-called 'Three Cities' of Nottingham, Derby and Leicester. The more remote rural areas are the most deprived, with higher levels of unemployment and a lower standard of living than the national and regional averages.

To the north, Stoke-on-Trent combines the six older towns of The Potteries, namely Burslem, Tunstall, Hanley, Stoke-upon-Trent, Longton, and Fenton. This became a world-renowned centre for the production of ceramics in the seventeenth century due to the combination of local clay and the innovative use of coal to fuel their kilns, which gave the local potters an advantage over those in other regions who were still burning

> My own parents had emigrated to New Zealand when they were newly married, which is over 50 years ago now. The family came from Warwickshire so I had cousins and aunts and uncles scattered across the Midlands and elsewhere. I had even been to the UK for a visit when I was about 12 so it wasn't much of a shock to come over here. Most of it was familiar although, obviously, it's different coming here to stay and work as an adult than it is to visit the place as a kid.
>
> John Livesey

wood. Stoke-on-Trent remains the UK's 'capital of china', with Royal Doulton, Spode and Wedgwood all based there and offering factory tours and shops, demonstrations and their own museums.

Although for some years Birmingham languished somewhat – its industrial roots and the domination of the notorious 'spaghetti junction' motorway network made this an unlovely city – along with other British cities it has in recent years undergone something of a renaissance, with the canalside and waterfront areas being regenerated by the introduction of bars, restaurants and residential areas. The Grand Union Canal linking Birmingham with London, an important means of freight transport in previous centuries, runs into the centre of the city.

The UK's first National Park, the Peak District, is here, and together with the Derbyshire Dales and the Lincolnshire Wolds, it contributes to the large expanses of natural beauty alongside the more built-up areas of the region.

Literary connections here are important, with Shakespeare's birthplace, Stratford-on-Avon, attracting thousands of visitors every year from around the world. Charles Dickens, another great British author – many would say second only after Shakespeare – was born and brought up in Shrewsbury, which is also a delightfully attractive town. Black and white half-timbered Tudor and Elizabethan buildings are a feature of many small towns in the region, evidence of their long history.

North

- **Major Towns:** Leeds, Sheffield, Bradford, Liverpool, Manchester, Sunderland, Newcastle upon Tyne.
- **Main Airports:** Manchester, Leeds/Bradford, Newcastle.
- **Regional Information Yorkshire and the Humber:** Government Office for Yorkshire and the Humber: www.gos.gov.uk/goyh
- **Regional Information North West:** Government Office for the North West: www.gos.gov.uk/gonw
- **Regional Information North East:** Government Office for the North East: www.gos.gov.uk/gone
- **Tourist Information Yorkshire:** www.enjoyengland.com/where/destinations/yorkshire/index.aspx
- **Tourist Information England's Northwest:** www.enjoyengland.com/where/destinations/englands-northwest/index.aspx
- **Tourist Information North East England:** www.enjoyengland.com/where/destinations/north-east-england/index.aspx
- **National Parks:** Lake District; Yorkshire Dales; North York Moors; Northumberland.
- **UNESCO World Heritage Sites:** Durham Castle and Cathedral; Hadrian's Wall; Liverpool, Maritime Mercantile City; Saltaire, West Yorkshire; Studley Royal Park and Ruins of Fountains Abbey.

There is something of a cultural and economic north-south divide in England. Northerners are reputed to be more warm and friendly people, while southerners are characterised as more reserved and stand-offish. Although there are always dangers in such blanket generalisations, there is an element of truth in this observation – largely to do, one suspects, with the higher density of population and faster pace of life in the south (particularly, London and the Home Counties which surround it). Although many of Britain's largest cities are in the north of England, there are also vast tracts of unspoiled countryside in the region with very low population densities.

It is certainly true that economically the north lags some distance behind the south. With London, England's capital city, attracting the majority of national and international business, and the people to work in those businesses, large parts of the north have seen depopulation in recent years. Over the past twenty to thirty years the region has suffered from the decline of traditional industries with substantial job losses in coal mining, steel production, manufacturing, engineering, and textiles. These are being replaced by growth in new areas, notably in the service sector and tourism. Regeneration is being carried out in many cities, as elsewhere in Britain, and they are gradually remodelling their run-down inner city and dockside areas as lively cosmopolitan places which help to attract new businesses and their high-flying employees. Leeds, England's third largest city, is one such success story, now being the second largest legal and financial centre outside London.

However, although metropolitan areas such as Manchester, Newcastle, Liverpool, and Leeds, and smaller historic cities such as Chester, Durham and York have a lot going for them, the main glory of the north of England is undoubtedly its countryside. All these towns and cities have unspoiled rural areas not far from their doorsteps – a fact which is confirmed by the existence of no fewer than four large national parks in the region, and several Areas of Outstanding Natural Beauty. As a result, the north is the best place in England for walking, climbing and other outdoor pursuits.

In the west of the region is the Lake District National Park which covers the whole of Cumbria, part of northern Lancashire and extends into the Yorkshire Dales. There are at least 16 lakes (most called 'meres' or 'waters') set amongst stunning scenery. England's five highest peaks are in the area. Hadrian's Wall (a World Heritage Site) runs through Cumbria and continues across to the northeast coast.

On the east, running from south to north, there are three National Parks: the Yorkshire Dales, the North York Moors, and Northumberland. Each has its own character: the Dales straddle the Pennines, the backbone of England; the North York Moors are full of wide open spaces criss-crossed with the characteristic drystone walls of the area; while Northumberland spreads across the hills and valleys at the very top of England. In all four

> I don't think I could stomach London, if I could I'd move to somewhere more remote. It's nice to live within reasonable reach of places where you can unwind away from people.
> Rainer Thonnes

> I'm a big outdoors man, so I love the north of England for hiking and climbing.
> John Livesey

parks ancient castles, hillforts and other archaeological sites are plentiful, as are picturesque villages and beautiful beaches.

Wales

- **Major Towns:** Cardiff, Swansea, Newport.
- **Main Airports:** Cardiff.
- **Regional Information:** Welsh Assembly: www.wales.gov.uk
- **Tourist Information:** Visit Wales: www.visitwales.co.uk
- **National Parks:** Brecon Beacons; Pembrokeshire Coast; Snowdonia.
- **UNESCO World Heritage Sites:** Blaenavon Industrial Landscape, Cardiff; Castles and Town Walls of King Edward in Gwynedd.

Wales is a Principality, with its titular head being the Prince of Wales, a ceremonial title traditionally held by the Heir Apparent to the throne. Unlike Scotland, Wales has never been a sovereign state and after nearly 500 years of being part of a unitary state its economy, infrastructure, legal and political systems are highly integrated with those of England. However, since the early 20th century there has been a marked revival in national consciousness, one of the most significant symbols of this being the establishment, as recently as 1955, of Cardiff as the capital of Wales. It took until 1999 for any form of autonomous government for Wales to be established, in the form of the Welsh Assembly.

Wales is officially bilingual, with over 20% of the population able to speak Welsh, claimed to be the widest spoken of the Celtic languages. Welsh and English are treated equally by law: all official documents are available in both languages, and place names on road signs are bilingual.

Wales is a predominantly rural country, much of it being very sparsely populated. The majority of its 2.95 million population is concentrated in its south-eastern corner, where the country's three largest cities, Cardiff, Swansea and Newport, are grouped quite close together. In contrast, Powys in the rural heartlands is one of the most thinly populated counties in Britain.

The industrialisation of parts of Wales started in the 18th century. Mining was an important industry in the country until early in the 20th century, with a wide range of ores being extracted, including coal, copper, iron, silver, lead, and gold. Now the mining and industry is all but dead, and manufacturing has declined also, with a greater percentage of the national income now coming from the service sector. The low-quality soil in the rural areas means that the majority of agriculture in Wales is livestock farming rather than crop-growing.

There are regeneration projects ongoing in Cardiff, Swansea and Newport, with plans to improve other towns also in the pipeline. At the time of writing Cardiff is the fastest-growing city in the EU as a direct result of new building and other ongoing projects.

The long and the short of it

Wales claims to have both the smallest town in Britain and the village with the longest name:

- Llanwrtyd Wells in mid-Wales had a population of 601 in the 2001 census.
- The island of Anglesey, situated just off the northwest coast, has a village with the name Llanfairpwllgwyngyllgogery chwyrndrobwllllantysiliogogogoch which means: The church of St. Mary in a hollow of white hazel near a rapid whirlpool and near St. Tysilio's church by the red cave. It is abbreviated to Llanfairpwll or Llanfair P.G. by the locals.

Tourism is very important to the Welsh economy. Wales is a beautiful country, with extensive mountainous areas; a 750 mile (1,207 km) coastline full of clean white-sand beaches and rocky bays; rare flora and fauna in many areas with environmental designations. The built heritage too is impressive, with the importance of the 'iron ring' of castles built by Edward I in the northern part of the country being recognised by their listing as a World Heritage Site.

Scotland

- **Major Towns:** Edinburgh, Glasgow, Aberdeen, Dundee, Inverness.
- **Main Airports:** Edinburgh, Glasgow, Aberdeen.
- **Regional Information:** Scottish Executive: www.scotland.gov.uk
- **Tourist Information:** Visit Scotland: www.visitscotland.com
- **National Parks:** Cairngorms; Loch Lomond and the Trossachs.
- **UNESCO World Heritage Sites:** Heart of Neolithic Orkney; New Lanark; Old and New Towns of Edinburgh; St Kilda.

The history of Scotland, both ancient and modern, has been so turbulent, with many waves of invaders and settlers, and a constantly changing political relationship with England and Europe, that the different regions have distinctive variations, historically, culturally, socially, and linguistically. These make Scotland a fascinating and diverse country.

Mainland Scotland is divided into three basic topographical regions: the southern uplands, the central lowlands, and the Highlands. In addition, there are the three major island groups, the Western Isles, Orkney and Shetland. There are about 790 islands and islets in total, only 130 of which are inhabited.

The central belt encompasses some very rural, fairly remote communities as well as the largest towns and cities of Scotland. The south of the country is rural and agricultural with small towns and villages dotted throughout. The Highlands is a vast region, within which there is a distinct difference between the far more accessible, populous east and the relatively isolated north and west. Even the weather differs significantly between the two sides of the country. In the Highlands the agricultural pattern is different, with the crofting tradition still strong. The poorer soils in the far northern regions mean that livestock production is more common than crop-growing.

As the business capital of Scotland and the seat of the Scottish Parliament, Edinburgh and the area around it contains Scotland's wealthiest parts, although as with any city, there are poorer, more downmarket, areas where unemployment is higher and average wages lower.

Glasgow, Scotland's largest city, is surrounded by easily accessible areas of beautiful scenery, both inland and along the Clyde coast. The city itself is not lacking in open spaces – it has over 70 parks and gardens, and handsome mature trees line many of the roads leading into the city centre.

There is a healthy sense of competition between Glasgow and Edinburgh: while the capital city has much of the international cachet as far as its political, historical and cultural heritage is concerned, Glasgow presents itself as the more vibrant, chic, altogether younger and livelier face of Scotland, than the somewhat staid, traditional image of Edinburgh.

Grampian in the north east is a diverse region, encompassing as it does the prosperous modern City of Aberdeen, the 'Oil Capital of Europe', and the rural hinterland of Aberdeenshire which, beyond the Aberdeen commuter belt, has areas where household incomes are well below the national average. In addition to the wealth produced by North Sea oil and gas, north east Scotland also produces around one third of Scotland's agricultural output.

With an area of nearly 10,000 square miles, the Highlands is a massive region, the largest of Scotland's local government areas. Despite its extent, the population is low, with just 4% of the population of Scotland living there. This makes it the least populated region of Europe with an average population density of only eight people per square kilometre. The region includes Inverness, where nearly one fifth of the population resides – if this is taken out of the figures the average density plummets.

The mountains, lochs and glens of the Highlands are the image which says 'Scotland' to the rest of the world, making this the most desirable region of the country for incomers and tourists alike.

Northern Ireland

- **Major Towns:** Belfast, Londonderry/Derry, Lisburn.
- **Main Airports:** Belfast International.

The natural politeness and hospitality of the Highlanders really made us fall in love with them – we'd already fallen in love with the scenery and the laid back way of life.
Pam and Tony Shinkins

> ❝ I find Scotland, and Edinburgh in particular, a great place to live –
> I often have friends visiting from Ireland, and they really enjoy
> the city and the surrounding countryside. The pace of life in
> Edinburgh is unlike that in other capital cities, but gives
> access to far greater amenities.
> Irishman Bob Grayson ❞

- **Regional Information:** Northern Ireland Executive: www.nics.gov.uk/index.htm
- **Tourist Information:** Northern Ireland Tourist Board: www.discovernorthernireland.com
- **UNESCO World Heritage Sites:** Giant's Causeway and Causeway Coast, County Antrim.

Northern Ireland, sometimes called Ulster, occupies 5,459 square miles (14,139 sq km) in the north-eastern corner of the island of Ireland. It has been an administrative division of the United Kingdom since 1920, while the Republic of Ireland occupying the remainder of the island is a self-governing country. In common with other regions of the UK, Northern Ireland has had its own devolved government, which was set up as a condition of the Good Friday Agreement of 1998.

For decades Northern Ireland has been riven by a violent dispute, known as 'The Troubles', between the Nationalists (predominantly Catholic) and the Unionists (mainly Protestant) . The Unionists want Northern Ireland to remain in the United Kingdom while the Nationalists think it should be part of the Republic. After years of abortive peace agreements between the two sides, the Good Friday Agreement finally succeeded where others have failed. As a result of it the main paramilitary bodies agreed to a ceasefire. There have been some minor setbacks – the Northern Irish Assembly is currently suspended due to a political dispute between the parties – but the province is enjoying the most settled period of peace for many years.

This has had a beneficial effect on the economy of Northern Ireland. The Troubles had kept both international investment and tourists away, but since the agreement both have seen an upturn.

▪ Don't Blame Us!

The doomed ship Titanic was built in Belfast's shipyards. The Irish sense of humour is evident in the local saying: 'She was all right when she left here.'

Much of the new investment has been focused on the capital, Belfast, and its surrounding areas, where millions of pounds have been spent redeveloping the city centre and the waterfront, in addition to other

FACT

Don't Blame Us!

▪ The doomed ship Titanic was built in Belfast's shipyards. The Irish sense of humour is evident in the local saying: 'She was all right when she left here.'

A giant step for mankind

The legend goes that the Giant's Causeway was built by the giant Finn McCool, commander of the army of the King of Ireland. He fell in love with a giant from Staffa, an island in the Scottish Hebrides which has similar basalt columns, and built the causeway between the two islands to bring her to live with him in Ulster.

projects. Belfast has been called 'Europe's friendliest regional capital' and the Irish people do have a reputation for their welcoming nature and love of a good time. Music, dancing, laughing, and drinking are all national pastimes, and all can be found in abundance throughout the region.

Londonderry or Derry (the name varies depending on where one's Unionist/Nationalist sympathies lie) is the region's second largest city and boasts the only complete city walls still standing in Ireland. The city has many other historic buildings and it was from here that thousands of Irish emigrants sailed for the New World.

The region has been inhabited for thousands of years and there is a great deal of evidence of them still to be seen. There are literally thousands of tombs and standing stones on the moors of the north west, and many Celtic and early Christian antiquities have been unearthed in the south west.

> I loved every minute of my stay in Belfast – highlights were visiting the castle and the cathedral, and shopping on the Lisburn Road. I found some great places to eat and the people were so friendly and entertaining – it's true what they say about Irish craic!
> Jo Penfold

Northern Ireland

Both scenically and climatically, Northern Ireland has much in common with the Scottish Highlands. It has many 'loughs' (the Irish Gaelic equivalent of the Scottish Gaelic 'loch'), including the massive Lough Neagh, the largest freshwater lake in the British Isles and the third largest in Western Europe. It has wild mountainous regions, although its peaks are not as high as on the mainland, with its highest being Slieve Donard (2782 feet/ 848m) in the Mountains of Mourne, and also has expanses of peat lands. Probably the most famous geographical feature of Northern Ireland is the striking Giant's Causeway, off the north east coast, comprising 40,000 natural stone columns, some reaching 40 feet tall and many of them hexagonal in shape.

■ POLITICAL AND ECONOMIC STRUCTURE

The UK Government

The United Kingdom is a constitutional monarchy, meaning it is governed by ministers of the crown in the name of the monarch (currently Queen Elizabeth II) who is head of the state and of the government. Today, the powers of the monarch are limited compared to what they once were, being restricted mainly to ceremonial and advisory roles. The main duties of the sovereign in relation to government are the summoning and dissolving of parliament at the beginning and end of each session; giving Royal Assent to bills passed by parliament; appointing important office-holders such as government ministers, judges and bishops; conferring honours such as peerages and knighthoods and granting pardons to people wrongly convicted of crimes.

The UK constitution is unwritten and has evolved over centuries through statute, common law and convention.

The government is made up of three strands:

- The Legislature – parliament.
- The Executive – Her Majesty's Government (comprising the cabinet and other ministers), government departments and local authorities.
- The Judiciary – legal system and law courts.

Parliament is the body which passes laws and scrutinises government policy and administration including expenditure proposals. There are two Houses of Parliament, the House of Commons (lower house) and the House of Lords (upper house, also known as the second chamber).

Parliament sits in the Palace of Westminster (also known as the Houses of Parliament), which is situated beside the River Thames in the centre of London. It was in former times the residence of the kings of England, although much of the original building burned down in 1834, being rebuilt over the following 30 years. The most famous feature of the current building is the clock tower, with its huge bell known as Big Ben. For more about the history of the Palace of Westminster, see www.parliament.uk/parliament/guide/palace.htm.

Britain is divided into geographical areas called constituencies, and each constituency is represented by a democratically elected Member of Parliament (MP) who sits in the House of Commons.

Members of Parliament (MPs) are elected by secret ballot at a General Election where every eligible UK citizen has one vote, although voting is not compulsory. A General Election must be held at least every five years. When a seat becomes vacant between General Elections, due to the death of the sitting MP, for example, a by-election is held for a replacement.

Most candidates for election represent a political party, but there is no requirement to have the backing of a party. Some stand as Independents, campaigning on their own set of issues, or sometimes on just one issue. Every candidate for election must be supported by the signatures of ten people registered in the constituency and must also deposit £500 with the returning officer. This money is only returned if the candidate polls more than 5% of the votes cast – this explains the term you may hear that a candidate 'lost his/her deposit'.

The areas covered by political constituencies are periodically reviewed by the Boundaries Commission, which may recommend changes in constituencies due to growth or depopulation of urban or rural areas, and the like. This means that the total number of MPs in the House of Commons fluctuates over the years, with eight changes over the last 60 years, between a low of 625 and a high of 659. There are currently 646 seats: 529 for England, 40 for Wales, 59 for Scotland and 18 for Northern Ireland. The Speaker of the House of Commons is the presiding officer of the Chamber and is elected by members at the beginning of each parliament. He or she, and a number of Deputy Speakers, are non-partisan and renounce affiliation with their former political party while in office.

> When I first moved here the divisions between left and right
> were far more marked than I had ever encountered, though
> the gradual erosion of ideological differences between parties is
> now more similar to the situation in Canada. But there is
> still a spirited left in Britain.
> Susan Griffith

Political Parties

The main political parties in the UK are Labour, Conservative and the Liberal Democrats. There are also a number of smaller parties, including some which are specific to Scotland, Wales and Northern Ireland.

In a general election, the candidate who wins the largest number of votes becomes the MP for that constituency. The government is formed by the party which wins most seats in a general election, this is known as the 'first past the post' system. If no party has a clear majority – i.e. at least 323 seats – then a coalition government is formed between two or more parties, but this is a rare occurrence in the UK. The government is headed by the leader of the winning party, and is known as the Prime Minister. He or she chooses a Cabinet of around 20 ministers, generally the heads of various government departments.

Make-up Of Parliament, June 2006	
Party	MPs
Labour	353
Conservative	196
Liberal Democrats	63
Plaid Cymru (Wales)	3
Scottish National Party	6
Sinn Fein (N.I.)	5
Social Democratic Labour Party	3
Democratic Unionist Party (N.I.)	9
Ulster Unionist (N.I.)	1
Respect	1
Independent	2
The Speaker and three Deputy Speakers	4
Total	646

Source: Whitaker's Concise Almanack 2007, A&C Black

The Leader of the Opposition (the party which holds the second largest number of seats) chooses a shadow cabinet. The role of the Leader of the Opposition and shadow ministers is to provide checks and balances to the Prime Minister and other government ministers, by constructive criticism or opposing all or part of proposed new, or changes in, legislation.

The Government and Opposition MPs sit on opposite sides of the House of Commons debating chamber, ministers and shadow ministers to the front, all other MPs on benches to the rear – thus being called 'back benchers'. MPs of the other parties generally sit in their party groups.

Draft legislation is introduced in the form of a bill, which is then debated and voted on, amendments being made during the various readings of the bill. Before it can become law it has also to be passed by the House of Lords. In some cases a bill may be passed back and forth between the two houses several times before it is sent to the sovereign for the royal assent. Only then does it become an Act of Parliament.

The House of Lords

This comprises a mixture of hereditary peers, life peers, law lords, archbishops, and bishops. Their main functions are to vet every bill brought before Parliament, revise legislation and provide independent expertise. The House of Lords is also the final court of appeal for Great Britain and

Northern Ireland, except for criminal cases in Scotland which go to the High Court of Justiciary in Edinburgh.

The lords choose whether to be affiliated to a political party or not. The archbishops and bishops are independent of political parties.

Many people think the whole idea of unelected persons overseeing the political process is outdated, and there has been an ongoing debate for many years about whether the House of Lords should be reformed or even abolished. In March 2007, 80% of MPs voted for a fully-elected second chamber, but the Lords overwhelmingly voted to remain fully appointed so this is a debate which will continue for some time to come.

Regional Government

There has been a significant change in the governing of Britain in the last decade, with the establishment of regional assemblies in Greater London, Wales and Northern Ireland and of a national parliament in Scotland. Each of these regions has different forms of devolution with different levels of devolved responsibilities.

There are ongoing plans to devolve some of the powers of central government to other regions in England, although it appears the residents of these areas are less positive about the benefits to them of such a move, so it remains to be seen what form any new regional assemblies might take, or when they are likely to be established, if at all.

London

On 7th May 1998 residents of the London boroughs voted to introduce a new layer of government for London, and the first elections to the Greater London Authority (GLA) were held on 4th May 2000. The GLA comprises the Mayor of London, whose role is to make overall decisions, and the London Assembly, which provides checks and balances on the mayor by scrutinising and regulating those decisions. They also have the power to amend the Mayor's budget. The Mayor and the 25 members of the Assembly are elected every four years, one member for each of the 14 London Boroughs and another 11 who represent political parties or who stand as Independents.

The main areas of responsibility devolved to the GLA are transport; planning; economic development and regeneration; environment; police; fire and emergency planning; culture; health.

Wales

In a referendum on 18th September 1997, the Welsh people voted in favour of the establishment of a National Assembly for Wales. The first elections were held on 6th May 1999 (the same day as the first Scottish Parliament elections were held).

The Assembly has powers to make secondary legislation on a range of matters including local government; planning and economic

development; industry; education and training; health; social services and housing; environment; ancient monuments and historic buildings; forestry, agriculture, fisheries, and food; tourism; highways and transport; water and flood defence; sport and recreation; culture and the Welsh language.

The Welsh Assembly Government is led by the First Minister and has a cabinet of nine ministers. It has 60 members in total: 40 constituency members and 20 additional regional members. It is responsible for most public expenditure in Wales but has no power to raise or lower income tax. Elections are held every four years.

In 2007 the powers of the Assembly were widened, with the formation of a Welsh Government executive body in addition to the Welsh Assembly, bringing it more into line with the structure of the Scottish Government.

Scotland

At a referendum on 11th September 1997 the Scottish people voted for devolution, and on 6th May 1999 they elected the first parliament to sit in the country since the government of Scotland was transferred to Westminster in 1707 under the Act of Union.

The Scottish Parliament is subordinate to Westminster and is empowered to legislate only on those matters devolved to it. These include local government; planning and economic development; criminal and civil law;

criminal justice and prosecution system; police and fire services; education; health; social work and housing; environment; natural and built heritage; forestry, agriculture and fisheries; food standards; tourism; some aspects of transport; sport and the arts.

The Scottish Executive, which governs Scotland in respect of all devolved matters, comprises the First Minister, the Lord Advocate and the Solicitor-General for Scotland and other Scottish Ministers appointed by the First Minister. There are in addition junior ministers appointed to assist the Scottish Ministers.

The Scottish Parliament has a single chamber with 129 members (MSPs). Seventy-three of these represent constituencies and are elected on a first past the post basis. An additional 56 regional members are elected on a proportional representation basis. The parliament has a fixed term of four years, with elections normally held on the first Thursday in May. It has made a commitment to operate in an open, accessible and transparent manner, and allows public access to meetings of the parliament and most of the committees.

In addition to MSPs, Scotland still elects representatives to Westminster (MPs), currently in 72 constituencies. For a more detailed discussion of the Scottish Parliament, see *Live & Work in Scotland* (Vacation Work 2005).

Northern Ireland

The Northern Ireland Assembly was established as a condition of the Belfast Agreement on 10th April 1998 (also known as the Good Friday Agreement). This agreement set out a plan for devolved government in Northern Ireland on a stable and inclusive basis and provided for the creation of Human Rights and Equality commissions, the early release of terrorist prisoners, the decommissioning of paramilitary weapons, and far-reaching reforms of criminal justice and policing. The people of Northern Ireland endorsed it at a referendum on 22nd May 1998 and the first assembly election was held on 25th June 1998.

Since that time, the assembly has been suspended by the Secretary of State on four occasions. The first three were due to delays in the process of weapons decommissioning, and the fourth took place in October 2002 after unionists walked out of the executive in protest at alleged misdemeanours by Sinn Fein. There are 108 members, six elected for each of 18 constituencies.

Local Government

Areas of the UK are governed at the local level by democratically elected local councils, also known as local authorities. They are responsible within their areas for such matters as state education; social work; strategic planning; local road provision and repair; consumer protection; flood prevention; coast protection; property valuation and rating; the police and fire services; emergency planning; electoral registration; public transport; registration of births, deaths and marriages; housing; leisure and recreation; building control and planning; environmental health; licensing; the administration of district courts.

Local Government in Britain is fairly complicated in structure, with single tier authorities in some areas, responsible for all local service provision, while in other areas the responsibility is split between two tiers of local government. To add to the confusion, these authorities have various different names.

Local authorities (or local councils – both terms are used interchangeably) are made up of directly elected councillors. The geographical area covered by the council is divided into a number of wards and a councillor is elected for each ward. Local government is financed from the council tax, non-domestic (business) rates, government grants, and income from charges for services.

Areas of Responsibility

They are responsible for a wide range of functions within their areas, which vary slightly from country to country, due to the differences between the remits of the various devolved governments. However, they are broadly similar, and include such things as education; social services; strategic planning; road provision and repair; consumer protection; flood prevention; coast protection; valuation and rating; the police and fire services; emergency planning; electoral registration; public transport; registration of births, deaths and marriages; housing; leisure and recreation; building control and planning; environmental health; licensing; public conveniences; the administration of district courts.

Overall policy is decided by the full council, while the administration of services is the responsibility of committees of councillors, who delegate day to day decisions to the council's officers.

Councils can be contacted in a number of ways. They all have their own websites, and can be contacted by email. Contact phone numbers are also given, and are listed in the local phone book. You can call in at the council offices and speak to staff in the various department directly – although it is probably best to ring or email first to arrange an appointment so you can be sure you speak with the best person to deal with your query. They may also have local offices, or 'one-stop shops', which can provide services and deal with queries from the public.

Alternatively, people may contact their own local councillor direct with any queries, comments, complaints or requests. If they are serving their ward properly, they should then ensure that the matter is dealt with.

Community, Town and Parish Councils

The lowest level of local government, in England, Wales and Scotland, are neighbourhood councils known variously as community, town or parish

councils. There is no equivalent of these in Northern Ireland. Their role is to ascertain and express the view of the communities which they represent on a range on matters pertaining to local government and other local services.

Local councils are committed to taking their representations seriously. They are constituted of locally elected community, town or parish councillors, who are unpaid but may claim small expenses for council work they carry out.

Useful Contacts

Local Government Association (England and Wales): 0207 664 3131; www.lga.gov.uk

Convention of Scottish Local Authorities (COSLA): 0131 474 9200; www.cosla.gov.uk

Northern Ireland Local Government Association: 02890 249286; www.nilga.org

National Association of Local Councils (England & Wales): 020 7637 1865; www.nalc.gov.uk

Association of Scottish Community Councils: 0131 225 4033; www.ascc.org.uk

The European Parliament

The UK has been electing Members of the European Parliament (MEPs) since 1979. Initially the elections were on a first past the post basis, but since 1999 a system of proportional representation has been used. The constituencies represented by UK MEPs cover much larger regions than those used in national elections, as is reflected in the number of MEPs elected. The number of seats fluctuates, partly due to the continuing growth in the number of member countries of the European Union. At the last European General Election on 10th June 2004, the number of seats stood at 78, of which 64 were in England, four in Wales, seven in Scotland and three in Northern Ireland.

Relations with the European Union are a reserved matter, so it is the UK Government that represents Scottish, Welsh and Northern Irish interests in the European Council of Ministers. This is the case even with those matters which are devolved to the regional governments within the UK – farming and fishing, for example. The Scottish Parliament and Welsh and Northern Irish Assemblies have a responsibility, therefore, to scrutinise EU proposals to ensure their interests are taken into consideration in these areas.

Economy

The UK economy is currently strong, and measured on Gross Domestic Product (GDP) it is currently the fourth largest economy in the world. In 2005 it had a GDP of US$2,133 billion. It is a member of the European Union, now the world's largest trading entity, and within the EU is the second largest economy after Germany. This healthy state of affairs has come about as a result of restructuring of the economy, after a period of far weaker performance, which began in the 1980s. Since that time the Government has greatly reduced public ownership of utility and communications companies, transport systems and the like, thereby increasing productivity and competitiveness in many sectors. Average annual growth is 2.2%.

Britain began the process of becoming an industrialised nation during the 19th century, and produced great wealth from heavy industries including coal mining, steel production, shipbuilding, and textiles. Britain dominated international trade during that period, sending its products to all corners of the Empire. Since the mid-20th century, however, Britain's dominance in the manufacturing sector has declined as other countries have grown in industrial strength and efficiency. As a result, the economic complexion of the United Kingdom has changed markedly since the end of the second world war as traditional industries have declined.

The strongest performing sector in the UK economy is business and financial services. Measured by 'Gross Value Added' (GVA), this sector represented over 33% of economic output in 2004 – more than double the size of the manufacturing sector at 14.1%. In contrast, agriculture's contribution remains below 1%. Information and Communication Technologies (ICT) contribute 6.4% of the total GVA.

Today, the service industries, in particular banking, insurance and business services, account for a huge proportion of GDP at around 73%. London is one of the largest financial centres in the world, and Edinburgh is also a big player in the field, being one of Europe's top cities for finance services.

Tourism is an important element within the service industries. The UK is ranked as the sixth major tourist destination in the world and attracts over 27 million tourists per year.

Compared with the rest of Europe the UK agriculture sector is small, accounting for only 0.9% of GDP. However, through the use of intensive, highly mechanised procedures, it is very efficient by European standards, and produces around 60% of its food requirements using just 2% of the work force.

With large reserves of coal, gas and oil, primary energy production accounts for about 10% of UK GDP, one of the highest proportions of any industrial nation.

Manufacturing accounts for a sixth of national output and over half of UK exports. The industry as a whole employs 3.5 million people directly, and many more indirectly through the connected supply chain and service industries.

Levels of taxation and regulation are comparatively low, so the UK attracts many international companies, especially to the London area. London is well-placed for travel to both Europe and the USA and has excellent communications – Heathrow is the busiest airport in the world with the highest number of international passengers, a number that will grow when the new Terminal 5 is completed in 2008 – which means that companies based in the UK are well placed to do business in the global marketplace. Over 100 of Europe's 500 largest companies have their headquarters in central London, as do more than half of the UK's top 100 companies. Furthermore, over 70% of the UK's top 100 companies are located within London's metropolitan area. In fact, a 2005 survey voted London the best European city in which to do business.

Many of these top UK companies have a global reach: of the 500 largest global companies, the third highest number are UK-owned, after only the USA and Japan.

A country built on trade, Britain is still one of the leading trading nations in the world. According to World Trade Organisation figures, it is the second largest exporter and third largest importer of commercial services, and the eighth largest exporter and fifth largest importer of merchandise. In 2005 it accounted for nearly 7% of world trade in services and 5% in goods.

In 2005 the UK received US$219 billion of foreign direct investment (FDI). This was the highest figure of any country in the world, and represented 24.4% of all global FDI, and 49% of all FDI in EU countries. At the same time, the UK is a large outward investor: during 2006 it invested at levels that made it the second largest outward investing country globally.

Over recent years the inflation and unemployment rates have been below the European averages, and despite Britons' ongoing complaints about levels of income tax and other taxes, the UK has among the lowest levels of personal taxation in Europe. This allows for a good standard of living for most UK residents, who find themselves relatively well off. Ten years ago Britain was at the bottom of the G7 nations on a measure of national income per head, but in 2005-6 Britain was second only to the USA. The mean annual income for a British subject in November 2006 was £19,840.

In 2006 the unemployment rate was 4.9%, well below the European Union average of 8.4%, one reason for which was the recent large influxes of economic migrants from other countries as they join the EU.

Breakdown of UK Manufacturing Industries

Food, drink and tobacco	15.0%
Paper, printing and publishing	13.6%
Chemicals and man-made fibres	11.0%
Transport equipment	10.9%
Electrical and optical equipment	10.7%
Basic metals and metal products	10.2%
Machinery and equipment	8.3%
Rubber and plastic products	5.2%
Textiles and clothing	3.0%
Non-metallic mineral products	3.8%
Wood and wood products	1.9%

> I feel that despite what people say, there is plenty of opportunity for someone to find work, if they have the will and are prepared to go out and search for it. After all, nearly a million people have come across from neighbouring EU states and most have managed to find jobs!
> Joe Rawal is perplexed by the high number of unemployed people in parts of Britain

Coke, refined petroleum and nuclear fuels	1.6%
Other manufacturing	4.4%
Leather and leather products	0.3%

Outlook

Although for the last few years the UK economy has been in a healthy situation, with steady growth while at the same time inflation and interest rates have been kept low, there have been signs of the economy over-heating somewhat. In December 2006 the Consumer Price Index rose to 3%, from 2.7% in November. This was a warning sign for the economy, as the Bank of England is charged by the Government with keeping inflation within the range of 1% above or below the target rate of 2%. The rise was partly caused by a rise in fuel costs, but the rate had been creeping upward for a while, a trend which the Bank had tried to address by raising the interest rate, in an attempt to dampen down the inflationary effects of a booming property market.

The property market in the UK has gone through an unprecedented boom in house prices, with average prices doubling between 2001 and 2007. Interest rate rises during 2004 had stabilised the market and put a brake on rising prices, but when the rate was lowered again in August 2005 the market took off once more. With plenty of money in their pockets, property became a favourite investment for the British, many people saying they found property a more secure investment than a pension. Record bonuses were paid to city bankers early in 2007 and this put further pressure on the housing market as they competed for expensive properties, many of them with over £500,000 to invest in property at home and abroad. In January 2007 the base lending rate was raised to 5.25%, the third rise in five months, bringing the overall rise to 0.75%.

Unemployment rates are also predicted to rise due to unusually strong growth in the labour force, due to high immigration, in particular from new members of the European Union – 10 new states joined in 2004, and a further two, Romania and Bulgaria, in January 2007. One prediction is that this should help to push back inflation levels and that this, together with interest rate rises, will bring inflation back to the 2% target.

The long term aim continues to be the reduction of the government deficit, to continue GDP growth at a rate of 2.5-2.75%, plus an improvement in workforce skills to aid employment levels and productivity.

■ LOCAL COUNCILS

Addresses of the upper tier of local authorities in England, and all councils in the rest of the UK, are given below. Links to all UK local authority websites, including district councils etc. can be found on the following websites:

> *i* **UK Local Government:** www.gwydir.demon.co.uk/uklocalgov/localtxt.
> htm#crown
> **Directgov:** www.direct.gov.uk/en/Dl1/Directories/Localcouncils/
> index.htm

England

Cornwall County Council: 01872 322000; www.cornwall.gov.uk
Bedfordshire County Council: 01234 363222; www.bedfordshire.gov.uk
Birmingham City Council: 0121 303 9944; www.birmingham.gov.uk
Buckinghamshire County Council: 0845 370 8090; www.buckscc.gov.uk
Cambridgeshire County Council: 0845 045 5200;
www.cambridgeshire.gov.uk
Coventry City Council: 024 7683 3333; www.coventry.gov.uk
Cumbria County Council: 01228 606060; www.cumbria.gov.uk
Derbyshire County Council: 01629 580000; www.derbyshire.gov.uk
Devon County Council: 0845 155 1015; www.devon.gov.uk
Dorset County Council: 01305 251000; www.dorsetforyou.com
Durham County Council: 0191 383 4567; www.durham.gov.uk
East Sussex County Council: 01273 481000; www.eastsussex.gov.uk
Essex County Council: 08457 430430; www.essexcc.gov.uk
Gloucestershire County Council: 01542 505345;
www.gloucestershire.gov.uk

Hampshire County Council: 01962 870500; www.hants.gov.uk
Herefordshire Council: 01432 260000; www.herefordshire.gov.uk
Hertfordshire County Council: 01992 555555; www.hertsdirect.org
Hull City Council: 01482 300300; www.hullcc.gov.uk
Isle of Wight Council: 01983 821000; www.iwight.gov.uk
Kent County Council: 08458 247247; www.kent.gov.uk
Lancashire County Council: 084 5 053 0000; www.lancashire.gov.uk
Leeds City Council: 0113 234 8080; www.leeds.gov.uk
Lincolnshire County Council: 01522 782060; www.lincolnshire.gov.uk
Liverpool City Council: 0151 233 3000; www.liverpool.gov.uk
London Assembly: 020 7983 4100; www.london.gov.uk/gla
Manchester City Council: 0161 234 5000; www.manchester.gov.uk
Newcastle City Council: 0191 232 8520; www.newcastle.gov.uk
Norfolk County Council: 0844 800 8020; www.norfolk.gov.uk
Northamptonshire County Council: 01604 236236;
www.northamptonshire.gov.uk
Northumberland County Council: 01670 533000;
www.northumberland.gov.uk
North Yorkshire County Council: 0160 780780; www.northyorks.gov.uk
Nottinghamshire County Council: 01777 713800;
www.nottinghamshire.gov.uk
Oxfordshire County Council: 01865 792422; www.oxfordshire.gov.uk
Royal Borough of Windsor and Maidenhead: 01628 683800;
www.rbwm.gov.uk
Rutland County Council: 01572 722577; www.rutland.gov.uk
Sheffield City Council: 0114 272 6444; www.sheffield.gov.uk
Shropshire County Council: 0845 678 9000; www.shropshire.gov.uk
Somerset County Council: 01823 355455; www.somerset.gov.uk
Staffordshire County Council: 01785 223121; www.staffordshire.gov.uk
Suffolk County Council: 01473583000; www.suffolk.gov.uk
Surrey County Council: 018456009009; www.surreycc.gov.uk
Sunderland City Council: 0191520 5555; www.sunderland.gov.uk
Warwickshire County Council: 01926 410410;
www.warwickshire.gov.uk
West Berkshire Council: 01635424000; www.westberks.gov.uk
West Sussex County Council: 01243777100; www.westsussex.gov.uk
Wiltshire County Council: 01225713000; www.wiltshire.gov.uk
Worcestershire County Council: 01905763763; www.worcestershire.
whub.org.uk

Wales

Bridgend County Borough Council: 01656 643643;
www.bridgend.gov.uk.

Blaenau Gwent County Borough Council: 01495 350555; www.blaenau-gwent.gov.uk

Caerphilly County Borough Council: 01443 815588 or 01495-226622; www.caerphilly.gov.uk

Cardiff Council: 029 2087 2000; www.cardiff.gov.uk

Carmarthenshire County Council: 0845 658 0445; www.carmarthenshire.gov.uk

Ceredigion County Council: 01970 617911; www.ceredigion.gov.uk

City and County of Swansea: 01792 636000; www.swansea.gov.uk

Conwy County Borough Council: 01492 574000; www.conwy.gov.uk

Denbighshire County Council: 01824 706000; www.denbighshire.gov.uk

Flintshire County Council: 01352 752121; www.flintshire.gov.uk

Gwynedd Council: 01286 672255; www.gwynedd.gov.uk

Isle of Anglesey County Council: 01248 750057; www.ynysmon.gov.uk

Merthyr Tydfil County Borough Council: 01685 725000; www.merthyr.gov.uk

Monmouthshire County Council: 01633 644644; www.monmouthshire.gov.uk

Neath Port Talbot County Borough Council: 01693 763333; www.neath-porttalbot.gov.uk

Newport City Council: 01633 656656; www.newport.gov.uk

Pembrokeshire County Council: 01437 764551; www.pembrokeshire.gov.uk

Powys County Council: 01597 826000; www.powys.gov.uk

Rhondda Cynon Taf County Borough Council: 01443 424000; www.rhondda-cynon-taf.gov.uk

Torfaen County Borough Council: 01495 762200; www.torfaen.gov.uk

Vale of Glamorgan Council: 01446 700111; www.valeofglamorgan.gov.uk

Wrexham County Borough Council: 01978-292000; www.wrexham.gov.uk

Scotland

Aberdeen City Council: 01224 522000; www.aberdeencity.gov.uk

Aberdeenshire Council: 01467 620981; www.aberdeenshire.gov.uk

Angus Council: 01307 461460; www.angus.gov.uk

Argyll and Bute Council: 01546 602127; www.argyll bute.gov.uk

City of Edinburgh Council: 0131 200 2000; www.edinburgh.gov.uk

Clackmannanshire Council: 01259 450000; www.clacks.gov.uk

Dumfries and Galloway Council: 01387 260000; www.dumgal.gov.uk

Dundee City Council: 01382 434000; www.dundeecity.gov.uk

East Ayrshire Council: 01563 576000; www.east ayrshire.gov.uk

East Dunbartonshire Council: 0141 578 8000; www.eastdunbarton.gov.uk

East Lothian Council: 01620 827827; www.eastlothian.gov.uk

East Renfrewshire Council: 0141 577 3000;
www.eastrenfrewshire.gov.uk

Comhairle nan Eilean Siar/Western Isles Council: 01851 703773;
www.cne siar.gov.uk

Falkirk Council: 01324 506070; www.falkirk.gov.uk

Fife Council: 01592 414141; www.fife.gov.uk

Glasgow City Council: 0141 287 2000; www.glasgow.gov.uk

Highland Council: 01463 702000; www.highland.gov.uk

Inverclyde Council: 01475 717171; www.inverclyde.gov.uk

Midlothian Council: 0131 271 7500; www.midlothian.gov.uk

Moray Council: 01343 543451; www.moray.org

North Ayrshire Council: 01294 324100; www.northayrshire.gov.uk

North Lanarkshire Council: 01698 302222; www.northlan.gov.uk

Orkney Islands Council: 01856 873535; www.orkney.com

Perth and Kinross Council: 01738 475000; www.pkc.gov.uk

Renfrewshire Council: 0141 842 5000; www.renfrewshire.gov.uk

Scottish Borders Council: 01835 824000; www.scotborders.gov.uk

Shetland Islands Council: 01595 693535; www.shetland.gov.uk

South Ayrshire Council: 01292 612000; www.south ayrshire.gov.uk

South Lanarkshire Council: 01698 454444;
www.southlanarkshire.gov.uk

Stirling Council: 0845 277700; www.stirling.gov.uk

West Dunbartonshire Council: 01389 737000;
www.west-dunbarton.gov.uk

West Lothian Council: 01506 777000; www.wlonline.org.uk

Northern Ireland

Antrim Borough Council: 028 9446 3113; www.antrim.gov.uk

Ards Borough Council: 028 9181 9628; www.ards council.gov.uk

Armagh City and District Council: 028 3752 9601; www.armagh.gov.uk

Ballymena Borough Council: 08456 581581; www.ballymena.gov.uk

Ballymoney Borough Council: 028 2766 0200; www.ballymoney.gov.uk

Banbridge Borough Council: 028 4066 0600; www.banbridge.com

Belfast City Council: 028 9032 0202; www.belfastcity.gov.uk

Carrickfergus Borough Council: 028 9335 8000; www.carrickfergus.org

Castlereagh Borough Council: 028 9049 4600; www.castlereagh.gov.uk

Coleraine Borough Council: 028 7034 7034; www.colerainebc.gov.uk

Cookstown District Council: 028 8676 2205; www.cookstown.gov.uk

Craigavon Borough Council: 028 3831 2400; www.craigavon.gov.uk

Derry City Council: 028 7136 5151; www.derrycity.gov.uk

Down District Council: 028 4461 0800; www.downdc.gov.uk

Dungannon and South Tyrone Borough Council: 028 7136 5151;
www.dungannon.gov.uk

Fermanagh District Council: 028 6632 5050; www.fermanagh.gov.uk

Larne Borough Council: 028 2827 2313; www.larne.gov.uk
Limavady Borough Council: 028 7772 2226; www.limavady.gov.uk
Lisburn City Council: 028 9250 9250; www.lisburncity.gov.uk
Magherafelt District Council: 028 7939 7979; www.magherafelt.gov.uk
Moyle District Council: 028 2076 2225; www.moyle council.org
Newry and Mourne District Council: 028 3031 3031;
www.newryandmournedc.gov.uk
Newtownabbey District Council: 028 9034 0000;
www.newtownabbey.gov.uk
North Down Borough Council: 028 9127 0371; www.northdown.gov.uk
Omagh District Council: 028 8224 5321; www.omagh.gov.uk
Strabane District Council: 028 7138 2204; www.strabanedc.org.uk

◼ RELIGION

The religious make-up of the UK is highly diverse, with over 170 distinct religions stated in the most recent (2001) Census. The majority, 71.6 per cent (42.1 million people), said they were Christians – this despite the fact that only half of British people claim to believe in God! The number who could be classed as 'active Christians', attending church regularly, is far fewer than either of these figures. Since the 1950s Britain has become increasingly secularised, with half of all Christians stopping going to church on a Sunday since 1979. In the 2001 census, 15.5 per cent said they had no religion, while another 7.3 per cent did not state their religious beliefs – or lack of them, together accounting for nearly one quarter of the population.

There are number of different Christian churches in Britain, the largest one being the Anglican (protestant) church. However, it is predicted that Roman Catholicism will become the dominant religion in Britain over the next few years with the ongoing influx of Catholic migrants from the new EU countries.

Adherents of other religions make up 5.4 per cent of the population. These include Buddhism, Hinduism, Islam, Judaism, and Sikhism. Muslims accounted for the second largest faith group, at 2.7 per cent.

Religious Beliefs in the UK

Religion	Thousand	per cent
Christian	42,079	71.6
No religion	9,104	15.5
Not stated	4,289	7.3
Muslim	1,591	2.7
Hindu	559	1.0
Sikh	336	0.6
Jewish	267	0.5
Buddhist	152	0.3
Other religion	179	0.3

Appendices

■ USEFUL BOOKS AND WEBSITES

Books

The Good Pub Guide, Alisdair Aird and Fiona Stapley (Ebury Press 2007).
I Never Knew That About England, Christopher Winn (Ebury Press 2005).
Note from a Small Island, Bill Bryson (Black Swan 1996).
The Good Schools Guide 2007, Ralph Lucas (Lucas Publications).
Michelin Guide GB & Ireland 2007, (Michelin Guides).
Guardian University Guide 2007, Jimmy Leach (Guardian Newspapers Ltd).
Coast: The Journey Continues, Christopher Somerville (BBC Books).

Websites

City News: Free classified ads sites for buying and selling in UK towns and cities. www.citynews.com/uk.html
Daily Life in England, Britain and the UK: www.woodlands-junior.kent.sch.uk/customs/questions/index/dailylife.htm
Direct Gov: Central Office of Information website, with information about and contacts to all Government departments and services. www.direct.gov.uk
UK Student Life: Study, work or travel in the UK. www.ukstudentlife.com
Villages Online: Directory of UK community websites. www.villagesonline.com
Where I Live: www.bbc.co.uk/whereilive

CONVERSIONS

In an attempt to bring the UK into step with Europe, because voluntary codes have not had much effect, in early 2000 shops were legally obliged to display the price per kilogram on their products; whether the price was also shown in pounds and ounces (avoirdupois) was optional. Fabric has been sold by the metre for decades, but still many shops will sell you fabric by the yard, and quote prices for both measurements.

Distances on road signs are in miles and speed limits are given in miles per hour. Road maps, however, do now show both miles and kilometres.

Weights and Measures: Metric Conversion

CONVERSION CHART

LENGTH (NB 12inches 1 foot, 10 mm 1 cm, 100 cm 1 metre)

inches	1	2	3	4	5	6	9	12		
cm	2.5	5	7.5	10	12.5	15.2	23	30		
cm	1	2	3	5	10	20	25	50	75	100
inches	0.4	0.8	1.2	2	4	8	10	20	30	39

WEIGHT (NB 14lb = 1 stone, 2240 lb = 1 ton, 1,000 kg = 1 metric tonne)

lb	1	2	3	5	10	14	44	100	2246
kg	0.45	0.9	1.4	2.3	4.5	6.4	20	45	1016
kg	1	2	3	5	10	25	50	100	1000
lb	2.2	4.4	6.6	11	22	55	110	220	2204

DISTANCE

mile	1	5	10	20	30	40	50	75	100	150
km	1.6	8	16	32	48	64	80	120	161	241
km	1	5	10	20	30	40	50	100	150	200
mile	0.6	3.1	6.2	12	19	25	31	62	93	124

(Continued on following page)

Appendices

VOLUME

1 litre = 0.2 UK gallons	1 UK gallon = 4.5 litres
1 litre = 0.26 US gallons	1 US gallon = 3.8 litres

CLOTHES

UK		8	10	12	14	16	18	20	
Europe		36	38	40	42	44	46	48	
USA		6	8	10	12	14	18		

SHOES

UK	3	4	5	6	7	8	9	10	11
Europe	36	37	38	39	40	41/42	43	44	45
USA	2.5	3.3	4.5	5.5	6.5	7.5	8.5	9.5	10.5

■ EMBASSIES IN LONDON

Australia
Tel: 020 7379 4334
Website: www.australia.org.uk
Email: info@australia.org.uk

Bangladesh
Tel: 020 7584 0081
Website: www.bangladeshhighcommission.org.uk
Email: bdesh.lon@dial.pipex.com

Canada
Tel: 020 7258 6600
Website: www.dfait-maeci.gc.ca/canada-europa/united_kingdom/
menu-en.asp
Email: ldn.consular@international.gc.ca

China
Tel: 020-7299 4049
Website: www.chinese-embassy.org.uk
Email: visa@chinese-embassy.co.uk

France
Tel: 020-7073 1000
Website: www.ambafrance-uk.org
Email: consulat.londres-fslt@diplomatie.fr

Germany
Tel: 020 7824 1300
Website: www.london.diplo.de
Email: info@german-embassy.org.uk

Irish Republic
Tel: 020 7235 2171
Website: http://ireland.embassyhomepage.com
Email: admin@embassyhomepage.com

India
Tel: 020 7836 8484
Website: www.hcilondon.net
Email: info@hcilondon.net

Italy
Tel: 020 7312 2200
Website: www.amblondra.esteri.it
Email: ambasciata.londra@esteri.it

New Zealand
Tel: 020 7930 8422
Website: www.nzembassy.com
Email: aboutnz@newzealandhc.org.uk

Nigeria
Tel: 020 7839 1244
Website: www.nigeriahc.org.uk
Email: information@nigeriahc.org.uk

Pakistan
Tel: 020 7664 9200
Website: www.pakmission-uk.gov.pk
Email: pareplondon@supanet.com

Phillippines
Tel: 020 7937 1600
Website: www.philemb.org.uk
Email: embassy@philemb.co.uk

Poland
Tel: 0870 774 2700
Website: www.polishembassy.org.uk
Email: polishembassy@polishembassy.org.uk

Portugal
Tel: 020 7235 5331
Website: http://portugal.embassyhomepage.com
Email: london@portembassy.co.uk

Russian Federation
Tel: 020 7229 2666/3628/6412
Website: www.great-britain.mid.ru
Email: info@rusemblon.org

South Africa
Tel: 020 7451 7299
Website: www.southafricahouse.com
Email: london.general@foreign.gov.za

Spain
Tel: 020 7235 5555
Website: http://spain.embassyhomepage.com
Email: admin@embassyhomepage.com

USA
Tel: 020 7499 9000
Website: www.usembassy.org.uk
Email: info@usembassy.org.uk

Zimbabwe
Tel: 020 7836 7755
Website: http://zimbabwe.embassyhomepage.com
Email: zimlondon@yahoo.co.uk

■ INDEX

More titles in the series:

Live & Work in Scotland

Detailing the scope of employment opportunities from the great cities of Edinburgh and Glasgow to the wonderfully mountainous Highlands, Live & Work in Scotland is a comprehensive guide for anyone considering moving to this country to live and work.

With business and industry reports, a regional employment guide and directory of major employers, Live & Work in Scotland provides priceless information on what makes Scotland tick; its political and economic structures, laws surrounding property purchase and immigration rules. Also included are the suggested pros and cons of moving to Scotland and personal case histories from people who have done it themselves.

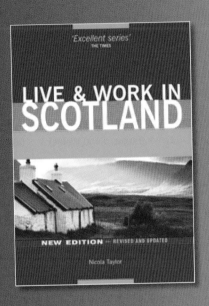

Author: Nicola Taylor
ISBN: 978 1 85458 334 5

"Essential information for anyone considering making the move"
The Times

"Full of advice"
Moneywise magazine

Essential Phone Numbers

Emergency Services

Fire service, Police, Ambulance	**999 or 112**
Coastguard, Cave rescue, Mountain rescue	**999 or 112**

Health

Doctors, Dentists, Chemists (24hr advice & assistance)

NHS Direct (England and Wales)	**0845 4647**
NHS24 (Scotland)	**08454 242424**

Utilities

Gas leak	**0800 111 999**
Emergency Heating Repairs	**08450 777 111**
Phone fault	**0800 800 151**

Phone Information

Directory Enquiries	**118 500**
Operator	**100**
International Access Code	**0044 + no. minus initial 0**

Travel

Heathrow Airport	**0870 000 0123**
Gatwick Airport	**0870 000.2468**
Cardiff Airport	**01446 711 111**
Edinburgh Airport	**0870 040 0007**
Glasgow Airport	**0870 040 0008**
Belfast Airport	**028 9448 4848**
American Airlines	**020 7365 0777**
British Airways	**0870 55 111 55**
KLM Royal Dutch Airlines	**020 4747 747**

Public Transport Information	**0871 200 22 33**
Train Information	**08457 48 49 50**
Eurostar (in Britain)	**08705 186 186**
Eurostar (outside Britain)	**01233 617 575**
Transport for London	**020 7222 1234**
London Taxis	**08700 802 902**
Cardiff Taxis	**029 2049 0000**
Glasgow Taxis	**0141 429 7070**
Edinburgh Taxis	**0131 229 2468**
Belfast Taxis	**028 9024 2000**

Other Information

Road traffic information	**08457 50 40 30**
Weather Report	**09068 500 400**
Floodline	**0845 988 1188**

Embassies

Australia	**020 7379 4334**
France	**020 7073 1000**
India	**020 7836 8484**
Ireland	**020 7235 2171**
Poland	**0870 774 2700**
South Africa	**020 7451 7299**
United States	**020 7499 9000**